TENNYSON: THE CRITICAL HERITAGE

THE CRITICAL HERITAGE SERIES

GENERAL EDITOR: B. C. SOUTHAM, M.A., B.LITT. (OXON.)
Formerly Department of English, Westfield College, University of London

Volumes in the series include

JANE AUSTEN   B. C. Southam

BYRON   Andrew Rutherford,
       University of Aberdeen

DICKENS   P. A. Collins, *University of Leicester*

HENRY JAMES   Roger Gard, *Queen Mary College,*
       University of London

TENNYSON   John D. Jump,
       University of Manchester

THACKERAY   Geoffrey Tillotson and Donald Hawes,
       Birkbeck College, University of London

TENNYSON

THE CRITICAL HERITAGE

Edited by

JOHN D. JUMP

John Edward Taylor Professor of English Literature
University of Manchester

LONDON: ROUTLEDGE & KEGAN PAUL
NEW YORK: BARNES & NOBLE INC

Published in England, 1967
by Routledge & Kegan Paul Limited
and in the United States of America
by Barnes & Noble, Inc

Printed in Great Britain
by C. Tinling & Co. Ltd
Liverpool, London and Prescot

TO

BARBARA

General Editor's Preface

The reception given to a writer by his contemporaries and near-contemporaries is evidence of considerable value to the student of literature. On one side, we learn a great deal about the state of criticism at large and in particular about the development of critical attitudes towards a single writer; at the same time, through private comments in letters, journals or marginalia, we gain an insight upon the tastes and literary thought of individual readers of the period. Evidence of this kind helps us to understand the writer's historical situation, the nature of his immediate reading-public, and his response to these pressures.

The separate volumes in *The Critical Heritage Series* present a record of this early criticism. Clearly, for many of the highly-productive and lengthily-reviewed nineteenth and twentieth-century writers, there exists an enormous body of material; and in these cases the volume editors have made a selection of the most important views, significant for their intrinsic critical worth or for their representative quality.

For writers of the eighteenth century and earlier, the materials are much scarcer and the historical period has been extended, sometimes far beyond the writer's life-time, in order to show the inception and growth of critical views which were initially slow to appear.

In each volume the documents are headed by an Introduction, discussing the material assembled and relating the early stages of the author's reception to what we have come to identify as the critical tradition. The volumes will make available much material which would otherwise be difficult of access and it is hoped that the modern reader will be thereby helped towards an informed understanding of the ways in which literature has been read and judged.

B.C.S.

Contents

CONTENTS

Introduction

There is no shortage of contemporary comment on Tennyson's work. Reviews of his publications are numerous and often extremely full; many articles deal with particular aspects of his achievement, especially during the latter half of his career; incidental references to him occur in letters, journals, and other writings; and he anticipates some of the poets of the twentieth century by himself serving as the subject of books issued during his lifetime. Nothing would have been easier than to fill the present volume with hundreds of short extracts from this mass of criticism. But it has seemed preferable to allow a relatively small number of critics to speak their minds at length. What they say about Tennyson himself becomes clearer in the context of their leisurely comparisons and confident generalizations.

So nearly half the items that follow this Introduction are essays reprinted without the omission of any of the critics' words. Even the articles and reviews that have had to be cut, and the extracts from writings on other subjects and from full-length books, run often to many thousands of words. Brief comments, and short extracts from longer discussions, have found places within the Introduction itself, where they help to illustrate an account of the reception of Tennyson's work by his contemporaries and of his reactions to that reception. Both in the Introduction and elsewhere, the serial numbers given to the thirty-five main items have provided a ready and compact means of cross-reference.

Tennyson's *Poems, Chiefly Lyrical* (1830) had a generally favourable reception. His Cambridge friends are sometimes given the credit for having organized this, and no doubt they did what they could for him. But only three or four reviews seem to have resulted from their efforts. A. H. Hallam's (No. 2) in the *Englishman's Magazine* was the most important of these. It is a persuasive manifesto on behalf of a poetry of suggestion as against a poetry of statement, and it anticipates in part the literary theory of the French symbolists and their English disciples.

W. J. Fox, whose highly laudatory notice (No. 1) appeared in the well-known *Westminster*, had no connection with Tennyson or his circle; his interest had sprung from his reading some of the poems in a newspaper. 'Christopher North' (John Wilson) was still more remote from Tennyson's group. In fact, he had been irritated by the excessive eulogies, as he considered them, of Fox and Hallam, and he distrusted the political tendencies of the periodicals for which they wrote. In *Blackwood's*, he derided both of these eulogies, and many of the poems of Tennyson, before proceeding to give high praise to what he held to be the better poems (No. 3). His concluding tribute, warm though it was, failed to placate Tennyson, who retorted with the epigram, 'To Christopher North'. Nevertheless, it is likely—Hallam certainly thought that it was the case—that this *Blackwood's* review helped rather than hindered the growth of Tennyson's reputation.

The reception of *Poems*, published at the end of 1832 but dated 1833, was distinctly less favourable, though on the whole not really hostile. Critics complained of Tennyson's obscurity, silliness, and affectation, related him to the so-called Cockney School, and praised him for his fancy, feeling, and imagination. One notice was violently destructive, however. This was J. W. Croker's (No. 4) in the *Quarterly*. Finding Tennyson extravagantly lauded in the circles represented by the liberal *Englishman's* and the radical *Westminster*, Croker concluded that the new poet belonged to the same literary and political movement as Keats, Shelley, and Leigh Hunt. His Tory susceptibilities were outraged, like those of 'Christopher North' a year earlier. The outcome was the famous review in which he hoped, in his own words, 'to make another Keats of' his victim (Myron F. Brightfield, *John Wilson Croker* (Berkeley, California, 1940), p. 350). The brutal sarcasm of his article deeply distressed Tennyson. The effect upon the public, however, was probably less great than some biographers—Harold Nicolson and Sir Charles Tennyson, for example—have supposed. The sales of the 1833 volume no doubt declined, but they did not stop. In part, this may have been because Tennyson did not lack defenders. The most able of them was John Stuart Mill, who contributed to the *London Review*, another radical organ, a discriminating article (No. 5) in which he recognized how rapidly Tennyson had progressed during the period represented by his volumes of 1830 and 1833.

Nevertheless, the adverse criticism of Croker and others affected Tennyson himself profoundly. It was evidently a major cause of the 'ten years' silence' which preceded his launching of his next collection of poems in 1842. His dread of publicity became acute. He even asked his friend, James Spedding, to discourage Mill from writing the review which was to defend him against Croker: '*I do not wish to be dragged forward again in any shape before the reading public at present*' (Hallam Tennyson, *Alfred Lord Tennyson: A Memoir. By his Son* (1897), ed. 1899, p. 121). Another friend, James Knowles, who knew him for the last thirty years of his life, described the habit of mind which produced this reluctance:

> Another frequent subject of his talk was the criticism on his own work, *when unfavourable*. All the mass of eulogy he took comparatively little notice of, but he never could forget an unfriendly word, even from the most obscure and insignificant and unknown quarter. He was hurt by it as a sensitive child might be hurt by the cross look of a passing stranger; or rather as a supersensitive skin is hurt by the sting of an invisible midge. He knew it was a weakness in him, and could be laughed out of it for a time, but it soon returned upon him, and had given him from his early youth exaggerated vexation. When remonstrated with . . ., he would grimly smile and say, '*Oh yes, I know. I'm black-blooded like all the Tennysons—I remember everything that has been said against me, and forget all the rest.*' (James Knowles, 'Aspects of Tennyson, II', *Nineteenth Century* (January 1893), xxxiii. 173–74).

Knowles' account receives confirmation from Julia Margaret Cameron, the well-known photographer, who was also a friend of Tennyson's: 'he was very sensitive to any critical opinion, so sensitive that I have heard him say, all the praise he had ever received didn't outweigh for the moment a spiteful and unkindly criticism, even though the criticism (he once added) was directed against the straightness of his toe-nail' (Hallam Tennyson, *op. cit.*, p. 490). Towards the end of his 'ten years' silence', Tennyson made it a condition of his appearing again in print, as his publisher desired, that Spedding should '*undertake to review him*'. Spedding agreed to do this and arrived at an understanding with the editor of the *Edinburgh*. His article was to be 'no puff—but an honest criticism', and the editor was to take it if it was not too fervent (E. F. Shannon, *Tennyson and the Reviewers: A Study of His Literary Reputation and of the Influence of the Critics upon His Poetry 1827–1851* (Cambridge, Mass., 1952), pp. 35–6). Since Spedding was out of the country at the crucial time, his review (No. 10) did not appear until nearly a year after the issue of the two volumes of *Poems* (1842).

Another consequence of Tennyson's habit of brooding upon hostile criticism was the very thorough revision to which he subjected his poems of 1830 and 1833. E. F. Shannon, whose exhaustive and invaluable *Tennyson and the Reviewers* has provided a good deal of the material used in the earlier sections of the present Introduction, concludes from a careful statistical investigation that

> he would not have revised so thoroughly or been so selective in reprinting had he not been so severely censured. With his self-criticism aroused, he went beyond the reviewers and produced incomparably superior work in the second versions of such poems as 'Oenone' and 'The Lady of Shalott'; but in these instances he was often correcting along lines the critics had indicated. Still, in most of the poems there were many more verbal changes and omissions than were suggested by his censors, and mere altering of criticized passages would not have accomplished what he did. When he could not agree with the reviewers, he ignored them. Yet both in his revisions and in the suppression of poems he accepted the opinion of the critics in more than half of their strictures. Finally, in the new poems of 1842, in both style and content, there is a significant concurrence with the advice of the reviewers. The periodicals expressed representative opinion; and more important than that, they had a large share in forming the literary taste of the public. An attentive consideration of the judgments of such organs was in order for a young poet who was determined to win recognition of his talents. (p. 59).

During his 'ten years' silence', Tennyson did not by any means disappear from public notice. Two poems which he contributed to annuals attracted some attention. Reviewers and others continued to refer to him. To twentieth-century readers, the most interesting of these printed allusions is probably the one that occurs in *Specimens of the Table Talk of the Late Samuel Taylor Coleridge* (1835), ii. 164–5:

> I have not read through all Mr. Tennyson's poems, which have been sent to me; but I think there are some things of a good deal of beauty in what I have seen. The misfortune is, that he has begun to write verses without very well understanding what metre is. Even if you write in a known and approved metre, the odds are, if you are not a metrist yourself, that you will not write harmonious verses; but to deal in new metres without considering what metre means and requires, is preposterous. What I would, with many wishes for success, prescribe to Tennyson,—indeed without it he can never be a poet in act,—is to write for the next two or three years in none but one or two well-known and strictly defined metres, such as the heroic couplet, the octave stanza, or the octo-syllabic measure of the

Allegro and Penseroso. He would, probably, thus get imbued with a sensation, if not a sense, of metre without knowing it, just as Eton boys get to write such good Latin verses by conning Ovid and Tibullus. As it is, I can scarcely scan his verses.

There is no record of Tennyson's immediate reaction to this verdict. But in later life he admitted that 'in the folly of youth' he had 'played some tricks with orthography and metre. But Coleridge ought (only old men get shut up in themselves) to have seen that it was from wanton-ness, not ignorance' (Sir Charles Tennyson, *Alfred Tennyson* (1949), p. 91).

Tennyson's 1842 collection contained, often in revised forms, such of his 1830 and 1833 poems as he wished at that date to preserve, together with a slightly greater quantity of new verse. The two volumes sold well; and from the start the reviewers gave them a reception which, though far from uncritical, was distinctly sympathetic. The efforts of Tennyson's friends undoubtedly contributed to this result. Moreover, suspicion of his politics had now faded; so critics were free to judge his work on its intrinsic merits.

An early review of special interest was that contributed, perhaps by Francis Garden, an old Cambridge acquaintance, to the *Christian Remembrancer*. This High Church monthly was running a series of articles under the general title, 'Poetry of the Year 1842'; after Words-worth and Campbell had shared an article in June, Tennyson received one to himself in July (No. 6). This recognized that he held 'the fore-most place' among the younger poets but complained that he had 'not yet become *human* enough'. The writer mentioned Hallam's review of 1831 (No. 2) as propounding a 'mistaken theory' that had perhaps misled Tennyson, the theory 'that to realize its aim, art should keep quite distinct from all that is not of itself—that poetry, therefore, as a branch of art, should admit nothing heterogeneous, such as persuasion to any particular line of belief or conduct, the inculcation of opinion, and so forth.'

The line taken by the writer in the *Christian Remembrancer* had al-ready been taken by W. J. Fox (No. 1) when he urged Tennyson in 1831 to keep 'distinct and worthy objects before him, and consecrate himself to their promotion'. Broadly similar advice occurs in one after another of the articles on the 1842 volumes. John Sterling's review (No. 7), with which the *Quarterly* made its public recantation of the error into which Croker had led it, embodies the assumption that great poetry must reflect the life of its time. Richard Monckton Milnes' somewhat disjointed notice (No. 9) in the *Westminster* concludes with an exhortation to Tennyson 'to show that he has substance (what Goethe used to call *stoff*) worthy of' his powers as a craftsman; and that 'he comprehends the function of the poet in this day of ours, to teach still more than he delights, and to suggest still more than he teaches'. In his delayed review in the *Edinburgh* (No. 10), Spedding argued that Tennyson was not lacking in 'a sound view of human life and the condition of man in the world' and urged him to incorporate this in 'a great work' of some length. These critics were directing Tennyson into various paths, but the paths all led in very much the same direction. Tennyson was being pressed to write a long poem, to handle an important contemporary subject, to display more human sympathy, and to inculcate sound doctrine. He was to respond with *The Princess* (1847).

In the meantime, the pressure continued. In *A New Spirit of the Age* (1844), R. H. Horne (No. 11) claimed for Tennyson 'the title of a true poet of the highest class of genius' but conceded that he was not yet 'in a fixed attitude; not resolute as to means, not determined as to end —sure of his power, sure of his activity, but not sure of his objects'. Thomas Carlyle, however, believed that Tennyson was growing more sure of these, was 'manufacturing [his chaos] into Cosmos'. In a letter of 1844 to Emerson, he wrote:

> Moxon informs me . . . that Tennyson is now in Town, and means to come and see me. Of this latter result I shall be very glad: Alfred is one of the few British or Foreign Figures (a not increasing number I think!) who are and remain beautiful to me;—a true human soul, or some authentic approximation thereto, to whom your own soul can say, Brother!—However, I doubt he will not come; he often skips me, in these brief visits to Town; skips everybody indeed; being a man solitary and sad, as certain men are, dwelling in an element of gloom,—carrying a bit of Chaos about him, in short, which he is manufacturing into Cosmos!

> . . . I think he must be under forty, not much under it. One of the finest-looking men in the world. A great shock of rough, dusty-dark hair; bright-laughing hazel eyes; massive aquiline face, most massive yet most delicate; of sallow-brown complexion, almost Indian-looking; clothes cynically loose, free-and-easy;—smokes infinite tobacco. His voice is musical metallic,—fit for loud laughter and piercing wail, and all that may lie between; speech and speculation free and plenteous: I do not meet, in these late decades, such company

over a pipe!—We shall see what he will grow to. He is often unwell; very chaotic,—his way is through Chaos and the Bottomless and Pathless; not handy for making out many miles upon. (*The Correspondence of Thomas Carlyle and Ralph Waldo Emerson 1834-1872* (1883), ii. 66-7)

George Gilfillan also praised him highly but finally limited his praise by stressing that Tennyson was 'less a prophet than an artist' ('Alfred Tennyson', *Tait's Edinburgh Magazine* (April 1847), N.S. xiv. 229-34). Henry Sutton, on the other hand, wrote sympathetically of 'The Lady of Shalott' as an allegorical rendering of the artist's need to 'keep his own island of individuality to himself' and resist 'the enticements of delusive Fame' (*Howitt's Journal* (15th January 1848), iii. 39-42).

The Princess (1847) had a mainly favourable reception. In *Fraser's*, Charles Kingsley (No. 13) welcomed it as mirroring the nineteenth century and embodying an essentially modern idea. But some of the reviewers saw things differently and regretted that Tennyson was still writing in the vein of art rather than in the vein of prophecy. A few, notably J. Westland Marston in the *Athenæum* (No. 12), complained of incongruities in the new work; and many more, of whom Marston again was one, felt that it marked no clear advance on its predecessors.

Contemporary criticism caused Tennyson to revise it extensively between 1847 and 1853, and even to some degree later; on the whole, the poem benefited from his alterations. He polished the metre and the wording in many places; he modified passages in the Prologue, the Interlude, and the Conclusion with a view to reducing incongruity— though George Brimley was still complaining of this in 1855; he tried to give more coherence and nobility to the character of the Princess; and he inserted the rhyming songs which now stand between the sections of the work.

Again and again during the eighteen-forties, both before and after the publication of *The Princess*, critics asserted that Tennyson's work was showing little or no progress. Despite the high reputation which he enjoyed at the end of the decade, he was still far from the peak of his fame. *In Memoriam* (1850) was to bring him close to that.

Although this was at first published anonymously, there was little doubt about its authorship. Its reception could hardly have been more enthusiastic than it was. George Henry Lewes expected it to become 'the solace and delight of every house where poetry is loved' and described its author as the 'greatest living poet' (*Leader* (22nd June 1850),

i. 303–04). Critics decided that *In Memoriam* could stand comparison even with Milton's 'Lycidas' and with the sonnets of Shakespeare. In welcoming it as a noble expression of Christian doctrines, Charles Kingsley (No. 13) was typical of the great majority of reviewers. Admittedly, there were some who felt misgivings about the firmness of Tennyson's religious faith; but, like their colleagues who found the work rather monotonous, they were few and had little influence. Agreement was almost complete that Tennyson had at last written the long prophetic poem, displaying deep human sympathies and inculcating sound doctrine in a form relevant to contemporary needs, for which his critics had been asking for years. Not surprisingly, the book sold very fast indeed, entering a fifth edition within eighteen months. There had been nothing like it since the period of Byron's greatest popular success.

Victorian readers came to use *In Memoriam* almost as a book of devotions. The Queen herself, during the earliest months of her widowhood, permitted the Duke of Argyll to inform Tennyson that 'She is finding much that she loves to dwell on in your "In Memoriam". She especially desired me to tell you this last night, and she gave me her copy to shew "how well it was read" and how many the passages she had marked. It will touch you, I think, to know that she had substituted "widow" for "widower" and "her" for "his" in the lines "Tears of a widower" ' (Sir Charles Tennyson, *op. cit.*, p. 336). 'I sometimes wonder,' wrote J. R. Green, the historian, 'whether poets ever have a glimpse of all the joy and comfort they give the world. There was a dark time in my life, when I could hardly have borne to go on with living, but for the quiet morning hour before breakfast when I read and re-read "In Memoriam" ' (Sir Charles Tennyson, *op. cit.*, p. 438). A. C. Bradley's valuable *Commentary on Tennyson's 'In Memoriam'* (1901) was by no means the earliest handbook to provide a detailed elucidation of the poem. Alfred Gatty, in *A Key to Tennyson's 'In Memoriam'* (1881), and Elizabeth Rachel Chapman, in *A Companion to 'In Memoriam'* (1888), were Bradley's most important predecessors. Gatty testifies that, since his 'home was darkened by death, the Poem has been a sublime resource and consolation' (p. iv); he feels certain that it will offer 'a rich legacy of comfort to all future generations of mourners' (p. 144). His commentary takes the form of a series of brief section-by-section paraphrases of the whole of *In Memoriam*. Elizabeth Rachel Chapman's takes the same form, but, since her paraphrases are less allusive than his, her volume is only one-half as long. In her Preface to the second edition (1901), she proudly records that Tennyson himself had declared his approval of it.

When Tennyson took the crucial decision to shape into a long philosophical poem the lyrics which he had begun writing in 1833 immediately on hearing of Hallam's death and about one-half of which existed by 1842, he was no doubt influenced by the insistent advice of his earlier critics. When the work was published in 1850, its reception was so favourable that he evidently felt little need to revise it further. He introduced few changes in later editions.

But *Maud* (1855) met with reprobation so widespread as almost to drown the voices raised on its behalf in the *Spectator* and elsewhere. Walter Bagehot (No. 18) states the case against it with some emphasis, and George Brimley (No. 15) and Robert James Mann (No. 16) summarize the case before going on to defend the poem. There were two principal allegations: that *Maud* is obscure and that *Maud* is morbid. A number of critics, including Goldwin Smith (No. 14) and W. E. Gladstone (No. 19), took particular exception to the views on peace and war which were announced by the hero of the poem and apparently shared in some degree by its author.

Revising his article for publication in book form some years later, Gladstone recanted his first criticisms. He still doubted whether the obscurity of *Maud* was justifiable; 'whether all that is put into the mouth of the Soliloquist . . . is within the lines of poetical verisimilitude; [and] whether this poem has the full moral equilibrium which is so marked a characteristic of the sister-works'. But he confessed that he had not at first 'done justice . . . to its rich and copious beauties of detail, nor to its great lyrical and metrical power. And what is worse, I . . . failed to comprehend rightly the relation between particular passages in the poem and its general scope. This is, I conceive, not to set forth any coherent strain, but to use for poetical ends all the moods and phases allowable under the laws of the art, in a special form of character, which is impassioned, fluctuating, and ill-grounded' (*Gleanings of Past Years 1845–76* (1879), ii. 146–7).

Gladstone's change of mind seems to have been shared by many. Peter Bayne, who had been disappointed and even repelled by *Maud* on its first appearance, admitted twenty-four years later that he had learned to think it 'well worthy of Tennyson's genius' (*Lessons from my Masters, Carlyle, Tennyson and Ruskin* (1879), p. 245). He wrote:

When Maud appeared, Tennyson's reputation rested upon the early

9

poems and In Memoriam, and the difference between these and the new work was hardly more startling than the inferiority of the new to the old seemed to be conspicuous. But now that Tennyson has written as much again as he had then given to the world, and when it has been proved that the somewhat crude realism of Maud was but a passing variation in his manner of composition, the right of such a poem to take its place in the totality of his works—to play its part in the general Tennysonian orchestra—is much more easily recognisable. What is still more important, the Maud of 1879 is a much more excellent poem than the Maud of 1855 . . . Tennyson listened to reasonable criticism, and mended his work. (pp. 232–3)

Bayne discusses Tennyson's revisions at some length. In his opinion, they help to clarify the plot, to give sharper definition to character and motivation, and to some extent to dissociate the poet from certain of the views expressed by his hero.

Bayne was certainly not alone in discovering that Tennyson's later work helped to reconcile him to Maud by convincing him that Maud exhibited no more than a 'passing variation' from the Tennysonian norm. In particular, Idylls of the King, four of which appeared in 1859, gave readers this reassurance. The poet seemed to be continuing from where he had left off on finishing In Memoriam, and review after review was highly enthusiastic. Among the most eloquent and laudatory was Gladstone's (No. 19); rather more independent in its judgments, but still deeply respectful, was Bagehot's (No. 18).

Hallam Tennyson, in his life of his father, quotes a number of letters containing the testimony of other leading men. Longfellow considered the Idylls 'a brilliant success. Rich tapestries, wrought as only Tennyson could have done them, and worthy to hang by the Faerie Queen' (p. 348); Thackeray declared, 'You have made me as happy as I was as a child with the Arabian Nights, every step I have walked in Elfland has been a sort of Paradise to me' (p. 374); Macaulay was 'delighted with' 'Guinevere' (p. 376); Benjamin Jowett thought 'Elaine' 'the fairest, purest, sweetest love-poem in the English language' (p. 377); and Arthur Hugh Clough described the Idylls as 'just what we had a right to hope for, better, because more fully given, without any disparagement to what went before' (p. 378). John Ruskin, however, coupled his praise of a great artist with a reservation:

I am not sure but I feel the art and finish in these poems a little more than I like to feel it. Yet I am not a fair judge quite, for I am so much of a realist as not by any possibility to interest myself much in an unreal subject to feel it as I should, and the very sweetness and stateliness of the words strike me all the more as *pure* workmanship.

As a description of various nobleness and tenderness the book is without price: but I shall always wish it had been nobleness independent of a romantic condition of externals in general.

'In Memoriam', 'Maud', 'The Miller's Daughter', and such like will always be my own pet rhymes, yet I am quite prepared to admit this to be as good as any, for its own peculiar audience. Treasures of wisdom there are in it, and word-painting such as never was yet for concentration, nevertheless it seems to me that so great power ought not to be spent on visions of things past but on the living present. For one hearer capable of feeling the depth of this poem I believe ten would feel a depth quite as great if the stream flowed through things nearer the hearer. (pp. 380-1)

Ruskin's statement of his preference for subjects belonging to 'the living present' echoes the earlier insistence of Sterling (No. 7) and others that great poetry must reflect the life of its time. By dismissing the 'Morte d'Arthur' in accordance with this view, Sterling had apparently helped to delay Tennyson's work on the Arthurian legend for a decade and a half. But Tennyson was soon to hear very much less of the doctrine. Bagehot (No. 18) rejected it in 1859; and, when Tennyson issued four more of the *Idylls* in 1869, hardly any of his reviewers complained that the subjects were remote from contemporary interests; they agreed, almost to a man, that the mediaeval setting did not prevent the poems from having an important message for the nineteenth century.

But as soon as they began to say exactly what that message was, especially in 'The Holy Grail', there was less agreement. So, when J. T. Knowles in a letter (No. 25) to the editor of the *Spectator* elucidated the Arthurian poems to their author's satisfaction, Tennyson not only wrote to Knowles in praise of '*the best, and indeed . . . the only true, critique of the Idylls*' but sent a copy of that critique by Dean Stanley to the Queen herself (James Knowles, 'Aspects of Tennyson, II', *Nineteenth Century* (January 1893), xxxiii. 181).

During the eighteen-sixties, public respect for Tennyson was almost unbounded. Reviewers in the *Spectator* thought him 'more likely than any living sovereign, and as likely as any living statesman, to give a name to the age' and hailed him as 'our only great living poet'. In a notice of F. T. Palgrave's *Golden Treasury* (1861), one of them stated that whenever it was possible to include some of Tennyson's lyrics in the anthology they would make the work complete by uniting again in themselves lyrical trends which had been dissociated since the time of Shakespeare. The *Saturday Review* agreed in regarding Tennyson as the great English poet of the period and held that he would be known to posterity 'as the poet of Arthur'. There was no reason why he should not write an excellent tragedy. To such a work 'he would bring passion, lofty or simple eloquence, constructive skill, familiarity with the phenomena of nature, with the moods of the human mind. What other qualities are demanded for the composition of *Œdipus* or *Lear*?' (See J. D. Jump, 'Weekly Reviewing in the Eighteen-Sixties', *Review of English Studies* (July 1952), N.S. iii. 244–62)

Not only was there less adverse criticism by this time but Tennyson himself had grown more resistant to such as there was. He completed the *Idylls* in accordance with his own maturely considered intentions, and he made the necessary final revisions of the instalments already published in the same independent spirit. This being so, the story of how his latest volumes were received, and of how he reacted to their reception, may remain untold here. What is now of greater interest is the development, among certain of his younger readers in particular, of two general criticisms of his work.

One of these obtained forcible expression shortly before the publication of *The Holy Grail, And other Poems* (1869, but dated 1870), the volume which contained the second instalment of four *Idylls*. In a drastic re-valuation of the Poet Laureate, a revaluation which was to provoke a reply from Henry Alford in the *Contemporary Review*, Alfred Austin (No. 24) acknowledges that the 'prevailing or universally expressed opinion' is that Tennyson 'is a great poet, a very great poet, perhaps as great a poet as ever lived'. But Austin finds his work tame: 'pretty, soothing, elegant', it is 'poetry of the drawing-room', some of it even 'namby-pamby'. This revives the old accusation underlying Edward Bulwer-Lytton's description of Tennyson, in *The New Timon* (1846), ii, as 'School-Miss Alfred'. In the same spirit, James Hain Friswell, in *Modern Men of Letters Honestly Criticised* (1879), disparages Tennyson as 'sugar sweet, pretty-pretty, full of womanly talk and feminine stuff' (p. 155). Swinburne, who in 'Tennyson and Musset' (No. 29) speaks up for his fellow-countryman against some of the strictures of the French literary historian, Hippolyte Taine (No. 21), nevertheless concedes in that essay as well as in his earlier polemic, *Under the Microscope* (No. 26), that Tennyson has diluted his Arthurian materials into a 'Morte d'Albert, or Idylls of the Prince Consort'. Gerard Manley Hopkins (No. 28) proposes the title, *Charades from the Middle Ages*; at the same time, he goes on to praise Tennyson as 'a glorious poet' and grieves 'to hear him depreciated, as of late years has often been done'. Matthew Arnold had sensed this depreciation ten years earlier, when he described Austin's essay (No. 24) 'as showing with what much greater independence' Tennyson was beginning to be judged (G. W. E. Russell (ed.), *Letters of Matthew Arnold 1848–1888* (1895), ii. 9).

The second of the two general criticisms had been formulated ten years earlier still in Ruskin's letter, already quoted, about the first four *Idylls*: 'I feel the art and finish in these poems a little more than I like to feel it.' Matthew Arnold (No. 20), finding in Tennyson's poetry 'an extreme subtlety and curious elaborateness of thought, an extreme subtlety and curious elaborateness of expression', was making a very similar point. So were Bagehot (No. 23), who took 'Enoch Arden' as his example of 'ornate' poetry, and Gerard Manley Hopkins (No. 22), who turned to the same new publication for his instance of Tennyson's 'Parnassian'. *Enoch Arden, Etc.* (1864) was an extraordinarily popular volume, perhaps more so than any other by its author. It confirmed the almost overwhelming prestige which Tennyson was to enjoy throughout the last third of his life; but there can be no doubt that it also helped to stimulate in a minority of readers the objection that his writing was too mannered and artificial.

This objection was often linked with the assertion that Tennyson was unduly dependent upon literary sources for his inspiration. To John Churton Collins (No. 35), for example, he was a minor, 'Alexandrian' poet. Collins argues that Tennyson's 'great achievements lie, not in original conceptions, but in elaborate workmanship, in assimilative skill', and he applies to him what Ovid says of Callimachus: '*Quamvis ingenio non valet arte valet*' (*Illustrations of Tennyson* (1891), pp. 117, 159–60). Understandably, Tennyson deeply resented such attentions. Shortly after the publication in the *Cornhill Magazine* for 1880 and 1881 of the articles in which Collins first tried to demonstrate this derivativeness, Tennyson complained to a correspondent: 'there is, I fear, a prosaic set growing up among us, editors of booklets, bookworms, index-hunters, or men of great memories and no imagination, who *impute themselves* to the poet, and so believe that *he*, too, has no imagination, but is for ever poking his nose between the pages of some old volume in order to see what he can appropriate' (Hallam Tennyson, *op. cit.*, p. 215).

The verb 'appropriate' fairly reports the allegations that some of these critics made. In his footnotes to the essay already mentioned (No. 24), Alfred Austin asserts that one phrase of Tennyson's is a 'bit of plagiarism from Shelley' and that another is 'copied from Keats, and spoiled in the copying'. Allegations of this kind provoked Browning to exclaim, 'Tennyson suspected of plagiarism! Why, you might as well suspect the Rothschilds of picking pockets' (Hallam Tennyson, *op. cit.*, p. 590).

During Tennyson's last years, parody became a favourite weapon of critics whose radicalism or rationalism brought them into opposition to him. Lewis Carroll had brilliantly parodied 'The Two Voices' in 1856:

> 'To dine!' she sneered in acid tone,
> 'To bend thy being to a bone
> Clothed in a radiance not its own!'
>
> The tear-drop trickled to his chin:
> There was a meaning in her grin
> That made him feel on fire within.
>
> 'Term it not "radiance",' said he:
> "Tis solid nutriment to me.
> Dinner is Dinner: Tea is Tea.'
>
> And she, 'Yea so? Yet wherefore cease!
> Let thy scant knowledge find increase.
> Say "Men are Men, and Geese are Geese".'
>
> He moaned: he knew not what to say.
> The thought 'That I could get away!'
> Strove with the thought 'But I must stay' . . .
>
> Pitying his obvious distress,
> Yet with a tinge of bitterness,
> She said 'The More exceeds the Less'.
>
> 'A truth of such undoubted weight',
> He urged, 'and so extreme in date,
> It were superfluous to state.'

Roused into sudden passion, she
In tone of cold malignity:
'To others, yea: but not to thee.'
('The Three Voices', ll. 22–36, 97–105)

But the parodists of the eighteen-eighties differed from Lewis Carroll in that they directed their attacks mainly against the poet's beliefs. Swinburne effectively opened their campaign with 'The Higher Pantheism in a Nutshell' (1880), in which mockery of Tennyson's metaphysics culminates in the lines:

God, whom we see not, is: and God, who is not, we see:
Fiddle, we know, is diddle: and diddle, we take it, is dee.

Other parodists attacked the man himself: 'And I'm to be one of the Peers, Vicky, I'm to be one of the Peers.'

On the whole, these travesties served to express the hostility of political and theological opponents. Adverse literary reactions tended to embody themselves in the complaints, already exemplified, of elegant tameness and mannered derivativeness. But these complaints came only from a small minority of Tennyson's readers during the last twenty or thirty years of his life. The vast majority steadily acknowledged what F. T. Palgrave called his 'imperial position in Poetry' (Hallam Tennyson, *op. cit.*, p. 837). R. C. Jebb, for example, exploring the relationship of Tennyson's 'Lucretius' to its subject's *De Rerum Natura*, does not seek to demonstrate plagiarism but simply to promote a fuller comprehension of an impressive English poem ('On Mr. Tennyson's "Lucretius",' *Macmillan's Magazine* (June 1868), xviii. 97–103). A similar admiration for the poet dominates the long and perceptive study by R. H. Hutton (No. 31), who defends against Swinburne (Nos. 26 and 29) the special interpretation which Tennyson placed upon his Arthurian materials and in so doing makes it clear that he esteems Tennyson as a great moral teacher. F. W. H. Myers (No. 32) sees him as 'the prophet simply of a Spiritual Universe', who has fulfilled his purpose more completely in his later than in his earlier poems. Admittedly, John M. Robertson (No. 33) has little use for Tennyson as a teacher or prophet; moreover, he finds his best work in the volumes up to and including *Maud*, 'which represents the high-water mark of the poet's lyrical achievement'; but he has a deep respect for the artistry shown in these earlier volumes. W. E. Henley's respect rests mainly on the later work, which brings to his mind 'the greater Shakespeare, the consummate Rembrandt, the unique Velasquez'

(No. 34). These critics differ on many particular points, but they are all at one in their admiration and even reverence for their great contemporary. Swinburne, who had made a habit of saying, 'I allow no one to laugh at Tennyson except myself' (Sir Charles Tennyson, *op. cit.*, p. 514), must have summed up the feelings of many when he wrote in his 'Threnody' on Tennyson's death:

> Far above us and all our love, beyond all reach of its voiceless praise,
> Shines for ever the name that never shall feel the shade of the changeful days
> Fall and chill the delight that still sees winter's light on it shine like May's.

Tennyson's popularity with American readers moved Walt Whitman (No. 30) to thank him on their behalf in 1887; and J. M. Robertson (No. 33), writing in the same year, had occasion to refer in a single essay to the printed comments of as many as three other American authors. No doubt the French had been quick off the mark with a friendly review of the volumes of 1830 and 1833 in the third number of the short-lived journal *L'Europe Littéraire* (6th March 1833, p. 13); but by the last years of Tennyson's life his principal foreign public was unquestionably transatlantic.

For thirty years after Tennyson's death, his poetry continued in great favour with readers generally. But the same period saw a considerable strengthening of the reaction against it which had been evident among sophisticated readers since the eighteen-sixties. New charges appeared in the indictment. In 1900, W. B. Yeats looked for a change 'in the manner of our poetry . . . A return to the way of our fathers, a casting out of descriptions of nature for the sake of nature, of the moral law for the sake of the moral law, a casting out of all anecdotes and of that brooding over scientific opinion that so often extinguished the central flame in Tennyson, and of that vehemence that would make us do or not do certain things' ('The Symbolism of Poetry', *Essays and Introductions* (1959), p. 163). Tennyson was felt to be too discursive and moralistic for twentieth-century needs.

Harold Nicolson's *Tennyson: Aspects of his Life, Character and Poetry* (1923) was taken by some to indicate that the reaction was coming to an end. While Nicolson was prepared to jettison a good deal of Tennyson's work, he made high claims for what he was ready to preserve. An interesting survey of the most original subsequent studies occupies the Introduction to John Killham's anthology, *Critical Essays on the Poetry of Tennyson* (1960). But we cannot claim that a marked revival of serious critical attention has yet occurred. Our symbolist assumptions seem still to inhibit us from making an appropriate response to Tennyson's work. Perhaps we can learn something from commentators whose assumptions are very different from our own.

A selection from the criticisms of Tennyson's poetry written between the date of his earliest publication and that of his death can serve several distinct purposes. It can illustrate the growth of his reputation and enable us to judge the extent to which particular developments in his work were stimulated by the praise and blame previous publications had attracted. It can dramatize the contemporary debates about his achievement by bringing Hallam into close proximity with 'Christopher North', Croker with Mill, Taine with Swinburne, and Swinburne with Hutton and with Robertson. It can give prominence to such significant presentations of theoretical principles as Hallam's sketch of a symbolist aesthetic, Sterling's insistence upon a close relationship between great poetry and the active life of its age, Swinburne's and Hutton's discussions of art and morality, and Robertson's effort to reconcile conflicting views by arguing that the poet needs a moral purpose to elicit his best energies but that a critic should judge the resultant poem in the spirit of art.

In addition, nineteenth-century criticism can illuminate particular poems for twentieth-century readers. It will not normally achieve this by close analysis of the poems in question—by 'minute criticism', as it was then called. The nearest that the nineteenth-century critics come to employing such a technique is represented in this selection by Mann's leisurely commentary upon one of the lyrics in *Maud*, by the fellow-craftsman's scrutiny of Tennyson's verse style undertaken by Hopkins, by Hutton's attempt to account in some detail for the success of 'Break, break, break', and by Robertson's investigation of the art of Tennyson by comparing revised and unrevised versions of his poems. At his most characteristic, the Victorian critic offers a rather more general account of the nature and the success of the poems with which he is concerned: Kingsley on *In Memoriam* and Gladstone on the *Idylls* are typical. At the same time, we must not underestimate the closeness of the reading that underlies many of these general formulations or the delicacy of the analysis which can be conducted in these general terms.

Goldwin Smith's essay on the war passages in *Maud* is a remarkable instance. The hero of *Maud* wants war, not because he believes it to be 'just and necessary', but because he thinks it will cure his country's Mammonism and his own neurosis—such is Goldwin Smith's summary; and this calling in of war to work a double cure is related to 'the general philosophy' of Tennyson's poems. Throughout these, 'we feel the force of circumstances, nowhere the energy of free will'. In Tennyson's hands, even the Homeric Ulysses merely 'intends to roam, but stands for ever a listless and melancholy figure on the shore'. Goldwin Smith, taking the war passages in *Maud* as his starting-point, has successfully moved out from them to a searching analysis of his author's outlook on life.

But comparison is one of the most useful of all tools in the hands of nineteenth-century critics. Though few of them can handle it with anything like the dexterity and tact shown by Matthew Arnold, many of them use it to very good effect. Taine compares Tennyson, to his disadvantage, with Musset; Swinburne repeats the manoeuvre in order to reverse the outcome. Critic after critic compares Tennyson with his immediate predecessors, Wordsworth, Byron, Shelley, and Keats, and with his contemporary, Browning. The *Idylls* are compared with the classical epics, *In Memoriam* with the classical elegies. Robertson gives his reasons for thinking Tennyson a finer artist than Gray; Austin and Collins introduce the names of minor poets in order to rank Tennyson no higher than them. Such are the means by which the critics communicate many of their most shrewd and most exact observations.

Nearly half of the items included in the present volume are separate articles reprinted without cuts. Both in these and in the other items, however, space has been saved by substituting references to the 'Oxford Standard Authors' edition for most of the longer quotations from Tennyson; and various reviewers' references to pages in the original editions have been silently deleted as unlikely to be serviceable to readers today. Three asterisks across the page are used to indicate an extensive omission. Obvious misprints have been corrected. In general, the earlier versions of reviews have been preferred to the later, but the revised versions of other articles have been preferred to the unrevised. Footnotes are invariably those of the authors of the texts to which they relate. Such editorial explanations as seem necessary have been placed in the head-notes to the items in question; and the assumption that readers will have access to standard works of reference has made it possible to keep their number very low. Each head-note opens with a reference to the complete book, article, lecture, or letter from which the passage in question has been taken; when necessary, a reference to the location of the passage within this work occurs in the second paragraph. The footnotes are those of the original texts.

For permission to quote two passages from the letters of Gerard Manley Hopkins as edited by C. C. Abbott and published by the Oxford University Press, I make grateful acknowledgement; full particulars are given in the relevant head-notes. I am also indebted to Messrs. Ernest Benn for kindly authorizing me to quote, from J. M. Robertson's *Essays Towards a Critical Method*, the whole of 'The Art of Tennyson'. My friends have been most generous in placing special knowledge and skill at my disposal. Mr. Christopher Ricks of Worcester College, Oxford, drew my attention to several important critical documents which he had met while preparing what is to be the first fully annotated edition of Tennyson's poems and also made a number of valuable detailed comments on an early draft of my Introduction. Dr. R. G. Cox of the University of Manchester kindly permitted me to take advantage of his extensive acquaintance with nineteenth-century periodical criticism. Others advised me and informed me in response to particular questions which I put to them. To all of these, I am deeply grateful.

JOHN D. JUMP

1. W. J. Fox on

Poems, Chiefly Lyrical [1830]

William Johnson Fox, unsigned review, *Westminster Review*
(January 1831), xiv. 210–24.

Fox (1786–1864) was a nonconformist preacher, politician,
and author. He contributed to the first number of the
Benthamite *Westminster Review*, and early in the present
essay he welcomes the appearance of 'the utilitarian spirit'
in literary criticism.

It would be a pity that poetry should be an exception to the great law of
progression that obtains in human affairs; and it is not. The machinery
of a poem is not less susceptible of improvement than the machinery of
a cotton-mill; nor is there any better reason why the one should retrograde from the days of Milton, than the other from those of Arkwright.
Of course we do not mean that the cases are precisely parallel, but the
difference is not so much in favour of the perfectibility of the cotton-
mill as is often imagined. Man cannot be less progressive than his own
works and contrivances; in fact it is by his improvement that they are
improved; and the mechanical arts are continually becoming superior
to what they were, just because the men who are occupied in or about
those arts have grown wiser than their predecessors, and have the advantage of a clearer knowledge of principles, an experience more
extended or more accurately recorded, and perhaps a stronger stimulus
to invention. Their progressiveness is merely a consequence from, a sort
of reflection of, the progressiveness of his nature; but poetry is far nearer
and dearer; it is essential to that nature itself; it is part and parcel of his
constitution; and can only retrograde in the retrogradation of humanity.

There is nothing mysterious, or anomalous, in the power of producing poetry, or in that of its enjoyment; neither the one nor the other is
a supernatural gift bestowed capriciously nobody knows how, when,

or why. It may be a compound, but it is not incapable of analysis; and although our detection of the component parts may not enable us to effect their combination at pleasure, it may yet guide us to many useful conclusions and well-grounded anticipations. The elements of poetry are universal. The exercise of the organs of sight and sense stimulates man to some degree of descriptive poetry; wherever there is passion, there is dramatic poetry; wherever enthusiasm, there is lyric poetry; wherever reflection, there is metaphysical poetry. It is as widely diffused as the electric fluid. It may be seen flashing out by fits and starts all the world over. The most ignorant talk poetry when they are in a state of excitement, the firmly-organized think and feel poetry with every breeze of sensation that sweeps over their well-tuned nerves. There is an unfathomable store of it in human nature; the species must fail before that can be exhausted; the only question is, whether there be any reason why these permanent elements should not be wrought into their combined form, in the future, with a facility and power which bear some direct ratio to the progress of society.

So far as poetry is dependent upon physical organization; and doubtless it is to some extent so dependent; there is no reason why it should deteriorate. Eyes and ears are organs which nature finishes off with very different gradations of excellence. Nervous systems vary from the finest degree of susceptibility down to the toughness of a coil of hempen cable. *Poeta nascitur* in a frame the most favourable to acute perception and intense enjoyment of the objects of sense; and it would be difficult to shew that poets are not, and will not continue to be, produced as excellent as they have been, and as frequently. Why, then, should not those species of poetry which may be termed its music and its painting, which spring from, and appeal to, our sense of the beautiful in form or colour and of harmonious modulation, abound as much as heretofore? He is no lover of nature who has any notion that the half of her loveliness has ever yet been told. Descriptive poetry is the most exhaustible; but our coal mines will fail us much sooner. No man ever yet saw all the beauty of a landscape. He may have watched it from the rising to the setting sun, and through the twilight, and the moonlight, and the starlight, and all round the seasons, but he is deceived if he thinks then that it has nothing more for him. Indeed it is not he who ever will think so, but the man who drove down one day and back the next because he found the place so dull. The world has tired of descriptive poetry because it has been deluged with what was neither poetical nor descriptive. The world was quite right to be no longer tolerant of the repetition of conventional, traditionary, unfelt, and unmeaning phrases. But Cowper did not find the ground preoccupied. Bucolics, and Georgics, and Eclogues, and Pastorals, all made reverential room for his honest verses; and the shelf on which they took their stand is far from crowded. Nature will never cease to be poetical, nor society either. Spears and shields; gods, goddesses, and muses; and all the old scenery and machinery may indeed wear out. That is of little consequence. The age of chivalry was but one, and poetry has many ages. The classical and romantic schools are both but sects of a religion which is universal. Even the fields which have been most frequently reaped will still bear harvests; and rich ones too. Bards began with battles some thousands of years ago, and yet nobody ever wrote the Fight of Flodden field till it was indited by Scott, nor did any one anticipate Campbell's glorious ballad of the battle of Hohenlinden. Genius is never anticipated. No wit ever complained that all the good things had been said; nor will any poet, to the world's end, find that all worthy themes have been sung. Is not the French Revolution as good as the siege of Troy? And the landing of the Pilgrim Fathers on the shores of America, as that of the Trojan fugitives on the coast of Italy? The world has never been more disposed to make the want of a hero 'an uncommon want' than in these supposed unpoetical days on which we are fallen. And were they not provided, poetry might do without them. The old epics will probably never be surpassed, any more than the old coats of mail; and for the same reason; nobody wants the article; its object is accomplished by other means; they are become mere curiosities. A long story, with a plot to be ravelled and unravelled, and characters to be developed, and descriptions to be introduced, and a great moral lesson at the end of it, is now always done, and best done, in prose. A large portion always was prose in fact, and necessarily so; but literary superstition kept up the old forms after every body felt them intolerably wearisome and soporific, though few dared be so heretical as to say so, until the utilitarian spirit shewed itself even in poetical criticism, and then the dull farce ended. This we take to be a great reformation. We have left off singing what ought only to be said, but the singing is neither the less nor the worse on that account. Nor will it be. The great principle of human improvement is at work in poetry as well as every where else. What is it that is reforming our criminal jurisprudence? What is shedding its lights over legislation? What purifies religions? What makes all arts and sciences more available for human comfort and enjoyment? Even that which will secure a succession of creations out of the unbounded and everlasting materials of poetry, our ever-growing acquaintance with the philosophy of mind and of man, and the increasing facility with which that philosophy is applied. This is the essence of poetic power, and he who possesses it never need furbish up ancient armour, or go to the East Kehama-hunting or bulbul-catching. Poetry, like charity, begins at home. Poetry, like morality, is founded on the precept, know thyself. Poetry, like happiness, is in the human heart. Its inspiration is of that which is in man, and it will never fail because there are changes in costume and grouping. What is the vitality of the *Iliad*? Character; nothing else. All the rest is only read either out of antiquarianism or of affectation. Why is Shakspeare the greatest of poets? Because he was one of the greatest of philosophers. We reason on the conduct of his characters with as little hesitation as if they were real living human beings. Extent of observation, accuracy of thought, and depth of reflection, were the qualities which won the prize of sovereignty for his imagination, and the effect of these qualities was practically to anticipate, so far as was needful for his purposes, the mental philosophy of a future age. Metaphysics must be the stem of poetry for the plant to thrive; but if the stem flourishes we are not likely to be at a loss for leaves, flowers, and fruit. Now whatever theories may have come into fashion, and gone out of fashion, the real science of mind advances with the progress of society like all other sciences. The poetry of the last forty years already shews symptoms of life in exact proportion as it is imbued with this science. There is least of it in the exotic legends of Southey, and the feudal romances of Scott. More if it, though in different ways, in Byron and Campbell. In Shelley there would have been more still, had he not devoted himself to unsound and mystical theories. Most of all in Coleridge and Wordsworth. They are all going or gone; but here is a little book as thoroughly and unitedly metaphysical and poetical in its spirit as any of them; and sorely shall we be disappointed in its author if it be not the precursor of a series of productions which shall beautifully illustrate our speculations, and convincingly prove their soundness.

Do not let our readers be alarmed. These poems are anything but heavy; anything but stiff and pedantic, except in one particular, which shall be noticed before we conclude; anything but cold and logical. They are graceful, very graceful; they are animated, touching, and impassioned. And they are so, precisely because they are philosophical; because they are not made up of metrical cant and conventional phraseology; because there is sincerity where the author writes from experience, and accuracy whether he writes from experience or observation;

and he only writes from experience or observation, because he has felt and thought, and learned to analyze thought and feeling; because his own mind is rich in poetical associations, and he has wisely been content with its riches; and because, in his composition, he has not sought to construct an elaborate and artificial harmony, but only to pour forth his thoughts in those expressive and simple melodies whose meaning, truth, and power, are the soonest recognized and the longest felt.

The most important department in which metaphysical science has been a pioneer for poetry is in the analysis of particular states of mind; a work which is now performed with ease, power, and utility as much increased, as in the grosser dissections of the anatomical lecturer. Hence the poet, more fortunate than the physician, has provision made for an inexhaustible supply of subjects. A new world is discovered for him to conquer. The poets of antiquity rarely did more than incidentally touch this class of topics; the external world had not yet lost its freshness; situations, and the outward expression of the thoughts, feelings and passions generated by those situations, were a province so much nearer at hand, and presented so much to be done and enjoyed, that they rested there content, like the two tribes and a half of Israel, who sought not to cross the narrow boundary that separated them from a better and richer country. Nor let them be blamed; it was for the philosophers to be the first discoverers and settlers, and for poetry afterwards to reap the advantage of their labours. This has only been done recently, or rather is only beginning to be done at all. Metaphysical systems and discussions in verse, there have been indeed, from Lucretius down to Akenside. But they have generally had just argument enough to spoil the poetry, and just poetry enough to spoil the argument. They resembled paintings of the bones, arteries, veins, and muscles; very bad as a substitute to the anatomist for the real substances in the human body, and still worse for the artist as the materials for a pleasant picture. Science, mental or physical, cannot be taught poetically; but the power derived from science may be used poetically; and metaphysics may do as much for the poet as anatomy has done for the painter,—in truth, more,—for the painter's knowledge of the human frame does not furnish him with distinct subjects for the exercise of his art; we have just re-marked the unfitness. The benefit which the painter derives is that of being able to delineate the external appearances of the living body with greater truth and effect. And while the poet has an analogous advantage from mental science in the greater truth and effect of his delineations of external action, character, passion, and all that belongs to situation and

25

grouping; he also finds in the phenomena exhibited in moral dissection (though not in the operation itself, in the application of the logical scalpel) some of the finest originals for his pictures; and they exist in infinite variety.

Mr. Tennyson has some excellent specimens of this class. He seems to obtain entrance into a mind as he would make his way into a landscape; he climbs the pineal gland as if it were a hill in the centre of the scene; looks around on all objects with their varieties of form, their movements, their shades of colour, and their mutual relations and influences; and forthwith produces as graphic a delineation in the one case as Wilson or Gainsborough could have done in the other, to the great enrichment of our gallery of intellectual scenery. In the 'Supposed Confessions of a second-rate sensitive mind not in unity with itself', there is an extraordinary combination of deep reflection, metaphysical analysis, picturesque description, dramatic transition, and strong emotion. The author personates (he can personate anything he pleases from an angel to a grasshopper) a timid sceptic, but who must evidently always remain such, and yet be miserable in his scepticism; whose early associations, and whose sympathies, make religion a necessity to his heart; yet who has not lost his pride in the prowess of his youthful infidelity; who is tossed hither and thither on the conflicting currents of feeling and doubt, without that vigorous intellectual decision which alone could 'ride in the whirlwind and direct the storm', until at last he disappears with an exclamation which remains on the ear like

> the bubbling cry
> Of some strong swimmer in his agony

Now without intruding any irreverent comparison or critical profanity we do honestly think this state of mind as good a subject for poetical description as even the shield of Achilles itself. Such topics are more in accordance with the spirit and intellect of the age than those about which poetry has been accustomed to be conversant; their adoption will effectually redeem it from the reproach of being frivolous and enervating; and of their affinity with the best pictorial qualities of poetry we have conclusive evidence in this very composition. The delineations of the trustful infant, the praying mother, the dying lamb, are as good as anything of the kind can be; while those of the supposed author's emotions as he gazes on 'Christians with happy countenances', or stands by the Christian grave, or realizes again, with a mixture of self-admiration and self-reproach, 'the unsunned freshness of his strength', when he 'went forth in quest of truth', are of a higher order, and are more powerfully, though not less gracefully finished.

Our author has the secret of the transmigration of the soul. He can cast his own spirit into any living thing, real or imaginary. Scarcely Vishnu himself becomes incarnate more easily, frequently, or perfectly. And there is singular refinement, as well as solid truth, in his impersonations, whether they be of inferior creatures or of such elemental beings as Syrens, as mermen and mermaidens. He does not merely assume their external shapes, and exhibit his own mind masquerading. He takes their senses, feelings, nerves, and brain, along with their names and local habitations; still it is himself in them, modified but not absorbed by their peculiar constitution and mode of being. In 'the merman' one seems to feel the principle of thought injected by a strong volition into the cranium of the finny worthy, and coming under all the influences, as thinking principles do, of the physical organization to which it is for the time allied: for a moment the identification is complete; and then a consciousness of contrast springs up between the reports of external objects brought to the mind by the senses and those which it has been accustomed to receive; and this consciousness gives to the description a most poetical colouring:

> There would be neither moon nor star;
> But the wave would make music above us afar—
> Low thunder and light in the magic night—
>   Neither moon nor star.
> We would call aloud in the dreary dells, &c.

The Mermaid is beautifully discriminated, and most delicately drawn. She is the younger sister of Undine; or Undine herself before she had a soul. And the Syrens,—who could resist these Sea Fairies, as the author prefers calling them? We must introduce a fragment of their song, though it is barbarous to break such a piece of coral for a specimen:

[Quotes the passage corresponding with ll. 9–42 in the final version of 'The Sea-Fairies'.]

The poet has here done, in the character of the Sea-Fairies, that which he has several times done in his own person, and always admirably; he has created a scene out of the character, and made the feeling within generate an appropriate assemblage of external objects. Every mood of the mind has its own outward world, or rather makes its own outward world. But it is not always, perhaps with sensitive and imaginative minds it is seldom, that the external objects, and their qualities will be seen through the medium of congeniality. It is thus in 'L'Allegro' and 'Il Penseroso'; but Milton was a happy man; the visions of both those poems were seen with the eyes of happiness, the only difference being that the one depicts a state of light-hearted, and the other of sober-minded enjoyment. There is not less truth, perhaps a more refined observation, in the opposite course which our author has taken in the two poems 'Nothing will die', and 'All things will die'. The outward objects, at the commencement of each, are precisely the same; the states of mind, are in contrast; and each seizes with avidity on some appearance which is uncongenial with itself. He who thinks that nothing will die, yet looks with wondering, and almost wearied eye on the ever-flowing stream, &c.; and he, who feels that all things must die, gazes mournfully on those same objects in the 'gayest, happiest attitude', which his own fancy has unconsciously compelled them to assume. There is this difference, however, that the felicitous conviction, in the first poem, enables the mind to recover itself with a sort of elastic bound; while in the second the external beauty and enjoyment, being at permanent variance with the tone of feeling, the mind after a melancholy recognition of their loveliness sinks into unmixed gloom, and surrounds itself with objects of deeper and darker shade. We shall be better understood by quoting the commencement of each.

[Quotes 'Nothing Will Die', ll. 1–13:

   'When will the stream be aweary of flowing . . .
   Nothing will die.'

and 'All Things Will Die', ll. 1–13:

   'Clearly the blue river chimes in its flowing . . .
   For all things must die.']

Both poems conclude nearly in the same terms, with the exception of a discriminative epithet or two; but expressing in the one case an exulting joyousness, 'So let the wind range'; and in the other a reckless and desperate gaiety, just as religion and infidelity sometimes approximate, in terms, to the inculcation of the same moral; and while the preacher of immortality cries 'rejoice evermore', the expectant of annihilation shouts, 'Let us eat and drink, for to-morrow we die.'

'Mariana' is, we are disposed to think, although there are several poems which rise up reproachfully in our recollection as we say so, altogether, the most perfect composition in the volume. The whole of this poem, of eighty-four lines, is generated by the legitimate process of poetical creation, as that process is conducted in a philosophical mind, from a half sentence in Shakespeare. There is no mere amplification; it is all production; and production from that single germ. That must be a rich intellect, in which thoughts thus take root and grow. Mariana, the forsaken betrothed of Angelo, is described in *Measure for Measure*, as living in seclusion at 'the moated grange'. Mr. Tennyson knows the place well; the ruinous, old, lonely house, the neglected garden, the forlorn stagnation of the locality.

> About a stonecast from the wall,
>   A sluice with blackened waters slept,
> And o'er it many, round and small,
>   The clustered marishmosses crept.
> Hard by a poplar shook alway,
>   All silvergreen with gnarled bark,
> For leagues no other tree did dark
>   The level waste, the rounding grey.

And here it was, that the deserted one lingered day after day in that 'hope deferred which maketh the heart sick'. The dreariness of the abode and the surrounding scenery was nothing to her;

> She only said, 'My life is dreary,
>   He cometh not,' she said;
> She said, 'I am aweary, aweary,
>   I would that I were dead!'

The poem takes us through the circuit of four-and-twenty hours of this dreary life. Through all the changes of the night and day she has but one feeling, the variation of which is only by different degrees of acuteness and intensity in the misery it produces; and again and again we feel, before its repetition, the coming of the melancholy burthen.

[Quotes 'Mariana', ll. 49–60:

> 'And ever when the moon was low . . .
> I would that I were dead." ']

The day, by its keener expectancy, was more harassing and agitating than the night; and by its sights and sounds, in that lonely place, and under the strange interpretations of a morbid fancy and a breaking heart, did yet more 'confound her sense'. Her deserted parents, the grey-headed domestics that had nursed her infancy in her father's house, seemed to be there; she recognized them, and what would they with her?

> Old faces glimmered through the doors,
> Old footsteps trod the upper floors,
> Old voices called her from without.

Again the hour passed at which Angelo used to arrive; again the evening is come when he used to be there, where he never would be again; the bright sunshiny evening, blazing and fading; and

> ——————most she loathed the hour
> When the thickmoted sunbeam lay
> Athwart the chambers, and the day
> Downsloped was westering in his bower.
> Then said she, 'I am very dreary,
> He will not come,' she said;
> She wept, 'I am aweary, aweary,
> Oh God, that I were dead!'

A considerable number of the poems are amatory; they are the expression not of heartless sensuality, nor of a sickly refinement, nor of fantastic devotion, but of manly love; and they illustrate the philosophy of the passion while they exhibit the various phases of its existence, and embody its power. An arrangement of them might be made which should depict the whole history of passion from its birth to its apotheosis, or its death.

[Quotes 'The Burial of Love', ll. 1–13:

> 'His eyes in eclipse . . .
> Love is dead.']

Had we space we should discuss this topic. It is of incalculable importance to society. Upon what love is, depends what woman is, and upon what woman is, depends what the world is, both in the present and the future. There is not a greater moral necessity in England than that of a reformation in female education. The boy is a son; the youth is a lover; and the man who thinks lightly of the elevation of character and the extension of happiness which woman's influence is capable of producing, and ought to be directed to the production of, in society, is neither the wisest of philosophers nor the best of patriots. How long will it be before we shall have read to better purpose the eloquent lessons, and the yet more eloquent history, of that gifted and glorious being, Mary Wollstonecraft?

Mr. Tennyson sketches females as well as ever did Sir Thomas Lawrence. His portraits are delicate, his likenesses (we will answer for them) perfect, and they have life, character, and individuality. They are nicely assorted also to all the different gradations of emotion and passion which are expressed in common with the descriptions of them. There is an appropriate object for every shade of feeling, from the light touch of a passing admiration, to the triumphant madness of soul and sense, or the deep and everlasting anguish of survivorship.

Lilian is the heroine of the first stage:

> Airy, fairy Lilian,
> Flitting, fairy Lilian,
> When I ask her if she love me,
> Claps her tiny hands above me,
> Laughing all she can;
> She'll not tell me if she love me,
> Cruel little Lilian.

Madeline indicates that another degree has been taken in the freemasonry of love, 'smiling frowning evermore'. And so we are conducted, through various gradations, to Isabel, 'the stately flower of female fortitude, and perfect wifehood', to the intense and splendid passion of 'Hero', and to the deep pathos of the ballad and dirge of 'Oriana'.

We had noted many other passages for extract or remark, but our limits are prescribed and almost arrived at. We should also have illustrated the felicitous effect often produced by the iteration of a word or sentence so posited that it conveys a different meaning or shade of meaning, excites a varied kind of emotion, and is involuntarily uttered in a different tone. There are many beautiful instances of this kind. In the ballad of Oriana, and in the songs, repetition, with a slight variation of epithet, is also practised with great power. Rousseau's *air des trois notes* is only a curiosity; Mr. Tennyson has made some very touching, and some very animating melodies, of little more than that number of words. He is a master of musical combinations. His songs set themselves, and generate their own tunes, as all songs do which are good for anything; but they are not many. Perhaps our author is only surpassed, among recent poets, by Coleridge, in the harmony of his versification.

It would also have been pleasant to have transcribed and analyzed such pictures as those of the Dying Swan, the Sleeping Beauty, Adeline, &c.; and to have shewn how the author can breathe his own spirit into unconscious things, making them instinct with life and feeling. One stanza of an autumnal song may intimate to some readers the facility and grace with which he identifies himself with nature.

[Quotes 'Song', ll. 1–12:

'A spirit haunts the year's last hours . . .
Heavily hangs the tigerlily.']

We must protest against the irregularities of measure, and the use of antiquated words and obsolete pronunciation, in which our author indulges so freely. He exposes himself thereby to the charge, and we think not unfairly, of indolence and affectation. There are few variations of effect which a skilful artist cannot produce, if he will but take the pains, —without deviating from that regularity of measure which is one of the original elements of poetical enjoyment; made so by the tendency of the human frame to periodical movements; and the continued sacrifice of which is but ill compensated to the disappointed ear by any occasional, and not otherwise attainable correspondence between the movement of a verse and the sense which it is intended to convey. Nor certainly is any thing gained by a song's being studded with words which to most readers may require a glossary.

Mr. Tennyson has the propensity which Shelley had, to use a word or two which young ladies of the present day are not accustomed to read or sing in the parlour; in singing, we believe, the toleration is greater than in reading or conversation; sentences, avoiding the words, but meaning much worse, are not generally proscribed.

That these poems will have a very rapid and extensive popularity we do not anticipate. Their very originality will prevent their being generally appreciated for a time. But that time will come, we hope, to a not far distant end. They demonstrate the possession of powers, to the future direction of which we look with some anxiety. A genuine poet has deep responsibilities to his country and the world, to the present and future generations, to earth and heaven. He, of all men, should have distinct and worthy objects before him, and consecrate himself to their promotion. It is thus that he best consults the glory of his art, and his own lasting fame. Mr. Tennyson has a dangerous quality in that facility of impersonation on which we have remarked, and by which he enters so thoroughly into the most strange and wayward idiosyncrasies of other men. It must not degrade him into a poetical harlequin. He has higher work to do than that of disporting himself amongst 'mystics' and

'flowing philosophers'. He knows that 'the poet's mind is holy ground';
he knows that the poet's portion is to be

> Dower'd with the hate of hate, the scorn of scorn,
> The love of love;

he has shown, in the lines from which we quote, his own just conception
of the grandeur of a poet's destiny; and we look to him for its fulfilment.
It is not for such men to sink into mere verse-makers for the amusement
of themselves or others. They can influence the associations of unnumbered minds; they can command the sympathies of unnumbered
hearts; they can disseminate principles; they can give those principles
power over men's imaginations; they can excite in a good cause the
sustained enthusiasm that is sure to conquer; they can blast the laurels
of the tyrants, and hallow the memories of the martyrs of patriotism;
they can act with a force, the extent of which it is difficult to estimate,
upon national feelings and character, and consequently upon national
happiness. If our estimate of Mr. Tennyson be correct, he too is a poet;
and many years hence may he read his juvenile description of that
character with the proud consciousness that it has become the description
and history of his own work:

[Quotes 'The Poet', ll. 29-38:

> 'So many minds did gird their orbs with beams . . .
> Her beautiful bold brow.']

2. A. H. Hallam on

Poems, Chiefly Lyrical [1830]

Arthur Henry Hallam, unsigned review, *Englishman's Magazine* (August 1831), i. 616–28.

Hallam (1811–33), a young man of extraordinary promise and a close friend of Tennyson, is now chiefly remembered as the subject of *In Memoriam*. In his opening sentences, Hallam refers to Robert Montgomery (1807–55), whose religious poems had been extravagantly praised. Montgomery's poem *The Omnipresence of the Deity* (1828) achieved twenty-eight editions in thirty years. But *Oxford*, published in the year in which Hallam was writing, was to be very much less successful.

So Mr. Montgomery's *Oxford*, by the help of some pretty illustrations, has contrived to prolong its miserable existence to a second edition! But this is slow work, compared to that triumphant progress of the *Omnipresence*, which, we concede to the author's friends, was 'truly astonishing'. We understand, moreover, that a new light has broken upon this 'desolator desolate'; and since the 'columns' have begun to follow the example of 'men and gods', by whom our poetaster has long been condemned, 'it is the fate of genius,' he begins to discover, 'to be unpopular'. Now, strongly as we protest against Mr. Montgomery's application of this maxim to his own case, we are much disposed to agree with him as to its abstract correctness. Indeed, the truth which it involves seems to afford the only solution of so curious a phenomenon as the success, partial and transient though it be, of himself, and others of his calibre. When Mr. Wordsworth, in his celebrated Preface to the *Lyrical Ballads*, asserted that immediate or rapid popularity was not the test of poetry, great was the consternation and clamour among those farmers of public favour, the established critics. Never had so audacious an attack been made upon their undoubted privileges and hereditary charter of oppression. 'What! *The Edinburgh Review* not infallible!' shrieked the amiable petulance of Mr. Jeffrey. '*The Gentleman's Magazine* incapable of decision!' faltered the feeble garrulity of Silvanus Urban. And straightway the whole sciolist herd, men of rank, men of letters, men of wealth, men of business, all the 'mob of gentlemen who think with ease', and a terrible number of old ladies and boarding-school misses began to scream in chorus, and prolonged the notes of execration with which they overwhelmed the new doctrine, until their wits and their voices fairly gave in from exhaustion. Much, no doubt, they did, for much persons will do when they fight for their dear selves: but there was one thing they could not do, and unfortunately it was the only one of any importance. They could not put down Mr. Wordsworth by clamour, or prevent his doctrine, once uttered, and enforced by his example, from awakening the minds of men, and giving a fresh impulse to art. It was the truth, and it prevailed; not only against the exasperation of that hydra, the Reading Public, whose vanity was hurt, and the blustering of its keepers, whose delusion was exposed, but even against the false glosses and narrow apprehensions of the Wordsworthians themselves. It is the madness of all who loosen some great principle, long buried under a snow-heap of custom and superstition, to imagine that they can restrain its operation, or circumscribe it by their purposes. But the right of private judgment was stronger than the will of Luther; and even the genius of Wordsworth cannot expand itself to the full periphery of poetic art.

It is not true, as his exclusive admirers would have it, that the highest species of poetry is the reflective: it is a gross fallacy, that, because certain opinions are acute or profound, the expression of them by the imagination must be eminently beautiful. Whenever the mind of the artist suffers itself to be occupied, during its periods of creation, by any other predominant motive than the desire of beauty, the result is false in art. Now there is undoubtedly no reason, why he may not find beauty in those moods of emotion, which arise from the combinations of reflective thought, and it is possible that he may delineate these with fidelity, and not be led astray by any suggestions of an unpoetical mood. But, though possible, it is hardly probable: for a man, whose reveries take a reasoning turn, and who is accustomed to measure his ideas by their logical relations rather than the congruity of the sentiments to which they refer, will be apt to mistake the pleasure he has in knowing a thing to be true, for the pleasure he would have in knowing it to be beautiful, and so will pile his thoughts in a rhetorical battery, that they may convince, instead of letting them glow in the natural course of contemplation, that they may enrapture. It would not be difficult to shew, by reference to the most admired poems of Wordsworth, that he is frequently chargeable with this error, and that much has been said by him which is good as philosophy, powerful as rhetoric, but false as poetry. Perhaps this very distortion of the truth did more in the peculiar juncture of our literary affairs to enlarge and liberalize the genius of our age, than could have been effected by a less sectarian temper. However this may be, a new school of reformers soon began to attract attention, who, professing the same independence of immediate favour, took their stand on a different region of Parnassus from that occupied by the Lakers,[1] and one, in our opinion, much less liable to perturbing currents of air from ungenial climates. We shall not hesitate to express our conviction, that the Cockney school (as it was termed in derision, from a cursory view of its accidental circumstances) contained more genuine inspiration, and adhered more speedily to that portion of truth which it embraced, than any *form* of art that has existed in this country since the day of Milton. Their *caposetta* was Mr. Leigh Hunt, who did little more than point the way, and was diverted from his aim by a thousand personal predilections and political habits of thought. But he was followed by two men of a very superior make; men who were born poets, lived poets, and went poets to their untimely graves. Shelley and Keats were, indeed, of opposite genius; that of the one was vast, impetuous, and sublime: the other seemed to be 'fed with honey-dew', and to have 'drunk the milk of Paradise'. Even the softness of Shelley comes out in bold, rapid, comprehensive strokes; he has no patience for minute beauties, unless they can be massed into a general effect of grandeur. On the other hand, the tenderness of Keats cannot sustain a lofty flight; he does not generalize or allegorize Nature; his imagination works with few symbols, and reposes willingly on what is given freely. Yet in this formal opposition of character there is, it seems to us, a ground-work of similarity sufficient for the purposes of classification, and constituting a remarkable point in the progress of literature. They are both poets of sensation rather than reflection. Susceptible of the slightest impulse from external nature, their fine organs trembled into emotion at colours, and sounds, and move-

[1] This cant term was justly ridiculed by Mr. Wordsworth's supporters; but it was not so easy to substitute an inoffensive denomination. We are not at all events the first who have used it without a contemptuous intention, for we remember to have heard a disciple quote Aristophanes in its behalf. Οὗτος οὐ τῶν ἠθάδων τῶνδ' ὧν ὁρᾶθ' ὑμεῖς ἀεί, ἀλλὰ ΛΙΜΝΑΙΟΣ. 'This is no common, no barn-door fowl: No, but a *Lakist*!'

ments, unperceived or unregarded by duller temperaments. Rich and clear were their perceptions of visible forms; full and deep their feelings of music. So vivid was the delight attending the simple exertions of eye and ear, that it became mingled more and more with their trains of active thought, and tended to absorb their whole being into the energy of sense. Other poets *seek* for images to illustrate their conceptions; these men had no need to seek; they lived in a world of images; for the most important and extensive portion of their life consisted in those emotions, which are immediately conversant with sensation. Like the hero of Goethe's novel, they would hardly have been affected by what are called the pathetic parts of a book; but the *merely beautiful* passages, 'those from which the spirit of the author looks clearly and mildly forth', would have melted them to tears. Hence they are not descriptive; they are picturesque. They are not smooth and *negatively* harmonious; they are full of deep and varied melodies. This powerful tendency of imagination to a life of immediate sympathy with the external universe, is not nearly so liable to false views of art as the opposite disposition of purely intellectual contemplation. For where beauty is constantly passing before 'that inward eye, which is the bliss of solitude'; where the soul seeks it as a perpetual and necessary refreshment to the sources of activity and intuition; where all the other sacred ideas of our nature, the idea of good, the idea of perfection, the idea of truth, are habitually contemplated through the medium of this predominant mood, so that they assume its colour, and are subject to its peculiar laws—there is little danger that the ruling passion of the whole mind will cease to direct its creative operations, or the energetic principle of love for the beautiful sink, even for a brief period, to the level of a mere notion in the understanding. We do not deny that it is, on other accounts, dangerous for frail humanity to linger with fond attachment in the vicinity of sense. Minds of this description are especially liable to moral temptations, and upon them, more than any, it is incumbent to remember that their mission as men, which they share with all their fellow-beings, is of infinitely higher interest than their mission as artists, which they possess by rare and exclusive privilege. But it is obvious that, critically speaking, such temptations are of slight moment. Not the gross and evident passions of our nature, but the elevated and less separable desires are the dangerous enemies which misguide the poetic spirit in its attempts at self-cultivation. That delicate sense of fitness, which grows with the growth of artist feelings, and strengthens with their strength, until it acquires a celerity and weight of decision hardly inferior to the correspondent judgments of conscience, is weakened by every indulgence of hetero-geneous aspirations, however pure they may be, however lofty, how-ever suitable to human nature. We are therefore decidedly of opinion that the heights and depths of art are most within the reach of those who have received from Nature the 'fearful and wonderful' constitution we have described, whose poetry is a sort of magic, producing a number of impressions too multiplied, too minute, and too diversified to allow of our tracing them to their causes, because just such was the effect, even so boundless, and so bewildering, produced on their imaginations by the real appearance of Nature. These things being so, our friends of the new school had evidently much reason to recur to the maxim laid down by Mr. Wordsworth, and to appeal from the immediate judgments of lettered or unlettered contemporaries to the decison of a more equitable posterity. How should they be popular, whose senses told them a richer and ampler tale than most men could understand, and who constantly expressed, because they constantly felt, sentiments of exquisite pleasure or pain, which most men were not permitted to experience? The public very naturally derided them as visionaries, and gibbeted *in terrorem* those inaccuracies of diction, occasioned sometimes by the speed of their con-ceptions, sometimes by the inadequacy of language to their peculiar conditions of thought. But, it may be asked, does not this line of argu-ment prove too much? Does it not prove that there is a barrier between these poets and all other persons, so strong and immoveable, that, as has been said of the Supreme Essence, we must be themselves before we can understand them in the least? Not only are they not liable to sudden and vulgar estimation, but the lapse of ages, it seems, will not consolidate their fame, nor the suffrages of the wise few produce any impression, however remote or slowly matured, on the judgments of the incapaci-tated many. We answer, this is not the import of our argument. Undoubtedly the true poet addresses himself, in all his conceptions, to the common nature of us all. Art is a lofty tree, and may shoot up far beyond our grasp, but its roots are in daily life and experience. Every bosom contains the elements of those complex emotions which the artist feels, and every head can, to a certain extent, go over in itself the process of their combination, so as to understand his expressions and sympathize with his state. But this requires exertion; more or less, indeed, according to the difference of occasion, but always some degree of exertion. For since the emotions of the poet, during composition, follow a regular law of association, it follows that to accompany their progress up to the harmonious prospect of the whole, and to perceive the proper dependence of every step on that which preceded, it is absolutely necessary *to start from the same point*, i.e., clearly to apprehend that leading sentiment in the poet's mind, by their conformity to which the host of suggestions are arranged. Now this requisite exertion is not willingly made by the large majority of readers. It is so easy to judge capriciously, and according to indolent impulse! For very many, therefore, it has become *morally* impossible to attain the author's point of vision, on account of their habits, or their prejudices, or their circumstances; but it is never *physically* impossible, because nature has placed in every man the simple elements, of which art is the sublimation. Since then this demand on the reader for activity, when he wants to peruse his author in a luxurious passiveness, is the very thing that moves his bile, it is obvious that those writers will always be most popular, who require the least degree of exertion. Hence, whatever is mixed up with art, and appears under its semblance, is always more favourably regarded than art free and unalloyed. Hence, half the fashionable poems in the world are mere rhetoric, and half the remainder are perhaps not liked by the generality for their substantial merits. Hence, likewise, of the really pure compositions those are most universally agreeable, which take for their primary subject the *usual* passions of the heart, and deal with them in a simple state, without applying the transforming powers of high imagination. Love, friendship, ambition, religion, &c., are matters of daily experience, even amongst imaginative tempers. The forces of association, therefore, are ready to work in these directions, and little effort of will is necessary to follow the artist. For the same reason such subjects often excite a partial power of composition, which is no sign of a truly poetic organization. We are very far from wishing to depreciate this class of poems, whose influence is so extensive, and communicates so refined a pleasure. We contend only that the facility with which its impressions are communicated, is no proof of its elevation as a form of art, but rather the contrary. What then, some may be ready to exclaim, is the pleasure derived by most men from Shakspeare, or Dante, or Homer, entirely false and factitious? If these are really masters of their art, must not the energy required of the ordinary intelligences, that come in contact with their mighty genius, be the greatest possible? How comes it then that they are popular? Shall we not say, after all, that the difference is in the power of the author, not in the tenor of his meditations? Those eminent spirits find no difficulty in conveying to common apprehension their lofty sense, and profound observation of Nature. They keep no aristocratic state, apart from the sentiments of society at large; they speak to the hearts of all, and by the magnetic force of their conceptions elevate inferior intellects into a higher and purer atmosphere. The truth contained in this objection is undoubtedly important; geniuses of the most universal order, and assigned by destiny to the most propitious eras of a nation's literary development, have a clearer and larger access to the minds of their compatriots, than can ever be open to those who are circumscribed by less fortunate circumstances. In the youthful periods of any literature there is an expansive and communicative tendency in mind, which produces unreservedness of communion, and reciprocity of vigour between different orders of intelligence. Without abandoning the ground which has always been defended by the partizans of Mr. Wordsworth, who declare with perfect truth that the number of real admirers of what is really admirable in Shakspeare and Milton are much fewer than the number of apparent admirers might lead one to imagine, we may safely assert that the intense thoughts set in circulation by those 'orbs of song', and their noble satellites, 'in great Eliza's golden time', did not fail to awaken a proportionable intensity in the natures of numberless auditors. Some might feel feebly, some strongly; the effect would vary according to the character of the recipient; but upon none was the stirring influence entirely unimpressive. The knowledge and power this imbibed, became a part of national existence; it was ours as Englishmen; and amid the flux of generations and customs we retain unimpaired this privilege of intercourse with greatness. But the age in which we live comes late in our national progress. That first raciness, and juvenile vigour of literature, when nature 'wantoned as in her prime, and played at will her virgin fancies', is gone, never to return. Since that day we have undergone a period of degradation. 'Every handicraftsman has worn the mark of Poesy.' It would be tedious to repeat the tale, so often related, of French contagion, and the heresies of the Popian school. With the close of the last century came an era of reaction, an era of painful struggle, to bring our overcivilised condition of thought into union with the fresh productive spirit that brightened the morning of our literature. But repentance is unlike innocence: the laborious endeavour to restore has more complicated methods of action, than the freedom of untainted nature. Those different powers of poetic disposition, the energies of Sensitive,[1] of Reflective, of Passionate

---

[1] We are aware that this is not the right word, being appropriated by common use to a different signification. Those who think the caution given by Caesar should not stand in the way of urgent occasion, may substitute 'sensuous', a word in use amongst our elder divines, and revived by a few bold writers in our own time.

Emotion, which in former times were intermingled, and derived from mutual support an extensive empire over the feelings of men, were now restrained within separate spheres of agency. The whole system no longer worked harmoniously, and by intrinsic harmony acquired external freedom; but there arose a violent and unusual action in the several component functions, each for itself, all striving to reproduce the regular power which the whole had once enjoyed. Hence the melancholy, which so evidently characterises the spirit of modern poetry; hence that return of the mind upon itself, and the habit of seeking relief in idiosyncracies rather than community of interest. In the old times the poetic impulse went along with the general impulse of the nation; in these, it is a reaction against it, a check acting for conservation against a propulsion towards change. We have indeed seen it urged in some of our fashionable publications, that the diffusion of poetry must necessarily be in the direct ratio of the diffusion of machinery, because a highly civilized people must have new objects of interest, and thus a new field will be opened to description. But this notable argument forgets that against this *objective* amelioration may be set the decrease of *subjective* power, arising from a prevalance of social activity, and a continual absorption of the higher feelings into the palpable interests of ordinary life. The French Revolution may be a finer theme than the war of Troy; but it does not so evidently follow that Homer is to find his superior. Our inference, therefore, from this change in the relative position of artists to the rest of the community is, that modern poetry, in proportion to its depth and truth, is likely to have little immediate authority over public opinion. Admirers it will have; sects consequently it will form; and these strong under-currents will in time sensibly affect the principal stream. Those writers, whose genius, though great, is not strictly and essentially poetic, become mediators between the votaries of art and the careless cravers for excitement.[1] Art herself, less manifestly glorious than in her periods of undisputed supremacy, retains her essential prerogatives, and forgets not to raise up chosen spirits, who may minister to her state, and vindicate her title.

One of this faithful Islam, a poet in the truest and highest sense, we are anxious to present to our readers. He has yet written little, and published less; but in these 'preludes of a loftier strain', we recognise the inspiring

---

[1] May we not compare them to the bright, but unsubstantial clouds which, in still evenings, girdle the sides of lofty mountains, and seem to form a natural connexion between the lowly vallies, spread out beneath, and those isolated peaks above, that hold the 'last parley with the setting sun'?

god. Mr. Tennyson belongs decidedly to the class we have already described as Poets of Sensation. He sees all the forms of nature with the '*eruditus oculus*', and his ear has a fairy fineness. There is a strange earnestness in his worship of beauty, which throws a charm over his impassioned song, more easily felt than described, and not to be escaped by those who have once felt it. We think he has more definiteness, and soundness of general conception, than the late Mr. Keats, and is much more free from blemishes of diction, and hasty capriccios of fancy. He has also this advantage over that poet, and his friend Shelley, that he comes before the public, unconnected with any political party, or peculiar system of opinions. Nevertheless, true to the theory we have stated, we believe his participation in their characteristic excellencies is sufficient to secure him a share in their unpopularity. The volume of *Poems, chiefly Lyrical* does not contain above 154 pages; but it shews us much more of the character of its parent mind, than many books we have known of much larger compass, and more boastful pretensions. The features of original genius are clearly and strongly marked. The author imitates nobody; we recognise the spirit of his age, but not the individual form of this or that writer. His thoughts bear no more resemblance to Byron or Scott, Shelley or Coleridge, than to Homer or Calderon, Ferdusi or Calidas. We have remarked five distinctive excellencies of his own manner. First, his luxuriance of imagination, and at the same time his control over it. Secondly, his power of embodying himself in ideal characters, or rather moods of character, with such extreme accuracy of adjustment, that the circumstances of the narration seem to have a natural correspondence with the predominant feeling, and, as it were, to be evolved from it by assimilative force. Thirdly, his vivid, picturesque delineation of objects, and the peculiar skill with which he holds all of them *fused*, to borrow a metaphor from science, in a medium of strong emotion. Fourthly, the variety of his lyrical measures, and exquisite modulation of harmonious words and cadences to the swell and fall of the feelings expressed. Fifthly, the elevated habits of thought, *implied* in these compositions, and imparting a mellow soberness of tone, more impressive, to our minds, than if the author had drawn up a set of opinions in verse, and sought to instruct the understanding, rather than to communicate the love of beauty to the heart. We shall proceed to give our readers some specimens in illustration of these remarks, and, if possible, we will give them entire; for no poet can fairly be judged of by fragments, least of all a poet, like Mr. Tennyson, whose mind conceives nothing isolated, nothing abrupt, but every part with reference to some other part, and in subservience to the idea of the whole.

'Recollections of the Arabian Nights!' What a delightful, endearing title! How we pity those to whom it calls up no reminiscence of early enjoyment, no sentiment of kindliness as towards one who sings a song they have loved, or mentions with affection a departed friend! But let nobody expect a multifarious enumeration of Viziers, Barmecides, Fireworshippers, and Cadis; trees that sing, horses that fly, and Goules that eat rice pudding! Our author knows what he is about: he has, with great judgment, selected our old acquaintance, 'the good Haroun Alraschid', as the most prominent object of our childish interest, and with him has called up one of those luxurious garden scenes, the account of which, in plain prose, used to make our mouths water for sherbet, since luckily we were too young to think much about Zobeide! We think this poem will be the favourite among Mr. Tennyson's admirers; perhaps upon the whole it is our own; at least we find ourselves recurring to it oftener than to any other, and every time we read it, we feel the freshness of its beauty increase, and are inclined to exclaim with Madame de Sévigné, *à force d'être ancien, il m'est nouveau.*' But let us draw the curtain.

[Quotes 'Recollections of the Arabian Nights', ll. 1–154:

'When the breeze of a joyful dawn blew free . . .
The good Haroun Alraschid!']

Criticism will sound but poorly after this; yet we cannot give silent votes. The first stanza, we beg leave to observe, places us at once in the position of feeling, which the poem requires. The scene is before us, around us; we cannot mistake its localities, or blind ourselves to its colours. That happy ductility of childhood returns for the moment; 'true Mussulmans are we, and sworn', and yet there is a latent knowledge, which heightens the pleasure, that to our change from really childish thought we owe the capacities by which we enjoy the recollection. As the poem proceeds, all is in perfect keeping. There is a solemn distinctness in every image, a majesty of slow motion in every cadence, that aids the illusion of thought, and steadies its contemplation of the complete picture. Originality of observation seems to cost nothing to our author's liberal genius; he lavishes images of exquisite accuracy and elaborate splendour, as a common writer throws about metaphorical truisms, and exhausted tropes. Amidst all the varied luxuriance of the sensations described, we are never permitted to lose sight of the idea which gives unity to this variety, and by the recurrence of which, as a sort of mysterious influence, at the close of every stanza, the mind is wrought up, with consummate art, to the final disclosure. This poem is a perfect gallery of pictures; and the concise boldness, with which in a few words an object is clearly painted, is sometimes (see the 6th stanza) majestic as Milton, sometimes (see the 12th) sublime as Æschylus. We have not, however, so far forgot our vocation as critics, that we would leave without notice the slight faults which adhere to this precious work. In the 8th stanza, we doubt the propriety of using the bold compound 'black-green', at least in such close vicinity to 'gold-green': nor is it perfectly clear by the term, although indicated by the context, that 'diamond plots' relates to shape rather than colour. We are perhaps very stupid, but 'vivid stars unrayed' [the reading of 1830] does not convey to us a very precise notion. 'Rosaries of scented thorn', in the 10th stanza, is, we believe, an entirely unauthorized use of the word. Would our author translate 'biferique rosaria Pæsti.'—'And rosaries of Pæstum, twice in bloom'? To the beautiful 13th stanza, we are sorry to find any objection: but even the bewitching loveliness of that 'Persian girl' shall not prevent our performing the rigid duty we have undertaken, and we must hint to Mr. Tennyson, that 'redolent' is no synonyme for 'fragrant'. Bees may be redolent of honey: spring may be 'redolent of youth and love', but the absolute use of the word has, we fear, neither in Latin nor English, any better authority than the monastic epitaph on Fair Rosamond. 'Hic jacet in tombâ Rosa Mundi, non Rosa Munda, non redolet, sed olet, quæ redolere solet.'

We are disposed to agree with Mr. Coleridge, when he says 'no adequate compensation can be made for the mischief a writer does by confounding the distinct senses of words'. At the same time our feelings in this instance rebel strongly in behalf of 'redolent'; for the melody of the passage, as it stands, is beyond the possibility of improvement, and unless he should chance to light upon a word very nearly resembling this in consonants and vowels, we can hardly quarrel with Mr. Tennyson if, in spite of our judgment, he retains the offender in his service.

Our next specimen is of a totally different character, but not less complete, we think, in its kind. Have we among our readers any who delight in the heroic poems of Old England, the inimitable ballads? Any to whom Sir Patrick Spens, and Clym of the Clough, and Glorious Robin, are consecrated names? Any who sigh with disgust at the miserable abortions of simpleness mistaken for simplicity, or florid weakness substituted for plain energy, which they may often have seen dignified with the title of Modern Ballads? Let such draw near, and read the 'Ballad of Oriana'. We know no more happy seizure of the antique spirit in the whole compass of our literature; yet there is no foolish self desertion, no attempt at obliterating the present, but every where a full discrimination of how much ought to be yielded, and how much retained. The author is well aware that the art of one generation cannot *become* that of another by any will or skill: but the artist may transfer the spirit of the past, making it a temporary form for his own spirit, and so effect, by idealizing power, a new and legitimate combination. If we were asked to name among the real antiques that which bears greatest resemblance to this gem, we should refer to the ballad of 'Fair Helen of Kirconnel Lea' in the *Minstrelsy of the Scottish Border*. It is a resemblance of mood, not of execution. They are both highly wrought lyrical expressions of pathos; and it is very remarkable with what intuitive art, every expression and cadence in 'Fair Helen' is accorded to the main feeling. The characters that distinguish the language of our *lyrical*, from that of our *epic* ballads, have never yet been examined with the accuracy they deserve. But, beyond question, the class of poems, which, in point of harmonious combination, 'Oriana' most resembles, is the Italian. Just thus the meditative tenderness of Dante and Petrarch is embodied in the clear, searching tones of Tuscan song. These mighty masters produce two-thirds of their effect by *sound*. Not that they sacrifice sense to sound, but that sound conveys their meaning, where words would not. There are innumerable shades of fine emotion in the human heart, especially when the senses are keen and vigilant, which are too subtle and too rapid to admit of corresponding phrases. The understanding takes no definite note of them; how then can they leave signatures in language? Yet they exist; in plenitude of being and beauty they exist; and in music they find a medium through which they pass from heart to heart. The tone becomes the sign of the feeling; and they reciprocally suggest each other. Analogous to this suggestive power, may be reckoned, perhaps, in a sister art, the effects of Venetian colouring. Titian *explains* by tints, as Petrarch by tones. Words would not have done the business of the one, nor any groupings, or *narration by form*, that of the other. But shame upon us! we are going back to our metaphysics, when that 'sweet, meek face' is waiting to be admitted.

[Quotes 'The Ballad of Oriana', ll. 1–99:

'My heart is wasted with my woe . . .
Oriana.']

We have heard it objected to this poem, that the name occurs once too often in every stanza. We have taken the plea into our judicial consideration, and the result is, that we overrule it, and pronounce that the proportion of the melodious cadences to the pathetic parts of the narration, could not be diminished without materially affecting the rich lyrical impression of the ballad. For what is the author's intention? To gratify our curiosity with a strange adventure? To shake our nerves with a painful story? Very far from it. Tears indeed may 'blind our sight', as we read; but they are 'blissful tears': the strong musical delight prevails over every painful feeling, and mingles them all in its deep swell, until they attain a composure of exalted sorrow, a mood in which the latest repose of agitation becomes visible, and the influence of beauty spreads like light, over the surface of the mind. The last line, with its dreamy wildness, reveals the design of the whole. It is transferred, if we mistake not, from an old ballad, (a freedom of immemorial usage with ballad mongers, as our readers doubtless know,) but the merit lies in the abrupt application of it to the leading sentiment, so as to flash upon us in a few little words a world of meaning, and to consecrate the passion that was beyond cure or hope, by resigning it to the accordance of inanimate Nature, who, like man, has her tempests, and occasions of horror, but august in their largeness of operation, awful by their dependence on a fixed and perpetual necessity.

We must give one more extract, and we are almost tempted to choose by lot among many that crowd on our recollection, and solicit our preference with such witchery, as it is not easy to withstand. The poems towards the middle of the volume seem to have been written at an earlier period than the rest. They display more unrestrained fancy, and are less evidently proportioned to their ruling ideas, than those which we think of later date. Yet in the 'Ode to Memory'—the only one which we have the poet's authority for referring to early life—there is a majesty of expression, united to a truth of thought, which almost confounds our preconceived distinctions. The 'Confessions of a second-rate, Sensitive Mind', are full of deep insight into human nature, and into those particular trials, which are sure to beset men who think and feel for themselves at this epoch of social development. The title is perhaps ill chosen: not only has it an appearance of quaintness, which has no sufficient reason, but it seems to us incorrect. The mood pourtrayed in this poem, unless the admirable skill of delineation has deceived us, is rather the clouded season of a strong mind, than the habitual condition of one feeble and 'second-rate'. Ordinary tempers build up fortresses of opinion on one side or another; they will see only what they choose to see; the distant glimpse of such an agony as is here brought out to view, is sufficient to keep them for ever in illusions, voluntarily raised at first, but soon trusted in with full reliance as inseparable parts of self. Perhaps, however, Mr. Tennyson's mode of 'rating' is different from ours. He may esteem none worthy of the first order, who has not attained a complete universality of thought, and such trustful reliance on a principle of repose, which lies beyond the war of conflicting opinions, that the grand ideas, 'qui planent sans cesse au dessus de l'humanité,' cease to affect him with bewildering impulses of hope and fear. We have not space to enter farther into this topic; but we should not despair of convincing Mr. Tennyson, that such a position of intellect would not be the most elevated, nor even the most conducive to perfection of art. 'The "How" and the "Why" ' appears to present the reverse of the same picture. It is the same mind still; the sensitive sceptic, whom we have looked upon in his hour of distress, now scoffing at his own state with an earnest mirth that borders on sorrow. It is exquisitely beautiful to see in this, as in the former portrait, how the feeling of art is kept ascendant in our minds over distressful realities, by constant reference to images of tranquil beauty, whether touched pathetically, as the Ox and the Lamb in the first piece, or with fine humour, as the 'great bird' and 'little bird' in the second. The 'Sea Fairies' is another strange title; but those who turn to it with the very natural curiosity of discovering who these new births of mythology may be, will be unpardonable if they do not linger over it with higher feelings. A stretch of lyrical power is here exhibited, which we did not think the English language had possessed. The proud swell of verse, as the harp tones 'run up the ridged sea', and the soft and melancholy lapse, as the sounds die along the widening space of waters, are instances of that right imitation which is becoming to art, but which in the hands of the unskilful, or the affecters of easy popularity, is often converted into a degrading mimicry, detrimental to the best interests of the imagination. A considerable portion of this book is taken up with a very singular, and very beautiful class of poems, on which the author has evidently bestowed much thought and elaboration. We allude to the female characters, every trait of which presumes an uncommon degree of observation and reflection. Mr. Tennyson's way of proceeding seems to be this. He collects the most striking phenomena of individual minds, until he arrives at some leading fact, which allows him to lay down an axiom, or law, and then, working on the law thus attained, he clearly discerns the tendency of what new particulars his invention suggests, and is enabled to impress an individual freshness and unity on ideal combinations. These expressions of character are brief and coherent: nothing extraneous to the dominant fact is admitted, nothing illustrative of it, and, as it were, growing out of it, is rejected. They are like summaries of mighty dramas. We do not say this method admits of such large luxuriance of power, as that of our real dramatists; but we contend that it is a new species of poetry, a graft of the lyric on the dramatic, and Mr. Tennyson deserves the laurel of an inventor, an enlarger of our modes of knowledge and power. We must hasten to make our election; so, passing by the 'airy, fairy Lilian', who 'clasps her hands' in vain to retain us; the 'stately flower' of matronly fortitude, 'revered Isabel'; Madeline, with her voluptuous alternation of smile and frown; Mariana, last, but oh not least—we swear by the memory of Shakspeare, to whom a monument of observant love has here been raised by simply expanding all the latent meanings and beauties contained in one stray thought of his genius—we shall fix on a lovely, albeit somewhat mysterious lady, who has fairly taken our 'heart from out our breast'.

[Quotes 'Adeline', ll. 1–64:

'Mystery of mysteries . . .
Spiritual Adeline.']

Is not this beautiful? When this Poet dies, will not the Graces and the Loves mourn over him, '*fortunatâque favillâ nascentur violæ*'? How original is the imagery, and how delicate! How wonderful the new world thus created for us, the region between real and unreal! The gardens of Armida were but poorly musical compared with the roses and lilies that bloom around thee, thou faint smiler, Adeline, on whom the glory of imagination reposes, endowing all thou lookest on with sudden and mysterious life. We could expatiate on the deep meaning of this poem, but it is time to twitch our critical mantles; and, as our trade is not that of mere enthusiasm, we shall take our leave with an objection (perhaps a cavil) to the language of cowslips, which we think too ambiguously spoken of for a subject on which nobody, except Mr. Tennyson, can have any information. The 'ringing bluebell' too, if it be not a pun, suggests one, and might probably be altered to advantage.

One word more, before we have done, and it shall be a word of praise. The language of this book, with one or two rare exceptions, is thorough and sterling English. A little more respect, perhaps, was due to the '*jus et norma loquendi*', but we are inclined to consider as venial a fault arising from generous enthusiasm for the principles of sound analogy, and for that Saxon element, which constitutes the intrinsic freedom and nervousness of our native tongue. We see no signs in what Mr. Tennyson has written of the Quixotic spirit which has led some persons to desire the reduction of English to a single form, by excluding nearly the whole of Latin and Roman derivatives. Ours is necessarily a compound language; as such alone it can flourish and increase; nor will the author of the poems we have extracted be likely to barter for a barren appearance of symmetrical structure that fertility of expression, and variety of harmony, which 'the speech, that Shakespeare spoke', derived from the sources of southern phraseology.

In presenting this young poet to the public, as one not studious of instant popularity, nor likely to obtain it, we may be thought to play the part of a fashionable lady, who deludes her refractory mate into doing what she chooses, by pretending to wish the exact contrary, or of a cunning pedagogue, who practises a similar manoeuvre on some self-willed Flibbertigibbet of the school-room. But the supposition would do us wrong. We have spoken in good faith, commending this volume to feeling hearts and imaginative tempers, not to the stupid readers, or the voracious readers, or the malignant readers, or the readers after dinner! We confess, indeed, we never knew an instance in which the theoretical abjurers of popularity have shewn themselves very reluctant to admit its actual advances; so much virtue is not, perhaps, in human nature; and if the world should take a fancy to buy up these poems, in order to be revenged on the *Englishman's Magazine*, who knows whether even we might not disappoint its malice by a cheerful adaptation of our theory to 'existing circumstances'.

3. Christopher North on

Poems, Chiefly Lyrical [*1830*]

'Christopher North', from an unsigned review, *Blackwood's Edinburgh Magazine* (May 1832), xxxi. 721–41.

As 'Christopher North', John Wilson (1785–1854) assumed the character of a captious, humorous, patronizing, and testy old man who was liable, when offended, to lay about him with his crutch. His habitual digressiveness has made it possible for his article to be severely cut for present purposes without any serious curtailment of his discussion of Tennyson.

'Maga' was the name by which *Blackwood's Edinburgh Magazine* was familiarly known.

. . . One of the saddest misfortunes that can befall a young poet, is to be the Pet of a Coterie; and the very saddest of all, if in Cockneydom. Such has been the unlucky lot of Alfred Tennyson. He has been elevated to the throne of Little Britain, and sonnets were showered over his coronation from the most remote regions of his empire, even from Hampstead Hill. Eulogies more elaborate than the architecture of the costliest gingerbread, have been built up into panegyrical piles, in commemoration of the Birth-day; and 'twould be a pity indeed with one's crutch to smash the gilt battlements, white too with sugar as with frost, and begemmed with comfits. The besetting sin of all periodical criticism, and now-a-days there is no other, is boundless extravagance of praise; but none splash it on like the trowelmen who have been bedaubing Mr. Tennyson. There is something wrong, however, with the compost. It won't stick; unseemly cracks deform the surface; it falls off piece by piece ere it has dried in the sun, or it hardens into blotches; and the worshippers have but discoloured and disfigured their Idol. The worst of it is, that they make the Bespattered not only feel, but look ridiculous; he seems as absurd as an Image in a tea-garden; and, bedizened with faded and fantastic garlands, the public cough on being told he is a Poet, for he has much more the appearance of a Post.

The Englishman's Magazine ought not to have died; for it threatened to be a very pleasant periodical. An Essay 'on the Genius of Alfred Tennyson' sent it to the grave. The superhuman—nay, supernatural—pomposity of that one paper, incapacitated the whole work for living one day longer in this unceremonious world. The solemnity with which the critic approached the object of his adoration, and the sanctity with which he laid his offerings on the shrine, were too much for our irreligious age. The Essay 'on the genius of Alfred Tennyson' awoke a general guffaw, and it expired in convulsions. Yet the Essay was exceedingly well-written—as well as if it had been 'on the Genius of Sir Isaac Newton'. Therein lay the mistake. Sir Isaac discovered the law of gravitation; Alfred had but written some pretty verses, and mankind were not prepared to set him among the stars. But that he has genius is proved by his being at this moment alive; for had he not, he must have breathed his last under that critique. The spirit of life must indeed be strong within him; for he has outlived a narcotic dose administered to him by a crazy charlatan in the *Westminster,* and after that he may sleep in safety with a pan of charcoal.

But the Old Man must see justice done to this ingenious lad, and save him from his worst enemies, his friends. Never are we so happy—nay, 'tis now almost our only happiness—as when scattering flowers in the sunshine that falls from the yet unclouded sky on the green path prepared by gracious Nature for the feet of enthusiastic youth. Yet we scatter them not in too lavish profusion; and we take care that the young poet shall see, along with the shadow of the spirit that cheers him on, that, too, of the accompanying crutch. Were we not afraid that our style might be thought to wax too figurative, we should say that Alfred is a promising plant; and that the day may come when, beneath sun and shower, his genius may grow up and expand into a stately tree, embowering a solemn shade within its wide circumference, while the daylight lies gorgeously on its crest, seen from afar in glory —itself a grove.

But that day will never come, if he hearken not to our advice, and, as far as his own nature will permit, regulate by it the movements of his genius. This may perhaps appear, at first sight or hearing, not a little unreasonable on our part; but not so, if Alfred will but lay our words to heart, and meditate on their spirit. We desire to see him prosper;

and we predict fame as the fruit of obedience. If he disobey, he assuredly goes to oblivion.

At present he has small power over the common feelings and thoughts of men. His feebleness is distressing at all times when he makes an appeal to their ordinary sympathies. And the reason is, that he fears to look such sympathies boldly in the face,—and will be—metaphysical. What all the human race see and feel, he seems to think cannot be poetical; he is not aware of the transcendant and eternal grandeur of common-place and all-time truths, which are the staple of all poetry. All human beings see the same light in heaven and in woman's eyes; and the great poets put it into language which rather records than reveals, spiritualizing while it embodies. They shun not the sights of common earth—witness Wordsworth. But beneath the magic of their eyes the celandine grows a star or a sun. What beauty is breathed over the daisy by lovingly blessing it because it is so common! 'Sweet flower! whose home is every where!' In like manner, Scott, when eulogizing our love of our native land, uses the simplest language, and gives vent to the simplest feelings—

> Lives there the man with soul so dead,
> Who never to himself hath said,
> This is my own, my native land?

What less—what more, could any man say? Yet translate these three lines—not omitting others that accompany them equally touching—into any language, living or dead—and they will instantly be felt by all hearts, savage or civilized, to be the most exquisite poetry. Of such power, conscious, as it kindles, of its dominion over men, because of their common humanity, would that there were finer and more frequent examples in the compositions—otherwise often exquisite—of this young poet. . . .

[Quotes 'National Song', 'English Warsong', ll. 1-11, 23-33, 'Song' ('The winds, as at their hour of birth'), 'Lost Hope', and 'Love, Pride, and Forgetfulness', with such comments as 'Miserable indeed' and 'That is drivel'. Then continues, with reference to the last three of these:]

The worst of all the above is, that they betray a painful and impotent straining after originality—an aversion from the straight-forward and strong simplicity of nature and truth. Such cold conceits—devoid of ingenuity—would seem to us of evil omen—but for our faith in genius, which can shake itself free even from the curse of Cockneyism, under the timeous administration of the exorcising crutch. . . .

[Quotes 'Sonnet' ('Shall the hag Evil die with child of Good'), 'The Poet's Mind', and 'The "How" and the "Why" ', commenting 'idiotic', 'silly', etc. Then continues, with reference to the last of these:]

Mr. Tennyson opines, that in these verses he displays his genius before an admiring, a delighted, and an instructed world, in the garb of an orthodox philosophy venturing for a while sportively to give utterance to its sense of the nothingness of all human knowledge, which is but another word for our ignorance of the mysteries of creation. But it is from beginning to end a clumsy and unwieldy failure, and shews no fancy in the region of metaphysics; though it is plain from many a page that he has deluded himself, and suffered others to delude him, into the belief that there lies his especial province. To some of his queries Thomas Aquinas himself, or any other celestial doctor, might be puzzled to give a satisfactory answer; but the first little boy or girl he may meet will set his mind at rest on the last two, though no man who has ever walked the streets of Edinburgh in a high wind, will be able to bring his mind to believe in the propriety—whatever he may think of the necessity—of a house with a chimney-pot, for which there is no substitute like an Old Woman.

Mr. Tennyson's admirers say he excels wondrously in personating mermen and mermaids, fairies, *et id genus omne*, inhabiting sea-caves and forest glades, 'in still or stormy weather', the 'gay creatures of the element', be that element air, earth, fire, or water, so that the denizens thereof be but of 'imagination all compact'. We beg of you to hear, for a few sentences, the quack in the *Westminster* 'Our author has the secret of the transmigration of the soul. He can cast his own spirit into any living thing, real or imaginary. Scarcely Vishnu himself becomes incarnate more easily, frequently, or perfectly. And there is singular refinement, as well as solid truth, in his impersonations, whether they be of inferior creatures, or of such elemental beings as sirens, as mermen, and mermaidens. He does not merely assume their external shapes, and exhibit his own mind masquerading. He takes their senses, feelings, nerves, and brain, along with their names and local habitations; still it is himself in them, modified but not absorbed by their peculiar constitution and mode of being. In the "Merman", one seems to feel the principle of thought injected by a strong volition into the cranium of the finny worthy, and coming under all the influences, as thinking principles do, of the physical organization to which it is for the time allied: for a moment the identification is complete; and then a consciousness of contrast springs up between the reports of external objects brought to the mind by the senses, and those which it has been accustomed to receive, and this consciousness gives to the description a most poetical colouring.' We could quote another couple of critics—but as the force of nature could no farther go, and as to make one fool she joined the other two, we keep to the *Westminster*. It is a perfect specimen of the super-hyperbolical ultra-extravagance of outrageous Cockney eulogistic foolishness, with which not even a quantity of common sense less than nothing has been suffered, for an indivisible moment of time, to mingle; the purest mere matter of moonshine ever mouthed by an idiot-lunatic, slavering in the palsied dotage of the extremest superannuation ever inflicted on a being, long ago, perhaps, in some slight respects and low degrees human, but now sensibly and audibly reduced below the level of the Pongos. 'Coming under all the influences, as thinking principles do, of the physical organization to which it is for the time allied'! There is a bit of Cockney materialism for you!...

Here is most of the poem which 'proves that our author has the secret of the transmigration of the soul'.

[Quotes 'The Merman', ll. 1–20:

'Who would be ...
Chasing each other merrily.'

and ll. 30–6:

'All night, merrily, merrily ...
Laughingly, laughingly.']

'Tis, after all, but a sorry affair—and were fifty of the Οἱ πολλοί to compose prize verses on 'The Merman', Oxford and Cambridge must be changed for the worse since our days, if two dozen copies did not prove about as bad as this—one dozen rather worse—one dozen far better, while the remaining brace, to the exclusion of Mr. Tennyson's attempt, had the prize divided between them, the authors having been found entitled to an equality of immortal fame. The pervading character of the verses is distinguished silliness; and Alfred cuts a foolish figure, 'modified but not absorbed by the peculiar constitution and mode of being' of a merman. He kisses like a cod-fish, and, we humbly presume, he is all the while stark-naked under the sea; though, for the sake of decency, we recommend next dip a pair of flannel drawers. Poetry and criticism must be at a low ebb indeed on the shores of the Thames. Should he persist in writing thus to the end of the Dean and Chapter, Alfred Tennyson may have a niche in the *Westminster Review*, but never in Westminster Abbey.

'The Mermaid', we are told by the Tailor's Trump, 'is beautifully discriminated and most delicately drawn. She is the younger sister of Undine; or Undine herself before she had a soul.' Here is a specimen of the sea-nymph without a soul, who is younger sister to herself, that is Undine. Her mother ought to keep a sharp look out upon her; for she is of an amorous temperament, and a strong Anti-Malthusian.

[Quotes 'The Mermaid', ll. 28–47:

'And all the mermen under the sea . . .
In the branching jaspers under the sea.']

So much for Mermen and Mermaidens, and for the style in which the Westminster Pet of the Fancy 'takes their senses, feelings, nerves, and brain, along with their local habitations and their names'. 'And the Sirens—who could resist these Sea-Fairies, as the author prefers calling them?' And pray what may be their alluring enticements?

[Quotes the passage corresponding with ll. 7–42 in the final version of 'The Sea-Fairies':

'Drop the oar, . . .
Whither away, whither away, whither away with the sail and the oar?']

Shakspeare — Spenser — Milton — Wordsworth—Coleridge—The Ettrick Shepherd—Allan Cunninghame, and some others, have loved, and been beloved by mermaidens, sirens, sea and land fairies, and revealed to the eyes of us who live in the thick atmosphere of this 'dim spot which men call earth', all the beautiful wonders of subterranean and submarine climes—and of the climes of Nowhere, lovelier than them all. It pains us to think, that with such names we cannot yet rank that of Alfred Tennyson. We shall soon see that he possesses feeling, fancy, imagination, genius. But in the preternatural lies not the sphere in which he excels. Much disappointed were we to find him weak where we expected him strong; yet we are willing to believe that his failure has been from 'affectations'. In place of trusting to the natural flow of his own fancies, he has followed some vague abstract idea, thin and delusive, which has escaped in mere words—words—words. Yet the Young Tailor in the *Westminster* thinks he could take the measure of the merman, and even make a riding-habit for the sirens to wear on gala days, when disposed for 'some horseback'. 'Tis indeed a jewel of a Snip. His protégé has indited two feeble and fantastic strains entitled 'Nothing will Die', 'All things will Die'. And them, Parsnip Junior, without the fear of the shears before his eyes, compares with 'L'Allegro' and 'Il Penseroso' of Milton, saying, that in Alfred's 'there is not less truth, and perhaps more refined observation!' That comes of sitting from childhood cross-legged on a board beneath a skylight.

The Young Tailor can with difficulty keep his seat with delight, when talking of Mr. Tennyson's descriptions of the sea. ''Tis barbarous', quoth he, 'to break such a piece of coral for a specimen'; and would fain cabbage the whole lump, with the view of placing it among other rarities, such as bits of Derbyshire spar and a brace of mandarins, on the chimney-piece of the shew-parlour in which he notches the dimensions of his visitors. So fired is his imagination, that he beholds in a shred of green fustian a swatch of the multitudinous sea; and on tearing a skreed, thinks he hears him roaring. But Mr. Tennyson should speak of the sea so as to rouse the souls of sailors, rather than the soles of tailors—the enthusiasm of the deck, rather than of the board. Unfortunately, he seems never to have seen a ship, or, if he did, to have forgotten it. The vessel in which the landlubbers were drifting, when the Sea-Fairies salute them with a song, must have been an old tub of a thing, unfit even for a transport. Such a jib! In the cut of her mainsail you smoke the old table-cloth. To be solemn—Alfred Tennyson is as poor on the sea as Barry Cornwall—and, of course, calls him a serpent. They both write like people who, on venturing upon the world of waters in a bathing machine, would ensure their lives by a cork-jacket. Barry swims on the surface of the Great Deep like a feather; Alfred dives less after the fashion of a duck than a bell; but the one sees few lights, the other few shadows, that are not seen just as well by an oyster-dredger. But the soul of the true sea-poet doth undergo a sea-change, soon as he sees Blue Peter; and is off in the gig,

> While bending back, away they pull,
> With measured strokes most beautiful—

There goes the Commodore!

'Our author having the secret of the transmigration of the soul', passes, like Indur, into the bodies of various animals, and

Three will I mention dearer than the rest,

the Swan, the Grashopper, and the Owl. The Swan is dying; and as we remember hearing Hartley Coleridge praise the lines, they must be fine; though their full meaning be to us like the moon 'hid in her vacant interlunar cave'. But Hartley, who is like the river Wye, a wanderer through the woods, is aye haunted with visions of the beautiful; and let Alfred console himself by that reflection, for the absent sympathy of Christopher. As for the Grashopper, Alfred, in that green grig, is for a while merry as a cricket, and chirps and chirrups, though with less meaning, with more monotony, than that hearth-loving insect, who is never so happy, you know, as when in the neighbourhood of a baker's oven. He says to himself as Tithon, though he disclaims that patronymic,

Thou art a mailed warrior, in youth and strength complete,

a line liable to two faults; first, absurdity, and, second, theft; for the mind is unprepared for the exaggeration of a grashopper into a Templar; and Wordsworth, looking at a beetle through the wonder-working glass of a wizard, beheld

A mailed angel on a battle-day.

But Tennyson out-Wordsworths Wordsworth, and pursues the knight, surnamed Longshanks, into the fields of chivalry.

> Arm'd cap-a-pie,
> Full fain to see;
> Unknowing fear,
> Undreading loss,
> A gallant cavalier,
> *Sans peur et sans reproche,*
> In sunlight and in shadow,
> THE BAYARD OF THE MEADOW!!

Conceived and executed in the spirit of the celebrated imitation— 'Dilly—dilly Duckling! Come and be killed!' But Alfred is greatest as an Owl.

[Quotes 'Song—The Owl', ll. 1–14:

> 'When the cats run home and light is come . . .
> The white owl in the belfry sits.'

and 'Second Song: To the Same', ll. 1–14:

> 'Thy tuwhits are lulled, I wot . . .
> Tuwhoo, tuwhit, tuwhit, tuwhoo-o-o.']

All that he wants is to be shot, stuffed, and stuck into a glass-case, to be made immortal in a museum.

But, mercy on us! Alfred becomes a—Kraken! Leviathan, 'wallowing unwieldy, enormous in his gait', he despises, as we would a minnow; his huge ambition will not suffer him to be 'very like a whale'; he must be a—Kraken. And such a Kraken, too, as would have astounded Pontoppidan.

[Quotes 'The Kraken', ll. 1–15:

> 'Below the thunders of the upper deep . . .
> In roaring he shall rise and on the surface die.']

The gentle reader who understands that sonnet, will perhaps have the goodness to interpret for us the following oracular sentence, which from childhood has been to us a great mystery.—'An old horse came in to be shaved; curse you, where's the suds? The estate was entailed to male heirs; and poor Mrs. Molly lost all her apple-dumplings.'

Thin as is this volume we are now reviewing, and sparse the letter-press on its tiny pages, 'twould yet be easy to extract from it much more unmeaningness; but having shewn by gentle chastisement that we love Alfred Tennyson, let us now shew by judicious eulogy that we admire him; and, by well-chosen specimens of his fine faculties, that he is worthy of our admiration.

Odes to Memory are mostly mummeries; but not so is the 'Ode to Memory' breathed by this young poet. In it, Memory and Imagination, like two angels, lead him by the hands back to the bowers of paradise. All the finest feelings and the finest faculties of his soul, are awakened under that heavenly guidance, as the 'green light' of early life again blesses his eyes; and he sees that the bowers of paradise are built on this common earth, that they are the very bushes near his father's house, where his boyhood revelled in the brightening dawn. We have many quotations yet to make—and therefore cannot give the whole ode, but the half of it; and none will deny, all will feel, that, with perhaps the exception of some harmless mannerisms—affectations we shall not call them—the lines are eminently beautiful.

[Quotes 'Ode to Memory', stanzas iv and v:

'Come forth, I charge thee, arise, . . .
Thou dewy dawn of memory.']

There is fine music there; the versification would be felt delightful to all poetical ears, even if they missed the many meanings of the well-chosen and happily-obedient words; for there is the sound as of a various-voiced river rejoicing in a sudden summer shower, that swells without staining its translucent waters. But the sound is echo to the sense; and the sense is sweet as that of life's dearest emotions enjoyed in 'a dream that is not all a dream'.

Mr. Tennyson, when he chooses, can say much in few words. A fine example of that is shewn in five few-syllabled four-lined stanzas on a Deserted House. Every word tells; and the short whole is most pathetic in its completeness—let us say perfection—like some old Scottish air sung by maiden at her wheel—or shepherd in the wilderness.

[Quotes 'The Deserted House', ll. 1–22:

'Life and Thought have gone away . . .
Would they could have stayed with us!']

Mr. Tennyson is sometimes too mystical; for sometimes we fear there is no meaning in his mysticism; or so little, that were it to be stated perspicuously and plainly, 'twould be but a point. But at other times he gives us sweet, still, obscure poems, like the gentle gloaming saddening all that is sad, and making nature's self pensive in her depth of peace. Such is the character of

[Quotes 'A Dirge', ll. 1–49:

'Now is done thy long day's work; . . .
Let them rave.']

Many such beautiful images float before us in his poetry, as 'youthful poets fancy when they love'. He has a delicate perception of the purity of the female character. Any one of his flesh and blood maidens, walking amongst flowers of our own earth, is worth a billowy wilderness of his Sea-Fairies. Their names and their natures are delightful—sound and sight are spiritualized—and yet, as Wordsworth divinely saith, are they

> Creatures not too bright or good
> For human nature's daily food,
> For transient sorrows, simple wiles,
> Praise, blame, love, kisses, tears and smiles!

We are in love—as an old man ought to be—as a father is with his ideal daughters—with them all—with Claribel, and Lilian, and Isabel, and Mariana, and Adeline, and Hero, and Almeida, and the Sleeping Beauty, and Oriana. What different beings from King Charles's beauties! Even in bodily charms far more loveable; in spiritual, pure

> As heavenly Una with her milk-white lamb—

objects, for a moment's thought, of passion; but of affection, for ever and a day. In face, form, figure, circumstance and character, delicately distinguished from one another are all the sweet sisterhood. 'Seven lilies in one garland wrought'—'alike, but oh, how different!' Budding, blossoming, full-blown; but if on leaf or flower any touch of decay, 'tis not the touch of time but of sorrow, and there is balmy beauty in the very blight—lovely to the last the lily of the garden, of the field, or of the valley. The rose is the queen of flowers—but should she ever die, the lily would wear the crown—and her name is

[Quotes 'Isabel', ll. 1–41:

> 'Eyes not down-dropt nor over-bright . . .
> Of such a finish'd chasten'd purity.']

There is profound pathos in 'Mariana'. The young poet had been dreaming of Shakspeare, and of *Measure for Measure*, and of the gentle lady all forlorn, the deserted of the false Angelo, of whom the Swan of Avon sings but some few low notes in her distress and desolation, as she wears away her lonely life in solitary tears at 'the moated grange'. On this hint Alfred Tennyson speaks; 'he has a vision of his own'; nor might Wordsworth's self in his youth have disdained to indite such melancholy strain. Scenery—state—emotion—character—are all in fine keeping; long, long, long indeed is the dreary day, but it will end at last; so finds the heart-broken prisoner who, from sunrise to sunset, has been leaning on the sun-dial in the centre of his narrow solitude!

[Quotes 'Mariana', ll. 1–84:

> 'With blackest moss the flower-plots . . .
> Oh God, that I were dead!"']

It is not at all necessary that we should understand fine poetry to feel and enjoy it, any more than fine music. That is to say, some sorts of fine poetry—the shadowy and the spiritual; where something glides before us ghostlike, 'now in glimmer and now in gloom', and then away into some still place of trees or tombs. Yet the poet who composes it, must weigh the force of every feeling word—in a balance true to a hair, for ever vibrating, and obedient to the touch of down or dew-drop. Think not that such process interrupts inspiration; it sustains and feeds it; for it becomes a habit of the heart and the soul in all their musings and meditations; and thus is the language of poetry, though human, heavenly speech. In reading it, we see new revelations on each rehearsal—all of them true, though haply different—and what we at first thought a hymn, we may at last feel to be an elegy—a breathing not about the quick, but the dead. So was it with us in reading over and over again 'Claribel'. We supposed the lady slept beneath the 'solemn oak-tree, thick-leaved, ambrosial'; and that the 'ancient melody' was dimly heard by her in her world of dreams. But we know now that only her dust is there; and that the character of her spirit, as it dwelt on earth, is shadowed forth by the congenial scenery of her burial-place. But 'Adeline' is alive—faintly-smiling—shadowy—dreaming—spiritual Adeline—such are the epithets bestowed by the poet on that Lady of Light who visits his visions—though doomed to die—or rather to melt away back to her native heaven.

[Quotes 'Adeline', ll. 1–64:

'Mystery of mysteries . . .
Spiritual Adeline.']

The life of Claribel was shadowed forth by images of death—the death of Adeline seemed predicted by images of life—and in the lovely lines on the Sleeping Beauty, life and death meet in the stillness of that sleep—so profound that it is felt as if it were immortal. And is there not this shading and blending of all feeling and all thought that regards the things we most tenderly and deeply love on this changeful earth?

[Quotes 'The Day-Dream: The Sleeping Beauty', ll. 1–24:

'Year after year unto her feet, . . .
A perfect form in perfect rest.']

Some of our old ballads, breathed in the gloom of forests or glens by shepherds or woodsmen, are in their earnest simplicity inimitable by genius born so many centuries since they died, and overshadowed by another life. Yet genius has often delighted to sink away into such moods as those in which it imagines those lowly men to have been lost when they sang their songs, 'the music of the heart', with nothing that moved around them but the antlers of the deer, undisturbed by the bard lying among the breckens or the broom, beneath the checkered light that came through the umbrage of the huge oak-tree, on which spring was hourly shedding a greener glory, or autumn a more golden decay. Shepherds and woodsmen, too, there have been in these later days, and other rural dwellers, who have sometimes caught the spirit of the antique strain—Robert, James, and Allan—whose happiest 'auld ballants' are as if obsolete forest-flowers were brought back to life on our banks and braes. Perhaps the most beautiful of all Alfred Tennyson's compositions, is the 'Ballad of Oriana'.

[Quotes 'The Ballad of Oriana', ll. 1–99:

'My heart is wasted with my woe, . . .
Oriana.']

But the highest of all this young poet's achievements, is the visionary and romantic strain, entitled, 'Recollections of the Arabian Nights'. It is delightful even to us, who read not the *Arabian Nights*, nor ever heard of them, till late in life—we think we must have been in our tenth year; the same heart-soul-mind-awakening year that brought us John Bunyan and *Robinson Crusoe*, and in which —we must not say with whom—we first fell in love. How it happened that we had lived so long in this world without seeing or hearing tell of these famous worthies, is a mystery . . . But so it was; we knew not that there was an Arabian Night in the whole world. Our souls, in stir or stillness, saw none but the sweet Scottish stars. We knew, indeed, that they rose, and set, too, upon other climes; and had we been asked the question, should have said that they certainly did so; but we felt that they and their heavens belonged to Scotland. And so feels the fond, foolish old man still, when standing by himself at midnight, with withered hands across his breast, and eyes lifted heavenwards, that show the brightest stars somewhat dim now, yet beautiful as ever; out walks the moon from behind a cloud, and he thinks of long Loch Lomond glittering afar off with lines of radiance that lift up in their loveliness, flush after flush—and each silvan pomp is statelier than the last—now one, now another, of her heron-haunted isles!

But in our egoism and egotism we have forgot Alfred Tennyson. To his heart, too, we doubt not that heaven seems almost always an English heaven; he, however, must have been familiar long before his tenth year with the *Arabian Nights' Entertainments*; for had he discovered them at that advanced period of life, he had not now so passionately and so imaginatively sung their wonders.

[Quotes 'Recollections of the Arabian Nights', ll. 1–154:

'When the breeze of a joyful dawn blew free . . .
The good Haroun Alraschid!']

Our critique is near its conclusion; and in correcting it for press, we see that its whole merit, which is great, consists in the extracts, which are 'beautiful exceedingly'. Perhaps, in the first part of our article, we may have exaggerated Mr. Tennyson's not unfrequent silliness, for we are apt to be carried away by the whim of the moment, and in our humorous moods, many things wear a queer look to our aged eyes, which fill young pupils with tears; but we feel assured that in the second part we have not exaggerated his strength—that we have done no more than justice to his fine faculties—and that the millions who delight in Maga will, with one voice, confirm our judgment—that Alfred Tennyson is a poet.

But, though it might be a mistake of ours, were we to say that he has much to learn, it can be no mistake to say that he has not a little to unlearn, and more to bring into practice, before his genius can achieve its destined triumphs. A puerile partiality for particular forms of expression, nay, modes of spelling and of pronunciation, may be easily overlooked in one whom *we* must look on as yet a mere boy; but if he carry it with him, and indulge it in manhood, why it will make him seem silly as his sheep; and should he continue to bleat so when his head and beard are as grey as ours, he will be truly a laughable old ram, and the ewes will care no more for him than if he were a wether.

Farther—he must consider that all the fancies that fleet across the imagination, like shadows on the grass or the tree-tops, are not entitled to be made small separate poems of—about the length of one's little finger; that many, nay, most of them, should be suffered to pass away with a silent 'God bless ye', like butterflies, single or in shoals, each family with its own hereditary character mottled on its wings; and that though thousands of those grave brown, and gay golden images will be blown back in showers, as if upon balmy breezes changing suddenly and softly to the *airt* whence inspiration at the moment breathes, yet not one in a thousand is worth being caught and pinned down on paper into poetry, 'gently as if you loved him'—only the few that are bright with the 'beauty still more beauteous'—and a few such belong to all the orders—from the little silly moth that extinguishes herself in your taper, up to the mighty Emperor of Morocco at meridian wavering his burnished downage in the unconsuming sun who glorifies the wondrous stranger.

Now, Mr. Tennyson does not seem to know this; or if he do, he is self-willed and perverse in his sometimes almost infantile vanity; (and how vain are most beautiful children!) and thinks that any Thought or Feeling or Fancy that has had the honour and the happiness to pass through *his* mind, must by that very act be worthy of everlasting commemoration. Heaven pity the poor world, were we to put into stanzas, and publish upon it, all our thoughts, thick as mots in the sun, or a summer evening atmosphere of midges!

Finally, Nature is mighty, and poets should deal with her on a grand scale. She lavishes her glorious gifts before their path in such profusion, that Genius—reverent as he is of the mysterious mother, and meeting her at sunrise on the mountains with grateful orisons—with grateful orisons bidding her farewell among the long shadows that stretch across the glens when sunset sinks into the sea—is yet privileged to tread with a seeming scorn in the midst of imagery that to common eyes would be as a revelation of wonders from another world. Familiar to him are they as the grass below his feet. In lowlier moods he looks at them—and in his love they grow beautiful. So did Burns beautify the daisy—'wee modest crimson-tipped flower!' But in loftier moods the 'violet by the mossy stone' is not 'half-hidden to the eye'—it is left unthought of to its own sweet existence. The poet then ranges wide and high, like Thomson, in his *Hymn* to the Seasons, which he had so gloriously sung, seeing in all the changes of the rolling year 'but the varied god'.—like Wordsworth, in his *Excursion*, communing too with the spirit 'whose dwelling is the light of setting suns'.

Those great men are indeed among the

Lights of the world and demigods of fame;

but all poets, ere they gain a bright name, must thus celebrate the worship of nature. So is it, too, with painters. They do well, even the greatest of them, to trace up the brooks to their source in stone-basin or mossy well, in the glen-head, where greensward glades among the heather seem the birthplace of the Silent People—the Fairies. But in their immortal works they must shew us how 'red comes the river down'; castles of rock or of cloud—long withdrawing vales, where midway between the flowery foreground, and in the distance of blue mountain ranges, some great city lifts up its dim-seen spires through the misty smoke beneath which imagination hears the hum of life—'peaceful as some immeasurable plain', the breast of old ocean sleeping in the sunshine—or as if an earthquake shook the pillars of his caverned depths, tumbling the foam of his breakers, mast-high, if mast be there, till the canvass ceases to be silent, and the gazer hears him howling over his prey—See—see!—the foundering wreck of a three-decker going down head-foremost to eternity.

With such admonition, we bid Alfred Tennyson farewell.

4. J. W. Croker on

Poems [1833]

John Wilson Croker, unsigned review, *Quarterly Review* (April 1833), xlix. 81–96.

Croker (1780–1857) was a prominent Tory politician and a regular contributor to the *Quarterly*, which published his notorious attack on Keats (1818).

This is, as some of his marginal notes intimate, Mr. Tennyson's second appearance. By some strange chance we have never seen his first publication, which, if it at all resembles its younger brother, must be by this time so popular that any notice of it on our part would seem idle and presumptuous; but we gladly seize this opportunity of repairing an unintentional neglect, and of introducing to the admiration of our more sequestered readers a new prodigy of genius—another and a brighter star of that galaxy or *milky way* of poetry of which the lamented Keats was the harbinger; and let us take this occasion to sing our palinode on the subject of 'Endymion'. We certainly did not[1] discover in that poem the same degree of merit that its more clear-sighted and prophetic admirers did. We did not foresee the unbounded popularity which has carried it through we know not how many editions; which has placed it on every table; and, what is still more unequivocal, familiarized it in every mouth. All this splendour of fame, however, though we had not the sagacity to anticipate, we have the candour to acknowledge; and we request that the publisher of the new and beautiful edition of Keats's works now in the press, with graphic illustrations by Calcott and Turner, will do us the favour and the justice to notice our conversion in his prolegomena.

Warned by our former mishap, wiser by experience, and improved, as we hope, in taste, we have to offer Mr. Tennyson our tribute of

[1] See *Quarterly Review*, vol. xix, p. 204.

unmingled approbation, and it is very agreeable to us, as well as to our readers, that our present task will be little more than the selection, for their delight, of a few specimens of Mr. Tennyson's singular genius, and the venturing to point out, now and then, the peculiar brilliancy of some of the gems that irradiate his poetical crown.

A prefatory sonnet opens to the reader the aspirations of the young author, in which, after the manner of sundry poets, ancient and modern, he expresses his own peculiar character, by wishing himself to be something that he is not. The amorous Catullus aspired to be a sparrow; the tuneful and convivial Anacreon (for we totally reject the supposition that attributes the ''Ειθε λύρη καλὴ γενοίμην to Alcæus) wished to be a lyre and a great drinking cup; a crowd of more modern sentimentalists have desired to approach their mistresses as flowers, tunicks, sandals, birds, breezes, and butterflies;—all poor conceits of narrow-minded poetasters! Mr. Tennyson (though he, too, would, as far as his true-love is concerned, not unwillingly be 'an earring', 'a girdle', and 'a necklace') in the more serious and solemn exordium of his works ambitions a bolder metamorphosis—he wishes to be—*a river*!

SONNET.

> Mine be the strength of spirit fierce and free,
> Like some broad river rushing down *alone*—

rivers that travel in company are too common for his taste—

> With the self-same impulse wherewith he was thrown—

a beautiful and harmonious line—

> From his loud fount upon the echoing lea:—
> Which, with *increasing* might, doth *forward flee*—

Every word of this line is valuable—the natural progress of human ambition is here strongly characterized—two lines ago he would have been satisfied with the *self-same* impulse—but now he must have *increasing* might; and indeed he would require all his might to accomplish his object of *fleeing forward*, that is, going backwards and forwards at the same time. Perhaps he uses the word *flee* for *flow*; which latter he could not well employ in *this* place, it being, as we shall see, essentially necessary to rhyme to *Mexico* towards the end of the sonnet—as an equivalent to *flow* he has, therefore, with great taste and ingenuity, hit on the combination of *forward flee*—

———————— doth forward flee
By town, and tower, and hill, and cape, and isle,
And in the middle of the green *salt* sea
Keeps his blue waters fresh for many a mile.

A noble wish, beautifully expressed, that he may not be confounded
with the deluge of ordinary poets, but, amidst their discoloured and
briny ocean, still preserve his own bright tints and sweet savor. He
may be at ease on this point—he never can be mistaken for any one else.
We have but too late become acquainted with him, yet we assure
ourselves that if a thousand anonymous specimens were presented to
us, we should unerringly distinguish his by the total absence of any
particle of *salt*. But again, his thoughts take another turn, and he
reverts to the insatiability of human ambition:—we have seen him just
now content to be a river, but as he *flees forward*, his desires expand into
sublimity, and he wishes to become the great Gulf-stream of the
Atlantic.

Mine be the power which ever to its sway
Will win *the wise at once*—

We, for once, are wise, and he has won *us*—

Will win the wise at once; and by degrees
May into uncongenial spirits flow,
Even as the great gulphstream of Flori*da*
Floats far away into the Northern seas
The lavish growths of southern Mexi*co*!

And so concludes the sonnet.

The next piece is a kind of testamentary paper, addressed 'To ———',
a friend, we presume, containing his wishes as to what his friend should
do for him when he (the poet) shall be dead—not, as we shall see, that
he quite thinks that such a poet can die outright.

Shake hands, my friend, across the brink
Of that deep grave to which I go.
Shake hands once more; I cannot sink
So far—far down, but I shall know
Thy voice, and answer from below!

Horace said 'non omnis moriar', meaning that his fame should survive
—Mr. Tennyson is still more vivacious, 'non *omnino* moriar'—'I will
not die at all; my body shall be as immortal as my verse, and however

low I may go, I warrant you I shall keep all my wits about me,—
therefore'

> When, in the darkness over me,
>   The four-handed mole shall scrape,
> Plant thou no dusky cypress tree,
>   Nor wreath thy cap with doleful crape,
>   But pledge me in the flowing grape.

Observe how all ages become present to the mind of a great poet;
and admire how naturally he combines the funeral cypress of classical
antiquity with the crape hatband of the modern undertaker.

He proceeds:—

> And when the sappy field and wood
>   Grow green beneath the *showery gray*,
> And rugged barks begin to bud,
>   And through damp holts, newflushed with May,
>   Ring sudden *laughters* of the jay!

Laughter, the philosophers tell us, is the peculiar attribute of man—
but as Shakspeare found 'tongues in trees and sermons in stones', this
true poet endows all nature not merely with human sensibilities but
with human functions—the jay *laughs*, and we find, indeed, a little
further on, that the woodpecker *laughs* also; but to mark the distinction
between their merriment and that of men, both jays and woodpeckers
laugh upon melancholy occasions. We are glad, moreover, to observe,
that Mr. Tennyson is prepared for, and therefore will not be disturbed
by, human laughter, if any silly reader should catch the infection from
the woodpeckers and jays.

> Then let wise Nature work her will,
>   And on my clay her darnels grow,
> Come only when the days are still,
>   And at my head-stone whisper low,
>   And tell me—

Now, what would an ordinary bard wish to be told under such circumstances?—why, perhaps, how his sweetheart was, or his child, or his
family, or how the Reform Bill worked, or whether the last edition of
the poems had been sold—*papæ*! our genuine poet's first wish is

> And tell me—*if the woodbines blow*!

When, indeed, he shall have been thus satisfied as to the *woodbines*, (of the blowing of which in their due season he may, we think, feel pretty secure,) he turns a passing thought to his friend—and another to his mother—

> If *thou* art blest, my *mother's* smile
> Undimmed——

but such inquiries, short as they are, seem too commonplace, and he immediately glides back into his curiosity as to the state of the weather and the forwardness of the spring—

> If thou art blessed—my mother's smile
> Undimmed—*if bees are on the wing?*

No, we believe the whole circle of poetry does not furnish such another instance of enthusiasm for the sights and sounds of the vernal season!—The sorrows of a bereaved mother rank *after* the blossoms of the *woodbine*, and just before the hummings of the *bee*; and this is *all* that he has any curiosity about; for he proceeds—

> Then cease, my friend, a little while
> That I may——

'send my love to my mother', or 'give you some hints about bees, which I have picked up from Aristæus, in the Elysian Fields', or 'tell you how I am situated as to my own personal comforts in the world below'?—oh no—

> That I may—hear the *throstle sing*
>   His bridal song—the boast of spring.
> Sweet as the noise, in parchèd plains,
>   Of bubbling wells that fret the stones,
> (*If any sense in me remains*)
>   Thy words will be—thy cheerful tones
>   As welcome to—my *crumbling bones*!

'*If any sense in me remains!*'—This doubt is inconsistent with the opening stanza of the piece, and, in fact, too modest; we take upon ourselves to re-assure Mr. Tennyson, that, even after he shall be dead and buried, as much '*sense*' will still remain as he has now the good fortune to possess.

  We have quoted these two first poems in *extenso*, to obviate any suspicion of our having made a partial or delusive selection. We cannot afford space—we wish we could—for an equally minute examination

of the rest of the volume, but we shall make a few extracts to show—
what we solemnly affirm—that every page teems with beauties hardly
less surprising.

'The Lady of Shalott' is a poem in four parts, the story of which
we decline to maim by such an analysis as we could give, but it opens
thus—

> On either side the river lie
> Long fields of barley and of rye,
> That clothe the wold and *meet the sky*—
> And *through* the field the road runs *by*.

The Lady of Shalott was, it seems, a spinster who had, under some
unnamed penalty, a certain web to weave.

> Underneath the bearded barley,
> The reaper, reaping late and early,
> Hears her ever chanting cheerly,
> Like an angel singing clearly . . .
> No time has she to sport or play,
> A charmèd web she weaves alway;
> A curse is on her if she stay
> Her weaving either night or day . . .
> She knows not—

Poor lady, nor we either—

> She knows not what that curse may be,
> Therefore she weaveth steadily;
> Therefore no other care has she,
> > The Lady of Shalott.

A knight, however, happens to ride past her window, coming
—— from Camelot;[1]

> From the bank, and *from* the *river*—
> He flashed *into* the crystal *mirror*—
> 'Tirra lirra, tirra *lirra*,' (*lirra?*)
> > Sang Sir Launcelot.

The lady stepped to the window to look at the stranger, and forgot
for an instant her web:—the curse fell on her, and she died; why, how,

---

[1] The same Camelot, in Somersetshire, we presume, which is alluded to by Kent in
King Lear—
> Goose! if I had thee upon Sarum plain,
> I'd drive thee cackling home to Camelot.

and wherefore, the following stanzas will clearly and pathetically
explain:—

> A long drawn carol, mournful, holy,
> She chanted loudly, chanted lowly,
> Till her eyes were darkened *wholly,*
> And her smooth face *sharpened slowly,*
> > Turned to towered Camelot.
> For ere she reached upon the tide
> The first house on the water side,
> Singing in her song she died,
> > The Lady of Shalott!
> Knight and burgher, lord and dame,
> To the plankèd wharfage came;
> Below *the stern* they read her name,
> > The Lady of Shalott.

We pass by two—what shall we call them?—tales, or odes, or
sketches, entitled 'Mariana in the South' and 'Eleänore', of which we
fear we could make no intelligible extract, so curiously are they run
together into one dreamy tissue—to a little novel in rhyme, called
'The Miller's Daughter'. Miller's daughters, poor things, have been so
generally betrayed by their sweethearts, that it is refreshing to find
that Mr. Tennyson has united himself to *his* miller's daughter in lawful
wedlock, and the poem is a history of his courtship and wedding. He
begins with a sketch of his own birth, parentage, and personal appearance—

> My father's mansion, mounted high,
> > Looked down upon the village-spire;
> I was a long and listless boy,
> > And son and heir unto the Squire.

But the son and heir of Squire Tennyson often descended from the
'mansion mounted high'; and

> I met in all the close green ways,
> > While walking with my line and rod,

A metonymy for 'rod and line'—

> The wealthy miller's mealy face,
> > Like the *moon in an ivytod.*
> He looked so jolly and so good—
> > While fishing in the mill-dam water,
> I laughed to see him as he stood,
> > And dreamt not of the miller's daughter.

He, however, soon saw, and, need we add, loved the miller's daughter,
whose countenance, we presume, bore no great resemblance either to
the 'mealy face' of the miller, or 'the moon in an ivy-tod'; and we
think our readers will be delighted at the way in which the impassioned
husband relates to his wife how his fancy mingled enthusiasm for
rural sights and sounds, with a prospect of the less romantic scene of
her father's occupation.

> How dear to me in youth, my love,
>   Was everything about the mill;
> The black, the silent pool above,
>   The pool beneath that ne'er stood still;
> The meal-sacks on the whitened floor,
>   The dark round of the dripping wheel,
> *The very air about the door,*
>   *Made misty with the floating meal!*

The accumulation of tender images in the following lines appears
not less wonderful:—

> Remember you that pleasant day
>   When, after roving in the woods,
> ('Twas April then) I came and lay
>   Beneath those *gummy* chestnut-buds?
> A water-rat from off the bank
>   Plunged in the stream. With idle care,
> Downlooking through the sedges rank,
>   I saw your troubled image there.
> If you remember, you had set,
>   Upon the narrow casement-edge,
> A *long green box* of mignonette,
>   And you were leaning on the ledge.

The poet's truth to Nature in his 'gummy' chestnut-buds, and to Art
in the 'long green box' of mignonette—and that masterly touch of
likening the first intrusion of love into the virgin bosom of the Miller's
daughter to the plunging of a water-rat into the mill-dam—these
are beauties which, we do not fear to say, equal anything even in
Keats.

We pass by several songs, sonnets, and small pieces, all of singular
merit, to arrive at a class, we may call them, of three poems derived
from mythological sources—Œnone, the Hesperides, and the Lotos-
eaters. But though the subjects are derived from classical antiquity,

Mr. Tennyson treats them with so much originality that he makes them exclusively his own. Œnone, deserted by

Beautiful Paris, evilhearted Paris,

sings a kind of dying soliloquy addressed to Mount Ida, in a formula which is *sixteen* times repeated in this short poem.

Dear mother Ida, hearken ere I die.

She tells her 'dear mother Ida', that when evilhearted Paris was about to judge between the three goddesses, he hid her (Œnone) behind a rock, whence she had a full view of the *naked* beauties of the rivals, which broke her heart.

Dear mother Ida, hearken ere I die:—
It was the deep mid noon: one silvery cloud
Had *lost his way* among the pined hills:
They came—*all three*—the Olympian goddesses.
Naked they came——

    ★   ★   ★   ★   ★   ★

How beautiful they were! too beautiful
To look upon; but Paris was to me
More lovelier than all the world beside.
O mother Ida, hearken ere I die.

In the place where we have indicated a pause, follows a description, long, rich, and luscious—Of the three naked goddesses? Fye for shame—no—of the 'lily flower violet-eyed', and the 'singing pine', and the 'overwandering ivy and vine', and 'festoons', and 'gnarlèd boughs', and 'tree tops', and 'berries', and 'flowers', and all the *inanimate* beauties of the scene. It would be unjust to the *ingenuus pudor* of the author not to observe the art with which he has veiled this ticklish interview behind such luxuriant trellis-work, and it is obvious that it is for our special sakes he has entered into these local details, because if there was one thing which 'mother Ida' knew better than another, it must have been her own bushes and brakes. We then have in detail the tempting speeches of, first—

The imperial Olympian,
With archèd eyebrow smiling sovranly,
Full-eyèd Here;

secondly of Pallas—

Her clear and barèd limbs
O'er-thwarted with the brazen-headed spear,

and thirdly—

> Idalian Aphrodite ocean-born,
> Fresh as the foam, new-bathed in Paphian *wells*—

for one dip, or even three dips in one well, would not have been enough on such an occasion—and her succinct and prevailing promise of—

> The fairest and most loving *wife* in Greece,—

upon evil-hearted Paris's catching at which prize, the tender and chaste Œnone exclaims her indignation, that she herself should not be considered fair enough, since only yesterday her charms had struck awe into—

> A wild and wanton pard,
> Eyed like the evening star, with playful tail—

and proceeds in this anti-Martineau rapture—

> *Most* loving is *she?*
> Ah me! my mountain shepherd, that my arms
> Were wound about thee, and my hot lips prest
> Close—close to thine in that quick-falling dew
> Of *fruitful* kisses . . .
> Dear mother Ida! hearken ere I die!

After such reiterated assurances that she was about to die on the spot, it appears that Œnone thought better of it, and the poem concludes with her taking the wiser course of going to town to consult her swain's sister, Cassandra—whose advice, we presume, prevailed upon her to live, as we can, from other sources, assure our readers she did to a good old age.

In the 'Hesperides' our author, with great judgment, rejects the common fable, which attributes to Hercules the slaying of the dragon and the plunder of the golden fruit. Nay, he supposes them to have existed to a comparatively recent period—namely, the voyage of Hanno, on the coarse canvas of whose log-book Mr. Tennyson has judiciously embroidered the Hesperian romance. The poem opens with a geographical description of the neighbourhood, which must be very clear and satisfactory to the English reader; indeed, it leaves far behind in accuracy of topography and melody of rhythm the heroics of Dionysius *Periegetes*.

> The north wind fall'n, in the new-starrèd night.

Here we must pause to observe a new species of *metabolé* with which

Mr. Tennyson has enriched our language. He suppresses the E in *fallen*, where it is usually written and where it must be pronounced, and transfers it to the word *new-starrèd*, where it would not be pronounced if he did not take due care to superfix a *grave* accent. This use of the grave accent is, as our readers may have already perceived, so habitual with Mr. Tennyson, and is so obvious an improvement, that we really wonder how the language has hitherto done without it. We are tempted to suggest, that if analogy to the accented languages is to be thought of, it is rather the acute (´) than the grave (`) which should be employed on such occasions; but we speak with profound diffidence; and as Mr. Tennyson is the inventor of the system, we shall bow with respect to whatever his final determination may be.

> The north wind fall'n, in the new-starrèd night
> Zidonian Hanno, voyaging beyond
> The hoary promontory of Soloë,
> Past Thymiaterion in calmèd bays.

We must here note specially the musical flow of this last line, which is the more creditable to Mr. Tennyson, because it was before the tuneless names of this very neighbourhood that the learned continuator of Dionysius retreated in despair—

> ———— ἐπωνυμίας νῦν ἔλλαχεν ἄλλας
> Αἰθιόπων γαίη, δυσφώνους οὐδ' ἐπιήρους
> Μούσαις, οὕνεκα τάσδ' ἐγὼ οὐκ ἀγορεύσομ' ἁπάσας.

but Mr. Tennyson is bolder and happier—

> Past Thymiaterion in calmèd bays,
> Between the southern and the western Horn,
> Heard neither——

We pause for a moment to consider what a sea-captain might have expected to hear, by night, in the Atlantic ocean—he heard

> ——neither the warbling of the *nightingale*
> Nor melody o' the Libyan lotusflute,

but he did hear the three daughters of Hesper singing the following song:—

> The golden apple, the golden apple, the hallowèd fruit,
> Guard it well, guard it warily,
> Singing airily,
> Standing about the charmèd root,
> Round about all is mute——

mute, though they sung so loud as to be heard some leagues out at sea—

—————————all is mute
As the snow-field on mountain peaks,
As the sand-field at the mountain foot.
Crocodiles in briny creeks
Sleep, and stir not: all is mute.

How admirably do these lines describe the peculiarities of this charmèd neighbourhood—fields of snow, so talkative when they happen to lie at the foot of the mountain, are quite out of breath when they get to to the top, and the sand, so noisy on the summit of a hill, is dumb at its foot. The very crocodiles, too, are *mute*—not dumb but *mute*. The 'red-combèd dragon curl'd' is next introduced—

Look to him, father, lest he wink, and the golden apple be stolen away,
For his ancient heart is drunk with overwatchings night and day,
Sing away, sing aloud evermore, in the wind, without stop.

The north wind, it appears, had by this time awaked again—

Lest his scalèd eyelid drop,
For he is older than the world——

older than the *hills*, besides not rhyming to 'curl'd', would hardly have been a sufficiently venerable phrase for this most harmonious of lyrics. It proceeds—

If ye sing not, if ye make false measure,
We shall lose eternal pleasure,
Worth eternal want of rest.
Laugh not loudly: watch the treasure
Of the wisdom of the west.
In *a corner* wisdom whispers. Five and three
(*Let it not be preached abroad*) make an awful mystery.

This recipe for keeping a secret, by singing it so loud as to be heard for miles, is almost the only point, in all Mr. Tennyson's poems, in which we can trace the remotest approach to anything like what other men have written, but it certainly does remind us of the 'chorus of conspirators' in the *Rovers*.

Hanno, however, who understood no language but Punic—(the Hesperides sang, we presume, either in Greek or in English)—appears to have kept on his way without taking any notice of the song, for the poem concludes,—

> The apple of gold hangs over the sea,
> Five links, a golden chain, are we,
> Hesper, the Dragon, and sisters three;
> Daughters three,
> Bound about
> All round about
> The gnarlèd bole of the charmèd tree,
> The golden apple, the golden apple, the hallowèd fruit.
> Guard it well, guard it warily,
> Watch it warily,
> Singing airily,
> Standing about the charmèd root.

We hardly think that, if Hanno had translated it into Punic, the song would have been more intelligible.

The 'Lotos-Eaters'—a kind of classical opium-eaters—are Ulysses and his crew. They land on the 'charmèd island', and eat of the 'charmèd root', and then they sing—

> Long enough the winedark wave our weary bark did carry.
> This is lovelier and sweeter,
> Men of Ithaca, this is meeter,
> In the hollow rosy vale to tarry,
> Like a dreamy Lotoseater—a delicious Lotoseater!
> We will eat the Lotos, sweet
> As the yellow honeycomb;
> In the valley some, and some
> On the ancient heights divine,
> And no more roam,
> On the loud hoar foam,
> To the melancholy home,
> At the limits of the brine,
> The little isle of Ithaca, beneath the day's decline.

Our readers will, we think, agree that this is admirably characteristic, and that the singers of this song must have made pretty free with the intoxicating fruit. How they got home you must read in Homer:— Mr. Tennyson—himself, we presume, a dreamy lotos-eater, a delicious lotos-eater—leaves them in full song.

Next comes another class of poems—Visions. The first is the 'Palace of Art', or a fine house, in which the poet *dreams* that he sees a very fine collection of well-known pictures. An ordinary versifier would, no doubt, have followed the old routine, and dully described himself as walking into the Louvre, or Buckingham Palace, and there seeing certain masterpieces of painting:—a true poet dreams it. We have not room to hang many of these *chefs-d'œuvre*, but for a few we must find space.—'The Madonna'—

> The maid mother by a crucifix,
> In yellow pastures sunny warm,
> Beneath branch work of costly sardonyx
> Sat smiling—*babe in arm*.

The use of this latter, apparently, colloquial phrase is a deep stroke of art. The form of expression is always used to express an habitual and characteristic action. A knight is described '*lance in rest*'—a dragoon, '*sword in hand*'—so, as the idea of the Virgin is inseparably connected with her child, Mr. Tennyson reverently describes her conventional position—'*babe in arm*'.

His gallery of illustrious portraits is thus admirably arranged: The Madonna — Ganymede — St. Cecilia — Europa — Deep-haired Milton — Shakspeare — Grim Dante — Michael Angelo — Luther — Lord Bacon — Cervantes — Calderon — King David — 'the Halicarnasseän' (*quære*, which of them?)—Alfred (not Alfred Tennyson, though no doubt in any other man's gallery *he* would have had a place) and finally—

> Isaïah, with fierce Ezekiel,
> Swarth Moses by the Coptic sea,
> Plato, *Petrarca*, Livy, and Raphaël,
> And eastern Confutzee!

We can hardly suspect the very original mind of Mr. Tennyson to have harboured any recollections of that celebrated Doric idyll, 'The groves of Blarney', but certainly there is a strong likeness between Mr. Tennyson's list of pictures and the Blarney collection of statues—

> Statues growing that noble place in,
> All heathen goddesses most rare,
> Homer, Plutarch, and Nebuchadnezzar,
> All standing naked in the open air!

In this poem we first observed a stroke of art (repeated afterwards) which we think very ingenious. No one who has ever written verse but must have felt the pain of erasing some happy line, some striking stanza, which, however excellent in itself, did not exactly suit the place for which it was destined. How curiously does an author mould and remould the plastic verse in order to fit in the favourite thought; and when he finds that he cannot introduce it, as Corporal Trim says, *any how*, with what reluctance does he at last reject the intractable, but still cherished offspring of his brain! Mr. Tennyson manages this delicate matter in a new and better way; he says, with great candour and simplicity, 'If this poem were not already too long, *I should have added* the following stanzas', and *then he adds them*,—or, 'the following lines are manifestly superfluous, as a part of the text, but they may be allowed to stand as a separate poem', *which they do*;—or, 'I intended to have added something on statuary, but I found it very difficult';—(he had, moreover, as we have seen, been anticipated in this line by the Blarney poet)—'but I had finished the statues of *Elijah* and *Olympias*—judge whether I have succeeded',—and then we have these two statues. This is certainly the most ingenious device that has ever come under our observation, for reconciling the rigour of criticism with the indulgence of parental partiality. It is economical too, and to the reader profitable, as by these means

We lose no drop of the immortal man.

The other vision is 'A Dream of Fair Women', in which the heroines of all ages—some, indeed, that belong to the times of 'heathen goddesses most rare'—pass before his view. We have not time to notice them all, but the second, whom we take to be Iphigenia, touches the heart with a stroke of nature more powerful than even the veil that the Grecian painter threw over the head of her father.

> ————dimly I could descry
> The stern blackbearded kings with wolfish eyes,
>   Watching to see me die.
> The tall masts quivered as they lay afloat;
>   The temples, and the people, and the shore;
> One drew a sharp knife through my tender throat—
>   Slowly—and *nothing more!*

What touching simplicity—what pathetic resignation—he cut my throat—'*nothing more!*' One might indeed ask, 'what *more*' she would have?

But we must hasten on; and to tranquillize the reader's mind after the last affecting scene, shall notice the only two pieces of a lighter strain which the volume affords. The first is elegant and playful; it is a

80

description of the author's study, which he affectionately calls his *Darling Room.*

> O darling room, my heart's delight;
> Dear room, the apple of my sight;
> With thy two couches, soft and white,
> There is no room so exqui*site*;
> No little room so warm and bright,
> Wherein to read, wherein to write.

We entreat our readers to note how, even in this little trifle, the singular taste and genius of Mr. Tennyson break forth. In such a dear *little* room a narrow-minded scribbler would have been content with *one* sofa, and that one he would probably have covered with black mohair, or red cloth, or a good striped chintz; how infinitely more characteristic is white dimity!—'tis as it were a type of the purity of the poet's mind. He proceeds—

> For I the Nonnenwerth have seen,
> And Oberwinter's vineyards green,
> Musical Lurlei; and between
> The hills to Bingen I have been,
> Bingen in Darmstadt, where the *Rhene*
> Curves towards Mentz, a woody scene.
> Yet never did there meet my sight,
> In any town, to left or right,
> A little room so exqui*site*,
> With *two* such couches soft and white;
> Not any room so warm and bright,
> Wherein to read, wherein to write.

A common poet would have said that he had been in London or in Paris—in the loveliest villa on the banks of the Thames, or the most gorgeous chateau on the Loire—that he had reclined in Madame de Staël's boudoir, and mused in Mr. Rogers's comfortable study; but the *darling room* of the poet of nature (which we must suppose to be endued with sensibility, or he would not have addressed it) would not be flattered with such common-place comparisons;—no, no, but it is something to have it said that there is no such room in the ruins of the Drachenfels, in the vineyard of Oberwinter, or even in the rapids of the *Rhene*, under the Lurleyberg. We have ourselves visited all these celebrated spots, and can testify, in corroboration of Mr. Tennyson, that we did not see in any of them anything like *this little room so exqui*SITE.

The second of the lighter pieces, and the last with which we shall delight our readers, is a severe retaliation on the editor of the *Edinburgh Magazine*, who, it seems, had not treated the first volume of Mr. Tennyson with the same respect that we have, we trust, evinced for the second.

TO CHRISTOPHER NORTH.

You did late review my lays,
　　Crusty Christopher;
You did mingle blame and praise,
　　Rusty Christopher.
When I learnt from whom it came
I forgave you all the blame,
　　Musty Christopher;
I could *not* forgive the praise,
　　Fusty Christopher.

Was there ever anything so genteelly turned—so terse—so sharp— and the point so stinging and *so true*?

I could not forgive the *praise*,
　　Fusty Christopher!

This leads us to observe on a phenomenon which we have frequently seen, but never been able to explain. It has been occasionally our painful lot to excite the displeasure of authors whom we have reviewed, and who have vented their dissatisfaction, some in prose, some in verse, and some in what we could not distinctly say whether it was verse or prose; but we have invariably found that the common formula of retort was that adopted by Mr. Tennyson against his northern critic, namely, that the author would always

—— Forgive us all the *blame*,
But could *not* forgive the *praise*.

Now this seems very surprising. It has sometimes, though we regret to say rarely, happened, that, as in the present instance, we have been able to deal out unqualified praise, but we never found that the dose in this case disagreed with the most squeamish stomach; on the contrary, the patient has always seemed exceedingly comfortable after he had swallowed it. He has been known to take the *Review* home and keep his wife from a ball, and his children from bed, till he could administer it to them, by reading the article aloud. He has even been heard to recommend the *Review* to his acquaintance at the clubs, as the best number which has yet appeared, and one, who happened to be an M.P. as well as an author, gave a *conditional* order, that in case his last work should be favourably noticed, a dozen copies should be sent down by the mail to the borough of ——. But, on the other hand, when it has happened that the general course of our criticism has been unfavourable, if by accident we happened to introduce the smallest spice of *praise*, the patient immediately fell into paroxysms—declaring that the part which we foolishly thought might offend him had, on the contrary, given him pleasure—positive pleasure, but *that* which he could not possibly either forget or forgive, was the grain of praise, be it ever so small, which we had dropped in, and for which, and *not for our censure*, he felt constrained, in honour and conscience, to visit us with his extreme indignation. Can any reader or writer inform us how it is that praise in the wholesale is so very agreeable to the very same stomach that rejects it with disgust and loathing, when it is scantily administered; and above all, can they tell us why it is, that the indignation and nausea should be in the exact inverse ratio to the quantity of the ingredient? These effects, of which we could quote several cases much more violent than Mr. Tennyson's, puzzle us exceedingly; but a learned friend, whom we have consulted, has, though he could not account for the phenomenon, pointed out what he thought an analogous case. It is related of Mr. Alderman Faulkener, of convivial memory, that one night when he expected his guests to sit late and try the strength of his claret and his head, he took the precaution of placing in his wine-glass a strawberry, which his doctor, he said, had recommended to him on account of its cooling qualities: on the faith of this specific, he drank even more deeply, and, as might be expected, was carried away at an earlier period and in rather a worse state, than was usual with him. When some of his friends condoled with him next day, and attributed his misfortune to six bottles of claret which he had imbibed, the Alderman was extremely indignant—'the claret', he said, 'was sound, and never could do any man any harm—his discomfiture was altogether caused by that damned single strawberry' which he had kept all night at the bottom of his glass.

5. J. S. Mill on

Poems, Chiefly Lyrical [1830]
Poems [1833]

John Stuart Mill, review signed 'A', *London Review* (July 1835), i. 402–24.

Mill (1806–73) had by this time deviated slightly from the strict utilitarianism in which his father, James Mill, had educated him. He wished to see the newly-established *London Review* an organ of all shades of philosophic radicalism and therefore 'made it one of the peculiarities of the work that every article should bear an initial, or some other signature, and be held to express the opinions solely of the individual writer; the editor being only responsible for its being worth publishing, and not in conflict with the objects for which the Review was set on foot' (*Autobiography*, vi).

Towards the close of the year 1830 appeared a small volume of poems, the work of a young and unknown author, and which, with considerable faults (some of them of a bad kind), gave evidence of powers such as had not for many years been displayed by any new aspirant to the character of a poet. This first publication was followed in due time by a second, in which the faults of its predecessor were still visible, but were evidently on the point of disappearing; while the positive excellence was not only greater and more uniformly sustained, but of a higher order. The imagination of the poet, and his reason, had alike advanced: the one had become more teeming and vigorous, while its resources had been brought more habitually and completely under the command of the other.

The notice which these poems have hitherto received from the more widely-circulated and influential organs of criticism consists, so far as we are aware, of two articles—a review of the first publication, in

Blackwood's Magazine, and of the second, in the *Quarterly Review*. The article in *Blackwood*, along with the usual flippancy and levity of that journal, evinced one of its better characteristics—a genuine appreciation and willing recognition of genius. It was not to be expected that a writer in *Blackwood* could accomplish a criticism on a volume of poetry, without cutting capers and exhibiting himself in postures, as Drawcansir says, 'because he dare'. The article on Mr. Tennyson is throughout in a strain of mocking exaggeration. Some reviewers write to extol their author, others to laugh at him; this writer was desirous to do both— first to make the book appear beyond all measure contemptible, next in the highest degree admirable—putting the whole force of his mind alternately into these two purposes. If we can forgive this audacious sporting with his reader and his subjects, the critique is otherwise not without merit. The praise and blame, though shovelled out rather than measured, are thrown into the right places; the real merits and defects of the poems are pointed out with discrimination, and a fair enough impression left of the proportion between the two; and it is evident that if the same writer were to review Mr. Tennyson's second publica- tion, his praise, instead of being about equally balanced by his censure, would be but slightly qualified by it.

Of Mr. Tennyson's two volumes, the second was the only one which fell into the hands of the *Quarterly* Reviewer; and his treatment of it, compared with the notice taken by *Blackwood* of its more juvenile pre- decessor, forms a contrast, characteristic of the two journals. Whatever may be in other respects our opinion of *Blackwood's Magazine*, it is im- possible to deny to its principal writers (or writer) a certain susceptibility of sense, a geniality of temperament. Their mode of writing about works of genius is that of a person who derives much enjoyment from them, and is grateful for it. Genuine powers of mind, with whatever opinions connected, seldom fail to meet with response and recognition from these writers. *The Quarterly Review*, on the other hand, both under its original and under its present management, has been no less character- ised by qualities directly the reverse of these. Every new claim upon its admiration, unless forced upon it by the public voice, or recommended by some party interest, it welcomes, not with a friendly extension of the hand, but with a curl of the lip: the critic (as we figure him to ourselves) taking up the book, in trusting anticipation of pleasure, not from the book, but from the contemplation of his own cleverness in making it contemptible. He has not missed the opportunity of admiring himself at the expense of Mr. Tennyson: although, as we have not heard that these poems have yet, like those of Mr. Robert Montgomery, reached the eleventh edition, nor that any apprehension is entertained of danger to the public taste from their extravagant popularity, we may well be astonished that performances so utterly worthless as this critic considers them, should have appeared to him deserving of so much attention from so superior a mind. The plan he adopts is no new one, but abundantly hacknied: he selects the few bad passages (not amounting to three pages in the whole), and such others as, by being separated from the context, may be made to look ridiculous; and, in a strain of dull irony, of which all the point consists in the ill-nature, he holds forth these as a specimen of the work. A piece of criticism, resembling, in all but their wit, the disgraceful articles in the early Numbers of the *Edinburgh Review*, on Wordsworth and Coleridge.

Meanwhile, these poems have been winning their way, by slow approaches, to a reputation, the exact limits and measure of which it would be hazardous at present to predict, but which, we believe, will not ultimately be inconsiderable. Desiring, so far as may depend upon us, to accelerate this progress, and also not without a desire to exhibit, to any who still have faith in the *Quarterly Review*, the value of its critical judgments, we propose to lay before those of our readers who are still unacquainted with the poems, such specimens as may justify the terms in which we have spoken of them—interspersing or subjoining a few remarks on the character and the present state of developement of Mr. Tennyson's poetic endowment.

Of all the capacities of a poet, that which seems to have arisen earliest in Mr. Tennyson, and in which he most excels, is that of scene-painting, in the higher sense of the term: not the mere power of producing that rather vapid species of composition usually termed descriptive poetry— for there is not in these volumes one passage of pure description: but the power of *creating* scenery, in keeping with some state of human feeling; so fitted to it as to be the embodied symbol of it, and to summon up the state of feeling itself, with a force not to be surpassed by anything but reality. Our first specimen, selected from the earlier of the two volumes, will illustrate chiefly this quality of Mr. Tennyson's productions. We do not anticipate that this little poem will be equally relished at first by all lovers of poetry: and indeed if it were, its merit could be but of the humblest kind; for sentiments and imagery which can be received at once, and with equal ease, into every mind, must necessarily be trite. Nevertheless, we do not hesitate to quote it at full length. The subject is Mariana, the Mariana of *Measure for Measure*, living deserted and in solitude in the 'moated grange'. The ideas which these two words suggest, impregnated with the feelings of the supposed inhabitant, have given rise to the following picture:

[Quotes 'Mariana', ll. 1–84:

'With blackest moss the flower-plots . . .
Oh God, that I were dead!'' ']

In the one peculiar and rare quality which we intended to illustrate by it, this poem appears to us to be pre-eminent. We do not, indeed, defend all the expressions in it, some of which seem to have been extorted from the author by the tyranny of rhyme; and we might find much more to say against the poem, if we insisted upon judging of it by a wrong standard. The nominal subject excites anticipations which the poem does not even attempt to fulfil. The humblest poet, who is a poet at all, could make more than is here made of the situation of a maiden abandoned by her lover. But that was not Mr. Tennyson's idea. The love-story is secondary in his mind. The words 'he cometh not' are almost the only words which allude to it at all. To place ourselves at the right point of view, we must drop the conception of Shakspeare's Mariana, and retain only that of a 'moated grange', and a solitary dweller within it, forgotten by mankind. And now see whether poetic imagery ever conveyed a more intense conception of such a place, or of the feelings of such an inmate. From the very first line, the rust of age and the solitude of desertion are on the whole picture. Words surely never excited a more vivid feeling of physical and spiritual dreariness: and not dreariness alone—for that might be felt under many other circumstances of solitude—but the dreariness which speaks not merely of being far from human converse and sympathy, but of being *deserted* by it.

Our next specimen shall be of a character remote from this. It is the second of two poems, 'The May Queen' and 'New Year's Eve'—the one expressing the wild, overflowing spirits of a light-hearted girl, just chosen Queen of the May; the latter, the feelings of the same girl some months afterwards, when dying by a gradual decay. We regret that the opening of the latter poem must lose in our pages the effect of contrast produced by its immediately succeeding the former:—

[Quotes 'The May Queen: New-Year's Eve', ll. 1–52:

'If you're waking, call me early, . . .
So, if you're waking, call me, call me early, mother dear.']

This poem is fitted for a more extensive popularity than any other in the two volumes. Simple, genuine pathos, arising out of the situations and feelings common to mankind generally, is of all kinds of poetic beauty that which can be most universally appreciated; and the genius implied in it is, in consequence, apt to be overrated, for it is also of all kinds that which can be most easily produced. In this poem there is not only the truest pathos, but (except in one passage[1]) perfect harmony and keeping.

The next poem which we shall quote is one of higher pretensions. Its length exceeds the usual dimensions of an extract. But the idea which would be given of the more perfect of Mr. Tennyson's poems, by detached passages, would be not merely an incomplete but a false idea. There is not a stanza in the following poem which can be felt or even understood as the poet intended, unless the reader's imagination and feelings are already in the state which results from the passage next preceding, or rather from all which precedes. The very breaks, which divide the story into parts, all tell.

If every one approached poetry in the spirit in which it ought to be approached, willing to feel it first and examine it afterwards, we should not premise another word. But there is a class of readers, (a class, too, on whose verdict the early success of a young poet mainly depends,) who dare not enjoy until they have first satisfied themselves that they have a warrant for enjoying; who read a poem with the critical understanding first, and only when they are convinced that it is right to be delighted, are willing to give their spontaneous feelings fair play. The consequence is, that they lose the general effect, while they higgle about the details, and never place themselves in the position in which, even with their mere understandings, they can estimate the poem as a whole. For the benefit of such readers, we tell them beforehand, that this is a tale of enchantment; and that they will never enter into the spirit of it unless they surrender their imagination to the guidance of the poet, with the same easy credulity with which they would read the *Arabian Nights*, or, what this story more resembles, the tales of magic of the middle ages.

Though the agency is supernatural, the scenery, as will be perceived, belongs to the actual world. No reader of any imagination will complain, that the precise nature of the enchantment is left in mystery.

[Quotes 'The Lady of Shalott', omitting the last stanza. A footnote

---

[1] We allude to the second line of the second stanza. The concluding words of the line appear to us altogether out of keeping with the rest of the poem.

refers to this omission of 'a "lame and impotent conclusion", where no conclusion was required.' (Tennyson later substituted the superior stanza which now ends the poem.) Two other footnotes defend passages attacked by Croker: ll. 100-8 and l. 148 (in its unrevised form, 'And her smooth face sharpened slowly'). Mill's footnote on l. 148 reads, 'This exquisite line, the egregious critic of the *Quarterly* distinguishes by italics as specially absurd! proving thereby what is his test of the truth of a description, even of a physical fact. He does not ask himself, Is the fact so? but, Have I ever seen the expression in the verses of any former poet of celebrity?']

In powers of narrative and scene-painting combined, this poem must be ranked among the very first of its class. The delineation of outward objects, as in the greater number of Mr. Tennyson's poems, is, not picturesque, but (if we may use the term) statuesque; with brilliancy of colour superadded. The forms are not, as in painting, of unequal degrees of definiteness; the tints do not melt gradually into each other, but each individual object stands out in bold relief, with a clear decided outline. This statue-like precision and distinctness, few artists have been able to give to so essentially vague a language as that of words: but if once this difficulty be got over, scene-painting by words has a wider range than either painting or sculpture; for it can represent (as the reader must have seen in the foregoing poem), not only with the vividness and strength of the one, but with the clearness and definiteness of the other, objects in motion. Along with all this, there is in the poem all that power of making a few touches do the whole work, which excites our admiration in Coleridge. Every line suggests so much more than it says, that much may be left unsaid: the concentration, which is the soul of narrative, is obtained, without the sacrifice of reality and life. Where the march of the story requires that the mind should pause, details are specified; where rapidity is necessary, they are all brought before us at a flash. Except that the versification is less exquisite, the 'Lady of Shalott' is entitled to a place by the side of the 'Ancient Mariner' and 'Christabel'.

Mr. Tennyson's two volumes contain a whole picture-gallery of lovely women: but we are drawing near to the limits of allowable quotation. The imagery of the following passage from the poem of 'Isabel', in the first volume, is beautifully typical of the nobler and gentler of two beings, upholding, purifying, and, as far as possible, assimilating to itself the grosser and ruder:—

A clear stream flowing with a muddy one,
  Till in its onward current it absorbs
    With swifter movement and in purer light
      The vexed eddies of its wayward brother—
  A leaning and upbearing parasite,
  Clothing the stem, which else had fallen quite,
    With clustered flowerbells and ambrosial orbs
      Of rich fruitbunches leaning on each other.

We venture upon a long extract from what we consider the finest of these ideal portraits, the 'Eleänore'. The reader must not, in this case, look for the definiteness of the 'Lady of Shalott'; there is nothing statuesque here. The object to be represented being more vague, there is greater vagueness and dimness in the expression. The loveliness of a graceful woman, words cannot make us see, but only feel. The individual expressions in the poem, from which the following is an extract, may not always bear a minute analysis; but ought they to be subjected to it? They are mere colours in a picture; nothing in themselves, but everything as they conduce to the general result.

[Quotes 'Eleänore', stanzas iv–vii:

  'How may fullsailed verse express, . . .
  Serene, imperial Eleänore.']

It has for some time been the fashion, though a fashion now happily on the decline, to consider a poet as a poet, only so far as he is supposed capable of delineating the more violent passions; meaning by violent passions, states of excitement approaching to monomania, and characters predisposed to such states. The poem which follows will show how powerfully, without the slightest straining, by a few touches which do not seem to cost him an effort, Mr. Tennyson can depict such a state and such a character.

[Quotes 'The Sisters', ll. 1–36:

  'We were two daughters of one race: . . .
  O the Earl was fair to see!']

The second publication contains several classical subjects treated with more or less felicity. The story of the Judgment of Paris, recited by Œnone, his deserted love, is introduced in the following stately manner:—

[Quotes the passage corresponding with ll. 1–21 ('There is a dale in

Ida, . . . Sloped downward to her seat from the upper cliff.') in the final version of 'Œnone' and adds a footnote defending Tennyson's use of repetition against Croker's attack.]

The length to which our quotations have extended, and the un-satisfactoriness of short extracts, prevent us from giving any specimen of one of the finest of Mr. Tennyson's poems, the 'Lotos-Eaters'. The subject is familiar to every reader of the *Odyssey*. The poem is not of such sustained merit in the execution as some of the others; but the general impression resembles an effect of climate in a landscape: we see the objects through a drowsy, relaxing, but dreamy atmosphere, and the inhabitants seem to have inhaled the like. Two lines near the com-mencement touch the key-note of the poem:

> In the afternoon they came unto a land
> Wherein it seemèd always afternoon.

The above extracts by no means afford an idea of all the variety of beauty to be found in these volumes. But the specimens we have given may, we hope, satisfy the reader, that if he explore further for himself, his search will be rewarded. We shall only subjoin a few remarks, tend-ing to an estimation of Mr. Tennyson's general character as a writer and as a poet.

There are in the character of every true poet, two elements, for one of which he is indebted to nature, for the other to cultivation. What he derives from nature, is fine senses: a nervous organization, not only adapted to make his outward impressions vivid and distinct (in which, however, practice does even more than nature), but so constituted, as to be, more easily than common organizations, thrown, either by physical or moral causes, into *states* of enjoyment or suffering, especially of en-joyment: states of a certain duration; often lasting long after the removal of the cause which produced them; and not local, nor consciously physical, but, in so far as organic, pervading the entire nervous system. This peculiar kind of nervous susceptibility seems to be the distinctive character of the poetic temperament. It constitutes the capacity for poetry; and not only produces, as has been shown from the known laws of the human mind, a predisposition to the poetic associations, but supplies the very materials out of which many of them are formed.[1]

---

[1] It may be thought, perhaps, that among the gifts of nature to a poet, ought also to be included a vivid and exuberant imagination. We believe, however, that vividness of imagination is no further a gift of nature, than in so far as it is a natural consequence of vivid sensations. All besides this, we incline to think, depends on habit and cultivation.

What the poet will afterwards construct out of these materials, or whether he will construct anything of value to any one but himself, depends upon the direction given, either by accident or design, to his habitual associations. Here, therefore, begins the province of culture; and, from this point upwards, we may lay it down as a principle, that the achievements of any poet in his art will be in proportion to the growth and perfection of his thinking faculty.

Every great poet, every poet who has extensively or permanently influenced mankind, has been a great thinker;—has had a philosophy, though perhaps he did not call it by that name;—has had his mind full of thoughts, derived not merely from passive sensibility, but from trains of reflection, from observation, analysis, and generalization; however remote the sphere of his observation and meditation may have lain from the studies of the schools. Where the poetic temperament exists in its greatest degree, while the systematic culture of the intellect has been neglected, we may expect to find, what we do find in the best poems of Shelley—vivid representations of states of passive and dreamy emotion, fitted to give extreme pleasure to persons of similar organization to the poet, but not likely to be sympathized in, because not understood, by any other persons; and scarcely conducing at all to the noblest end of poetry as an intellectual pursuit, that of acting upon the desires and characters of mankind through their emotions, to raise them towards the perfection of their nature. This, like every other adaptation of means to ends, is the work of cultivated reason; and the poet's success in it will be in proportion to the intrinsic value of his thoughts, and to the command which he has acquired over the materials of his imagination, for placing those thoughts in a strong light before the intellect, and impressing them on the feelings.

The poems which we have quoted from Mr. Tennyson prove incontestably that he possesses, in an eminent degree, the natural endowment of a poet—the poetic temperament. And it appears clearly, not only from a comparison of the two volumes, but of different poems in the same volume, that, with him, the other element of poetic excellence—intellectual culture—is advancing both steadily and rapidly; that he is not destined, like so many others, to be remembered for what he might have done, rather than for what he did; that he will not remain a poet of mere temperament, but is ripening into a true artist. Mr. Tennyson may not be conscious of the wide difference in maturity of intellect, which is apparent in his various poems. Though he now writes from greater fulness and clearness of thought, it by no means follows that he has learnt to detect the absence of those qualities in some of his earlier effusions. Indeed, he himself, in one of the most beautiful poems of his first volume (though, as a work of art, very imperfect), the 'Ode to Memory', confesses a parental predilection for the 'first-born' of his genius. But to us it is evident, not only that his second volume differs from his first as early manhood from youth, but that the various poems in the first volume belong to different, and even distant stages of intellectual development;—distant, not perhaps in years—for a mind like Mr. Tennyson's advances rapidly—but corresponding to very different states of the intellectual powers, both in respect of their strength and of their proportions.

From the very first, like all writers of his natural gifts, he luxuriates in sensuous[1] imagery; his nominal subject sometimes lies buried in a heap of it. From the first, too, we see his intellect, with every successive degree of strength, struggling upwards to shape this sensuous imagery to a spiritual meaning;[2] to bring the materials which sense supplies, and fancy summons up, under the command of a central and controlling thought or feeling. We have seen, by the poem of 'Mariana', with what success he could occasionally do this, even in the period which answers to his first volume; but that volume contains various instances in which he has attempted the same thing, and failed. Such, for example, are, in our opinion, the opening poem, 'Claribel', and the verses headed 'Elegiacs'. In both, there is what is commonly called imagination—namely, fancy: the imagery and the melody actually haunt us; but there is no harmonizing principle in either;—no appropriateness to the spiritual elements of the scene. If the one poem had been called 'A solitary Place in a Wood', and the other, 'An Evening Landscape', they would not have lost, but gained. In another poem, in the same volume, called 'A Dirge', and intended for a person who, when alive, had suffered from calumny—a subject which a poet of maturer powers would have made so much of, Mr. Tennyson merely glances at the topics of thought and

---

[1] *Sensuous*, a word revived by Coleridge, as he himself states, 'from our elder classics'. It is used by Milton, who, in his little tract on Education, says of poetry, as compared with rhetoric, that it is 'less subtile and fine, but more simple, *sensuous*, and passionate'. The word *sensual* is irretrievably diverted to another meaning; and a term seems to be required, which (without exciting any ethical associations) shall denote all things pertaining to the bodily senses, in contradistinction to things pertaining to the intellect and the mental feelings. To this use, the word *sensuous* seems as well adapted as any other which could be chosen.

[2] We conceive ourselves warranted, both by usage and the necessity of the case, in using the word *spiritual* as the converse of *sensuous*. It is scarcely necessary to say that we do not mean *religious*.

emotion which his subject suggested, and expatiates in the mere scenery about the grave.[1]

Some of the smaller poems have a fault which in any but a very juvenile production would be the worst fault of all: they are altogether without meaning: none at least can be discerned in them by persons otherwise competent judges of poetry; if the author had any meaning, he has not been able to express it. Such, for instance, are the two songs on the Owl; such, also, are the verses headed 'The "How" and the "Why"', in the first volume, and the lines on To-day and Yesterday, in the second. If in the former of these productions Mr. Tennyson aimed at shadowing forth the vague aspirations to a knowledge beyond the reach of man—the yearnings for a solution of all questions, soluble or insoluble, which concern our nature and destiny—the impatience under the insufficiency of the human faculties to penetrate the secret of our being here, and being what we are—which are natural in a certain state of the human mind; if this was what he sought to typify, he has only proved that he knows not the feeling—that he has neither experienced it, nor realized it in imagination. The questions which a Faust calls upon earth and heaven, and all powers supernal and infernal, to resolve for him, are not the ridiculous ones which Mr. Tennyson asks himself in these verses.

But enough of faults which the poet has almost entirely thrown off merely by the natural expansion of his intellect. We have alluded to them chiefly to show how rapidly progressive that intellect has been.[2]

[1] There are instances in the volume, of far worse failures than these. Such are the two poems 'The Merman' and 'The Mermaid'. When a poet attempts to represent to us any of the beings either of religious or of popular mythology, we expect from him, that, under the conditions prescribed by the received notion of those beings, some mode of spiritual existence will be figured, which we shall recognise as in harmony with the general laws of spirit, but exhibiting those laws in action among a new set of elements. The faculty of thus bringing home to us a coherent conception of beings unknown to our experience, not by logically *characterizing* them, but by a living *representation* of them, such as they would, in fact, *be*, if the hypothesis of their possibility could be realized—is what is meant, when anything is meant, by the words creative imagination. Mr. Tennyson not only fails in this, but makes nothing even of the sensuous elements of the scene: he does not even produce, what he in no other instance misses—a suitable representation of outward scenery. He is actually puerile.

Of the two productions (the most juvenile, we should think, of the set)—'An English War Song', and 'National Song', we can only say, that unless they are meant for bitter ridicule of vulgar nationality, and of the poverty of intellect which usually accompanies it, their appearance here is unaccountable. The sonnet, 'Buonaparte', in the second volume, though not so childish in manner, has still something of the same spirit which was manifested in the two just cited (if they are to be taken as serious).

[2] With the trifling exceptions already mentioned, the only pieces in the second volume which we could have wished omitted are, the little piece of childishness beginning 'O darling room', and the verses to Christopher North, which express, in rather a common-

There are traces, we think, of a continuance of the same progression, throughout the second as well as the first volume.

In the art of painting a picture to the inward eye, the improvement is not so conspicuous as in other qualities; so high a degree of excellence having been already attained in the first volume. Besides the poems which we have quoted, we may refer, in that volume, to those entitled, 'Recollections of the Arabian Nights', 'The Dying Swan', 'The Kraken', and 'The Sleeping Beauty'. The beautiful poems (songs they are called, but are not) 'In the glooming light', and 'A spirit haunts the year's last hours', are (like the 'Mariana') not mere pictures, but states of emotion, embodied in sensuous imagery. From these, however, to the command over the materials of outward sense for the purpose of bodying forth states of feeling, evinced by some of the poems in the second volume, especially 'The Lady of Shalott' and 'The Lotos-eaters', there is a considerable distance; and Mr. Tennyson seems, as he proceeded, to have raised his aims still higher—to have aspired to render his poems not only vivid representations of spiritual states, but symbolical of spiritual truths. His longest poem, 'The Palace of Art', is an attempt of this sort. As such, we do not think it wholly successful, though rich in beauties of detail; but we deem it of the most favourable augury for Mr. Tennyson's future achievements, since it proves a continually increasing endeavour towards the highest excellence, and a constantly rising standard of it.

We predict, that, as Mr. Tennyson advances in general spiritual culture, these higher aims will become more and more predominant in his writings; that he will strive more and more diligently, and, even without striving, will be more and more impelled by the natural tendencies of an expanding character, towards what has been described as the highest object of poetry, 'to incorporate the everlasting reason of man in forms visible to his sense, and suitable to it'. For the fulfilment of this exalted purpose, what we have already seen of him authorizes us to foretell with confidence, that powers of execution will not fail him; it rests with himself to see that his powers of thought may keep pace with them. To render his poetic endowment the means of giving impressive-

---

place way, the author's resentment against a critique, which merited no resentment from him, but rather (all things considered) a directly contrary feeling.

One or two poems, of greater pretension than the above, may be considered not indeed as absolute, but as comparative failures. Among these we must place the second poem in the volume (which affords to the *Quarterly* critic the opportunities for almost his only just criticisms); and even, notwithstanding its fine sonorous opening, the 'Hesperides'.

ness to important truths, he must, by continual study and meditation, strengthen his intellect for the discrimination of such truths; he must see that his theory of life and the world be no chimera of the brain, but the well-grounded result of solid and mature thinking;— he must cultivate, and with no half devotion, philosophy as well as poetry.

It may not be superfluous to add, that he should guard himself against an error, to which the philosophical speculations of poets are peculiarly liable—that of embracing as truth, not the conclusions which are recommended by the strongest evidence, but those which have the most poetical appearance;—not those which arise from the deductions of impartial reason, but those which are most captivating to an imagination, biassed perhaps by education and conventional associations. That whatever philosophy he adopts will leave ample materials for poetry, he may be well assured. Whatever is comprehensive, whatever is commanding, whatever is on a great scale, is poetical. Let our philosophical system be what it may, human feelings exist: human nature, with all its enjoyments and sufferings, its strugglings, its victories and defeats, still remain to us; and these are the materials of all poetry. Whoever, in the greatest concerns of human life, pursues truth with unbiassed feelings, and an intellect adequate to discern it, will not find that the resources of poetry are lost to him because he has learnt to use, and not abuse them. They are as open to him as they are to the sentimental weakling, who has no test of the true but the ornamental. And when he once has them under his command, he can wield them for purposes, and with a power, of which neither the dilettante nor the visionary have the slightest conception.

We will not conclude without reminding Mr. Tennyson, that if he wishes his poems to live, he has still much to do in order to perfect himself in the merely mechanical parts of his craft. In a prose-writer, great beauties bespeak forgiveness for innumerable negligences; but poems, especially short poems, attain permanent fame only by the most finished perfection in the details. In some of the most beautiful of Mr. Tennyson's productions there are awkwardnesses and feeblenesses of expression, occasionally even absurdities, to be corrected; and which generally might be corrected without impairing a single beauty. His powers of versification are not yet of the highest order. In one great secret of his art, the adaptation of the music of his verse to the character of his subject, he is far from being a master: he often seems to take his metres almost at random. But this is little to set in the balance against so much excellence; and needed not have been mentioned, except to indicate to Mr. Tennyson the points on which some of his warmest admirers see most room and most necessity for further effort on his part, if he would secure to himself the high place in our poetic literature for which so many of the qualifications are already his own.

6. F. Garden [?] on
Poems [1842]

Francis Garden (?), from an unsigned article, *Christian Remembrancer* (July 1842), iv. 42–58.

Garden (1810–84), a theologian, was intimate with F. D. Maurice and John Sterling. He became an editor of the *Christian Remembrancer* in 1841 and very likely wrote the article from which a short passage (pp. 46–9) is here reprinted.

. . . We are glad to see the effervescence of Mr. Tennyson's youthful style tamed down, his mannerisms nearly all disappeared, (especially one which we once feared was destined to grow upon him—a passion for compound words,) and to find him writing on the whole such genuine and vigorous English.

Still we are unsatisfied. Though there is positive progress, there is not the amount we could have wished or expected. 'The Two Voices' may in itself be a finer poem than the 'Recollections of the Arabian Nights'; but the latter gave a promise of something better still,—a promise which yet remains to be kept by the poet. And Mr. Tennyson has not yet become *human* enough for our cravings. We desiderate 'the common growth of mother earth' in his stanzas. He is still too fantastic,—too removed from 'familiar matters of today'—from the ordinary fountains of mirth and woe,—still too much a 'dweller in a baseless world of dream, that is not earth nor heaven'. There is much, we can assure him, in the alternative presented in our last quotation. The great poet dwells in heaven or earth, but never long out of the one or the other. He is of those,

who soar, but never roam,
True to the kindred points of heaven and home.

If he quits for a long while our ordinary, our homebred scenes, it is to be sublime, not to be fantastic.

We cannot help suspecting that Mr. Tennyson's mind has been led astray on this matter, not only by natural bias, but by a mistaken theory. At least, one that was in our judgment such had some prevalence, if we mistake not, among his fervent admirers, and was ably propounded and advocated by one of them[1]—the most richly endowed with gifts natural and acquired—the noblest and the loveliest of spirits, but, alas for us! not destined to yield in this world the harvest of which his spring gave so wondrous a promise.

The theory to which we allude is somewhat to this effect:—that to realize its aim, art should keep quite distinct from all that is not of itself—that poetry, therefore, as a branch of art, should admit nothing heterogeneous, such as persuasion to any particular line of belief or conduct, the inculcation of opinion, and so forth. Whether rightly or wrongly, it is but too easy to infer from this, that the poet should be a kind of being altogether distinct from his fellows,—that he should neither participate in their duties nor their cares,—that the strife of opinion should be to him but as the other sounds of the world around him, the rustling of the leaves, the stir of the wind, or the murmuring of streams,—that he should, as a poet, 'dwell apart, holding no form of creed, but contemplating all'.

From facts, this theory can, we think, get but scanty support. Few things are more remarkable than the extent to which the transcendant poets of the world have been, also, in a good sense, men of the world,—practical men, capable of ordinary business-like exertion of every sort,—stirred by domestic and public interests like others, and more than others, fireside men,—and patriots alive to duty, and ready for exertion in any way. We do not know too much of Homer, or whatever the name may stand for; but surely thus much, that it represents no fantastic dreamer or set of dreamers; we have no warrant in the Homeric poems for deadness to ordinary human interests. Neither have we in Shakespeare. When we turn to our great poet, we find ourselves in contact with one who had not exactly lived the life of an ascetic—who had been loose on the world and had got soiled perhaps with a few of its stains,—who probably found ample cause for penitence in his early retirement from the arena in which he won his immortality,[2]—but

---

[1] In a periodical entitled *The Englishman's Magazine*, which had a brief existence two years ago. The essay to which we allude was a review of the *Poems chiefly Lyrical*, of which it has never been made a secret that the author was Arthur Henry Hallam.

[2] What was the meaning of Shakespeare's early retirement? We often please ourselves by imagining that it was for purposes of more decided penitence, and more consistent religion than, with all his religious feelings, he had found practicable in his theatrical occupations.

who never seems to have fancied that either he or any one else could be a privileged person, exempt from ordinary rules or obligations; one who doubtless had his wayward moods and strange fancies, but the roots of whose being were far from fantastic, but, on the contrary, energetic, human, and sympathizing, beyond the average degree. Pindar, Æschylus, Sophocles, Euripides, Dante, Milton, rightly or wrongly, were *men* in their whole course, warriors or statesmen, anything and everything except isolated from their fellows. Even the morbid Petrarch was a man of business, and an active and zealous patriot. Need we speak of Wordsworth and Coleridge?—the former, one who has interested himself in everything vitally concerning his country and his species,—the latter, seemingly disabled, indeed, from action by some strange and sad disease of his temperament, but yet all a-glow with the feelings of an Englishmen, a European, and a Christian. Surely it was because they were, in the first place, so genuinely, so deeply, and so pervadingly *men*, that all these were such surpassingly great poets. And it is precisely this deep fervent humanity that we miss in Mr. Tennyson. He brings visions of wondrous beauty before us, but all is icy cold. His subjects seem all equidistant from himself and from us, as if his Adelines and Lilians were no nearer or dearer than the Lotos-eaters or than St. Simeon Stylites.

But let us examine more closely the theory of poetry to which we have alluded, and which we cannot help suspecting Mr. Tennyson has consciously adopted. That art is something distinct, and cannot be made directly subservient to purposes external to itself, we fully admit. The great end of most of the arts is the manifestation of ideal beauty, and all other ends can be subserved by them only indirectly; their only legitimate moral must consist in their ultimate influence on the character. But a striking difference is to be noticed between poetry and the other arts, which the critics in question have overlooked. The aim of each of the others is to idealize some part of the world around. Thus, music idealizes sound; architecture inanimate, and sculpture animate, forms; painting, forms and colours together. But what does poetry idealize? Properly speaking, nothing but human discourse; though, as that is capable of describing external things, of bringing pictures before us, poetry, whose instrument it is, can perform in a measure the function of each of the other arts—more faintly and feebly in regard to each taken separately than its peculiar art, but, as being capable of uniting them all, with a greater range and more comprehensive scope. Thus, when we praise poetry,—when we say, *What a beautiful passage!*—we often refer to two things—first, and primarily, the passage itself; secondly, the images it presents to us. Thus:

> A violet by a mossy stone,
> Half-hidden from the eye;
> Fair as a star when only one
> Is shining in the sky.

We call this a beautiful stanza; and we thereby mean mainly that it contains beautiful thoughts, beautifully expressed; but we also have our minds charmed with the beauty of a violet half hidden by a mossy stone, with the 'meek splendour' of a single star, with the loveliness of the maiden who is compared to these things. And the artist is often considered ποιητής, or creative, because of his power of bringing such visions before us. But is not the following beautiful?

> I travell'd among unknown men,
> In lands beyond the sea;
> Nor, England, did I know till then
> What love I bore to thee.

> 'Tis past, that melancholy dream!
> Nor will I quit thy shore
> A second time; for still I seem
> To love thee more and more.

> Among thy mountains did I feel
> The joy of my desire;
> And she I cherish'd turned her wheel
> Beside an English fire.

> Thy mornings show'd, thy nights conceal'd,
> The bower where Lucy play'd;
> And thine, too, is the last green field,
> That Lucy's eyes survey'd.

Here we may say that the whole beauty is in the discourse; that the poem is, as we have said all poetry is, an idealization of human utterance; in this case the utterance of passionate and bereaved affection. Now, if this be so,—if poetry be the idealization of human speech, and no otherwise of external forms and objects than as speech has power to bring them vividly before us,—it is easy to see that, whereas the scope of other arts, such as sculpture and painting, can be easily laid down, that of poetry is very indefinite, and that a criticism which narrows it to a certain range of subjects proceeds on a false analogy. It is easy to see also, what brings us to the subject more directly before us, that, whereas sculpture and painting have no opinions to profess, no persuasions to urge, few direct *duties* of any sort, poetry is in a predicament altogether different. Call it a fine art as much as you will,—it is discourse; it is utterance; it is man speaking to man, man telling man his thoughts and feelings. Now, speech can never be long without having a direct moral character, without having aims in themselves foreign to art, without having a good deal to do that is not out of place in poetry, but that yet cannot easily be brought within a definition of it. And, therefore, while even the cultivators of the more simple arts are greatly the better, as artists, for having many daily thoughts, feelings, and occupations similar to the rest of men, for the poet this is almost necessary.

It would indeed be doing Mr. Tennyson great injustice to impute to him such an opinion, as that a poet, or any other artist, has a right as a man to wash his hands of ordinary duties and sympathies. So far is he from this, that he has written a noble poem to show the contrary. But we do not think he sees clearly how such duties and sympathies find their way into poetry. Undoubtedly it is natural for the poet to call up pictures, to revel amid visions of the beautiful, to surround himself with unreal images,—so natural, that many, as we have seen, consider it the very essence of his occupation to do so. But, though no man would be a poet who had not such a tendency, it is yet, like gold, comparatively useless for the purposes designed, unless accompanied by the alloy of something firmer, though it may be coarser. And therefore it is, that, with all their manifold beauties, the poetry of Keats and Tennyson so seldom penetrates to the heart. It is because they so separate the world and the actings of the imagination from this real world, and all the actings that relate to it.

This, however, is not uniformly the case with Mr. Tennyson. . . .

7. J. Sterling on

Poems [1842]

John Sterling, unsigned review, *Quarterly Review* (September 1842), lxx. 385–416.

Sterling (1806–44) had been a leading member of the Apostles, the Cambridge club to which Tennyson was later elected; he was a friend of Carlyle's.

William Huskisson, the statesman, to whom Sterling refers early in the present review, was run over by an engine at the opening of the Manchester and Liverpool Railway and died on the same day. Exeter Hall, to which Sterling alludes a little later, was a large hall in the Strand, London, used for religious and philanthropic meetings. It was a centre of Evangelical Protestantism.

What poetry might be in our time and land, if a man of the highest powers and most complete cultivation exercised the art among us, will be hard to say until after the fact of such a man's existence. Waiting for this desirable event, we may at least see that poetry, to be for us what it has sometimes been among mankind, must wear a new form, and probably comprise elements hardly found in our recent writings, and impossible in former ones.

Of verses, indeed, of every sort but the excellent there is no want: almost all, however, so helpless in skill, so faint in meaning, that one might almost fancy the authors wrote metre from mere incapacity of expressing themselves at all in prose—as boys at school sometimes make nonsense-verses before they can construct a rational sentence. Yet it is plain that even our magazine stanzas, album sonnets, and rhymes in corners of newspapers aim at the forms of emotion, and use some of the words in which men of genius have symbolized profound thoughts. The whole, indeed, is generally a lump of blunder and imbecility, but in the midst there is often some turn of cadence, some attempt at an epithet of more significance and beauty than perhaps a much finer mind would have hit on a hundred years ago. The crowds of stammering children are yet the offspring of an age that would fain teach them —if it knew how—a richer, clearer language than they can learn to speak.

It is hard in this state of things not to conceive that the time, among us at least, is an essentially unpoetic one—one which, whatever may be the worth of its feelings, finds no utterance for them in melodious words.

Yet our age is not asleep. Great movements, various activities, are heard and seen on all sides. In the lowest department, that of mere mechanics, consider what fifteen years have done. It was only in the autumn of 1830, following close on the French three memorable days of July, that the Duke of Wellington opened the Manchester and Liverpool Railroad. The population of the busiest region on this earth were assembled round him, whom all acknowledged as the greatest man in England, at the inauguration of a new physical power, then felt to double the strength and swiftness of human beings. While, among myriads of gravely joyous faces, the new machines travelled at a speed matching that of eagles, the life of a great statesman shot off on a darker and more distant journey, and the thrill of fear and pain at his destruction gave the last human tragic touch to an event which would at any rate have retained for ever an historic importance. The death of Mr. Huskisson startled the fixed bosom of the veteran soldier, and those who were near perceived a quiver of the lip, a movement of the eye, such as had hardly been caused by the most unlooked-for and dreadful chances of his mighty wars. To a calm observer, the emotion of the whole multitude, great and small, might strangely have recalled far-distant ages and the feelings with which ancient peoples held every great event as incomplete, wanting the blood of a victim—too often human—solemnly shed. In the most prosperous and peaceful of national triumphs the dark powers again claimed a share, and would not be forgotten.

Since then, about twelve years have passed, and behold what they have brought forth. Some seventy millions of money have been expended—more, at the lowest estimate, than four times as much as the Papacy was able to raise in a century and a half for the construction of its greatest monument, the costliest the world has ever seen. These seventy millions of pounds have been subscribed by private persons at their own choice in one small country, and have created nearly fifteen hundred miles of railroads—structures that surpass all pyramids and Cyclopean walls, and machines that would puzzle Archimedes, by which myriads of men are perpetually travelling like the heroes of fairy tales. It is probable that the roads of the Roman empire, the work of many centuries, did not cost so much of human labour, and they certainly did not exhibit so much greatness of thought, as those that we have built in less than twenty years.—In the state of society that has produced such results there may be, we know there is, enough torpor, even rottenness. But it cannot be, on the whole, an insignificant stage of human existence, one barren for imaginative eyes.

Or look at one of our general elections. The absurdities are plain, no doubt—has not the ocean froth and bubbles? But take the thing altogether, and observe the mixture and spread of interests and faculties brought into action—above all, the open boldness with which a nation throws itself into the streets and markets, casting off, in the faith that it can reproduce, its company of rulers, and letting the fools clamour, the poor groan, the rich humble themselves, and all men bring all to judgment, without a moment's fear but that quiet will spring out of the tumult, and a government be born from a mob. From the castle of the highest peer to the clay-stained tipplers in the alehouse, from the bench of bishops to the ranters in the moor-side smithy, all are stirred and fluttered, feverish with the same anxieties, debating in their different dialects the same questions, and all alike dependent on the omnipotence of an event which no man can absolutely control. Most of what they say is folly—most of their objects of hope and fear chimeras: but how full of throbbing business is the whole land, how braced are all the wishes and devices of all! Among so much of make-believe and sound, it is a great thing that the whole country must at least be willingly deceived if it is to be gained over—must seem to itself rationally persuaded; and that the most futile pretender can only cheat by aping, and so strengthening in others, the qualities in which he is most deficient. At the blast of the newsmen's tin trumpets all shadows must walk out of their darkness into sunshine, and there be tried; when if many of the umbratile fraudulently pass muster, there is at least a public recognition of the laws of light.

Not merely is there a debate and seeming adjudication in every country-town on all matters over the whole globe which any tailor or brazier may choose to argue, but at last the tailor's and the brazier's voice does really influence the course of human affairs. The vote of the cobbler in an alley turns the poll for a candidate; the vote of the member gains the triumph of his party; and the success of his party decides on every question of peace or war over the globe, makes commercial treaties with Abyssinia, creates a white commonwealth among the savages of the Pacific Ocean, sends armaments to Pekin, and raises or lowers the price of silk grown among the Druses of Lebanon, and of opium sold on the frontiers of Tartary. Within a year after the election in an English village, its result is felt in the more or less cost of food and clothes in Kaffer huts, and in the value of the copper saucepan trafficked at Timbuctoo for palm-oil and black babies. This is not a vapid, insubstantial political existence for the mass of men, not one devoid of topics and emotions, however little they may hitherto have been used in any books but those of statistics and trade.

Or glance at the matter in another of its phases. In the midmost rush of London business, and all the clatter of its vehicles, turn aside through an open door, and what do we see? A large and lofty room, every yard of its floor and galleries crammed with human, chiefly female life—a prodigious sea of bonnets, and under each of these a separate sentient sea of notions, and feelings, and passions, all in some measure stirred by the same tides and gales—every one of them, however narrow at the surface, in depth unfathomable.

Altogether irrespectively of our present purpose, and on the most general grounds, it may be safely said that in one of these great Exeter Hall meetings there is more to strike us than almost anywhere else we know. The room is said to hold 4,000 persons, and from its form they are all clearly visible at once—all of the middle or upper classes, well dressed, though often many of them in Quaker uniform, and at these times probably three-fourths of them women. Such assemblages are in truth, for a large part of the members, by far the most exciting outward events of life. The faces themselves are alone quite enough to prove no small share of moral culture in the mass. The delicately-curved mouths and nostrils, the open yet quiet and observant eyes, and a look of serious yet pleasurable elevation, mark very clearly a chosen class of our country. The men are of course less pure and single in their stamp of feeling—business has marked on them its contractedness with its strength. Yet these also have an appearance of thought, although with some coxcombical importance and complacent theological primness. Take, however, the whole assemblage, all it is and all it represents, we know not where anything like it could be discovered. No Roman Catholic, no despotic, no poor, no barbarous, no thoroughly demoralised, we fear we must add no very instructed and well-organised community could ever exhibit such a gathering—voluntary be it remembered, chiefly female, all with money to spare, united for such remote and often fantastic objects: above all, under such leaders. For in the kind of persons guiding these bodies, and in their discourse, consists more than half the wonder. In the House of Commons, in the Courts of Law, we may hear nonsense enough. But in these places it is not the most vehement, the most chimerical—in other words, the most outrageous and silly, who bear the chiefest sway, but much the contrary. Now in such Strand-Meetings, for the purest and noblest purposes, it is plain enough that a loud tongue, combined with a certain unctuous silkiness of profession, and the most dismal obscuration of brain, may venture with success upon the maddest assertions, the most desperate appeals; and will draw sighs and even tears of sympathy, by the coarsest nonsense, from hundreds of the amiable and thoughtful persons dieted at home on Cowper, Fénelon, Wordsworth, and tuned to Nature's softest melodies. The carrier's horse (or was it ass?) that could draw inferences, is but a brute symbol of the spoken stuff that at religious meetings can draw admiration from the finest female bosoms. Such is the charm of twilight meanings and monstrous images used in behalf of some remote and generous object, and strengthened by the oneness of feeling in a multitude of accordant hearts. Very strange it is to witness the single thrill of some two thousand bonnets, to hear the deep long sigh from as many warm and gentle breasts, all inspired by the raving folly of some declaimer, or by the gravely numerical statements of moral facts as to distant countries proceeding from ill-informed and well-paid agents, and which those who know their falsity are sure enough not to seek the odium of refuting. The sure tact of goodness leads the greater part of the hearers right in home-concerns, but has no measure of probability for new experiments in remote lands. The faith which lives in the Infinite and Eternal, and is perpetually baffled in its search among present things, adds joyfully its charms, the transcendant element of all romance, to the faintest glimpse between distant clouds, and feels it a duty and delight to believe in the realised visions of credulous fancy.

Yet who can think without a certain approval of the immense annual revenue, larger than that of some continental kingdoms, raised by these marvellous addresses to our best feelings? Who can compare, without some admiration mixed in his contempt, the coarse and brainless weakness of the talk on these occasions with the honest virtue, the moral elegance of heart in those whom it influences? Or who that lives in England can be unaware that very many among the auditors of these brazen mouth-pieces show in the whole course of their private lives, and in hard stern trials of all kinds, a simple self-forgetting nobleness and truth, beautifully contrasted with the ostentatious emptiness of the charitable melodrame?

On the whole, the country in which these varieties of good and evil are found mixed on such a scale can hardly be considered in a state of lifeless inertness. Its want cannot be of themes and interest, but rather of those able to seize what lies before them, and turn it to right imaginative use. For every one indeed knows that all our activities, mechanical, political, missionary, celestial, or diabolical, are the immediate outgrowths of the human beings engaged in such matters, and might be found with much more inside and beneath them in the hearts and lives of the individuals. This is all the poet requires; a busy, vigorous, various existence is the matter *sine quâ non* of his work. All else comes from within, and from himself alone. Now, strangely as our time is racked and torn, haunted by ghosts, and errant in search of lost realities, poor in genuine culture, incoherent among its own chief elements, untrained to social facility and epicurean quiet, yet unable to unite its means in pursuit of any lofty blessing, half-sick, half-dreaming, and whole confused—he would be not only misanthropic, but ignorant, who should maintain it to be a poor, dull, and altogether helpless age, and not rather one full of great though conflicting energies, seething with high feelings, and struggling towards the light with piercing though still hooded eyes. The fierce, too often mad force, that wars itself away among the labouring poor, the manifold skill and talent and unwearied patience of the middle classes, and the still unshaken solidity of domestic life among them—these are facts open to all, though by none perhaps sufficiently estimated. And over and among all society the wealth of our richer people is gathered and diffused as it has never been before anywhere else, shaping itself into a thousand arts of luxury, a million modes of social pleasure, which the moralist may have much to object against, but which the poet, had we a truly great one now rising among us, would well know how to employ for his own purposes.

Then, too, if we reflect that the empire and nation seated here as in its centre, and at home so moving and multifarious, spreads its dominions all round the globe, daily sending forth its children to mix in the life of every race of man, seek adventures in every climate, and fit themselves to every form of polity, or it to them—whereafter they return in body, or at least reflect their mental influences among us—it cannot be in point of diversity and meaning that Britain disappoints any one capable of handling what it supplies.

See how Chaucer exhibits to us all that lay around him, the roughness and ignorance, the honour, faith, fancy, joyousness of a strong mind and a strong age, both tranquil within bounds which, as large enough for their uses, neither had tried to pass. How strikingly for us are those grating contrasts of social condition harmonised by the homebred feeling that men as they then were had the liberty and space they then needed: the king and priest the all-sufficient guides of men's higher life, and all powers and even wishes finding ample room, each within the range marked out by custom! Every figure is struck off by as clear and cutting a stroke as that of a practised mower with his scythe—and of all these peculiarities of character, so blended in that world are strength and unconsciousness, not one ever rises into individuality of principle. In clearness, freedom, fulness, what delineation of our actual life can be at all compared with this? Of this poet how truly may it be said,

> O'er Chaucer's blithe old world, for ever new,
> In noon's broad sunbeam shines the morning dew;
> And while tired ages float in shade away,
> Unwearied glows with joy that clear to-day.

In Shakespeare again, who never meant anything of the kind, that period, with its far deeper wants and more abundant forces, all lies softly, firmly drawn by every random jotting of his pen. For that, with all his unmatched reflectiveness, much was thus lightly done, seems no less certain at the hundredth perusal than obvious at the first. The stately courtesies and consecrated forms of the past, all still untroubled, but a new spirit rising within those antique walls, and as yet professing peaceful reverence, though it must one day shake them down; the heaven-storming imagination still toiling and sporting on the ground; the aimless bravery of knighthood still wearing its blazon of the starry cross, but going forth on real adventures for the conquest of our actual earth in east and west; thought blending, though almost unmarked, with all the romance of passion—and fancy, no longer gathering flowers and strewing them in childish sport, but weaving them into garlands for victorious conscience, and using them for the charactery of knowledge: all this is undeniably there, though unintended, and only because the great mind of that and all time necessarily comprised and reproduced whatever was essential in his age. Ranks were still apart, customs unquestioned, forms holy, and natural truth and wisdom only the uncanonical but inevitable comment by which men undesignedly interpreted the page of prescription. And he who has best shown us all this as it truly was, yet sent forth at every breath a fiery element, of which he was himself scarce conscious, that should some day kindle and burn much still dear and venerable to him.

A gulf of generations lies between us and him, and the world is all changed around his tomb. But whom have we had to feel and express like this man the secret of our modern England, and to roll all out before him the immense reality of things as his own small embroidered carpet, on which he merely cared to sit down at his ease and smoke his pipe?

There have been but two writers among us whom every Englishman with a tincture of letters has read or heard of, aiming to shape poetically an image of human life. These are of course Sir Walter Scott and Lord Byron. But see how different their aim has been from such a one as we hint at. The elder poet, with his wholesome sense and clear felicity, has indeed given us much of human fact, and this, as it could not be otherwise, in the colours of the time that he himself belonged to. But he has swayed the sympathies of the world in a great measure through their curiosity after the past, which he, more than all men in the annals of mankind, has taught us all to regard as alive and still throbbing in spirit, though its bones be turned to dust.

Byron has sought, through distance of place and foreign costume, the interest which Scott obtained from the strangeness of past ages; and it is but a small though a profound and irrepressible part of our far-spread modern mind that he has so well embodied in his scornful Harolds and despairing Giaours.

We have indeed one of his works, the only one, which is a splendid attempt at a creative survey of modern life, and contains all the essential elements of such performance. And in spite of the puerile egotisms and dawdling prate into which the poem so often wanders, the first five cantos of *Don Juan*, forming in point of bulk about a half, have more of fiery beauty and native sweetness in them than anything we know of in our modern literature. There is also a wide range and keenness of observation; and were some trivialities struck out, as they so easily might be, no capital defect would remain but the weakness of speculative culture visible in all Lord Byron's philosophical excursions. In the latter half of the poem, and unhappily when he is on English ground, the lax shapelessness of structure, the endless slipshod, yawny

loungings, and vapid carelessness of execution, become very disagreeable in spite of passages rich with imperishable beauty, wit, and
vigour, such as no other modern Englishman or man could have
approached. On the whole, with all its faults, moral and poetic, the
earlier portion of this singular book will probably remain, like the first
half of *Faust,* the most genuine and striking monument of a whole
recent national literature. But the weakness as to all deeper thought, and
the incomplete groundplan, place it somewhat lower than could be
wished. And at best it is but one book, in an age that produces annual
thousands.

Little therefore as is all that has been done towards the poetic representation of our time—even in the looser and readier form of prose
romance—it is hard to suppose that it is incapable of such treatment.
The still unadulterated purity of home among large circles of the
nation presents an endless abundance of the feelings and characters, the
want of which nothing else in existence can supply even to a poet.
And these soft and steady lights strike an observer all the more from
the restless activity and freedom of social ambition, the shifting
changes of station, and the wealth gathered on one hand and spent on
the other with an intenseness and amplitude of will to which there is
at least nothing now comparable among mankind. The power of self-
subjection combined with almost boundless liberty, indeed necessitated
by it, and the habit of self-denial with wealth beyond all calculation—
these are indubitable facts in modern England. But while recognised as
facts, how far do they still remain from that development as thoughts
which philosophy desires, or that vividness as images which is the aim
of poetry! It is easy to say that the severity of conscience in the best
minds checks all play of fancy, and the fierceness of the outward
struggle for power and riches absorbs the energies that would otherwise exert themselves in shapeful melody. But had we minds full of
the idea and the strength requisite for such work, they would find in
this huge, harassed, and luxurious national existence the nourishment,
not the poison, of creative art. The death-struggle of commercial and
political rivalry, the brooding doubt and remorse, the gas-jet flame of
faith irradiating its own coal-mine darkness—in a word, our over-
wrought materialism fevered by its own excess into spiritual dreams—
all this might serve the purposes of a bold imagination, no less than the
creed of the antipoetic Puritans became poetry in the mind of Milton,
and all bigotries, superstitions, and gore-dyed horrors were flames that
kindled steady light in Shakespeare's humane and meditative song.

Of all our recent writers the one who might seem at first sight to have most nearly succeeded in this quest after the poetic *Sangreal* is Crabbe. No one has ranged so widely through all classes, employed so many diverse elements of circumstance and character. But nowhere, or very, very rarely, do we find in him that eager sweetness, a fiery spirituous essence, yet bland as honey, wanting which all poetry is but an attempt more or less laudable, and after all, a failure. Shooting arrows at the moon, one man's bow shoots higher than another's; but the shafts of all alike fall back to earth, and bring us no light upon their points. It needs a strange supernatural power to achieve the impossible, and fix the silver shaft within the orb that shoots in turn its rays of silver back into our human bosoms.

Crabbe is always an instructive and forceful, almost always even an interesting writer. His works have an imperishable value as records of his time; and it even may be said that few parts of them but would have found an appropriate place in some of the reports of our various commissions for inquiring into the state of the country. Observation, prudence, acuteness, uprightness, self-balancing vigour of mind are everywhere seen, and are exerted on the whole wide field of common life. All that is wanting is the enthusiastic sympathy, the jubilant love, whose utterance is melody, and without which all art is little better than a laborious ploughing of the sand, and then sowing the sand itself for seed along the fruitless furrow.

In poetry we seek, and find, a refuge from the hardness and narrowness of the actual world. But using the very substance of this Actual for poetry, its positiveness, shrewdness, detailedness, incongruity, and adding no new peculiar power from within, we do no otherwise than if we should take shelter from rain under the end of a roof-spout.

To Mr. Wordsworth of course these remarks on Crabbe would be by no means applicable. Yet even he has exhibited only one limited, however lofty region of life, and has made it far less his aim to represent what lies around him by means of self-transference into all its feelings, than to choose therefrom what suits his spirit of ethical meditation, and so compel mankind, out alike of their toilsome daily paths and pleasant nightly dreams, into his own severe and stately school of thought. The present movements of human life, nay its varied and spontaneous joys, to him are little, save so far as they afford a text for a mind in which fixed will, and stern speculation, and a heart austere and measured even in its pity, are far more obvious powers than fancy, emotion, or keen and versatile sympathy. He discourses indeed with divine wisdom of life and nature, and all their sweet and various impulses; but the impression of his own great calm judicial soul is always far too mighty for any all-powerful feeling of the objects he presents to us. In his latest volume there is a poem with the date of 1803, 'At the Grave of Burns', full of *reflective* tenderness. But it is noticeable that even here Burns is interesting, not for his own sake and in his own splendid personality, but with reference to Mr. Wordsworth's mind and the effect of the peasant's poetry on him. We are glad indeed to have any pretext for citing this beautiful stanza:—

> Well might I mourn that he was gone
> Whose light I hail'd when first it shone,
> When, breaking forth as Nature's own,
>   It show'd my youth
> How verse may build a princely throne
>   On humble truth.

In thus pointing to the problem which poetry now holds out, and maintaining that it has been but partially solved by our most illustrious writers, there is no design of setting up an unattainable standard, and then blaming any one in particular for inevitably falling short of it. Out of an age so diversified and as yet so unshapely, he who draws forth any graceful and expressive forms is well entitled to high praise. Turning into fixed beauty any part of the shifting and mingled matter of our time, he does what in itself is very difficult, and affords very valuable help to all his future fellow-labourers. If he has not given us back our age as a whole transmuted into crystalline clearness and lustre, a work accomplished only by a few of the greatest minds under the happiest circumstances for their art, yet we scarce know to whom we should be equally grateful as to him who has enriched us with any shapes of lasting loveliness 'won from the vague and formless infinite'.

Mr. Tennyson has done more of this kind than almost any one that has appeared among us during the last twenty years. And in such a task of alchemy a really successful experiment, even on a small scale, is of great worth compared with the thousands of fruitless efforts or pretences on the largest plan, which are daily clamouring for all men's admiration of their nothingness.

The first of these two volumes consists of republished poems, and may be regarded, we presume, as all that Mr. Tennyson wishes to preserve of his former editions. He has sifted in most cases his earlier harvests, and kept the better grain. There are some additions of verses and stanzas here and there, many minute changes, and also beneficial shortenings and condensations. The second volume, however, is on the whole far advanced in merit beyond the first. There is more clearness, solidity, and certainty of mind visible in it throughout: especially some of the blank-verse poems—a style almost unattempted in the earlier series—have a quiet completeness and depth, a sweetness arising from the happy balance of thought, feeling, and expression, that ranks them among the riches of our recent literature.

The collection includes poems of four markedly different kinds:— 1. The Idyllic, in which there is sometimes an epic calmness in representing some event or situation of private life, sometimes a flow of lyrical feeling, but still expanding itself in a narrative or description of the persons, events, and objects that fill the poet's imagination. 2. The purely Lyrical—odes, songs, and the more rapid ballads, where the emotion is not only uppermost, but all in all, and the occasions and interests involved appear but casually and in hints. 3. Fancy pieces; those, namely, of which the theme is borrowed or imitated from those conceptions of past ages that have now become extremely strange or quite incredible for us. In these the principal charm of the work can spring only from the vividness and grace of the imagery, the main idea making no direct impression on our feelings. 4. There is a class of Allegories, Moralities, didactic poems. We might add another, of Facetiæ; but in these the writer, though not unmeaning or without talent, seems far inferior to himself, and they happily fill but a small part of his pages.

The first and third of these classes—the Idylls and Fancies—are, in our view, of the greatest merit, and differ in little but the stranger and more legendary themes of the latter series, while they resemble each other in a somewhat spacious and detailed style of description, with, however, an evident general predominance of personal feeling, sometimes masked by the substitution of an imaginary narrator for the real poet.

We shall speak first of the second class, which we have called Odes. 'Claribel', 'Lilian', 'Isabel', 'Madeline', 'Adeline', 'Eleänore', and 'Margaret',—all are raptures in honour of ladies. 'Isabel' is similar in style and plan to the rest, but differs by being addressed to a matron, not a maiden; and though, like the others euphuistic enough, and coldly ingenious, is pleasant as a relief from the unrealities of rhetorical sentiment. There is a beautiful idea in it—with much verbal melody and many dainty phrases, far beyond the reach of any but a man of

genius, however inaptly genius may be spent in dressing make-believe
emotions with far-fetched rhythmic ornament. 'Claribel' is a sort of
lament over a dead woman. The other young ladies seem to have the
advantage of being still alive, but their poetic environment is not for
that the less ghostly and preternatural. In all of these pieces the will to
write poetry seems to us to have supplied (insufficiently) the place of
poetic feeling; though one sees that only a poet could have written
them. The heroines are moonshine maidens, in the number of whom
Mr. Tennyson is really as unconscionable as Solomon or Mahomet.
It may be suspected that neither the Arab prophet nor Jewish king
would much have approved such questionable charms as *black-beaded
eyes*, and *crimson-threaded* lips. We of a more metaphysical generation
grow heartily weary of the delicacies, and subtleties, and super-fineries
of so many mysterious passions, and phantom objects, as carefully
discriminated as varieties of insects by Ehrenberg, or fossils by Owen.
The whole style smells of musk, and is not without glimpses of rouge
and pearl-powder. We have found nothing here at once more distinct
and graceful than the following lines, and these are marred by the two
final epithets:—

His bowstring slacken'd, languid Love,
Leaning his cheek upon his hand,
Droops both his wings, regarding thee;
And so would languish evermore,
Serene, imperial Eleänore.

Of the poem 'To ——', much need not be said. '*Clear-headed friend*'
is the most ludicrously flat beginning of a serious poem that we have
ever seen proceed from a real poet; and the construction of the final
strophe is so obscure that we have in vain attempted to disentangle it
into any meaning. Yet few readers can be required to spend as much
time on such a matter as we are both bound and glad so to employ.
In the same verses '*kingly intellect*' is at least in that connection a phrase
of vague rhetoric. The two little poems to the 'Owl' are at best ingenious imitations of the manner of some of Shakespeare's and his
contemporaries' songs; well done enough, but not worth doing.

The 'Recollections of the Arabian Nights' is a better kind. The
writer does not in this seem painfully striving after topics, images,
variations, and originalities, but writing from lively conception of a
theme which offered in abundance the material suited to his fancy and
ear. The poem is at once brilliant and pleasing: but we may remark that
its merit is of a kind which presents itself somewhat too easily to a

reader of the tales it recalls; that there is little progress in imagery, and none in thought, beyond the first stanza, in all the following thirteen; and that some meaning adapted to our modern European brains might perhaps have been insinuated under those gorgeous eastern emblems without injury to their genuine Asiatic import. The gold and red arabesque repeats itself, square after square of the pattern, with undeniable splendour, but somewhat wearying monotony.

The 'Ode to Memory' aims at a far higher sort of excellence. Had it preceded, instead of following, Mr. Wordsworth's 'Platonic Ode', it would have been a memorable poem. The elder poet's solemn rapture on the 'Recollections of Childhood' is comparable, in its way, to the Portland funeral vase, were that lighted, as it ought to be, from within: on a purple ground, dark as midnight, still and graceful snow-white figures, admitting of endless interpretations, all more or less fitting, but none, perhaps, conclusive. Mr. Tennyson has caught some of the same feeling, and much of the rhythm, but has not even earned what was still within his power, the praise of a greater variety and richness of painting, nor has precipitated with Shelleyan passion the stream that slept so calmly in Mr. Wordsworth's mountain-lake.

There could hardly be a more decisive proof of Mr. Tennyson's inaptitude for *Orphic* song than the last six lines of this poem:

> My friend, with thee to live alone,
> Methinks were better than to own
> A crown, a sceptre, and a throne.
> O strengthen me, enlighten me!
> I faint in this obscurity,
> Thou dewy dawn of memory.

To tell Memory, the mystic prophetess to whom in these transcendant initiations we owe all notices connecting our small individuality with the Infinite Eternal, that converse with her were better than crowns and sceptres! Memory might perhaps reply—'My friend, if you have not, after encircling the universe, traversing the abyss of ages, and uttering more than a hundred lines, forgotten that there are such toys on that poor earth as crowns and sceptres, it were better for you to be alone, not with, but without me.' Think how sublime a doctrine, that to have the beatific vision is really better than the power and pomp of the world. Philosophy, that sounds all depths, has seldom approached a deeper *bathos*.

Of the little poem called 'Circumstance' we shall quote the whole, pleased to find something that we can produce in support of our admiration for a large class of Mr. Tennyson's poems, on which we have not yet touched:—

> Two children in two neighbouring villages
> Playing mad pranks along the heathy leas;
> Two strangers meeting at a festival;
> Two lovers whispering by an orchard wall;
> Two lives bound fast in one with golden ease;
> Two graves grass-green beside a gray church-tower,
> Wash'd with still rains, and daisy-blossomed;
> Two children in one hamlet born and bred;—
> So runs the round of life from hour to hour.

Much is not attempted here, but the more performed. How simple is the language; how quietly flowing the rhythm; how clear the images; and with what pleasant enigmatic openness do the few lines set before us all the little tale of the two villagers, playing, parted, meeting, loving, wedding, dying, and leaving behind them two orphan children! It is a small tone of natural feeling, caught and preserved with genuine art, and coming home to every bosom that sweet words can penetrate at all.

'Fatima' is of a far higher pitch, but seems oddly misnamed. It is full of true and vehement, yet musical passion; and it suggests the strong flow of Lesbian poetry, and particularly the well-known fragment of Sappho addressed to a woman. Whence, then, the name? Lesbos has hardly gained by becoming a part of Turkey, or Sappho by turning into Fatima. But the poem is beautiful: we scarcely know where in English we could find anything so excellent, as expressing the deep-hearted fulness of a woman's conscious love. Many will read it as if it belonged only to some Fatima or Sappho to feel with this entireness of abandonment. But there are hundreds of women in the West end of London—and in the East end too—who would find it only a strain that nature had already taught them.

'Lady Clara Vere de Vere' aims at less, and though of no very rare cast, is successful in all that it attempts. Mr. Tennyson seems to have intended to be very severe in this remonstrance to a flirt. But the damsel who deserved it would certainly rather have been flattered than provoked by such a tribute to her powers.

'The Blackbird', 'The Death of the Old Year', and 'Edward Gray', are all sufficiently good for publication, but not for detailed criticism. 'Sir Launcelot and Queen Guinevere' is of similar tone, but not extraordinary merit. The last but one appears to be the best stanza:

Now on some twisted ivy-net,
Now by some tinkling rivulet,
On mosses thick with violet,
Her cream-white mule his pastern set:
    And now more fleet she skimmed the plains
Than she whose elfin prancer springs
By night to eery warblings,
When all the glimmering moorland rings
    With jingling bridle-reins.

In one less careful of his melody—and we have few very recent writers so successfully careful of it—we should hardly make any remark on the harsh *r's* in these latter lines, so unsuitable to the vague and gliding fluency of the image.

Under the head of FANCIES we class all those poems relating to distant and marvellous circumstances and persons such as we can only conceive, and that very imperfectly, by a conscious removal of our thoughts into regions of which we have no experience, and which seem to us half impossible. In some instances the poet only attempts to reproduce outward relations of society and a kind of feeling which have departed from our common life—as in 'The Sisters', 'The Beggar Maid', 'St. Simeon', and 'St. Agnes'. In others, and the greater number of these pieces, he rushes away with us into the ruins and sepulchres of old supernatural beliefs—dear to him, however, not as still partly credible, or as ever having been sacred and awful to mankind, but for the graceful strangeness of the figures that they suggest and are linked with. This mythological poetry is not of equal interest and difficulty with that which produces as brilliant and deep effects from the ordinary realities of our own lives. But it is far from worthless. Some German ballads of this kind by Goethe and Schiller—nay, by Bürger and by Heine—have great power over every one, from the art with which the imagination is won to accept as true what we still feel to be so strange. This is done mainly by a potent use of the mysterious relation between man and nature, and between all men towards each other, which always must show itself on fitting occasions as the visionary, the ominous, the spectral, the 'eery', and awful consciousness of a supernatural somewhat within our own homely flesh. It appears to us that Mr. Tennyson has neither felt so deeply as some other poets—Coleridge, for instance, in 'Christabel'—the moral ground on which this oracular introsentient part of man is firmly built, nor has employed its phantasmagoric power with such startling witchery. But there is almost always a vivid elegance and inward sweetness in his elfin song, whether Gothic or Grecian, and he sometimes even uses the legends of Pagan antiquity with a high perfection of dreamy music.

'The Dying Swan', 'The Merman', and 'The Mermaid', are figments which he has not connected with any feeling that could render us willing to believe, nor with any meaning that would give them value as symbols. There is a kind of unhappy materialism in some of these attempts at spiritualizing nature, and in the midst of some beautiful images we are stopped short by fancies equally farsought and unpleasant.

There are, however, hardly any of these legendary poems that might not well be cited as examples of solid and luminous painting. We must admit that Mr. Tennyson has scarcely succeeded, perhaps has not tried, to unite any powerful impression on the feelings with his coloured blaze. It is painted—though well painted—fire. But in animated pomp of imagery, all in movement, like a work of Paolo Veronese, few things that we know could rival these compositions. His figures are distinct as those of brazen statuary on tombs, brilliant as stained glass, musical as the organ-tones of chapels. And as some of these romantic songs remind us of Paul Cagliari, others—those especially that have been dreamt upon the lap of the Greek Muse—are akin to the creations of a still greater painter than the Veronese, Correggio. So mild and mournful in interest are these, so perfect in harmony of images and rhythm, we almost grieve at last to waken from our trance and find we have been deluded by a Pagan vision, and by the echoes of oracles now dumb. Scarcely fabled magic could be more successful. The effect is the result evidently of great labour, but also of admirable art. As minstrel conjurations, perhaps, in English, 'Kubla Khan' alone exceeds them. The verse is full of liquid intoxication, and the language of golden oneness. While we read, we too are wandering, led by nymphs, among the thousand isles of old mythology, and the present fades away from us into a pale vapour. To bewitch us with our own daily realities, and not with their unreal opposites, is a still higher task; but it could not be more thoroughly performed.

The 'Morte d'Arthur', the first poem in the second volume, seems to us less costly jewel-work, with fewer of the broad flashes of passionate imagery, than some others, and not compensating for this inferiority by any stronger human interest. The miraculous legend of 'Excalibur' does not come very near to us, and as reproduced by any modern writer must be a mere ingenious exercise of fancy. The poem, however, is full of distinct and striking description, perfectly expressed; and a tone of mild, dignified sweetness attracts, though it hardly avails to enchant us. The poet might perhaps have made the loss of the magic sword, the death of Arthur, and dissolution of the Round Table, a symbol for the departure from earth of the whole old Gothic world, with its half-pagan, all-poetic faith, and rude yet mystic blazonries. But it would be tyrannical exaction to require more philosophy in union with so fiery and productive a fancy. No one but Coleridge among us has ever combined a thoroughly speculative intellect with so restless an abundance of beautiful imagery as we find in Mr. Tennyson; and the younger minstrel has as much of the reflection proper to an age like ours as any living poet except Mr. Wordsworth, and as any but a very few deceased ones.

The gift of comprehensive thoughtfulness does not, however, show itself to advantage in 'St. Simeon Stylites', a kind of monological personation of a filthy and mad ascetic. We find exhibited, with the seriousness of bitter poetic irony, his loathsome, yet ridiculous attempts at saintship, all founded on an idea of the Divinity fit only for an African worshipping a scarecrow fetish made of dog's bones, goose-feathers, and dunghill-rags. This is no topic for Poetry: she has better tasks than to wrap her mantle round a sordid, greedy lunatic.

How different, how superior is 'Ulysses'! There is in this work a delightful epic tone, and a clear unimpassioned wisdom quietly carving its sage words and graceful figures on pale but lasting marble. Yet we know not why, except from schoolboy recollections, a modern English poet should write of Ulysses rather than of the great voyagers of the modern world, Columbus, Gama, or even Drake. Their feelings and aims lie far nearer to our comprehension—reach us by a far shorter line. Even of 'Godiva', different as is the theme, a similar observation holds. It also is admirably well done; but the singularity and barbarousness of the fact spur, no doubt, the fancy, even told in plain prose, yet are far from rendering the topic favourable for poetry. The 'Day-Dream', the old and pretty tale of the 'Sleeping Beauty', is open to no such objection. Here the poetry was made to the writer's hand, and one cannot but wish that his grace, liveliness, and splendour had been employed on a matter of his own invention;[1] or, if borrowed, of some

[1] It is difficult to suppose that the poem was written before the exhibition of Mr. Maclise's picture of 'The Sleeping Beauty', (1841)—a work displaying, like most of that rising artist's, great wealth and boldness of fancy and execution, but, like too many both of the paintings and the poems of our day, too ambitiously crowded, and forced and glaring in its περιεργία.

more earnest meaning. Yet, as graceful and lively description, as truth playing behind the mask of fairy-tale, the whole poem is most agreeable. . . .

[Quotes 'The Day-Dream: The Sleeping Palace, The Revival, and The Departure'.]

The poems which we would class under the head MORALITIES, in which Reflection lifts the rod to silence Feeling, are scattered up and down the volumes under various titles. They almost all appear to us decided and remarkable failures, and only one or two of the shorter and slighter at all worthy of Mr. Tennyson.

The 'Palace of Art', indeed, has the tints and force of poetry, and shows the author's characteristic power of distinct and deeply-dyed painting. But there is considerable affectation in some of the groupings both of words and things, and what is worse, the meaning, the *morality*, is trivial, and even mistaken. The writer's doctrine seems to be, that the soul, while by its own energy surrounding itself with all the most beautiful and expressive images that the history of mankind has produced, and sympathizing wholly with the world's best thoughts, is perpetrating some prodigious moral offence for which it is bound to repent in sackcloth and ashes. A more rational and not less religious view would seem to be, that we should repent of the errors we commit from the *in*activity of our higher powers and feelings. We hardly know a notion worthier of Simeon [Stylites], or of some crack-brained sot repenting in the stocks, than this doctrine that the use of our noblest faculties on their right objects is an outrage against our best duties. Happily, Mr. Tennyson's practice is wiser than the theory propounded in this piece; and his theory itself, if we may judge from the doctrinal parts of his second and more mature volume, is also much improved. The long and dull production called the 'Two Voices', a dispute on immortality, adding nothing to our previous knowledge, and of which the substance might have been better given in three pages (or one) than thirty, has yet no such folly in it as the many-coloured mistake of the 'Palace of Art'.

In all Mr. Tennyson's didactic writing one sees too clearly that, unless when the Image enchains his heart, the Thought has far too little hold upon him to produce any lively movement of soul. His speculations have the commonplaceness, vagueness, and emptiness of dreams, though the dreams of genius; and hopefully do we trust that the poet will not again throw off his magic mantle for either the monkish gown or stoic robe.

We have now reached that class of poems which stand first in our list, and which we have entitled IDYLLS. We have reserved till now all special mention of them, as holding them the most valuable part of Mr. Tennyson's writings, a real addition to our literature. They have all more or less of the properly Idyllic character, though in three or four of them marked with the rapid and suggestive style of the ballad. In all we find some warm feeling, most often love, a clear and faithful eye for visible nature, skilful art and completeness of construction, and a mould of verse which for smoothness and play of melody has seldom been equalled in the language. The heartfelt tenderness, the glow, the gracefulness, the strong sense, the lively painting, in many of these compositions, drawn from the heart of our actual English life, set them far above the glittering marvels and musical phantasms of Mr. Tennyson's mythological romances, at first sight the most striking portion of his works.

Among the happier specimens of this class two are pre-eminent— the 'Gardener's Daughter', and 'Dora'. These are both of them Idylls in the strictest sense of the term, and might rank with the eclogues of Theocritus and Virgil, and with some poems of Goethe—as anecdotes drawn from rustic life and rounded into song. Especially, as compared with the antique models, we see in them all the gain that Christianity and civilization have brought to the relation of the sexes, and to the characters of women.

The 'Gardener's Daughter' is a husband's recollection of his successful love, the object of which has been withdrawn from him by death. The unrhymed verse has a quiet fulness of sound, and all the delineation a clear yet rich completeness of truth, that render the little work, though far from the loftiest, yet one of the most delightful we know. As English landscape-painting, what can exceed this?

[Quotes 'The Gardener's Daughter', ll. 33–47:

'Not wholly in the busy world, . . .
The lime a summer home of murmurous wings.']

Or take the companion picture, where this view is alive with human passion:—

[Quotes 'The Gardener's Daughter', ll. 209–20:

'There sat we down . . .
. . . until we settled there.']

'Dora', though not so luxuriously beautiful, has less, indeed nothing, that could be spared without serious loss, and being only half the length of the former one, we shall extract it entire:—

[Quotes 'Dora', ll. 1–167:

'With farmer Allan at the farm abode . . .
But Dora lived unmarried till her death.']

We shall leave this without comment, which, we trust, is needless.
'Audley Court', and 'Walking to the Mail', are in a lighter style, and with less of interest. 'The Talking Oak' is more important, but does not satisfy us so well. This also, like most of Mr. Tennyson's better poems, is love-inspired and love-breathing. But an ancient oak, that is won by a poet to utter Dodonæan oracles, would hardly, we conceive, be so prolix and minute in its responses. In 'Locksley Hall' the fancy is again at home. It is, perhaps, on the whole, the one of all these poems in which far-extended thought is best involved in genuine and ardent imagination. A quick and generous heart pours out through the lips of a young man who has been deceived by the woman he loved, and who, inflamed with disappointment, reviews at passionate speed—far unlike the prosaic slowness of professional reviewers—the images that the darkened world now presents to him, and the diverse paths of action that he is tempted to try. We know not what the author means by his hero's talk of comrades and bugle-horns; for all the rest is the direct outbirth and reflection of our own age. The speaker tells his former happiness in the following lines:—

[Quotes 'Locksley Hall', ll. 21–44:

'Then her cheek was pale and thinner . . .
. . . and a narrower heart than mine!']

The images that haunt him, of the faithless maiden's married life with a despised husband, are full of bitter strength; but we prefer a small specimen of his more indistinct and wider notions:—

[Quotes 'Locksley Hall', ll. 107–26:

'Can I but relive in sadness? . . .
. . . plunging thro' the thunder-storm.']

'Lady Clare' is not memorable; but the 'Lord of Burleigh' well deserves citation, as an example of the skill with which a poet can find a true and complete imaginative interest in an anecdote of our actual refined life:—

[Quotes 'The Lord of Burleigh'.]

Every thoughtful reader of the poems which we have thus glanced through will be led to compare them with those on similar themes, of present human existence in the country, by the most profoundly reflective of our living poets, Mr. Wordsworth. 'Michael', 'The Brothers', the story of Margaret in the beginning of *The Excursion,* 'Ruth',—these also are English Idylls, drawn from the well-springs of Nature, and finished with the painful care of a great artist. How naked and bare they all are in their solemn stillness! Nor is it only in these poems, but even in works of lighter and gladder movement, that we are compelled to listen to the bard as to a grave teacher of moral truth, whom the spirit of spontaneous enjoyment, and even the sympathy with whatever is pathetic or grand in man, cannot hurry beyond the school of his compassionate but austere stoicism. Ignorance only, or lunacy, could deny him a deep internal power of true poetry. But even this, and not merely the manly passions and the soft affections, even the shaping and inspired imagination itself, is always subject to the considerate dominion of the moral idea. *Emotion,* the most general and obvious, the necessary impulse of all poetry in every age, is restrained in all his writings by the awful presence of self-centred will. The feelings are described rather than shared; the tragic passions summoned up only to be rebuked by a more solemn conjuration than their own; the free enjoyment of life and nature approved only within the bounds of unrelaxing caution; and love—the name bubbled by every wave of Hippocrene, and thundered in all the floods and storms of the main ocean of our being—is here a grave ritual sound spoken over the still waters drawn from the well of Truth for a penitential baptism.

Of course it would be far from our design to charge this great writer with want of feeling. A poet without feeling! Fire without warmth, and a heart without pulsation! But it is clear that his feelings are always strictly watched by his meditative conscience, too strictly, not for wisdom, but for rapture. Not a prophet in the wilderness lifting up his testimony against an evil generation, for the heart of the seer must be red and fierce as molten iron—not a hermit in his cave retired from human joys, for the anchorite floats above his rocky floor, forgetful of laws and retributions, in an ecstasy of self-denying love, that supplies the place of decalogue and duties—but like the prophet and the monk, this poet turns aside from the busy ways of life to speculate, in sage and sometimes awful rhetoric, on the wondrousness of existence, and the care with which we must tend the purity of its fountain in the heart. There is no face so lovely, no act so gushing over with keen life, that it can kindle at once the minstrel into song, hurrying him beyond all thought of wrong and right, and having warrant enough in the zealous heat which it inspires. Only in communion with the stars, the mountains, and the sea, the flowers of spring and autumn leaves, and all the simple mysteries of natural things, does his heart pour, without pause, a stream of melodious gladness, and fear no danger in its own happy ecstasies. Even in these solemn elevations of soul he does not forget to impose a scheme of toils on human life. Among streams and rocks he begins with discourse of virtue; and when he has risen on the ladder of his vision to the stars, we still hear him singing from the solar way, that it is by temperance, soberness, and chastity of soul he has so climbed, and that the praise of this heroic discipline is his last message to mankind. A noble temper of heart! A truly great man! He has strangely wedded his philosophic lore to the sweetness of poetry. But the poetry would have streamed out in a freer gush, and flushed the heart with ampler joy, had the moral been less *obtruded* as its constant aim.

In the younger of these two idyllic writers, on the whole the most genial poet of English rural life that we know—for Burns was of another language and country, no less than school—there is a very different stamp of soul. In his works there has been art enough required and used to give such clear and graceful roundness; but all skill of labour, all intellectual purpose, kept behind the sweet and fervid impulse of the heart. Thus, all that we call affection, imagination, intellect, melts out as one long happy sigh into union with the visibly beautiful, and with every glowing breath of human life. In all his better poems there is this same character—this fusion of his own fresh feeling with the delightful affections, baffled or blessed, of others—and with the fairest images of the real world as it lies before us all to-day. To this same tendency all legend and mystery are subordinate—to this the understanding, theorizing and dogmatizing, yet ever ministers, a loyal giant to a fairy mistress. In his better and later works the fantastic and ingenious brain, abounding in gold-dust and diamond-powder, and the playmate of sphinxes and hieroglyphic beasts, pours out its wealth, and yokes its monsters only for the service of that homely northern nature, without whose smile all wealth is for us but dead stones, and all mysteries but weary task-like puzzles.

8. Leigh Hunt on

Poems [1842]

James Henry Leigh Hunt, unsigned review, *Church of England Quarterly Review* (October 1842), xii. 361–76.

Hunt (1784–1859), poet, essayist, and friend of Shelley and Keats, had reviewed Tennyson's 1830 volume very favourably in the *Tatler* (24th and 26th February 1831), ii. 593–4, 601–02. His review of the 1842 volumes, while also favourable, is more discriminating. Towards its conclusion, the title 'Head Waiter' refers to 'Will Waterproof's Lyrical Monologue'.

Only one of these volumes is entirely new. The first, as the author intimates in two successive dates at the beginning and middle of it, and a little more copious bit of information in four lines at the conclusion, is for the most part a collection of former volumes, and some of the poems in it have been 'considerably altered'. Others, he might have added, have been left out; and, retaining what he has, we do not see good reason for the omission: so that the present publication is neither an entire collection, nor a thoroughly satisfactory selection, which is a pity.

We state our objections first, that we may get rid of the unpleasant part of our task, and enjoy the subsequent approbation with more comfort; for, though reviewers are supposed to take a special delight in censure, and we ourselves must in candour confess that we know what it is to be tempted to go the way of all critical flesh, and how strong the desire in the young reviewer is to make the importance of the judgment-seat felt; but a little more Christian reflection made us discern the danger which our love of truth was undergoing, especially towards persons who differed with us in opinion; and, though we must never cease to find fault where truth demands it, and where the book is of importance enough to render fault-finding necessary (for wretched books may surely be left to their own natural death, without exciting a shabby desire to kill them), yet, so far from giving either into this once reigning bad habit of reviews, or into the other pick-thank extreme of indiscriminate praise, or following the still more common and servile practice of giving the greatest praise to none but authors in fashion, and being afraid of doing justice to others perhaps far superior, we shall make it our business to give as cheerful and even reverential eulogy to genius, in whatever quarter we find it, as we shall jealously guard that right and sincerity of objection which alone can render it thoroughly valuable. We would not give wholesale, indiscriminate laudation to Shakspeare himself, as long as human nature is what it is, and no man perfect. Neither, on the other hand, shall any reigning fashion induce us to take common-place for invention, or the soothing of the languors of soft ears for a masculine versification.

We are compelled to say, then, in justice to the very respect which we entertain, and the more which we desire to entertain, for the genius of Mr. Tennyson, that the above 'lettings out of the bag' of his dates and alterations, are a little too characteristic of a certain mixture of timidity and misgiving with his otherwise somewhat defying demands upon our assent to his figments and his *hyphens*, and that we have greater objections to a certain air of literary dandyism, or fine-gentlemanism, or fastidiousness, or whatever he may *not* be pleased to call it, which leads him to usher in his compositions with such exordiums as those to 'Morte d'Arthur', and 'Godiva'; in the former of which he gives us to understand that he should have burnt his poem but for the 'request of friends'; and, in the latter, that he 'shaped' it while he was waiting 'for the train at Coventry', and hanging on the bridge 'with grooms and porters'. Really this is little better than the rhyming fine-ladyism of Miss Seward, who said that she used to translate an ode of Horace 'while her hair was curling'. And, if the 'grooms and porters' have any meaning beyond a superfluous bit of the graphic, not in keeping with his subject, it is a little worse, for why should not Mr. Tennyson, in the universality of his poetry, be as content to be waiting on a bridge, among 'grooms and porters', as with any other assortment of his fellow-men? Doubtless he would disclaim any such want of philosophy; but this kind of mixed tone of contempt and nonchalance, or, at best, of fine-life phrases with better fellowship, looks a little instructive, and is, at all events, a little perilous. There is a drawl of Bond-street in it. We suspect that these poems of 'Morte d'Arthur' and 'Godiva' are among those which Mr. Tennyson thinks his best, and is most anxious that others should regard as he does; and therefore it is that he would affect to make trifles of them. The reader's opinion is at once to be of great importance to him, and yet none at all. There is a boyishness in this, which we shall be happy to see Mr. Tennyson, who is no longer a boy, outgrow.

So of his hyphens and his dots, his *seërs*, *low-lieths*, and *Eleänores*, and the intensifications of his prefix *a*—*aweary*, *amany*, *anear;* it is 'affectations, 'oman', as Sir Hugh says; and a very unnecessary bad compliment both to his readers and himself, as if they did not know how to read, or could never enough see the merit of his quantities and qualities without the help of his lackadaisical particle. Upon a like principle we object to his excessive fondness for repeating a lyrical 'burthen'. His 'aweary, aweary', in the 'Moated Grange', may indeed help us to sympathise with the fatigue of the inhabitant; but four 'Orianas' to every stanza, in the ballad of that name, amounting to forty-four in all, burlesque all music and feeling, and become a parrot-cry instead of a melody. This, too, in a poem full of beauty!

We trust that in his next publication Mr. Tennyson will show that he has acquired energy enough to get rid of these mixtures of weakness with his strength. We do not wish him, merely because critics object to them, to leave out some of his second or third-best productions, as he seems to have done, and this, too, while retaining his most objectionable; we desire to see him once for all at ease both with his critics and himself, acknowledge what is juvenile or faulty, or rather perceive it without saying anything about the matter; and, whether he discountenances anything or nothing of what he has done, cease to combine misgiving with rashness, and airs of the drawing-room with the enlargement he really possesses, and give us a good, wholesome, satisfactory, and enduring quintessence of the best part of him. He has fancy, imagination, expression, thought, knowledge, and music, too—in short, all the materials of an admirable contemplative poet, and in some instances his success has been already great, and his name, we trust, will be lasting. But at present he still shows a little too much of the spoiled child. He is indolent, over-refining, is in danger of neutralizing his earnestness altogether by the scepticism of thought not too strong, but not strong enough to lead or combine, and he runs, or rather reposes, altogether upon feelings (not to speak it offensively) too sensual. His mind lives in an atmosphere heavy with perfumes. He grows lazy by the side of his Lincolnshire water-lilies; and, with a genius of his own sufficient for original and enduring purposes (at least we hope so), subjects himself to the charge of helping it too much with the poets gone before him, from Homer to Wordsworth, and to Shelley and Keats. But we will touch upon most of the poems in their order, and thus best show what we mean. The beautiful passages that we shall have to quote in eulogy will luckily far more than repay the reader and ourselves for any unpleasant necessity of finding fault.

'Claribel', who 'low-lieth' where the 'beetle *boometh*' (not a good word), and the 'wild bee hummeth', and the 'lintwhite smelleth', and the 'mavis dwelleth', *et cetera, et cetera*, is rather a series of descriptive items in obsolete language than a dirge in earnest.

'Lilian' is as light and pretty as its subject; but

> Till the lightning laughters dimple
> The baby roses in her cheeks,

is an instance of that injudicious crowding of images which sometimes results from Mr. Tennyson's desire to impress upon us the abundance of his thoughts.

The style of 'Isabel' reminds us both of Wordsworth's solemnity and Shelley's Grecisms and penultimate accents. It is a panegyric of chastity in that ultra-super-exalting spirit of Beaumont and Fletcher, which renders the sincerity of it suspicious; and the conclusion unluckily corroborates the impression by informing us that 'the world hath not such another', for a 'finished, chastened purity', as this lady! This is awkward for the sex in general, and for their gratitude to the poet. The expression '*blanched* tablets of the heart', will not do at all after its beautiful original in the old poet, 'the *red-leaved* tablets of the heart'. There is a charming verisimilitude and warmth of feeling in the latter image, full of grace and cordiality.

'Mariana', in the 'Moated Grange', brings us at once into the thick of the real beauties of the author; and, as we have not noticed him in this publication before, and wish our article to give as thorough an idea of his genius as it can, we will quote the whole of it, though at the hazard of the reader's having seen it years ago. The loose, rusty nails on the garden wall, the 'glooming flats', the low of the oxen coming from the dark fens, the blue fly singing in the pane, and the mouse shrieking behind the mouldering wainscot, are part of a heap of images all painted from nature, and true to the feeling of the subject.

[Quotes 'Mariana', ll. 1–84:

'With blackest moss the flower-plots . . .
Oh God, that I were dead!'']

Mr. Tennyson seems to have felt, that these descriptions, beautiful as they were, were rather native than foreign; and he has accordingly given us a 'Mariana in the South'; which, though more Catholic in one sense is less so in another; and though not without its truth too, and beauty, must undergo the fate of all sequels, in being considered very inferior to its prototype.

'Madeline' is held forth to us a lady, who 'smiling frowning evermore', is considered 'perfect in love'. 'Delicious spites and darling angers' are here; things such as Tasso took delight in praising; and as long as they only amused him, they were very well; but when he came to take a deeper interest, adieu to the lovingness of the lady and to his own happiness. So with this ever frowning and smiling coquette of Mr. Tennyson's, who fixes a smile at him if he offers to go, and then 'blushes angerly' if he offers to kiss the tips of her fingers. We confess we have no faith in the lady's knowledge of love at all, nor any vast deal in the loveability of Mr. Tennyson's ladies in general. They remind us too much of the fine young ladies in souvenirs and beauty-books, with rapturous eyes, dark locks and tresses, and all that—ready made to conquer between the meretricious and the moral—between a boarding-school education, and prudential, and in truth cold contradictions to it. He has a whole seraglio of them. The list would make a song of itself. There is Mariana, Eleänore, Oriana, Fatima, Dora, Margaret, Olivia, Rose, Emilia, Claribel, Isabel, Adeline, Madeline, Lady Clara, and Lady Flora. Poets are bound to be admirers of the fair sex; but Mr. Tennyson talks as if he really loved most of these ladies, while it is pretty clear that his admiration is of a very ordinary sort, and that he makes the poor creatures pegs to hang characters upon; for which we are not surprised that they seldom appear to return his passion. We think him more ingenious than happy in these portraitures. There is sometimes a good deal of observation in them, and metaphysical acuteness; but it is too ostentatiously shown, often in numbers affectedly musical; and he makes them so very conscious, or fastidious, or stately, or in some way or other almost always puts some such unpleasant contradiction to their loveability in the midst of their exuberant airs and graces, that they end in impressing us as a sort of poetical milliners, or artificial idealisms full dressed. And how can he condescend to write such fantastic nothings, pretending to be intense somethings, as the following:—

[Quotes 'Adeline', stanza v, commenting, 'The meaning?' after its eleventh line.]

We have read of lettered hyacinths in Theocritus (alluding to the

story in the Mythology), and of 'shuttles of the morn', in a very different poet, one Mr. Merry, hight Della Crusca, who described them as
'weaving an airy lay upon a cobwebbed thorn'; and we must say that in
such verses as these, Mr. Tennyson reminds us far more of the gossamer
fancies of that gentleman, than of his worthier and more kindred asso-
ciate. Could any one suppose that the writer who would allow himself
to put forth such lines as these was the same who painted the following
masterly portrait? It is very different from those of his young ladies, and
evidently taken entirely from the life. We have heard of its original being
disowned in a late admirable poet and metaphysician. If so, it is after all
but a one-sided, and in great measure even superficial portrait, for the
whole humanity at the bottom of his heart is left out, together with his
lovely imagination. But still it is a masterly show-up of the worldly side
of a man who is understood by most people to have had an esoterical
and an exoterical creed; and it is very like his manner and his book.

[Quotes 'A Character', ll. 1–30:

'With a half-glance upon the sky . . .
With chisell'd features clear and sleek.']

We look upon the above, after its kind, as a faultless composition;
and its kind is no mean one. Considered as a poetical satire, it brings an
atmosphere of imagination round the coldest matter of fact; and the
delicate *blank* effect of the disposition of the rhymes completes the
seemingly passionless exposure of its passionless object.

The 'Poet' reminds us of Shelley; and we are not sure whether,
though it has in some respects a look of generality, it was not intended
for his portrait. If so, whatever objections this publication would have
to make to the original, we should have admired Mr. Tennyson's
boldness more had he spoken out.

The 'Merman' and 'Mermaid' are true bits of half-human, half-fishy
sympathy. But even under the water there is too much vanity and
consciousness mixed up with the author's actions of love. The 'Lady of
Shalott', we confess, we do not very well understand, except as a series
of long-drawn musical reiterations; and as such, it is very successful.
Oenone lamenting the infidelity of Paris is as beautiful and graceful as if
it had been painted by one of the Italian masters. It reminds us of a
lovely comparison by a brother critic, the other day, of Raphael, cut
off in the flower of his years, to a broken orange-tree (something more
than an imitation of Homer's simile of the fallen warrior with the young
olive-tree.) Select beauty is in it; not the less true for being select; and a

golden warmth pervades the grace, like Titian shining upon the Caracci, or the hue of the orange upon the beauty of its orb. The 'Recollections of the Arabian Nights', compared with this elegant bit of paganism, is not a true oriental contrast. It runs too much into mere luxury and exuberance. We are oppressed as with a nook of Lincolnshire weeds. The better part of the stateliness and drapery of the East is not in it, much less the human variety of that wonderful set of stories. When Mr. Tennyson's subject is spiritual, he is apt to become sensuous enough; and very beautiful he *then* is in his sensuousness. When his subject is *sensual*, it is to his detriment; for his luxury tends to rankness.

Of the 'Goose' we shall only say that humour and jest are not Mr. Tennyson's forte, and that the less he meddles with them the better. These, like his vaticinations on the future glory of one of the Kemble family—the *only one* without a ray of talent or genius, presumptuous, overbearing, a self-conceited coxcomb and liberal—Mr. T. should relinquish. We can assure him he has not the prophetic portion of the ancient Vates, as this unlucky mistake of a goose for a god, a block for a brain, a braggart for a brave, indicates—proving him to possess less than vulpine astuteness into the real character of objects.

We now come to the principal poems in the second or *new* volume; and of these we may observe in general that, although we do not recognize any advancement upon the best of the former ones, we can testify to a very considerable negative improvement in the articles of fantasticism and whimsicality. We have no longer such passages as the one quoted from 'Adeline', nor the same propensity to hyphens, quaint lyrics, and other juvenilities. The only difference for the worse is, that Mr. Tennyson has become more misgiving, not in what he omits, but in what he has at the same time a special inclination to do, and that not liking the misgiving, and fearing it will commit his dignity, he takes to a kind of unpoetical nonchalance or indifferent superiority to himself over his own performances. We have already noticed this involuntary exhibition of uneasiness in speaking of two of the new poems, the 'Morte d'Arthur' and 'Godiva'. We confess that, with all our admiration of particular passages, we do not like either of these poems so well as the author, by his studious airs of indifference about them, seems to wish we should. The 'Morte d'Arthur', as he truly designates it, is an 'Homeric echo'. It treats the modes and feelings of one generation in the style of another, always a thing fatal, unless it be reconciled with something of self-banter in the course of the poem itself, or the mixture of light with grave, as in Pulci and others. The impossibility of a thorough earnestness must, somehow or other, be self-acknowledged. The peculiar exoterical delicacy, or, as a prophane critic would say, the ticklishness of the position of Lady Godiva, is exceedingly well characterized. The very 'stones' of the city streets and walls 'prate of her whereabouts', or, at least, hold their tongues, and open their eyes with an eloquent intensity of dumbness. But the true spirit of the master, we conceive, is not hit in this treatment of the subject. The feelings of the heroine's heart ought to have been more spoken of, and those of the good people inside the houses, who did not think of 'peeping', like the rascally tailor, but wept, and prayed, and loved the unseen angel that was going along. This would have been the way to do honour to the glorious Coventry heroine; and this is what few could have done better than Mr. Tennyson, had he been less in the habit of writing about a hundred Adelines and Madelines, and done more justice to the spiritual part of his fine genius. The best passage in this poem is the characteristic sketch of Godiva's husband and his dialogue, ending with a truly Homeric bit of human animal painting.

[Quotes 'Godiva', ll. 19–31:

'She told him of their tears, . . .
He parted with great strides among his dogs.']

The poem entitled 'St. Simeon Stylites' is a powerfully graphic, and in some respects appalling satire on the pseudo-aspirations of egotistical ascetism and superstition. Poetry had need mix up the beautiful with the horrible, or, sometimes, in the enjoyment of its power to detect and punish, it would appear cruel. We do not recollect to have met with a more startling picture of the sordid and the aspiring—the selfish and the self-sacrificing—the wretched, weak body and mind and resolute soul—the abject, the dominant, the stupid, the imaginative—and, alas, the misgiving (don't let Mr. Tennyson suppose that we are applying any other of these bad epithets to him)—all mixed up in the poor phantom-like person of the almost incredible Saint of the Pillar—the almost solitary Christian counterpart of the Yogees of the Hindoos, who let birds build in their hair, and the nails of their fingers grow through the palms of their hands. We say Christian, out of Christian charity; for though real Christianity is a quintessence of good sense, both in its human and angelical aspirations, as the flower of it in due time will make manifest, yet these and other dark absurdities have, no doubt, lurked about its roots, and for a time, with equal absurdity, been confounded with the flower.

But our favourite poem in the new volume is 'The Two Voices'. The humour of the 'Head Waiter' we cannot relish, though we like its good fellowship; and 'Amphion' is but a fancy of Monk Lewis's run to seed. We prefer the original ballad, in which—

> An arm of the sea,
> Introduc'd by a tree,
> To a fair young whale advances,
> And, making a leg,
> Says, 'Miss, may I beg
> Your fin for the next two dances.'

'The Two Voices' is a summary of the argument, *pro* and *con*, about suicide, capitally well put on both sides, and ending, as they ought to do, in the victory of a cheerful wisdom befitting the beauty of the universe and the goodness of its Creator. We admire it so much, that we would fain extract the whole of it, did it not amount to upwards of thirty pages—a good bit of the volume; so that we must content ourselves with recommending the reader to buy the work, if it were only for this single poem, though his money would be well laid out were it not among the contents. Unluckily, the more we admire it, the more we are compelled to do so at the expense of the volume that contains it, for, on looking at the last stanza, we suddenly discover a date which informs us that it was written in the year 1833; so that we must qualify in some respects what we have intimated about the progress of Mr. Tennyson's genius, the new volume assuredly containing nothing either in feeling or thought which is superior to the old one, if, indeed, it can be said to equal it. We will quote the beginning and the conclusion of 'The Two Voices', that we may have pleasure of shewing the reader of what sort of stuff it is made, and then say a word or two more on this point, in bringing our remarks to an end.

[Quotes 'The Two Voices', ll. 1–45:

> 'A still small voice spake unto me, . . .
> Rain'd thro' my sight its overflow.']

That is very beautiful. But we must hasten to the conclusion, always begging the reader to become acquainted with the rest for himself.

[Quotes 'The Two Voices', ll. 385–462:

> 'The still voice laugh'd . . .
> . . ."Rejoice! Rejoice!"',

omitting ll. 430–9, 445–7.]

This is genuine, Christian, manly, and poetical philosophy, far better than a hundred elaborate luxuries, whether of voluptuousness or woe, and in a style more advanced than that which heaps up compound epithets and an ostentation of thoughts. There has been a reaction of late years in favour both of thought and feeling, and a very salutary reaction it is, against the unthinking common-place that prevailed at the beginning of the century; but, with the usual tendency of revolutions, it has gone to an extreme, and young poets are in danger of exchanging one set of impertinences, that is to say, irrelevancies, for another. They *think* they must *think* at any rate, and be in an incessant state of exuberant remark and imagery, in order to shew what is in them. But real abundance is not under the necessity of taking those violent measures to prove itself. Everything even said well is not said fitly. The real feeling is apt to become smothered in the false; thought takes its place, and that alone is perilous; genuine powers prematurely exhibit themselves, taking pains to shew they have come to their full growth, with airs of universality, and profundity, and final judgments; till at last they are in danger of meeting with a very awkward 'extreme', and, instead of hitting the real points of their subject, whirl their giddy heads round towards the gentle outer-pole of the heroes of the *Dunciad*,

Who wrote *about* it, goddess, and *about* it.

Now, one thing said with thorough truth, and to the purpose, is worth millions of half-apposite fancies, and similes, and collateralities, which do but end, as Ovid calls it, in a poverty-stricken abundance—*inops copia*, and leave every poem of necessity unfinished: for where so many things are said *about* things, why not say more? or where is to be the end of them? Writers of this kind are apt to look with scorn on such poets as Gray and Collins, much more on Pope and the other poets of the French school. We ourselves are adherents to poetry in all its grades, and love the miniatures of Pope, notwithstanding our far greater love and delight in Spenser and Shakspeare, and our admiration of all the genuine intermediate good stuff, whether of thought or feeling, or both, in Beaumont and Fletcher, and Webster, and Marlowe, and Donne, and Daniel, and Drayton; but we cannot blind ourselves to the fact, that completeness is completeness—judgment, a thing select—and passion, a thing with 'no nonsense'—and imagination, not to be confounded with thoughts and fancies, any more than quantity is quality, or profession performance. And the danger to these gentlemen is, that the Grays and Collinses, and even that of the simply natural in Goldsmith, will survive them, and see most of them even speedily perish, unless they 'change their hand and check their pride', simply because those writers are consistent with the truth that is in them, and are not always provoking and disappointing the degree of expectation which they have undertaken to raise.

Mr. Tennyson is at present a kind of philosophical Keats, without the later judgment of that extraordinary genius, and of a turn of mind less naturally and thoroughly given to poetry, in its essence. But there can be no doubt that he is a genuine poet too in his degree (a sacred name—pray let him know how to value it, and be at his ease with it): and there is a class of poetry in which we think he may obtain for himself a name, perhaps as great in its way as that of the other, and one of an independent sort, and that is in a mixture of thought and feeling, more abundant in the former respect than Keats, and more pleasurable and luxuriant in the latter than Wordsworth. We have already characterized, at the beginning of our article, his poetical merits as well as defects, and surely out of all these he might produce another volume which, if less in bulk than the two before us, would have a far greater real abundance. His poems of 'Mariana', and 'A Character', and the 'Merman' and 'Mermaid', and 'Oriana' (in spite of its burden), and the 'Miller's Daughter', and 'Simeon Stylites', and the 'Two Voices', are almost all written in a style as clear and compact as the fancy and imagination are poetical, and the thinking profound; and we hope to see the day when Mr. Moxon will oblige us with a volume including these, and containing new ones nothing inferior to the old.

Such is the position, in the opinion of poets and lovers of genuine poetry (the opinion of critics, and of the public, may not as yet be quite in accordance with the former), which Mr. Tennyson has attained after having been before the world during ten or twelve years. With the first class his genius was at once recognized—with the critics and the public it has, as usual, been matter of slow progress and much contest; but we think that, on the whole, he has little reason to be dissatisfied, and no reason at all, when we consider the ill treatment and tardy admission of the claims of Shelley, of Keats, and of Wordsworth.

9. R. M. Milnes on

Poems [1842]

Richard Monckton Milnes, from a review signed 'R.M.M.', *Westminster Review* (October 1842), xxxviii. 371–90.

Milnes (1809–85) had great social and literary gifts. He was an early champion of Keats and of Swinburne, and he pursued an active political career. His review of Tennyson ends with the following paragraphs.

. . . Poetry is surely now more respectable than it has ever been before in this country; no man, of whatever gravity of station or character, would be ashamed of having written good verse; the insolent cant about Grub street is gone by; aristocratic patronage, which, while it comforted the body, degraded the mind of its object, has ceased, and the poet enjoys the dignity and is subject to the responsibilities of independence. No Gay would now write pitifully regretting that he had written fables for the infant Duke of Cumberland instead of taking Pope's advice, 'rather to write them for some young nobleman'. London lionism still remains,—the last stage of that condescension of ignorance and folly to wisdom and knowledge, by which wealth and power flatter themselves into the notion that they have something to give, while, in truth, they are hardly capable to receive.

Among the large and intelligent middle classes of this country there is much poetry read and enjoyed. It is on this broad basis, not on the clatter of a coterie, nor even on the comprehension of cognate minds, that the fame of Wordsworth rests. Poetry every day becomes more human, more true to the common heart of man; Byronism is past as a school, and the taint of factitious and unreal feeling which lies on its master is going far to dethrone him from popular interest. Take up any magazine, and see not only how comparatively high is the general character of its poetry in diction and execution, but how healthy even its commonplaces are, how reflective or affectionate or pious, how free from appeals to the baser passions and the lower conditions of our nature. The imaginative power may at other periods have been more deeply concentrated in individuals, but it has never been so widely diffused and so freely cultivated as now; and thus it is a genuine source of national congratulation, that of the rising poets of our time there is no single one whose influence can be called immoral or irreligious. It rests with Mr. Tennyson to prove that he can place himself at the head of all these his contemporaries. His command of diction is complete, his sense and execution of the harmonies of verse accurate and admirable; he has only to show that he has substance (what Goethe used to call *stoff*) worthy of these media; that he will not content himself with any ingenuity of conceit or fancifulness of illustration; that, in fine, he comprehends the function of the poet in this day of ours, to teach still more than he delights, and to suggest still more than he teaches.

10. J. Spedding on
Poems [1842]

James Spedding, unsigned review, *Edinburgh Review* (April 1843), lxxvii. 373–91.

Spedding (1808–81), editor and biographer of Francis Bacon, was an intimate friend of Tennyson. In his *Reviews and Discussions* (1879), p. 297, he gives the original version of the opening lines of the last paragraph of his review, which the editor of the *Edinburgh Review* had altered. From this, it appears that Spedding started with 'We cannot, however, conclude' and that the following sentence began, 'Powers are displayed in these volumes, adequate to the production of a very great work'.

One of the severest tests by which a poet can try the true worth of his book, is to let it continue for two or three years out of print. The first flush of popularity cannot be trusted. Admiration is contagious, and means often little more than sympathy with the general feeling—the pleasure of being in the fashion. A book which is praised in all the Reviews, thousands will not only buy but be delighted with; and thus a judicious publisher may contrive, by keeping it cleverly in people's way, to preserve for years a popularity which is merely accidental and ephemeral. But if this be all, the interest in it will cease as soon as it becomes difficult to procure. Let a man ask for it two or three times without getting it, he will take to something else; and his curiosity, unless founded on something more substantial than a wish to see what others are looking at, and a disposition to be pleased with what others praise, will die away. If, on the other hand, a new edition be perseveringly demanded, and when it comes, be eagerly bought, we may safely conclude that the work has something in it of abiding interest and permanent value; for then we know that many people have been so pleased or so edified by the reading that they cannot be content without the possession. To this severe test, the author of the unpretending volumes before us has submitted an infant, and what seemed to many a baseless and precarious, reputation; and so well has it stood the test—for we understand that preparations are already making for another edition—as to give him an undeniable claim to the respectful attention of all critics.

The book must not be treated as one collection of poems, but as three separate ones, belonging to three different periods in the development of his mind, and to be judged accordingly. Mr. Tennyson's first book was published in 1830, when he was at college. His second followed in 1832. Their reception, though far from triumphant, was not inauspicious; for while they gained him many warm admirers, they were treated even by those critics whose admiration, like their charity, begins and ends at home, as sufficiently notable to be worth some not unelaborate ridicule. The admiration and the ridicule served alike to bring them into notice, and they have both been for some years out of print. As many of these productions as Mr. Tennyson has cared to preserve, are contained in the first volume of the present edition. The second consists entirely of poems not hitherto published; which, though composed probably at various intervals during the ten intervening years, have all, we presume, had the benefit of his latest correcting hand. In subject, style, and the kinds of excellence which they severally attain or aim at, they are at once so various and so peculiar, that we cannot affect to convey any adequate idea of the general character of the collection; unless we should go through the table of contents, giving as we go a description and a sample of each poem. Neither shall we trouble ourselves to assign to the author his exact rank among the poets of the day. We trust we have room enough in our hearts for as many true poets, each moving in his just and entire orbit, as the land can produce; we are not, therefore, concerned to enquire how far one differs from another in glory: Πάντα δέ τ᾽ εἴδεται ἄστρα. γέγηθε δέ τε φρένα ποιμήν. We shall content ourselves with endeavouring to form a true estimate of the man himself, and his claims upon the public attention, both for what he has done and for what is to be expected of him hereafter;—which, if we are not much mistaken, (and supposing, what as yet however we have no absolute assurance of, that he possesses the one great faculty of holding all his other faculties in full and sustained exertion,) is something that will make all he has yet produced appear only like preliminary essays and experiments. For the indications of improving taste and increasing power exhibited not only in the results of his later labours, but in the omission of some and the alteration of others among his earlier, lead us to infer that his faculties have not yet reached their highest development; and, even as they are now, he has not yet ventured upon a subject large enough to bring them all into play together.

His earliest published volume—though it contains one or two poems, as 'Mariana' for instance, which must always rank among his very best—is to be referred to rather as a point from which to measure his subsequent progress, than for specimens of what he is. The very vigour and abundance of a poet's powers will commonly be in his way at first, and produce faults. But such faults are by no means unpromising. Indeed it is better that the genius should be allowed to run rather wild and wanton during its nonage; for a poet will hardly have the free command of his faculties when full grown, unless he allow them free play during growth. Too severe a repression of their young activities will stunt and cripple them, so that their aid will not be forthcoming when it is wanted; while, on the other hand, a free indulgence of them will bring in the end a double advantage—they will be not only more fully developed by exercise, but (having sown their wild oats) more readily brought into discipline when business begins.

Regarded as a crop of wild oats, Mr. Tennyson's first collection of poems, as originally published, cannot but be accounted a production of unusual promise. The natural faults of youth—exuberance, prodigality, lightness of heart and head, ingenuity wasted upon nothing, the want of sustained effort and a determined course, together with some vanities and fopperies—it may well afford to be charged with. The untried genius needed to be assured of its powers by putting them forth—to feel itself alive through all its capacities by living acts of creation. Hence his early efforts are, many of them, rather exercises than works—gymnastic exercises for the fancy, the intellect, the imagination, the power of language, and even for the feelings—valuable, as the games and tasks of schoolboys are valuable, not for the thing done, but for the practice, strength, and dexterity acquired in doing it. Here we have a succession of vague melodies, in which the power of musical expression tries how far it can go; there a group of abstract ideas, turned, for the satisfaction of the creative genius, into shapes ready for the sculptor:—here a conceit, in which the fancy admires its own ingenuity; there a thought, of no great worth or novelty perhaps, but expressed with curious felicity:—presently we find ourselves surrounded by a bevy of first-loves—Adelines, Madelines, and Lilians, more than we can remem-

ber—phantoms of female grace in every style, but all belonging to the
land of shadows: then again come delineations of every state of mind,
from that of the mystic who has nearly reached the highest circle, to
the 'second-rate sensitive mind not at unity with itself'; and of every
variety of untried being, on earth or in water, or on the earth under the
water, from the grashopper with his 'short youth, sunny and free', to
the kraken sleeping for ages in the central depths, among millennial
sponges and giant-finned polypi: whilst at intervals we recognize a
genuine touch of common humanity—a 'Character',—a 'Circumstance',—or a sketch truly drawn from homeliest nature, which needs,
however, no fancy dress to make it beautiful, but will remain for ever
fresh when all that 'airy stream of lively portraiture' has faded before
the increasing daylight:—

[Quotes 'Ode to Memory', ll. 95–104:

'No matter what the sketch might be . . .
The trenched waters run from sky to sky.'

and ll. 55–71:

'Come from the woods . . .
Forth gushes from beneath a low-hung cloud.']

In the course of these exercises, though Mr. Tennyson may not have
produced much that he now sets any high value on, yet he made himself master of a great variety of intruments; and his next appearance,
only two years after, showed manifest symptoms of the benefit derived
both from what he had acquired and from what he had thrown off.
The superiority of his second collection of poems lay not so much in the
superior workmanship, (it contained perhaps fewer that were equally
perfect in their kind,) as in the general aim and character. If some of the
blossom was gone, it was amply repaid by the more certain promise of
fruit. Not only was the aim generally larger, the subjects and interest
more substantial, and the endeavour more sustained; but the original
and distinctive character of the man appeared more plainly. His genius
was manifestly shaping a peculiar course for itself, and finding out its
proper business; the moral soul was beginning more and more to assume
its due predominance—not in the way of formal preaching, (the proper
vehicle of which is prose,)—but in the shape and colour which his creations unconsciously took, and the feelings which they were made
insensibly to suggest. Considerable faults, however, still remained; a
tendency, for example, arising from the fulness of a mind which had not

yet learned to master its resources freely, to overcrowd his composition
with imagery; a habit also (caused by that dissatisfaction with himself,
which, so long as it does not depress the spirits too much, a poet ought
to cultivate rather than to repress) of adding, altering, and retouching,
till in trying to improve the form he lost the spirit and freshness of his
work, and blurred the impression;—to which may be added an over-
indulgence in the luxuries of the senses—a profusion of splendours,
harmonies, perfumes, gorgeous apparel, luscious meats and drinks, and
such 'creature comforts', which rather pall upon the sense, and make the
glories of the outward world a little to obscure and overshadow the
world within.

In all these respects, the decade during which Mr. Tennyson has
remained silent has wrought a great improvement. The handling in his
later pieces is much lighter and freer; the interest deeper and purer;—
there is more humanity with less imagery and drapery; a closer adherence to truth; a greater reliance for effect upon the simplicity of
nature. Moral and spiritual traits of character are more dwelt upon, in
place of external scenery and circumstance. He addresses himself more
to the heart, and less to the ear and eye. This change, which is felt in its
results throughout the second volume, may in the latter half of the first
be traced in its process. The poems originally published in 1832, are
many of them largely altered; generally with great judgment, and always
with a view to strip off redundancies—to make the expression simpler
and clearer, to substitute thought for imagery, and substance for shadow.
'The Lady of Shalott', for instance, is stripped of all her finery; her pearl
garland, her velvet bed, her royal apparel, and her 'blinding diamond
bright,' are all gone; and certainly, in the simple white robe which she
now wears, her native beauty shows to much greater advantage. The
'Miller's Daughter', again, is greatly enriched by the introduction of
the mother of the lover; and the following beautiful stanzas (which
many people, however, will be ill satisfied to miss) are displaced, to make
room for beauty of a much higher order:—

> Remember you the clear moonlight
>   That whiten'd all the eastern ridge,
> When o'er the water, dancing white,
>   I stepp'd upon the old mill-bridge?
> I heard you whisper from above,
>   A lute-toned whisper, 'I am here!'
> I murmur'd, 'Speak again, my love,
>   The stream is loud: I cannot hear!'

I heard, as I have seem'd to hear
When all the under-air was still,
The low voice of the glad new year
Call to the freshly-flowered hill.
I heard, as I have often heard
The nightingale in leafy woods
Call to its mate, when nothing stirr'd
To left or right but falling floods.

These, we observe, are away; and the following graceful and tender picture, full of the spirit of English rural life, appears in their place. (The late squire's son, we should premise, is bent on marrying the daughter of the wealthy miller:—)

[Quotes 'The Miller's Daughter', ll. 137–60:

'And slowly was my mother brought ...
Approaching, press'd you heart to heart.']

In the song of the 'Lotos-Eaters'—which, as an expression of the loathing of exertion supposed to be produced by that plant, and as a picturesque and melodious assemblage of all images in nature that can suggest or persuade repose, hardly admitted of improvement—Mr. Tennyson has added some touches of deeper significance, indicating the first effects of the physical disease upon the moral and intellectual nature:—

[Quotes 'The Lotos-Eaters', stanza vi:

'Dear is the memory of our wedded lives, ...
And eyes grown dim with gazing on the pilot-stars.']

At the end of the same poem there will be found an alteration of similar tendency, but of still more awful import; where for the flow of triumphant enjoyment, in the contemplation of merely sensual ease and luxurious repose, with which it originally closed, a higher strain is substituted, which is meant apparently to show the effect of lotos-eating upon the religious feelings. The gods of the Lotos-eaters, it is worth knowing, are altogether Lucretian.

Another instance, more convenient for quotation, of Mr. Tennyson's growing tendency to seek deeper for sources of interest is the third and concluding part (which is entirely new) of the 'May Queen'. Many of our readers are probably familiar with the first two parts of this poem; in the latter of which the natural pathos of the situation—a beautiful girl dying in her prime, before life has lost its freshness, before decay and sorrow have made her familiar with the thought of death—is wrought up with so much truth and tenderness, that there seemed to be little room for more. It is a picture of resignation to a fate felt to be a hard one—the reluctant abandonment of pleasures which she is content to resign since she needs must, but would fain be permitted to keep;—the case of thousands, the rudest delineation of which must always be affecting. With Mr. Tennyson's treatment of it, no fault can be found. The homely pleasures, the sports, the cares, the vanities of her little life—the familiar places she must leave, the familiar process of the seasons, hitherto bringing to the delighted spirit only a succession of delights, now sad and sacred, because watched for the last time—all her shining world, as it was when she moved the centre of it, as it will be when she is no longer there—pass over her mind like shadows, and are touched with exquisite sweetness and simplicity. But he saw in the situation materials for a deeper and loftier strain. Hitherto so full of life, what should she know of death? A blank negation it seemed; the non-existence to her of all that existed; no positive image. But as she grows familiar with the thought of total separation from all she knows, new interests disclose themselves, and death appears but as the passage to a new life. That life she has long known of, indeed, and looked forward to; but idly, as a thing far off, which did not yet practically concern her; a proposition assented to, but not comprehended; a book possessed and known to contain precious things, but not yet read—or, at most, read with a truant attention,

> Like words
> That leave upon the still susceptive sense
> A message undeliver'd, till the mind
> Awakes to apprehensiveness, and takes it.

But now the formless void takes shape and substance as she gazes into it, and draws her whole spirit that way, until already in imagination death is swallowed up in victory. The theme is as trite as can be, and the treatment as simple; but it is not the less original. There are probably not less than a thousand persons now living who could have made elegant and touching verses upon it—one set, perhaps, not greatly differing from another. But of all the thousand poems, we will venture to say that not one would have resembled this:—

[Quotes 'The May Queen: Conclusion', omitting the fourth, eleventh, and twelfth stanzas.]

These specimens may serve to show that the full blossom which distinguished the *Poems chiefly Lyrical*, contained no deceitful promise.

But it is a small thing that the genius possesses the command of all its intruments, if it be not itself in tune with nature. All that is of true and lasting worth in poetry, must have its root in a sound view of human life and the condition of man in the world; a just feeling with regard to the things in which we are all concerned. Where this is not, the most consummate art can produce nothing which men will long care for—where it is, the rudest will never want audience; for then nothing is trivial—the most ordinary incidents of daily life are invested with an interest as deep as the springs of emotion in the heart—as deep as pity, and love, and fear, and awe. In this requisite Mr. Tennyson will not be found wanting. The human soul, in its infinite variety of moods and trials, is his favourite haunt; nor can he dwell long upon any subject, however apparently remote from the scenes and objects of modern sympathy, without touching some string which brings it within the range of our common life. His moral views, whether directly or indirectly conveyed, are healthy, manly, and simple; and the truth and delicacy of his sentiments is attested by the depth of the pathos which he can evoke from the commonest incidents, told in the simplest manner, yet deriving all their interest from the manner of telling. See, for instance, the story of 'Dora', and 'The Lord of Burleigh'. What is there in these that should so move us? Quarrels and reconciliations among kindred happen daily. Hopeless affection, secretly, without complaint, cherished to the end, is a grief commoner than we know of. Many a woman marries above her natural rank, and afterwards dies of a decline. How is it that we do not pass these stories by as *commonplace*—so like what we see every day that we want no more of them? It is because they are disclosed to us, not as *we* are in the habit of seeing such things, through the face they present to the outward world—but as they stand recorded in the silent heart, to whose tragic theatre none but itself (and the poet) may be admitted as a spectator. And many a lighted drawing-room is doubtless the scene of tragedies as deep as *Hamlet*, which pass into the long night unwept, only for want of some *vates sacer* to make them visible. As a specimen of the same kind of power in quite another style, take the following stanzas, entitled 'A Farewell', the pathos of which, if it be difficult to account for, it is not the less impossible to resist:—

[Quotes 'A Farewell', ll. 1–16:

    'Flow down, cold rivulet, to the sea . . .
    For ever and for ever.']

A simple touch this—a mere ejaculation of tender emotion, which seems as if it might have escaped from any body; yet it shows, as well as a more elaborate performance could have done, how truly the poet's feeling vibrates in sympathy with nature; otherwise how should so simple a tone out of his heart awaken such an echo in our own?

But there are four poems in which Mr. Tennyson has expressly treated of certain morbid states of the mind; and from these we may gather, not indeed his creed, but some hints concerning his moral theory of life and its issues, and of that which constitutes a sound condition of the soul. These are the 'Palace of Art', the 'St. Simeon Stylites', the 'Two Voices', and the 'Vision of Sin'. The 'Palace of Art' represents allegorically the condition of a mind which, in the love of beauty and the triumphant consciousness of knowledge and intellectual supremacy, in the intense enjoyment of its own power and glory has lost sight of its relation to man and to God.

> I built my soul a lordly pleasure-house,
> Wherein at ease for aye to dwell.
> I said, 'O soul, make merry and carouse,
> Dear soul, for all is well!'
>
> To which my soul made answer readily:
> 'Trust me, in bliss I shall abide
> In this great mansion, that is built for me,
> So royal-rich, and wide.'

There she gathers round her whatever is beautiful in nature, perfect in art, noble and moving in history—all objects, from all climates and ages, that can inspire the imagination, flatter the senses, or charm the heart; in the midst of which she 'lives alone unto herself', till she feels beyond the reach of change or chance.

> Then of the moral instinct would she prate,
> And of the rising from the dead,
> As hers by right of full accomplished Fate;
> And at the last she said:
>
> 'I take possession of men's minds and deeds.
> I live in all things great and small.
> I sit apart, holding no forms of creeds,
> But contemplating all.'

The very remembrance of human misery and weakness—'the riddle of the painful earth'—though it crosses her thoughts, does not disturb her triumph. But such immunity from the common yoke of mortality is not given to mortal; for a man (as our author expresses it elsewhere)

is not as God;
But then most Godlike, being most a man.

The sin of self-absolution from human cares and duties, finds its appropriate retribution in the despair which the sense of being cut off from human sympathy, when it once forces itself on the mind, inevitably brings;—a truth which Shakspeare has indicated in the case of Richard III.; when he 'that had no brother, that was like no brother',—'he that had neither pity, love, nor fear,'—was shaken by his conscience in sleep.

There is no creature loves me;
And if I die no soul shall pity me:—
I shall despair.

We have not room for the whole passage in which Mr. Tennyson describes the despair of this soul, when, in the midst of her solitary delights, 'deep dread and loathing of her solitude' fell upon her. But the concluding stanzas (as conveying the moral, and especially as showing that it is not the enjoyment, but the *selfish* enjoyment, of her intellectual supremacy—not the gifts, but the gifts as divorced from charity —which he holds to be sinful) must find a place.

[Quotes 'The Palace of Art', ll. 257–96:

'Back on herself . . .
. . . purged my guilt." ']

As the 'Palace of Art' represents the pride of voluptuous enjoyment in its noblest form, the 'St. Simeon Stylites' represents the pride of asceticism in its basest. To shadow forth dramatically the faith, the feelings, and the hopes, which support the man who, being taught that the rewards of another life will be proportioned to the misery voluntarily undergone in this, is bent on qualifying himself for the best place —appears to be the design, or the running idea, of the poem. It is done with great force and effect; and, as far as we can guess, with great fidelity to nature. Of this, however, we must confess that we are not competent judges. Holding, as we do, that all self-torment inflicted for its own sake—all mortification beyond what is necessary to keep the powers of self-command and self-restraint in exercise, and the lower parts of our nature in due subjection to the higher—is a thing unblest; and that the man who thinks to propitiate God by degrading his image and making his temple loathsome, must have his whole heart out of tune, and be in the right way to the wrong place—we must confess that we cannot so expand our human sympathy as to reach the case of St. Simeon. We notice the poem for the light it throws on Mr. Tennyson's feeling with regard to this disease of the mind; which, if we collect it rightly—(for, as the saint has all the talk to himself, it cannot of course be conveyed directly)—is, that selfishness, sensuality, and carnal pride, are really at the bottom of it; and this, however paradoxical it may appear, we believe to be quite true.

In the 'Two Voices' we have a history of the agitations, the suggestions, and counter-suggestions, of a mind sunk in hopeless despondency, and meditating self-destruction; together with the manner of its recovery to a more healthy condition. Though not one of the most perfect, it is one of the most remarkable of Mr. Tennyson's productions. An analysis of the arguments urged on either side, would present nothing very new or striking; and in point of poetical management—though rising occasionally into passages of great power and beauty, and though indicating throughout a subtle and comprehensive intellect, well fitted for handling such questions—it appears to us to be too long drawn out, and too full of a certain tender and passionate eloquence, hardly compatible with that dreary and barren misery in which the mind is supposed to be languishing. The dry and severe style with which the poem begins, should have been kept up, we think, through the greater portion of the dialogue, especially on the part of the 'dull and bitter' voice, which sustains the character of a tempting Mephistopheles. These, however, are points of minute criticism, into which we have not room to enter. What we are at present concerned with, is the moral bearing of the poem. The disease is familiar; but where are we to look for the remedy? Many persons would have thought it enough to administer a little religious consolation to the diseased mind; but unfortunately despondency is no more like ignorance than atrophy is like hunger; and as the most nutritious food will not nourish the latter, so the most comfortable doctrine will not refresh the former. Not the want of consoling topics, but the incapacity to receive consolation, constitutes the disease. Others would have been content to give the bad voice the worst of the argument; but, unhappily, all moral reasoning must ultimately rest on the internal evidence of the moral sense; and where this is disordered, the most unquestionable logic can conclude nothing, because it is the first principles which are at issue;—the *major* is not admitted. Mr. Tennyson's treatment of the case is more scientific. We quote it, not indeed as new or original,—(it has been anticipated, and may perhaps have been sug-

gested, by Mr. Wordsworth, in the memorable passage at the close of
the fourth book of the *Excursion*,)—but for the soundness of the
philosophy, and the poetic beauty of the handling. The dialogue ends,
(as such a dialogue, if truly reported, must always do,) leaving every
thing unsettled, and nothing concluded. Then the speaker, having
answered the tempter's arguments, but gathered no practical assurance
from his own, opens the window and looks forth into the early Sabbath
morning:—

[Quotes 'The Two Voices', ll. 403–62:

    'And I arose . . . Rejoice!" ']

The 'Vision of Sin' touches upon a more awful subject than any of
these;—the end, here and hereafter, of the merely sensual man:—

    I had a vision when the night was late:
    A youth came riding toward a palace-gate.
    He rode a horse with wings, that would have flown,
    But that his heavy rider kept him down.
    And from the palace came a child of sin,
    And took him by the curls, and led him in.

Then follows a passage of great lyrical power, representing, under the
figure of Music, the gradual yielding up of the soul to sensual excitement, in its successive stages of languor, luxury, agitations, madness,
and triumph:—

    Till, kill'd with some luxurious agony,
    The nerve-dissolving melody
    Flutter'd headlong from the sky.

This is the sensual life to which the youth is supposed to be given up.
Meantime, the inevitable, irrevocable judgment comes slowly on,—
not without due token and warning, but without regard:—

[Quotes 'The Vision of Sin', stanza iii:

    'And then I look'd up . . .
    And lighted at a ruin'd inn.']

This is the youth, the winged steed, and the palace—the warm blood,
the mounting spirit, and the lustful body—now chilled, jaded, and
ruined; the cup of pleasure drained to the dregs; the senses exhausted of
their power to enjoy, the spirit of its wish to aspire: nothing left but

'loathing, craving, and rottenness'.[1] His mental and moral state is developed in a song, or rather a lyric speech, too long to quote; and of which, without quoting, we cannot attempt to convey an idea;—a ghastly picture (lightened only by a seasoning of wild inhuman humour) of misery and mockery, impotent malice and impenitent regret; 'languid enjoyment of evil with utter incapacity to 'good'.'[2] Such is his end on earth. But the end of all?

[Quotes 'The Vision of Sin', stanza v:

'The voice grew faint: . . .
God made Himself an awful rose of dawn.']

Into the final mysteries of judgment and of mercy let no man presume to enquire further. Enough for us to know what for us is evil. Be the rest left to Him with whom nothing is impossible!

We have dwelt longer on these four poems than either their prominence or their relative poetic merit would have led us to do; because, though they may not show the author's art in its most perfect or most attractive form, they show the depth from which it springs; they show that it is no trick of these versifying times—born of a superficial sensibility to beauty and a turn for setting to music the current doctrines and fashionable feelings of the day; but a genuine growth of nature, having its root deep in the pensive heart—a heart accustomed to meditate earnestly, and feel truly, upon the prime duties and interests of man.

Having ascertained the depth and quality, we should next enquire into the compass, of his power, and the manner in which it has hitherto been most completely and characteristically developed. But we have already transgressed our limits, and must leave the book to speak for itself on these points. Such poems as the 'Morte d'Arthur', the 'Pictures', the 'Talking Oak', the 'Day Dream', and many others, could derive no additional interest from any comment of ours; and if there be persons to whom a few of the lighter pieces—such as 'Audley Court', 'Walking to the Mail', 'Will Waterproof', or 'Amphion'—appear idle and foolish, we see no help for it; nor, in the mean time, any harm. Those whose humours (to borrow Falstaff's phrase) they happen to 'jump with', will relish them: the rest may pass on.

We cannot conclude without reminding Mr. Tennyson, that highly as we value the Poems which he has produced, we cannot accept them as a satisfactory account of the gifts which they show that he possesses; any more than we could take a painter's collection of *studies* for a picture,

[1] Berkeley.   [2] Lamb.

in place of the picture itself. Powers are displayed in these volumes, adequate, if we do not deceive ourselves, to the production of a great work; at least we should find it difficult to say which of the requisite powers is wanting. But they are displayed in fragments and snatches, having no connexion, and therefore deriving no light or fresh interest the one from the other. By this their effective value is incalculably diminished. Take the very best scenes in Shakspeare—detach them from the context—and suppose all the rest to have perished, or never to have been written—where would be the evidence of the power which created *Lear* and *Hamlet*? Yet, perhaps, not one of those scenes could have been produced by a man who was not capable of producing the whole. If Mr. Tennyson can find a subject large enough to take the entire impress of his mind, and energy persevering enough to work it faithfully out as one whole, we are convinced that he may produce a work, which, though occupying no larger space than the contents of these volumes, shall as much exceed them in value, as a series of quantities multiplied into each other exceeds in value the same series simply added together.

11. R. H. Horne

'Alfred Tennyson'

Richard Henry, or Hengist, Horne, from 'Alfred Tennyson', *A New Spirit of the Age* (1844), ii. 3–32.

Horne (1802–84) led an active and adventurous life. Elizabeth Barrett, later Mrs. Browning, collaborated with him in his *New Spirit of the Age*. The cuts made in his article for present purposes leave his discussion of Tennyson virtually untouched.

. . . We are about to claim for Alfred Tennyson—living as he is, and solely on account of what he has already accomplished—the title of a true poet of the highest class of genius, and one whose writings may be considered as peculiarly lucid to all competent understandings that have cultivated a love for poetry.

It may fairly be assumed that the position of Alfred Tennyson, as a poet of fine genius, is now thoroughly established in the minds of all sincere and qualified lovers of the higher classes of poetry in this country. But what is his position in the public mind? Or, rather, to what extent is he known to the great mass of general readers? Choice and limited is the audience, we apprehend, to whom this favoured son of Apollo pours forth his melodious song. It is true, however, that the public is 'a rising man' in its gradual appreciation, perhaps of every genius of the present time; and certainly this appreciation is really on the rise with respect to the poetry of Tennyson. It is only some thirteen years since he published his first volume, and if it require all this time for 'the best judges' to discover his existence, and determine 'in one way, and the other', upon some of his most original features, the public may be excused for not knowing more about his poems than they do at present. That they desire to know more is apparent from many circumstances.

The name of Alfred Tennyson is pressing slowly, calmly, but surely,—

with certain recognition but no loud shouts of greeting,—from the lips of the discerners of poets, of whom there remain a few, even in the cast-iron ages, along the lips of the less informed public, 'to its own place' in the starry house of names. That it is the name of a true poet, the drowsy world exerts itself to acknowledge; testifying with a heavy lifting of the eyelid, to its consciousness of a new light in one of the nearer sconces. This poet's public is certainly awake to him, although you would not think so. And this public's poet, standing upon the recognition of his own genius, begins to feel the ground firm beneath his feet, after no worse persecution than is comprised in those charges of affectation, quaintness, and mannerism, which were bleated down the ranks of the innocent 'sillie' critics as they went one after another to water. Let the toleration be chronicled to the honor of England.[1] And who knows?—There may be hope from this, and a few similar instances of misprision of the high treason of poetry, that our country may conclude her grand experience of a succession of poetical writers unequalled in the modern world, by learning some ages hence to know a poet when she sees one. Certainly if we looked only to the peculiar genius of Tennyson, with the eyes of our forefathers, and some others rather nearer to our own day, we should find it absolutely worthy of being either starved or stoned, or as Shelley said of Keats, 'hooted into the grave'.

. . . How much of the peculiar genius of Keats is visible in Alfred Tennyson, must have been apparent to all those who are familiar with their writings; and yet it is equally certain that Tennyson, so far from being an imitator of any one, is undoubtedly one of the most original poets that ever lived. Wordsworth has had many imitators, some of whom have been tolerably successful—especially in the simplicity. They thought *that* was the grand secret. A few who had genuine *ideas* have been more worthy followers of the great poet of profound sentiment. Tennyson has also had followers; but only such as have felt his spirit, nor is he likely to have any mere imitators, for the dainty trivialities and mannerism of his early productions have been abandoned, and now let those imitate who can. They must have some fine poetical elements of *their own*, as in the recent instance of Mr. Patmore, in order to be at all successful.

[1] One or two exceptions should be noticed. The *Examiner*, in a graceful and appreciating notice of the recent publication of Leigh Hunt's collected works, says, that he was the first to hail the appearance of Alfred Tennyson in the *Tatler*. In 1833 a philosophical criticism appeared on Tennyson, in the *Monthly Repository* written by W. J. Fox, which unhesitatingly recognised his genius.

If a matter-of-fact philosopher who prided himself upon the hardness of his head, and an exclusive faculty of understanding actual things, were to apply to us for the signification of the word 'Poetry', we could not do better than thrust into his hand, widely opened for the expected brick, one of Alfred Tennyson's volumes. His poetry is poetry in the intense sense, and admits of no equivocal definitions. The hard-headed realist might perhaps accept Macaulay's *Lays of Ancient Rome*, as good martial music, (with the help of a little prompting from a friend of some imagination,) or Mr. Henry Taylor's *Philip van Artevelde* as excellent steady thinking; or a considerable portion even of Wordsworth's works as sound good sense, though in verse, (a great admission); but if he did not understand Tennyson's poems to be 'Poetry', he would not be very likely to misunderstand them for anything else. The essence and element of them are poetry. The poetry of the matter strikes though the manner. The Art stands up in his poems, self-proclaimed, and not as any mere modification of thought and language, but the operation of a separate and definite power in the human faculties. A similar observation attaches itself to the poetry of Shelley, to the later productions of Keats, to certain poems of Coleridge. But Tennyson and Shelley, more particularly, walk in the common day-light in their 'singing clothes'; they are silver-voiced when they ask for salt, and say 'Good-morrow to you' in a cadence. They each have a poetical dialect; not such a one as Wordsworth deprecated when he overthrew a system; not a conventional poetical idiom, but the very reverse of it—each poet fashioning his phrases upon his own individuality; and speaking as if he were making a language then, for the first time, under those 'purple eyes' of the muse, which tinted every syllable as it was uttered, with a separate benediction.

Perhaps the first spell cast by Mr. Tennyson, the master of many spells, he cast upon the ear. His power as a lyrical versifier is remarkable. The measures flow softly or roll nobly to his pen; as well one as the other. He can gather up his strength, like a serpent, in the gleaming coil of a line; or dart it out straight and free. Nay, he will write you a poem with nothing in it except music, and as if its music were everything, it shall charm your soul. Be this said, not in reproach,—but in honour of him and of the English language, for the learned sweetness of his numbers. The Italian lyrists may take counsel, or at once enjoy,—

Where Claribel low lieth.

But if sweetness of melody, and richness of harmony be the most exquisitely sensuous of Tennyson's characteristics, he is no less able to 'pipe to the spirit ditties of no tone', for certainly his works are equally characterized by their thoughtful grace, depth of sentiment, and ideal beauty. And he not only has the most musical words at his command (without having recourse to exotic terminologies) but he possesses the power of conveying a sense of colour, and a precision of outline by means of words, to an extraordinary degree. In music and colour he was equalled by Shelley; but in *form*, clearly defined, with no apparent effort, and no harsh shades or lines, Tennyson stands unrivalled.

His ideality is both adornative and creative, although up to this period it is ostensibly rather the former than the latter. His ideal faculty is either satisfied with an exquisitely delicate Arabesque painting, or clears the ground before him so as to melt and disperse all other objects into a suitable atmosphere, or aerial perspective, while he takes horse on a passionate impulse, as in some of his ballads which seem to have been panted through without a single pause. This is the case in 'Oriana', in 'Locksley Hall', in 'The Sisters', &c. Or, at other times, selecting some ancient theme, he stands collected and self-contained, and rolls out with an impressive sense of dignity, orb after orb of that grand melancholy music of blank verse which leaves long vibrations in the reader's memory; as in 'Ulysses', the divine 'Œnone', or the 'Morte D'Arthur'. The idea of the death, or fading away of Fairy-land, allegorically conveyed in the latter poem, is apparently the main basis of the design, and probably original; but it is observable that Tennyson scarcely ever invents any elaborate design of moving characters. The two other poems just named, with the 'Lord of Burleigh', 'Lady Clare', 'Dora', 'Godiva', and most of those which contain human character in a progressive story, are taken from various sources; but they are taken by a master-hand, and infused with new life and beauty, new thought and emotion. The same peculiarity as to ground-plot is observable in Shakspere and Chaucer, who never invented their subjects or stories; but filled them up as nobody else ever had done, or could do. It was exactly the converse with Scott, who invented nearly all his stories, but borrowed materials to fill them up from all possible sources. Tennyson does not appear to possess much inventive construction. He has burnt his epic, or this would have settled the question. We would almost venture to predict that he will never write another; nor a five-act tragedy, nor a long heroic poem. Why should he?

Alfred Tennyson may be considered generally under four different aspects,—developed separately or in collective harmony, according to the nature of his subject—that is to say, as a poet of fairy-land and enchantment; as a poet of profound sentiment in the affections (as Wordsworth is in the intellect and moral feelings); as a painter of pastoral nature; and as the delineator and representer of tragic emotions, chiefly with reference to one particular passion.

With regard to the first of these aspects of his genius, it may be admitted at the outset that Tennyson is not the portrayer of individual, nor of active practical character. His characters, with few exceptions, are generalizations, or refined abstractions, clearly developing certain thoughts, feelings, and forms, and bringing them home to all competent sympathies. This is almost exclusively the case in the first volume, published in 1830. Those critics, therefore, who have seized upon the poet's early loves—his Claribels, Lilians, Adelines, Madelines —and comparing them with real women, and the lady-loves of the actual world, have declared that they were not natural beings of flesh and blood, have tried them by a false standard. They do not belong to the flesh-and-blood class. There is no such substance in them. They are creatures of the elements of poetry. And, for that reason, they have a sensuous life of their own; as far removed from ordinary bodily condition as from pure spirit. They are transcendentalisms of the senses; examples of the Homeric εἴδωλα, or rather—if we may venture to trace the genealogical history of such fragile creatures—the descendants of those εἴδωλα, as modified by the influence of the romantic ages. Standing or seated, flying or floating, laughing or weeping, sighing or singing, pouting or kissing, they are lovely underbodies, which no German critic would for a moment hesitate to take to his visionary arms; but we are such a people for 'beef'. We cry aloud for soul—we want more soul—we want to be inspired—and the instant anything is floated before our ken which might serve as an aerial guide to the Elysian Valley, or the Temple of the Spirit, then we intantly begin to utter the war-cry of 'dreamy folly!' 'mystical mystery!' and urged by the faith (the beef) that is in us, continue our lowing for the calf, that surely cometh, but cannot satisfy our better cravings.

Continuing our inquiries into the fruits of Tennyson's early excursions in dream-land, we perceive that he was inclined, even when upon commoner ground, to accept the fantasy of things, for the things themselves. His Muse was his own Lady of Shalott,—she was metamorphosed into the Merman and the Mermaid; they reunited at the bottom of the sea in the form of the Kraken, and lay swelling with the sense of ages beneath enormous growths floating upon the surface. Why this 'Kraken' should have been omitted in the present collection puzzles and annoys us as much as his insertion of 'the Goose', and one or two other such things. But nothing in this class of subjects is more remarkable, than the power he possesses of communicating to simple incidents and objects of reality, a preternatural spirit as part of the enchantment of the scene. Of this kind, in the dim and desolate chamber of the moated grange, where Mariana, in the anguish of mingled hope and despair, moaned away her dreary life—of this kind, to her morbid fancy, was the blue fly that 'sung i' the pane'; and the mouse that 'behind the mouldering wainscot shrieked'. We have heard it asked—as such questions always are asked by numbers—what more there was in this than the mere details of a description of squalidness and desertion? The best answer was recently made by ——.'Why,' said he, 'don't you know that this ghastly fly had been bred of a corpse— and knew it? As for the mouse, it had clearly been the poor starved niece of a witch, and the witch had murdered her, her soul passing into the body of a mouse by reason of foul relationship.' This, at least, was accepting a suggestion at full. In such a spirit of imaginative promptitude and coincidence should such things be read, or nothing will come of the reading.

> Old faces glimmer'd through the doors,
> Old footsteps trod the upper floors,
> Old voices called her from without!

But since 'the low sky raining' in the autumn eve, when the white-robed dying form of the Lady of Shalott floated in the boat towards the many-towered palaces of the Knights, a marked change has come over the genius of this poet with regard to his female characters. Instead of the scions of the fairy-race, most of whom seem to have been the poet's 'cousin'—a consanguinity which evidently haunts him—we had in the volume of 1832, some equally beautiful women, such as the 'Miller's Daughter', 'Margaret', and the proud 'Lady Clara Vere de Vere'; while in the volume last given to the public, there are several more, and not a single additional sylph. Here we find him not only awake to the actual world, but awake with a set of totally new experiences. In no writer is the calm intensity of pure affection, both in its extreme tenderness and continuity, more exquisitely portrayed, than in the poems of the 'Miller's Daughter', 'Dora', and the 'Gardener's

Daughter'. They are steeped in the very sweetest fountains of the human heart.

In the description of pastoral nature in England, no one has ever surpassed Tennyson. The union of fidelity to nature and extreme beauty is scarcely to be found in an equal degree in any other writer. There may sometimes be a tone of colour, and the sense of a sustained warmth in the temperature, which is rather Italian; and this is a peculiarity of our poets, who invariably evade notice or consciousness of the four seasons in each day, which is a characteristic of our climate. The version which all English poets give of 'Spring', more especially, is directly at variance with what everybody feels and knows of that bitter season in this country. But allowing for this determination to make the best of what we have, no poet more closely adheres to nature. He is generally as sweet, and fresh, and faithful in his drawing and colouring of a landscape, as the prose pastorals of Miss Mitford, which is saying the utmost we can for a possessor of those qualifications. But besides this, Tennyson idealizes, as a poet should, wherever his subject needs it— not so much as Shelley and Keats, but as much as the occasion will bear, without undue preponderance, or interfering with the harmony of his general design. His landscapes often have the truthful ideality of Claude, combined with the refined reality of Calcott, or the homely richness of Gainsborough. The landscape-painting of Keats was more like the back grounds of Titian and Annibal Carracci; as that of Shelley often resembled the pictures of Turner. We think the extraordinary power of language in Shelley sometimes even accomplished, not only the wild brilliancy of colouring, but the apparently impossible effect, by words, of the wonderful aerial perspective of Turner—as where he speaks of the loftiest star of heaven 'pinnacled dim in the intense inane'. But with Tennyson there is no tendency to inventiveness in his descriptions of scenery; he contents himself with the loveliness of the truth seen through the medium of such emotion as belongs to the subject he has in hand. But as these emotions are often of profound passion, sentiment, reflection, or tenderness, it may well be conceived that his painting is of that kind which is least common in art. The opening of 'Œnone' is a good example, and is a fine prelude to love's delirium, which follows it.

> There lies a vale in Ida, lovelier
> Than all the valleys of Ionian hills.
> The swimming vapour slopes athwart the glen,
> Puts forth an arm and creeps from pine to pine,

And loiters, slowly drawn. On either hand
The lawns and meadow-ledges midway down
Hang rich in flowers, and far below them roars
The long brook falling thro' the clov'n ravine
In cataract after cataract to the sea.

If Alfred Tennyson became awake to the actual world in his second
volume of 1832, his publication in 1843 showed him more completely
so; awake after the storm, after the wrecks, the deepest experiences of
life. In the ten years' interval he has known and suffered. So far from
any of his private personal feelings being paraded before the public,
either directly, or by means of characters which everybody shall
recognise as identical, after the fashion of Lord Byron, there is a
withdrawal from every identification, and generally a veil of ideality
cast over the whole. Certainly Tennyson is not at all dramatic. That he
can be intensely tragic, in pure emotion and deep passion of expression,
we shall presently show; that he has great power of concentration, will
be equally apparent; and that in his powerful monodrama of 'St.
Simeon Stylites', and in the various imaginative or fanciful personages
he introduces, he presents full evidence of the faculty of self-absorption
in the identity of other idiosyncrasies, we think also to be incontestible.
Still, he only selects a peculiar class of characters—those in whom it
shall not be requisite to dispossess himself of beauty (Stylites being the
only exception); nor can he speak without singing. His style of blank
verse is elegiac, epic, heroic, or suited to the idyl; and not at all
dramatic. His characters, as we have said before, are generalizations or
abstractions; they pass before the imagination, and often into the very
centre of the heart and all its emotions; they do not stand forth conspicuous in bone or muscle, nor in solidity, nor roundness, nor substantial identity. They have no little incidental touches of character,
and we should not know them if we met them out of his poetry. They
do not eat and drink. One never thought of that before; and it seems an
offence to hint at such a thing concerning them. But besides all this,
our poet cannot laugh outright in his verses; not joyously, and with
self-abandonment. His comic, grotesque, or burlesque pieces, are
neither natural nor wild. They are absolute failures by dint of ingenuity.
His 'Amphion' and 'the Goose' have everything but that which such
attempts most need—animal spirits. There is something intermediate,
however, which he can do, and which is ten thousand times more uncommon,—that of an harmonious blending of the poetical and familiar,
so that the latter shall neither destroy the former, nor vex the taste of

the reader. As an instance of this, we would quote 'Will Waterproof's Lyrical Monologue', which is perfection; as also were Shelley's poetical 'Letter to ——', and his 'Julian and Maddalo'. Of the constructive power, and the distribution of action required in a dramatic composition, there is no need to speak; but it is time to consider the tragic faculties of our author, and his power over the passions by description.

The frequent tendency to the development or illustration of tragic emotion has been less noticed than any other important feature of Tennyson's poetry. In his first volume (1830) we find a 'Dirge'; the 'Death of Love'; the 'Ballad of Oriana'; the 'Supposed Confessions'; and 'Mariana'; all of which are full of the emotions and thoughts which lead directly to, if they do not involve, tragic results. The same may be said of the following poems in the second volume (1832):—the 'Lady of Shalott'; 'Eleänore'; 'Sappho' (called 'Fatima' in the new edition!); 'Œnone'; the 'New Year's Eve'; and the 'Sisters'. Upon this last-named poem we will venture a few remarks and suggestions.

'The Sisters' is a ballad poem of six stanzas, each of only four lines, with two lines of a chorus sung by the changeful roaring of the wind 'in turret and tree'—which is made to appear conscious of the passions that are at work. In this brief space is comprised, fully told, and with many suggestions beyond, a deep tragedy.

The story is briefly this. A youthful earl of great personal attractions, seduces a young lady of family, deserts her, and she dies. Her sister, probably an elder sister, and not of equal beauty, had, apparently, also loved the earl. When, therefore, she found that not only had her love been in vain, but her self-sacrifice in favour of her sister had only led to the misery and degradation of the latter, she resolved on the earl's destruction. She exerted herself to the utmost to attract his regard; she 'hated him with the hate of hell', but, it is added, that she 'loved his beauty passing well', for the earl 'was fair to see'. Abandoning herself in every way to the accomplishment of her purpose, she finally lulled him to sleep, with his head in her lap, and then stabbed him 'through and through'. She composed and smoothed the curls upon 'his comely head', admiring to see that 'he looked so grand when he was dead'; and wrapping him in a winding sheet, she carried him to his proud ancestral hall, and 'laid him at his mother's feet'.

We have no space to enter into any psychological examination of the peculiar character of this sister; with regard, however, to her actions, the view that seems most feasible, and the most poetical, if not equally tragic, is that she did not actually commit the self-abandonment and murder; but went mad on the death of her sister, and imagined in her delirium all that has been related. But 'read the part' how we may, there never was a deeper thing told in briefer words.

The third volume of *Tennyson's Poems*, (that is, the Vol. II. of the new edition last issued), contains several tragic subjects. The one most penetrating to the heart, the most continuous, and most persevered in with passionate intensity, so that it becomes ineradicable from the sensibility and the memory, is 'Locksley Hall'. The story is very simple; not narrative, but told by the soliloquy of anguish poured out by a young man amid the hollow weed-grown courts of a ruined mansion. He loved passionately; his love was returned; and the girl married another,—a dull, every-day sort of husband. The story is a familiar one in the world—too familiar; but in Tennyson's hands it becomes invested with yet deeper life, a vitality of hopeless desolation. The sufferer invoking his betrayer, her beauty and her falsehood, by the memory of their former happiness, says that such a memory is the very crown of sorrow:—

Drug thy memories, lest thou learn it, lest thy heart be put to proof,
In the dead unhappy night, and when the rain is on the roof.

Like a dog he hunts in dreams, and thou art staring at the wall,
Where the dying night-lamp flickers, and the shadows rise and fall.

Then a hand shall pass before thee, pointing to his drunken sleep,
To thy widowed marriage-pillow, to the tears that thou shalt weep.

Thou shalt hear the 'Never! never!' whispered by the phantom years,
And a song from out the distance, in the ringing of thine ears;

And an eye shall vex thee, looking ancient kindness on thy pain.

Of similar character and depth of tone is the poem of 'Lady Clara Vere de Vere', who impelled to suicide one of the victims of her heartless beauty. The long-drawn music of her very name is suggestive of the proud pedigree to which she was ready to offer up any sacrifice. For continuity of affectionate tenderness and deep pathos in the closing scene, we should mention 'The Lord of Burleigh', and the idyl of 'Dora',—the style of both being studiously artless, the latter, indeed, having a Scriptural simplicity which presents a curious contrast to the poet's early manner. In the poem of 'Love and Duty' there is a general tone of suppressed emotion, and a violent effort against nature which is deeply painful. The equal tenderness and bitterness of the anguish renders it the more difficult to receive with that feeling of resignation and sense of right which one would wish for, on such heart-breaking occasions. It is to be feared that some conventionalities have been erected into undue tyrannies over the noblest and most impassioned impulses, although the poet, not choosing to be more explicit in his story, or its suggestions, may not have intended to illustrate any such principle. The clear course of feeling in the two preceding poems, which are equally pathetic and conclusive, will generally be preferable, even to the more intensely tragic emotion of this latter one.

It remains to offer a remark on two or three other poems which also form the most striking features of the present collection.

With respect to 'Œnone', it is an exquisitely successful attempt of the poet to infuse his own beating heart's blood into the pale blind statues of the antique times; and loses no jot of the majesty, while the vitality informs the grace. It is not surpassed by anything of the kind in Keats, or Shelley, or Landor. The 'Morte D'Arthur' precisely reverses the design of the Greek revival; and, with equal success, draws back the Homeric blood and spirit to inspire a romantic legend.

Of the 'Ulysses' we would say that the mild dignity and placid resolve—the steady wisdom after the storms of life, and with the prospect of future storms—the melancholy fortitude, yet kingly resignation to his destiny which gives him a restless passion for wandering—the unaffected and unostentatious modesty and self-conscious power,—the long softened shadows of memory cast from the remote vistas of practical knowledge and experience, with a suffusing tone of ideality breathing over the whole, and giving a saddened charm even to the suggestion of a watery grave,—all this, and much more, independent of the beautiful picturesqueness of the scenery, render the poem of 'Ulysses' one of the most exquisite (as it has hitherto been one of the least noticed) poems in the language.

It would be impossible to give that full consideration to the extraordinary poem of 'St. Simeon Stylites', which as a work of genius it merits, without entering into complexities of the passions, mind, and human character, under the excitement and involuntary as well as wilful hallucinations of fanaticism, for which we could afford no adequate space. We must content ourselves with saying that it is a great and original 'study'.

There are no qualities in Tennyson more characteristic than those of delicacy and refinement. How very few are the poets who could equally well have dealt with the visible loveliness of the story of 'Godiva',—

we say visible, as distinguished from the deeper loveliness of heart which gave her courage to go through such a trial.

[Quotes 'Godiva', ll. 5–11, 32–5, 42–51.]

The mind which can force up a vital flower of ideality through the heavy fermenting earth of human experiences, must have a deep intellectual root and active life. Among these experiences we must of course include those inner struggles of the soul with its own thoughts; dealings with the revelations that seem to come from other states of existence; difficult contests between the mortal promptings and resistances that breed so many doubts and hopes, and things inscrutable; and thoughts that often present themselves in appalling whispers, against the will and general tone and current of the mind. Tennyson's intellectual habit is of great strength; his thoughts can grow with large progressive purpose either up or down, and the peculiarity is that in him they commonly do so to 'a haunting music'. No argument was ever conducted in verse with more admirable power and clearness than that of the 'Two Voices'. The very poetry of it magnifies itself into a share of the demonstration: take away the poetry and the music, and you essentially diminish the logic.

Though Tennyson often writes, or rather sings apparently from his own personality, you generally find that he does not refer to himself, but to some imaginary person. He permits the reader to behold the workings of his individuality, only by its reflex action. He comes out of himself to sing a poem, and goes back again; or rather sends his song out from his shadow under the leaf, as other nightingales do; and refuses to be expansive to his public, opening his heart on the hinges of music, as other poets do. We know nothing of him except that he is a poet; and this, although it is something to be sure of, does not help us to pronounce distinctly upon what may be called the mental intention of his poetry.

Whatever he writes is a complete work: he holds the unity of it as firmly in his hand as his Œnone's Paris holds the apple—and there is nothing broken or incomplete in his two full volumes. His few 'fragments' are entire in themselves, and suggest the remainder. But for all this unity of every separate poem produced by him, there is, or appears to be, some vacillation of intention, in his poetry as a mass. To any question upon the character of his early works, the reply rises obviously, —they are from dream-land; and of the majority of those which he has since produced, the same answer should be returned. The exceptive instances are like those of one who has not long awakened from his Dreams. But what dreams these have been—of what loveliness of music, form, and colour, and what thoughtfulness—our foregoing remarks have very faintly expressed and declared. In the absence of any marked and perceptible design in his poetical faith and purposes, Tennyson is not singular. It would be equally difficult to decide the same question with regard to several others; nor perhaps is it necessary to be decided. As the matter rests in this instance, we have the idea of a poet (his volumes in our hands) who is not in a fixed attitude; not resolute as to means, not determined as to end—sure of his power, sure of his activity, but not sure of his objects. There appears to be some want of the sanctification of a spiritual consistency; or a liability at intervals to resign himself to the 'Lotos-Eaters'. We seem to look on, while a man stands in preparation for some loftier course—while he tries the edge of his various arms and examines the wheels of his chariots, and meditates, full of youth and capability, down the long slope of glory. He constantly gives us the impression of something greater than his works. And this must be his own soul. He may do greater things than he has yet done; but we do not expect it. If he do no more, he has already done enough to deserve the lasting love and admiration of posterity. . . .

12. J. W. Marston on

The Princess [1847]

John Westland Marston, unsigned review, *Athenæum*
(1st January 1848), xxi. 6–8.

Marston (1819–90) was a dramatic poet.

There is so much to admire in this volume that we cannot wish it
unwritten,—but so much also to censure that, while we could recognize
the whole if tendered as a pledge of genius, we cannot accept it as a due
consummation of that faculty. To those whom occasional revelations
of rare and genuine beauty compensate for much that is marred by
affectation, wasted by neglect, or destroyed by incongruity *The
Princess* will be welcome:—but it will be read with some disappointment
by all who expected from its author harmony of design and sustained
merit in its exposition.

We find in these pages little which denotes advance. In many shorter
poems from the same source the aim is as exalted, the insight as deep,
as in this elaborate one! No wholesome severity has discarded former
puerilities. Nor does the poet in all cases retain his admitted and peculiar
excellencies. That charming modulation which gave added effect to
his felicitous conceptions, and not seldom substituted them, is often
remorselessly violated in the book before us. False or deficient quantities
occur with a frequency which suggests that they have been deliberately
adopted. If, as we suspect, they have been introduced for relief, we
would caution Mr. Tennyson that correct monotony is less displeasing
than awkward and unmusical licence. The only new attribute of the
writer's mind revealed in *The Princess* is a certain fertility of incident—
which, however, does not extend to happiness of combination.

The absence of this latter quality is, indeed, the chief defect in the
poem. Notwithstanding passages of occasional baldness, harsh or careless versification, and sentences so inverted or elliptical as frequently to

be ambiguous,—there is in this production a wealth and pictorial beauty and a delicate apprehension of motive and feeling to which our current poetry can furnish few parallels. The grand error of the story is the incoherency of its characteristics. Its different parts refuse to amalgamate. They are derived from standards foreign to each other. The familiar and conventional impair the earnestness of the ideal:—and what might else have been appreciated as genial satire loses its force from its juxtaposition to tragic emotion. Nor are these opposite elements used as contrasts to each other. It is sought to identify them; but in the attempt to fuse both, each parts with its distinctiveness.

At the commencement, for example, the Princess is a modern blue, to be quizzed and bantered. At a later period, she is transformed into a stately Amazon. Yet even in her metamorphosis, the details of ordinary life are so frequently obtruded that we lose all faith in her individuality. The effect is similar to that which would result from investing some antique divinity with a cashmere shawl; or as if while her port bespoke the goddess—

Et vera incessu patuit dea—

she should expose at every step the satin slipper of the drawing-room.

But we would not have this objection misinterpreted. We do not blame Mr. Tennyson for having introduced into his poem the associations and feelings of modern life. We should have rejoiced had he so evolved for us the truth and passion which underlie the present no less than the past. But with this design, the poet should grapple boldly with the actualities of his subjects, redeem them from their prosaic suggestions, and change them into the symbols of Man. All forms become poetic when humanity inspires them. The fastidiousness which cannot feel genuine emotion because conveyed through a familiar medium discredits the ideal on which it insists. Limited by its sensuous associations, it doubts the power of genius to alter or exalt them. It sees the formless and flaccid bag on the earth, and will not believe that the subtle gas can dilate it into a sphere and lift it toward the stars. With such scepticism, its own bondage to the actual is its gauge for the possible. Its affinity to the electric fluid is small,—and for this reason it is often squeamish as to the conductor.

From the benefit of this hypothetical defence Mr. Tennyson has, however, excluded himself. When he deals with contemporary life he touches on its customs apart from its passions. Hence, with all his decorative skill, the prosaic material is sadly conspicuous through the former half of his book. But even had the feelings as well as the habits of these times been expounded in the tale, its subsequent transition to formal dignity and old heroics would have destroyed all mental congruity.

It is true that the author has anticipated our exceptions. His very title-page declares *The Princess* to be a 'Medley'. In the Prologue we have this avowal in detail. Wishing to adapt his narrative to the time and place of its relation, the speaker exclaims—

> But one that really suited time and place
> Were such a medley, we should have him back
> Who told the Winter's Tale to do it for us:
> A Gothic ruin and a Grecian house,
> A talk of college and of ladies' rights,
> A feudal knight in silken masquerade,
> And there with shrieks and strange experiments,
> For which the good Sir Ralph had burnt them all,
> The nineteenth century gambols on the grass.

But this consciousness of an eccentric plan can scarcely excuse it. We fancy that the Prologue is in reality an apologetic supplement. If so, there is hope that an error spontaneously discerned and confessed will in future be avoided.

The story is of a Prince and a Princess Ida contracted to each other by their parents in infancy. The pair have never met; but, as the Prince approaches manhood, he becomes enamoured of the lady from her portrait. In due time she is demanded for him in marriage,—but her father answers evasively. The latter is shortly afterwards surprised by a visit from the prince:—who then learns that his affianced has withdrawn to the borders of the kingdom and there established a college of women. Penetrated by a sense of the injustice of man towards her sex, Ida displays her resentment by excluding him from her retreat. The penalty of death is denounced against masculine intrusion. Nothing daunted, the Prince and his companions gain admission to the college in feminine disguise,—and are inrolled amongst her subjects and pupils. Considerable humour is exhibited in these details. Then follows the interview with the Princess; who is thus described:—

[Quotes *The Princess*, ii. 32–41:

> 'There at a board . . .
> And to her feet.']

The Princess [1847]

In the following extract the Prince and his attendants are introduced to the occupations of the college:—

[Quotes *The Princess*, ii. 360–80:

'And then we stroll'd . . .
We issued gorged with knowledge.']

As may be imagined, the Prince avails himself of his *incognito* to plead his own cause in his assumed character. He finds the lady obdurate,— but willing to hear the arguments of the supposed maiden. A logical combat ensues, in which Ida proves herself a biting satirist and a subtle metaphysician. Eventually, the disputants repose under a tent of satin, and music is commanded. The song which follows is full of plaintive beauty; and delicately indicates that bias of Woman's heart towards the affections which neither the example nor the discipline of the Princess had been able effectively to counteract.—

[Quotes 'Tears, idle tears' from *The Princess*, iv.]

In the same scene, by an inadvertence which we need not relate, the sex of the Prince and his companions is discovered. The heroine and her maidens at once betake themselves to horse and fly. In her 'blind rage', the former misses the plank across the river, and is suddenly immersed. From this peril she is delivered by the hero,—who with great temerity returns to the college. He is eventually arrested in its gardens by the feminine officials, and led before the indignant president. A scene follows which, though unequal and in some parts tedious, contains much vivid description. Had the story been told by the pencil, its lights and groupings could scarcely have been more effective than those here produced by the pen. The Prince defends himself in this court of beauty before its queen. While his fate is yet undecided, despatches are delivered to Ida. One from her father acquaints her that he is a captive to the father of the Prince. The other, from the latter potentate, threatens her with prompt vengeance unless she deliver up his son unscathed and fulfil her contract. The effect of these motives on the Princess and the character of the entire scene are thus disclosed:—

[Quotes *The Princess*, iv. 468–94:

'a tide of fierce . . .
. . . and the tumult fell.']

Nothing can be finer than the instantaneous calm described in the concluding line. The silence is broken by Ida; who harangues her subjects on the claims of woman, and concludes with an indignant repudiation of the Prince. It is to be lamented that, when her scorn at his treachery has attained a passionate climax, the illusion should be dispelled by an incident of the broadest farce. Eight stalwart women lay hands upon the hero and his comrade. These 'mighty daughters of the plough', though admirable examples of fantastic humour, encroach fatally on a serious interest. Of their unfitness for their position some notion may be collected from their subsequent proceedings. A herald is despatched with pacific overtures to the college. He is warned to retire,—but neglects the admonition. Then

> ————those eight daughters of the plough
> Came sallying through the gates, and caught his hair,
> And so belabour'd him on rib and cheek
> *They made him wild.*

Eventually, the claims of the Prince on Ida are settled by a tourney,— in which the champions of the lady are victorious. The Prince is un- horsed, and lies senseless on the field. What follows is happily conceived. The empire of force is not the empire of woman. The resolution of the Princess is defeated by her triumph. Pity succeeds to scorn,—love to pity. She nurses the wounded Prince, and grants to suffering what she had refused to enterprise and intimidation. The growth and maturity of her affection are charmingly developed and described.—

[Quotes 'Now sleeps the crimson petal' and 'Come down, O maid' from *The Princess*, vii.]

Of these extracts we can speak with unqualified praise. The com- mencing lyric breathes the very luxury of tenderness, and floats to us in sighs of music. Nor shall we readily find an example of the pastoral at once more rich and chaste than the instance which succeeds.—The following lines convey the moral of the poem.—

[Quotes *The Princess*, vii. 274–85:

'For woman is not . . .
. . . music unto noble words.']

We have left ourselves little space to notice the collateral incidents and characters of the story. The latter are nicely, though somewhat too finely, discriminated; but they all suffer from the artistic defects of which we have already complained. The heterogeneous combination that mars the conception throughout sometimes extends to the detail.

Here is a striking instance. A mother who has long been separated from her child, finds it on the plain of battle.—

> Red grief and mother's anger in her eye,
> And down dead heavy sank her curls, and half
> The sacred mother's bosom panting *burst*
> *The laces towards her babe.*

Our analysis of the poem will have sufficiently exhibited the discordant nature of its elements. Lecture rooms and chivalric lists, modern pedantry and ancient romance, are antagonisms which no art can reconcile. With the power which Mr. Tennyson has here evinced for the familiar and the ideal regarded separately, it is much to be deplored that by their unskilful combination he has produced simply—the grotesque.

13. C. Kingsley on *In Memoriam* [1850] and Earlier Works

Charles Kingsley, from an unsigned review, *Fraser's Magazine* (September 1850), xlii. 245–55.

Kingsley (1819–75) took a vigorous interest, both as a writer and as a member of the Anglican clergy, in the movement for social reform during the middle years of the nineteenth century. Like most other reviewers, he welcomed *In Memoriam* warmly. Such opposition as existed may be represented here by George Gilfillan (1813–78): 'Nor do we admire so much as the public his "In Memoriam". It is a succession of fine quaint moralisings, with many timid gleams of thought, but with no adequate subject, no consecutive power, no new insight, no free, strong motion, no real unity, and discovering rather an elaborate and imitative ingenuity than original genius' ('Alfred Tennyson', *Galleries of Literary Portraits* (1856), i. 230). At a later date, Tennyson spoke of the poem to James Knowles: '*It is rather the cry of the whole human race than mine. In the poem altogether private grief swells out into thought of, and hope for, the whole world. It begins with a funeral and ends with a marriage—begins with death and ends in promise of a new life—a sort of Divine Comedy, cheerful at the close. It is a very impersonal poem as well as personal. There is more about myself in "Ulysses", which was written under the sense of loss and that all had gone by, but that still life must be fought out to the end. It was more written with the feeling of his loss upon me than many poems in "In Memoriam". . . . It's too hopeful, this poem, more than I am myself.*' (Knowles, 'Aspects of Tennyson, II', *Nineteenth Century* (January 1893), xxxiii. 182). The cuts made in Kingsley's review for present purposes do not significantly affect his discussion of Tennyson.

Critics cannot in general be too punctilious in their respect for an *incognito*. If an author intended us to know his name, he would put it on his title-page. If he does not choose to do that, we have no more right to pry into his secret than we have to discuss his family affairs or open his letters. But every rule has its exceptional cases; and the book which stands first upon our list is surely such. All the world, somehow or other, knows the author. His name has been mentioned unhesitatingly by several reviews already, whether from private information, or from the certainty which every well-read person must feel, that there is but one man in England possessed at once of poetic talent and artistic experience sufficient for so noble a creation. We hope, therefore, that we shall not be considered impertinent if we ignore an incognito which all England has ignored before us, and attribute *In Memoriam* to the pen of the author of *The Princess*.

Such a course will probably be the more useful one to our readers; for this last work of our only living great poet seems to us at once the culmination of all his efforts and the key to many difficulties in his former writings. Heaven forbid that we should say that it completes the circle of his powers. On the contrary, it gives us hope of vaster effort in new fields of thought and forms of art. But it brings the development of his Muse and of his Creed to a positive and definite point. It enables us to claim one who has been hitherto regarded as belonging to a merely speculative and peirastic school as the willing and deliberate champion of vital Christianity, and of an orthodoxy the more sincere because it has worked upward through the abyss of doubt; the more mighty for good because it justifies and consecrates the æsthetics and the philosophy of the present age. We are sure, moreover, that the author, whatever right reasons he may have had for concealing his own name, would have no quarrel against us for alluding to it, were he aware of the absolute idolatry with which every utterance of his is regarded by the cultivated young men of our day, especially at the universities, and of the infinite service of which this *In Memoriam* may be to them, if they are taught by it that their superiors are not ashamed of Faith, and that they will rise instead of falling, fulfil instead of denying the cravings of their hearts and intellects, if they will pass upwards with their teacher from the vague though noble expectations of 'Locksley Hall', to the assured and everlasting facts of the proem to *In Memoriam*,—in our eyes, the noblest Christian poem which England has produced for two centuries.

To explain our meaning, it will be necessary, perhaps, to go back to

Mr. Tennyson's earlier writings, of which he is said to be somewhat ashamed now—a fastidiousness with which we will not quarrel; for it should be the rule of the poet as well as of the apostle, 'forgetting those things which are behind, to press on to those things which are before', and 'to count not himself to have apprehended, but' —— no, we will not finish the quotation: let the readers of *In Memoriam* finish it for themselves, and see how after all the poet, if he would reach perfection, must be found by Him who found St. Paul of old. In the meantime, as the poet must necessarily be in advance of his age, Mr. Tennyson's earlier poems, rather than these latter ones, coincide with the tastes and speculations of the young men of this day. And in proportion, we believe, as they thoroughly appreciate the distinctive peculiarities of those poems, will they be able to follow the author of them on his upward path.

Some of our readers, we would fain hope, remember as an era in their lives the first day on which they read those earlier poems; how, fifteen years ago, 'Mariana in the Moated Grange', 'The Dying Swan', 'The Lady of Shalott', came to them as revelations. They seemed to themselves to have found at last a poet who promised not only to combine the cunning melody of Moore, the rich fulness of Keats, and the simplicity of Wordsworth, but one who was introducing a method of observing Nature different from that of all the three, and yet succeeding in everything which they had attempted, often in vain.

. . . Mr. Tennyson . . . seems, like most other great artists, to have first tried imitations of various styles which already existed, before he learnt the art of incorporating them into his own, and learning from all his predecessors, without losing his own individual peculiarities. But there are descriptive passages . . . also which neither Keats nor Wordsworth could have written, combining the honest sensuous observation which is common to them both, with a self-restrained simplicity which Keats did not live long enough to attain, and a stately and accurate melody, an earnest songfulness (to coin a word) which Wordsworth seldom attained, and from his inaccurate and uncertain ear, still seldomer preserved without the occurrence of a jar or a rattle, a false quantity, a false rapture, or a bathos. And above all, or rather beneath all—for we suspect that this has been throughout the very secret of Mr. Tennyson's power—there was a hushed and a reverent awe, a sense of the mystery, the infinitude, the awfulness, as well as of the mere beauty of wayside things, which invested these poems as wholes with a peculiar richness, depth, and majesty of *tone*, beside which both Keats's and Wordsworth's methods of handling pastoral subjects looked like the colouring of Julio Romano or Watteau, by the side of Correggio or Titian.

This deep, simple faith in the divineness of Nature as she appears, which, in our eyes, is Mr. Tennyson's *differentia*, is really the natural accompaniment of a quality at first sight its very opposite, and for which he is often blamed by a prosaic world; namely, his subjective and transcendental mysticism. It is the mystic, after all, who will describe Nature most simply, because he sees most in her; because he is most ready to believe that she will reveal to others the same message which she has revealed to him. Men like Boehme, Novalis, and Fourier, who can soar into the inner cloud-world of man's spirit, even though they lose their way there, dazzled by excess of wonder—men who, like Wordsworth, can give utterance to such subtle anthropologic wisdom as the 'Ode to the Intimations of Immortality', will for that very reason most humbly and patiently 'consider the lilies of the field, how they grow'. And even so it is just because Mr. Tennyson is, far more than Wordsworth, mystical, and what an ignorant and money-getting generation, idolatrous of mere sensuous activity, calls 'dreamy', that he has become the greatest naturalistic poet which England has seen for several centuries: the same faculty which enabled him to draw such subtle subjective pictures of womanhood as 'Adeline', 'Isabel', and 'Eleänore' enabled him to see, and, therefore simply to describe in one of the most distinctive and successful of his earlier poems, how

> The creeping mosses and clambering weeds,
>   And the willow branches hoar and dank,
> And the wavy swell of the soughing reeds,
>   And the wave-worn horns of the echoing bank,
> And the silvery marish-flowers that throng
> The desolate creeks and pools among,
> Were flooded over with eddying song.

No doubt there are in the earlier poems exceptions to this style,—attempts to adorn Nature, and dazzle with a barbaric splendour akin to that of Keats,—as, for instance, in the 'Recollections of the Arabian Nights'. But how cold and gaudy, in spite of individual beauties, is that poem by the side of either of the 'Marianas', and especially of that one in which the scenery is drawn, simply and faithfully, from those

counties which the world considers the quintessence of the prosaic—
the English fens.

> Upon the middle of the night
>   Waking she heard the night-fowl crow;
> The cock sung out an hour ere light:
>   From the dark fen the oxen's low
> Came to her: without hope of change,
>   In sleep she seem'd to walk forlorn,
>   Till cold winds woke the grey-eyed morn
> About the lonely moated grange.
>
> About a stone-cast from the wall
>   A sluice with blacken'd waters slept,
> And o'er it many, round and small,
>   The cluster'd marish-mosses crept.
> Hard by a poplar shook alway,
>   All silver-green with gnarled bark,
>   For leagues no other tree did dark
> The level waste, the rounding gray.

Throughout all these exquisite lines occurs but one instance of what
the vulgar call 'poetic diction'. All is simple description, in short and
Saxon words, and yet who can deny the effect to be perfect—superior
to almost any similar passage in Wordsworth? And why? Because the
passage quoted, and indeed the whole poem, is perfect in what artists
call *tone*—tone in the metre and in the sound of the words, as well as
in the images and the feelings expressed. The weariness, the dreariness,
the dark mysterious waste, exist alike within and without, in the slow
monotonous pace of the metre and the words, as well as in the boundless
fen, and the heart of her who, 'without hope of change, in sleep did
seem to walk forlorn'. The same faith in Nature, the same instinctive
correctness in melody, springing from that correct insight into Nature,
ran through the poems inspired by mediæval legends. The very spirit
of the old ballad writers, with their combinations of mysticism and
objectivity, their freedom from any self-conscious attempt at reflective
epithets or figures, runs through them all. We are never jarred in them,
as we are in all the attempts at ballad-writing and ballad-restoring
before Mr. Tennyson's time, by discordant touches of the reflective in
thought, the picturesque in Nature, or the theatric in action. To
illustrate our meaning, readers may remember the ballad of 'Fair
Emmeline', in Bishop Percy's *Reliques*. The bishop confesses, if we
mistake not, to have patched the end of the ballad. He need not have

informed us of that fact, while such lines as these following met our
eyes,—

> The Baron turned aside,
> And wiped away the rising tears
> He proudly strove to hide (!!!)

Conceive an old ballad writer dealing in such a complicated concetto!
As another, and even a worse instance, did any of our readers ever
remark the difference between the old and new versions of the grand
ballad of 'Glasgerion'? In the original, we hear how the elfin harper
could

> Harp fish out of the water,
> And water out of a stone,
> And milk out of a maiden's breast
> That bairn had never none.

For which some benighted 'restorer' substitutes,—

> Oh, there was magic in his touch,
> And sorcery in his string!

No doubt there was. But while the new *poetaster* informs you of the
abstract notion, the ancient *poet* gives you the concrete fact; as Mr.
Tennyson has done with wonderful art in his exquisite 'St. Agnes',
where the saint's subjective mysticism appears only as embodied in
objective pictures,—

> *Break up the heavens*, oh, Lord! and *far*
> Through all *yon starlight keen*
> Draw me, thy bride, *a glittering star*,
> In *raiment white* and clean.

Sir Walter Scott's ballads fail just on the same point. Even Campbell
cannot avoid an occasional false note of sentiment. In Mr. Tennyson
alone, as we think, the spirit of the middle age is perfectly reflected.—
Its delight, not in the 'sublime and picturesque', but in the green leaves
and spring flowers for their own sake,—the spirit of Chaucer and of
the *Robin Hood Garland*,—the naturalism which revels as much in the
hedgerow and garden as in alps, and cataracts, and Italian skies, and
the other strong stimulants to the faculty of admiration which the
palled taste of an unhealthy age, from Keats and Byron down to
Browning, has rushed abroad to seek. It is enough for Mr. Tennyson's
truly English spirit to see how

On either side the river lie
Long fields of barley and of rye,
That clothe the wold and meet the sky;
And through the field the road runs by
    To many-tower'd Camelot.

Or how,

In the stormy east-wind straining,
The pale yellow woods were waning,
The broad stream in his banks complaining,
Heavily the low sky raining
    Over tower'd Camelot.

Give him but such scenery as that, which he can see in every parish
in England, and he will find it a fit scene for an ideal myth, subtler
than a casuist's questionings, deep as the deepest heart of woman.

But in this earlier volume we have only the *disjecta membra poetæ*.
The poet has not yet arrived at the art of combining his new speculations on man with his new mode of viewing Nature. His objective
pieces are too exclusively objective, his subjective too exclusively
subjective; and where he deals with natural imagery in these latter, he
is too apt, as in 'Eleänore', to fall back upon the old and received method
of poetic diction, though he never indulges in a commonplace or a
stock epithet. But in the interval between 1830 and 1842 the needful
interfusion of the two elements took place. And in 'Locksley Hall'
and the 'Two Voices' we find the new doubts and questions of the time
embodied naturally and organically, in his own method of simple
natural expression. For instance, from the 'Search for Truth' in the
'Two Voices',—

Cry, faint not, climb: the summits slope
Beyond the furthest flights of hope,
Wrapt in dense cloud from base to cope.

Sometimes a little corner shines,
As over rainy mist inclines
A gleaming crag with belts of pines.

'I will go forward,' sayest thou;
'I shall not fail to find her now.
Look up, the fold is on her brow.'

Or, again, in 'Locksley Hall', the poem which, as we think deservedly, has had most influence on the minds of the young men of our
day,—

Eager-hearted as a boy when first he leaves his father's field,
And at night along the dusky highway near and nearer drawn,
Sees in heaven the light of London flaring like a dreary dawn;
And his spirit leaps within him to be gone before him then,
Underneath the light he looks at, in among the throngs of men;
Men, my brothers, men the workers, ever reaping something new:
That which they have done but earnest of the things which they
 shall do:

and all the grand prophetic passage following, which is said, we know
not how truly, to have won for the poet the respect of that great
statesman whose loss all good men this day deplore.

In saying that 'Locksley Hall' has deservedly had so great an influence
over the minds of the young, we shall, we are afraid, have offended
some who are accustomed to consider that poem as Werterian and
unhealthy. But, in reality, the spirit of the poem is simply anti-
Werterian. It is man rising out of sickness into health,—not conquered
by Werterism, but conquering his selfish sorrow, and the moral and
intellectual paralysis which it produces, by faith and hope,—faith in
the progress of science and civilization, hope in the final triumph of
good. Doubtless, that is not the highest deliverance,—not a permanent
deliverance at all. Faith in God and hope in Christ alone can deliver a
man once and for all, from Werterism, or any other moral disease;
that truth was reserved for *In Memoriam*: but as far as 'Locksley Hall'
goes, it is a step forward—a whole moral æon beyond Byron and
Shelley; and a step, too, in the right direction, just because it *is* a step
forward,—because the path of deliverance is, as 'Locksley Hall' sets
forth, not backwards towards a fancied paradise of childhood—not
backward to grope after an unconsciousness which is now impossible,
an implicit faith which would be unworthy of the man, but forward
on the road on which God has been leading him, carrying upward with
him the aspirations of childhood, and the bitter experience of youth,
to help the organized and trustful labour of manhood. There are, in
fact, only two deliverances from Werterism possible in the nineteenth
century; one is into Popery, and the other is—

Forward, forward, let us range;
Let the peoples spin for ever down the ringing grooves of change;
Through the shadow of the world we sweep into the younger day:
Better fifty years of Europe than a cycle of Cathay.

But such a combination of powers as Mr. Tennyson's naturally
develope themselves into a high idyllic faculty; for it is the very essence

of the idyl to set forth the poetry which lies in the simpler manifesta-tions of Man and Nature; yet not explicitly, by a reflective moralizing on them, as almost all our idyllists—Cowper, Gray, Crabbe, and Wordsworth—have been in the habit of doing, but implicitly, by investing them all with a rich and delightful tone of colouring, perfect grace of manner, perfect melody of rhythm, which, like a gorgeous summer atmosphere, shall glorify without altering the most trivial and homely sights. And it is this very power, as exhibited in the 'Lord of Burleigh', 'Audley Court', and the 'Gardener's Daughter', which has made Mr. Tennyson, not merely the only English rival of Theo-critus and Bion, but, in our opinion, as much their superior as modern England is superior to ancient Greece.

Yet in *The Princess*, perhaps, Mr. Tennyson rises higher still. The idyllic manner alternates with the satiric, the pathetic, even the sublime, by such imperceptible gradations, and continual delicate variations of key, that the harmonious medley of his style becomes the fit outward expression of the bizarre and yet harmonious fairy-land, in which his fancy ranges. In this work, too, Mr. Tennyson shows himself more than ever the poet of the day. In it more than ever the old is interpenetrated with the new—the domestic and scientific with the ideal and senti-mental. He dares, in every page, to make use of modern words and notions, from which the mingled clumsiness and archaism of his com-peers shrinks, as unpoetical. Though, as we just said, his stage is an ideal fairy-land, yet he has reached the ideal by the only true method,—by bringing the Middle age forward to the Present one, and not by ignor-ing the Present to fall back on a cold and galvanized Mediævalism; and thus he makes his 'Medley' a mirror of the nineteenth century, pos-sessed of its own new art and science, its own new temptations and aspirations, and yet grounded on, and continually striving to reproduce, the forms and experiences of all past time. The idea, too, of *The Princess* is an essentially modern one. In every age women have been tempted, by the possession of superior beauty, intellect, or strength of will, to deny their own womanhood, and attempt to stand alone as men, whether on the ground of political intrigue, ascetic saintship, or philo-sophic pride. Cleopatra and St. Hedwiga, Madame de Staël and the Princess, are merely different manifestations of the same self-willed and proud longing of woman to unsex herself, and realize, single and self-sustained, some distorted and partial notion of her own as to what the 'angelic life' should be. Cleopatra acted out the pagan idea of an angel; St. Hedwiga, the mediæval one; Madame de Staël hers, with the peculiar notions of her time as to what *'spirituel'* might mean; and in *The Princess* Mr. Tennyson has embodied the ideal of that nobler, wider, purer, yet equally fallacious, because equally unnatural analogue, which we may meet too often up and down England now. He shows us the woman, when she takes her stand on the false masculine ground of intellect, working out her own moral punishment, by destroying in herself the tender heart of flesh: not even her vast purposes of philanthropy can preserve her, for they are built up, not on the womanhood which God has given her, but on her own self-will; they change, they fall, they become inconsistent, even as she does herself, till, at last, she loses all feminine sensibility; scornfully and stupidly she rejects and misunderstands the heart of man; and then falling from pride to sternness, from sternness to sheer inhumanity, she punishes sisterly love as a crime, robs the mother of her child, and becomes all but a vengeful fury, with all the peculiar faults of woman, and none of the peculiar excellencies of man.

The poem being, as its title imports, a medley of jest and earnest, allows a metrical license, of which we are often tempted to wish that its author had not availed himself; yet the most unmetrical and apparently careless passages flow with a grace, a lightness, a colloquial ease and frolic, which perhaps only heighten the effect of the serious parts, and serve as a foil to set off the unrivalled finish and melody of these latter. In these come out all Mr. Tennyson's instinctive choice of tone, his mastery of language, which always fits the right word to the right thing, and that word always the simplest one, and the perfect ear for melody which makes it superfluous to set to music poetry which, read by the veriest schoolboy, makes music of itself. The poem, we are glad to say, is so well-known that it seems unnecessary to quote from it; yet there are here and there gems of sound and expression of which, however well our readers may know them, we cannot forbear reminding them again. For instance, the end of the Idyl in book vii., beginning 'Come down, O maid' (the whole of which is perhaps one of the most perfect fruits of the poet's genius):—

> Myriads of rivulets hurrying through the lawn,
> The moan of doves in immemorial elms,
> And murmuring of innumerable bees.

Who, after three such lines, will talk of English as a harsh and clumsy language, and seek in the effeminate and monotonous Italian for expressive melody of sound? Who cannot *hear* in them the rapid rippling of the water, the stately calmness of the wood-dove's note, and, in the repetition of short syllables and soft liquids in the last line, the

> Murmuring of innumerable bees?

Or again, what extraordinary combination of richness with simplicity in such a passage as this:—

> Breathe upon my brows;
> In that fine air I tremble, all the past
> Melts mist-like into this bright hour, and this
> I scarce believe, and all the rich to come
> Reels, as the golden Autumn woodland reels
> Athwart the smoke of burning leaves.

How Mr. Tennyson can have attained the prodigal fulness of thought and imagery which distinguishes this poem, and especially the last canto, without his style ever becoming overloaded, seldom even confused, is perhaps one of the greatest marvels of the whole production. The songs themselves, which have been inserted between the cantos in the last edition of the book, seem, perfect as they are, wasted and smothered among the surrounding fertility; till we discover that they stand there, not merely for the sake of their intrinsic beauty, but serve to call back the reader's mind, at every pause in the tale of the princess's folly, to that very healthy ideal of womanhood which she had spurned.

[Quotes, with comments, 'As thro' the land at eve we went' from *The Princess*, ii; 'Sweet and low' from *The Princess*, iii; and 'Ask me no more: the moon may draw the sea' from *The Princess*, vii.]

We now come to ... *In Memoriam*; a collection of poems on a vast variety of subjects, but all united, as their name implies, to the memory of a departed friend. We know not whether to envy more—the poet the object of his admiration, or that object the monument which has been consecrated to his nobleness. For in this latest and highest volume, written at various intervals during a long series of years, all the poet's peculiar excellencies, with all that he has acquired from others, seem to have been fused down into a perfect unity, and brought to bear on his subject with that care and finish which only a labour of love can inspire. We only now know the whole man, all his art, all his insight, all his faculty of discerning the *più nell' uno*, and the *uno nel più*. As he says himself:—

> My love has talked with rocks and trees,
> He finds on misty mountain-ground
> His own vast shadow glory-crowned;
> He sees himself in all he sees.

Everything reminds him of the dead. Every joy or sorrow of man, every aspect of nature, from

> The forest crack'd, the waters curl'd
> The cattle huddled on the lea,

to

> The thousand waves of wheat
> That ripple round the lonely grange.

In every place where in old days they had met and conversed; in every dark wrestling of the spirit with the doubts and fears of manhood, throughout the whole outward universe of nature, and the whole inward universe of spirit, the soul of his dead friend broods—at first a memory shrouded in blank despair, then a living presence, a ministering spirit, answering doubts, calming fears, stirring up noble aspirations, utter humility, leading the poet upward step by step to faith, and peace, and hope. Not that there runs throughout the book a conscious or organic method. The poems seem often merely to be united by the identity of their metre, so exquisitely chosen, that while the major rhyme in the second and third lines of each stanza gives the solidity and self-restraint required by such deep themes, the mournful minor rhyme of each first and fourth line always leads the ear to expect something beyond, and enables the poet's thoughts to wander sadly on, from stanza to stanza and poem to poem, in an endless chain of

> Linked sweetness long drawn out.

There are records of risings and fallings again, of alternate cloud and sunshine, throughout the book; earnest and passionate, yet never bitter; humble, yet never abject; with a depth and vehemence of affection 'passing the love of woman', yet without a taint of sentimentality; self-restrained and dignified, without ever narrowing into artificial coldness; altogether rivalling the sonnets of Shakespeare.—Why should we not say boldly, surpassing—for the sake of the superior faith into which it rises, for the sake of the proem at the opening of the volume—in our eyes, the noblest English Christian poem which several centuries have seen?

But we must quote, and let the poet tell his own tale; though the very poems which we should most wish to transcribe are just those about which we feel a delicacy, perhaps morbid, in dissecting critically before the public eye. They are fit only to be read solemnly in our purest and most thoughtful moods, in the solitude of our chamber, or by the side of those we love, with thanks to the great heart who has taken courage to bestow on us the record of his own love, doubt, and triumph.

We shall make no comments on our extracts. It were an injustice to the poet to think they needed any.

[Quotes *In Memoriam*, v, xix, lx, lxx, lxxxvi, lxxxviii, xciii, ci, cvi, cxviii, cxxix, cxxxi.]

From the proem, or from the exquisite epithalamium at the end of the volume, we shall not quote; they are too long to be inserted at length, and too perfect wholes for us to mar them by any curtailment.

It has been often asked why Mr. Tennyson's great and varied powers had never been concentrated on one immortal work. The epic, the lyric, the idyllic faculties, perhaps the dramatic also, seemed to be all there, and yet all sundered, scattered about in small fragmentary poems. *In Memoriam*, as we think, explains the paradox. Mr. Tennyson could not write an epos or a drama while he was living one. It was true, as people said, that his secluded habits had shut him out from that knowledge of human character necessary for the popular dramatist; but he had been talking all the while with angels. Within the unseen world which underlies and explains this mere time-shadow, which men call Reality and Fact, he had been going down into the depths, and ascending into the heights, led, like Dante of old, by the guiding of a mighty spirit. And in this volume, the record of seventeen years, we have the result of those spiritual experiences in a form calculated, as we believe, to be a priceless benefit to many an earnest seeker in this generation, and perhaps to stir up some who are priding themselves on a cold dilettantism and barren epicurism, into something like a living faith and hope. Blessed and delightful it is to find, that even in these new ages the creeds which so many fancy to be at their last gasp, are still the final and highest succour, not merely of the peasant and the outcast, but of the subtle artist and the daring speculator! Blessed it is to find the most cunning poet of our day able to combine the complicated rhythm and melody of modern times with the old truths which gave heart to martyrs at the stake, to see in the science and the history of the nineteenth century new and living fulfilments of the words which we learnt at our mothers' knee! Blessed, thrice blessed, to find that hero-worship is not yet passed away; that the heart of man still beats young and fresh; that the old tales of David and Jonathan, Damon and Pythias, Socrates and Alcibiades, Shakespeare and his nameless friend, of 'love passing the love of woman', ennobled by its own humility, deeper than death, and mightier than the grave, can still blossom out if it be but in one heart here and there to show men still how sooner or later 'he that loveth knoweth God, for God is Love!'

14. Goldwin Smith

'The War Passages in

Maud' [1855]

Goldwin Smith, 'The War Passages in "Maud" ' (unsigned article), *Saturday Review* (3rd November 1855), i. 14–15.

Smith (1823–1910), a Liberal controversialist of puritanic fervour, was a guest of Lady Ashburton at the end of 1855, when Tennyson was also present. 'I cannot say I find his presence particularly annoying', wrote Tennyson to his wife with evident surprise (Sir Charles Tennyson, *op. cit.*, p. 290).

Our readers will allow us to say a few words on these passages, regarded merely in a moral and poetical point of view, without the slightest reference to the present question of peace or war.

To the hero of *Maud* himself, indeed, the justice of the war is only a parenthesis between more real motives—

> And as months ran on, and rumour of battle grew,
> It is time, it is time, O passionate heart, said I,
> (For I cleaved to a cause that I felt to be pure and true,)
> It is time, O passionate heart and morbid eye,
> That old hysterical mock-disease should die.

The relief of the passionate heart and morbid eye is his first object. What he wants is not a just and necessary war, but war in itself—war, as a cure, first, for the Mammonism of a nation which has still enough of the spiritual left in it to produce and honour a great poet, and secondly, for the hysterical mock-disease of a heart-broken and, one must add, guilty man.

To the glorification of war as a remedy for the canker of peace, the common sense of the nation, even of the most warlike part of it, has answered, that war, though to be faced, and even to be accepted with enthusiasm, for other ends, is not to be incurred for this. The violent passions scarcely suspend, much less do they cure, the mean ones. Strahan, Paul, and Co. did not change their ways when we sat down before Sebastopol. Swindling, burglary, adulteration of food, wife-beating, are as rife as ever. To the common list of rogueries you have to add those of commissaries and contractors. The poor are more ground than ever when taxes drain the charities, and bread is high. As for stock-jobbing, which drove the father of the hero to suicide, and the hero himself to misanthropy, war is the element in which it revels. The heart of the *bulls* does not 'beat with the same desire' as that of the *bears*, nor does the heart of the Opposition beat with the same desire as that of the Government, unless it be desire of the same places.

People have felt also that the moral blister of war is rather partially applied. We do not, like the nations of antiquity to whom Tyrtæus sung, literally *go* to war. We send our hired soldiers to attack a nation which may not be in need of the same regimen as ourselves. To most of us, the self-sacrifice involved in war with an enemy who cannot get at us consists in paying rather more taxes. Mr. Tennyson paints him-self, in the 'Lines to the Rev. F. D. Maurice', sitting with his friend in a charming cottage in the Isle of Wight, and chatting of the war over his wine, while the men-of-war sailing outwards lend another charm to the beautiful sea view. This blister is not very severe, and therefore it cannot be very efficacious.

That which, however, has rather escaped notice is the consilience between the two passages—that in which war is called in to cure the vices of a nation, and that in which it is called in to cure a broken heart —and the connexion of both with the general philosophy of Mr. Tennyson's poems. In both cases, an external sensation—and that a sensation to be obtained at a terrible cost to others—is sought where an internal effort is the obvious and the true cure. Let the nation commence the work of self-reform; let it choose better rulers, make better laws, transport swindlers, institute a strict medical police. Let the hero who has compromised a woman's character by his selfishness, and killed her brother, try a more natural mode of regaining peace of mind than that of shedding more blood and inflicting more misery on the world. This is the better course—it is also the more poetical. To wage 'war with a thousand battles and shaking a hundred thrones', in order to cure a hypochondriac and get rid of the chicory in coffee, is a bathos.

To rely on external sensations instead of internal efforts for a moral cure, is natural to that character which, whether dramatically or otherwise, is presented to us throughout Mr. Tennyson's poems—sometimes directly as in *Maud* and 'Locksley Hall', everywhere as the medium through which the world is viewed. It is the character of a man of high intellect and exquisite sensibility, keenly alive to all impressions, but wanting in the power of action and active sympathies, dependent on the world without him for happiness, and cynical because it is not afforded. Not once throughout the poems is active life painted with real zest. Not once are we called to witness the happiness or the moral cures which result from self-exertion. Everywhere we feel the force of circumstances, nowhere the energy of free will. The meditated suicide in the 'Two Voices' is arrested, not by an effort of reason or an act of faith, but by the sound of the church bells, and the sight of happy people going to church. Women seem to have no function but that of casting out the demon of hypochondria from the breast of the solitary, and relieving him of the melancholy which flows to him from all around him—from his home and history, from nature, from philosophy, from science. They are the 'counter-charms of space and hollow sky', without active life or interests of their own; we can scarcely think of them as wives, much less as daughters or as mothers. Marriage itself, though painted as the gate of virtue and happiness, seems to lead, not from melancholy listlessness into activity, but only from an unhappy dream into a happy one. We see the visionary and his wife in the 'Miller's Daughter', leading the life of lotus eaters. Even children would bore them. They have had one, which has died, and become a pensive reminiscence, adding the luxury of melancholy to their happy thoughts, as they sit at evening looking into each other's eyes, or wander out to see the sunset.

You may trace the hues of this character tinging everything in the poems. Even the Homeric Ulysses, the man of purpose and action, seeking with most definite aim to regain his own home and that of his companions, becomes a 'hungry heart', roaming aimlessly to 'lands beyond the sunset', in the vain hope of being 'washed down by the gulf to the Happy Isles', merely to relieve his *ennui*, and dragging his companions with him. We say he roams aimlessly—we should rather say, he intends to roam, but stands for ever a listless and melancholy figure on the shore. Even in *In Memoriam*, the deepest and most beautiful, in our opinion, of all Mr. Tennyson's works, we have the image of a mind abandoning itself to a noble but vain regret, without a thought of offering, by good action, the highest tribute to the beloved and lamented shade.

It is natural to such a character to be averse to the mental efforts which lead to conviction, as well as to the moral efforts which lead to action. He may be keenly alive to the picturesque in philosophy and theology as well as in nature. He may paint exquisitely all the phases of historical character as well as all the aspects of nature. He may draw knights-errant and saints as well as modern philosophers, though he will turn them all into still life, as he turns the flash of the cannon into 'the blood-red blossom of war with a heart of fire'. But his own philosophy is to leave that which is amiss in the world to unriddle itself by-and-by. Death, not reason, for him, keeps the keys of all the creeds. In politics he does not care whether it is aristocrat, democrat, or auto-crat, so long as there is a strong man to save him from the necessity of performing the active duties of a citizen.

Such a character has in it some pure and noble elements. It is one for which, where all is imperfect, the world will often have reason to be grateful. It is one in which, when presented by Mr. Tennyson with all the luxury of melancholy and cynicism, every man of sensibility must feel a deep and even painful interest. We will not stop to ask whether the poems in which all the morbid tendencies and cravings of such men find their full indulgence do more to heal or increase the malady. But thus much must be clear to every man who has sense as well as sensi-bility, that this is not the right medium through which to view the world for serious purposes—that it is not to satisfy the cravings of such a character that we can rightly bring war upon mankind. The only right judge in such questions is a mind which decides by the rule of active duty and practical religion.

We do not for a moment charge the author of *Maud* with in-humanity, though he speaks somewhat lightly of 'the heart of the citizen hissing on his hearthstone'; and there are other passages in the poem which show that he is endowed not only with the 'love of love', but also with the 'hate of hate' and the 'scorn of scorn'. He has too much sense and solidity of intellect not to know that the manhood of a poet, if it is a little compromised by the softness of his calling, must be redeemed, not by talking lightly of blood, but by true tenderness, self-control, obedience to the moral law, and fidelity to the end of his mission, such as lent heroism to the soft and, in some respects, weak nature of Wordsworth. A painful impression has been created in the minds of some readers by that which appears to be bloodthirstiness, because it is unconnected with any general activity of political or social aspirations. In Milton, Byron, Shelley, Wordsworth, a passionate cry for a just war would have seemed like the foam on the wave—in Mr. Tennyson it seems a little like the foam without the wave.

In rejecting the author of *Maud* as a practical adviser, let us render full, though superfluous, homage to his poetical powers. Only on the theory that a moral purpose is indispensable to poetry, can it be denied that he is one of the greatest of poets. His works are perhaps the most exquisite intellectual luxury the world ever enjoyed. His cynicism completes their exquisiteness; for the supreme luxury of an age like ours is a cynic. Only let us protest against any attempt to bring all poetry under the Tennysonian yoke. To say that we will accept no verses which are not as exquisitely elaborated as his, would be to shut the door against a great deal of enjoyment. There was a poet dear to the heart of antiquity, who sang

> Inter arma
> Sive jactatam religârat udo
> Littore navim.

Let such poets sing still, though they may not even have the leisure, to say nothing of the power, to contrive the exquisite harmonies, and distil the luscious language, which charm and almost overpower the sense in reading *Maud*, but which still leave us to wish for something nearer as well as more bracing to the heart.

15. G. Brimley on
Maud [*1855*]

George Brimley, from 'Alfred Tennyson's Poems', *Cambridge Essays* (1855), pp. 226–81.

Brimley (1819–57) was librarian of Trinity College, Cambridge. His essay contains a long, sensitive, and appreciative analysis of Tennyson's 'Morte d'Arthur'. It also contains a protest against the indiscriminate use in literary criticism of the term 'morbid', which 'has acquired a perfectly new meaning of late years, and is made to include all works of art, and all views of life that are coloured by other than comfortable feelings' (p. 260). His remarks on *Maud* (pp. 263–9) elicited a letter of approval from the poet (Hallam Tennyson, *op. cit.*, pp. 344–5).

. . . Nothing that can with any propriety be called morbid or unhealthy belongs to any of the great love poems in the [1842] collection; and surely the view of the relation of the sexes in *The Princess* is as sound a basis for a noble life as was ever propounded. It would be singular if, with such antecedents, Mr. Tennyson should, in the maturity of his intellect and experience, have descended to exhibit the influence of love upon a weak and worthless character, and have chosen for that purpose a melodramatic story of suicide, murder, and madness, dished up for popular applause with vehement invective on the vices of the English nation, and claptrap appeals to the war-feeling of the day. This, however, is what we are asked to believe of Mr. Tennyson's latest production, *Maud*, by the loudest professional critics of the journals and magazines. The critics give us some gauge of their opinion by tracing Mr. Tennyson's gradual degradation through *The Princess*, lower still in *In Memoriam*, to its climax of weakness and absurdity in *Maud*; and it is but justice to say that these opinions are not now for the first time put forth on the provocation of the last-named poem, but appear to be the deliberate convictions of the writers. We believe that both *The Princess* and *In Memoriam* are in their sixth edition, which, apart from private experience, necessarily limited, of the impression the works have produced, leads to the conclusion that these writers do not in this case fairly represent the opinion of the English public. Whether they represent it any better in respect to *Maud* remains to be seen. Meanwhile it is well not to be frightened out of the enjoyment of fine poetry, and out of the instruction to be gained from a great poet's views of life, as exhibited dramatically in the destiny of a particular sort of character subjected to a particular set of influences, by such epithets as 'morbid', 'hysterical', 'spasmodic', which may mean one thing or another, according to the sense, discrimination, and sympathy of the man who applies them.

There is little question as to the artistic merits of *Maud*. It is only the aim of the poet that has been assailed; his execution is generally admitted to be successful. It may be at once conceded that the writer of the fragments of a life which tell the story of *Maud*, is not in a comfortable state of mind when he begins his record; and that if a gentleman were to utter such sentiments at a board of railway directors, or at a marriage breakfast, he might not improperly be called hysterical. Like the hero of 'Locksley Hall', his view of the life around him, of the world in which his lot is cast, has been coloured by a grievous personal calamity; and the character of the man is originally one in which the sensibilities are keen and delicate, the speculative element strong, the practical judgment unsteady, the will and active energies comparatively feeble. A Shelley or a Keats may stand for example of his type; not perfect men, certainly, but scarcely so contemptible as not to possess both dramatic interest and some claim to human sympathy. Chatterton, a much lower type than either, has been thought a subject of psychological and moral interest, in spite or in consequence of the vulgar, petulant, weak melodrama of his life and death. You see, God makes these morbid, hysterical, spasmodic individuals occasionally, and they have various fates; some die without a sign; others try the world, and dash themselves dead against its bars; some few utter their passionate desires, their weak complaints, their ecstatic raptures in snatches of song that make the world delirious with delight,—and somehow, for their sake the class becomes interesting, and we are at times inclined to measure the spiritual capacity of an age by its treatment of these weak souls,—by the fact, whether the general constitution of society cherishes such souls into divine lovers and singers of the beautiful, or lashes and starves and chains them into moping idiots and howling madmen. The autobiographer of *Maud* belongs to this class by temperament, as anyone may understand from the turn of his angry thoughts to those social evils which must and ought to excite indignation and scorn in gentle and loving natures that are at the same time inspired with generous and lofty ideas; from the speculative enigmas he torments himself with at the prevalence of rapine and pain in creation, at the insignificance of man in a boundless universe, subject to iron laws; from the penetrating tenderness, the rich fancy, the childlike *naïveté* of his love for the young girl who saves him from himself and his dark dreams. There lies in such a character, from the beginning, the capacity for weakness and misery, for crime and madness. That capacity is inseparable from keen sensibility, powerful emotions, and active imagination; and if events happen which paralyze the will already feeble, turn the flow of feeling into a stream of bitterness, and present to the imagination a world of wrong and suffering, the capacity fulfils itself according to the force and direction of the events. In *Maud* the tendency meets with events that carry it on through these stages; and the question is, whether any one of these events is impossible or improbable, whether English society is misrepresented when it is made capable of furnishing the unwholesome nutriment for such a character. It would rather seem as if the only improbable incident in the whole story were that which redeems society from a wholesale charge; as if the daughter of the millionaire, the sister of 'the dandy-despot, the oiled and curled Assyrian bull', were the least likely character of the whole group. God be thanked, however, there are such girls; and many a noble woman—like the Princess Ida—has given her heart out of pity to a man whose energy and hope she saw crushed for want of sympathy, and would endorse these lines:

> Perhaps the smile and tender tone
>   Came out of her pitying womanhood,
> For am I not, am I not, here alone
>   So many a summer since she died,
> My mother, who was so gentle and good?

And many a man who seems to himself to be living on without motive, 'a death in life', could say,

> Ah! what shall I be at fifty,
>   Should Nature keep me alive,
> If I find the world so bitter
>   When I am but twenty-five?

Yet, if she were not a cheat,
If Maud were all that she seem'd,
And her smile were all that I dream'd,
Then the world were not so bitter
But a smile could make it sweet.

No doubt it is only weak characters who are affected in this way. To strong men the world is not made bitter by a father's ruin and suicide, by the prevalence of meanness and cruelty, by contemptuous neglect, and general absence of sympathy. Nor would a girl's smile atone to them for such calamities as do affect them. So weakness has its compensation.

But then, some one will say, if the poet's intention were to exhibit the restorative power of love over a delicate and beautiful mind overthrown by circumstances,

Like sweet bells jangled, out of tune, and harsh,—

and if, in respect to this intention, we allow the exhibition of the disease in order to feel the full force of the restoring influence, and of course are prepared that the love should be of a kind corresponding to the character,—rapturous, fanciful, childish, fitted more for a Southern woman like Juliet, as one of the best critics of *Maud* has remarked, than for an Englishman,—why does not the poet carry out his intention, and conduct his story to a happy close? Why, good sir or madam, does not Shakspeare let Juliet and her Romeo adorn Verona with troops of little Juliets and Romeos, to do as their papa and mamma did before them? Why does not Cordelia live to comfort Lear in his old age, restored to true appreciation of his daughters? Why does Ophelia drown in a ditch; and Hamlet, after murdering Polonius, die by chance medley? Why are not Othello's eyes opened before, instead of after his fatal deed, and he and Desdemona allowed to spend the rest of their days in peace and mutual trust? Is it, think you, because Shakspeare belongs to the hysterical, morbid, spasmodic school, and likes the violent excitement of melo-dramatic incident? We should be sorry to stake much upon the reception any of these poetic issues would meet with from certain critics, if they now for the first time came up for judgment. Perhaps in all these cases he had some vague design of moving certain passions which the older critics knew by the name of pity and terror, and to which one who was himself something of a poet—the author of *Samson Agonistes*—refers approvingly, on the authority of Aristotle, as the justifying motive of tragedy. Perhaps, too, he might think it his business, in delineating particular characters, to express in their destiny his view of the general condition of society, as tested by the fate and fortunes of such characters. And possibly Mr. Tennyson may think himself justified in presenting a story that does not end happily, for both these reasons. It may appear to him that 'the course of true love' would be unlikely to 'run smooth' under the circumstances of Maud and her lover, combined with the conditions of English modern life; that the man had not the coolness and self-control to master the circumstances; and that there was not in society the generosity and disregard of rank and money necessary to allow the restorative influence of Maud's affection to work out its cure. Divest the story for a moment of its lyric elevation, and compare it with our greatest novelist's treatment of a somewhat kindred case. Suppose Mr. Barnes Newcome had not been a coward as well as a brute, and had found his sister Ethel holding a *tête-à-tête* in the garden with her cousin Clive, after an evening party to which the Most Noble the Marquis of Farintosh had been invited expressly to conclude his courtship,—is it not possible that Mr. Barnes and his cousin might have enacted the scene between the 'Assyrian bull' and Maud's lover? The physical courage of the Assyrian bull is quite as true, to say the least, to the real types of his class as the physical cowardice of Barnes Newcome. But the object of the novelist not being to excite pity and terror, he developes the selfishness and Mammon-worship of English rich people to other consequences and in another direction. The poet takes his course, too, with equal effect towards carrying out his design, and without violating, so far as we see, the essential contemporary truth of his story; while he is thus enabled to exhibit some of the eternal elements of tragedy still in operation among us.

We need say nothing of the skill and beauty with which the remorse of the murderer is painted. The wonderful power of the strains in which the successive stages of this feeling are represented, is admitted on all hands. English literature has nothing more dramatically expressive of a mind on the verge of overthrow, than the verses in which the shell on the Brittany coast serves as text; nothing that presents the incipient stage of madness, springing from the wrecked affections, with more of reality and pathos than the poem, 'Oh! that 'twere possible', now recovered from the pages of a long-forgotten miscellany, and set as a jewel amid jewels; nothing that surpasses in truth and terrible force the madhouse soliloquy, 'Dead, long dead!' If the poem had ended there, 'the strangest anti-climax that we ever remember to have read' would not have offended the critic of *The Times*. We fear that in that case, true enough to nature as it might have been, the climax would have come in for blame of the opposite character, and the poet have been found fault with for leaving his readers to dwell upon horrible impressions without relief. We are sure that no poet deserving the name would choose such an ending where any other was possible. But men do recover from madness, and can—though with an awe-struck sense of their unfitness for life, a nervous apprehension that paralyzes energy and action,—be roused to interest themselves in something out of themselves and their miseries. And Mr. Tennyson, who introduces his hero breathing scorn and indignation on the meanness and littleness of a society, where the vices of individuals are not obscured and compensated by any conscious noble aim of the commonwealth, dismisses him, cheered and strengthened by knowing that the British nation has risen for a time to a consciousness of a great purpose,—has awaked out of its commercial epicureanism, and roused itself to fight a battle for the right and the good. In sympathy with a grand purpose and a high resolve animating his countrymen, the dreary phantom that had haunted him departs; he knows that his love has forgiven him the injury that his passionate heart caused her; and he can wait, calm and hopeful, till death re-unites them.

The fact is, that Mr. Tennyson, without abandoning his lyric forms, has in *Maud* written a tragedy—a work, that is, which demands to be judged, not by the intrinsic goodness and beauty of the actions and emotions depicted, but by their relation to character; that character, again, being not only an interesting study in itself and moving our sympathy, but being related dynamically to the society of the time which serves as the back-ground of the picture, and thus displaying the characteristics of the society by showing its influence, under particular circumstances, upon the character selected. Mr. Tennyson's critics have for the most part read the poem as if its purpose were to hold up an example for our imitation, and have condemned it because, viewed in this light, it offers nothing but a nature of over-excitable sensibilities, first rendered moody by misfortune, then driven mad by its own crime, and finally recovered to a weak exultation in a noble enterprise it has not the manliness to share. But no one feels that Shakspeare is immoral in making Othello kill himself; no one attributes the cynicism of Mephistopheles to Goethe. . . .

16. R. J. Mann on

Maud [1855]

Robert James Mann, from *Tennyson's 'Maud' Vindicated: An Explanatory Essay* (1856).

Mann (1817–86) was a popular scientific writer. Tennyson described his book on *Maud* as being 'as true as it is full' (Hallam Tennyson, *op. cit.*, p. 342). Rather less than one-third of it is reprinted here: a passage from near the beginning (pp. 6–9), Mann's fullest analysis of a single lyric (pp. 35–50), and a passage from near the end (pp. 71–75).

. . . A poet, who has long held a sure place in popular estimation, won for himself by long years of service, after due deliberation and a judicious exercise of the refined care which is an inherent characteristic of his nature, a few months since presented to the world a work which it is to be presumed he believed was worthy of favourable acceptance. The world, if it had been left to its own inclinations and tendencies, would no doubt have received this production of his fancy and intellect reverentially, and with some measure of gratitude—taking occasion, perchance, in its own slow-paced way to master the full purport of the work, but, in the meantime, giving credit both for sense and excellence, until its perceptions had been matured in the legitimate way, through reflection and study. The guild of critics, however, true to its traditions, and to its own idea of its craft, acted upon the assumption that it held the vested right of seeing at a glance what high genius had only perfected through the expenditure of prolonged and patient labour, and proceeded forthwith to deliver its Protean judgments. One member of the fraternity immediately pronounced the poem to be *a spasm*; another acutely discovered that it was a careless, visionary, and unreal *allegory of the Russian war*; a third could not quite make up his mind whether the adjective *mud* or *mad* would best apply to the work, but thought, as there was only one small vowel redundant in the title in either case, both might do. A fourth found that the mud concealed *irony*; and a fifth, leaning rather to the mad hypothesis, nevertheless held that the madness was only assumed as *an excuse for* pitching the tone of the poetry in *a key of extravagant sensibility*. Others of the multifold judgments were that it was *an ægis covering startling propositions* from too close philosophic scrutiny;—a *political fever*;—an *epidemic* caught from the prevalent carelessness of thought and rambling contemplativeness of the time;—*obscurity mistaken for profundity*;—the *dead level of prose run mad;—circumstance proclaimed dominant* over free-will; *matrimony exhibited* as the soother of troubled dreams;—*absurdity, such as even partial friendship must blush to tolerate,* (and, therefore, it is to be presumed, exceeding even the seemingly unapproachable accomplishments of criticism in this line;)—rampant and rabid *bloodthirstiness of soul.* These are but a few of the pleasant suggestions which critical acumen brought forward as its explanations of the inspiration of numbers that most nevertheless admitted to be musical. When time shall have accomplished its appointed task of beneficence,—the crumbling of dry and unvital substance into indistinguishable vapour and harmless dust, the statement will never be believed that such were the views professed critics offered as interpretations of the object and meaning of Mr. Tennyson's *Maud*, at the period of its first appearance. That they were so is, however, strictly, soberly, and sadly a literary fact.

To the high and impartial court of candid and enquiring readers, who desire to be free from those trammels of contradictory casuistry and shallow pretence, which are erroneously called criticism, the following earnest appeal is humbly, yet trustfully, tendered in behalf of the much abused, but much deserving *Maud*; and it is confidently anticipated that there is a very wide public to whom this simple résumé of the real argument, spirit, and purpose of the poem will prove a welcome companion and helpful guide.

Maud is a drama;—that is, an action;—in which an exquisite tale of love and sorrow is revealed in a form that bears upon itself the impress at once of consummate art, and of simple nature. The *dramatis persona* of the action,—for there is but one individual who is ever brought forward in it *in person*,—exhibits his story through the mental influences its several incidents work in himself, and this exhibition is made, not directly and connectedly, but, as it were, inferentially and interruptedly, through a series of distinct scenes, which are as varied as the circumstances involved. It is in this peculiarity of the poem,—the one person revealing to the reader his own sad and momentous history, by fits and starts, which are themselves but so many impulsive utterances naturally called forth from a mind strung to the pitch of keen poetic sensibility,—that its absolute originality and the surpassing skill of the Laureate are displayed. Nothing can be more exquisitely consonant to the proceedings of nature than that such utterances should be made in fitful and broken strains, rather than that they should march steadily on to the measure of equal lines, and regularly recurring rhymes. It is one of the necessities of the poet-temperament that it must feel, what it does feel, to its inmost core, and that it must speak, when it does speak, in words that are actually articulate casts of what it feels. Every utterance, whether it be of sentiment, passion, or reflection, is an impulsive outburst; but it is an outburst that involuntarily clothes itself in language of the most appropriate character and vivid power. Such, both in the matter of sense and of music, is the language of *Maud*. The syllables and lines of the several stanzas actually trip and halt with abrupt fervour, tremble with passion, swell with emotion, and dance with joy, as each separate phase of mental experience comes on the scene. The power of language to symbolize in sound mental states and perceptions, has never before been so magically proved. In the success-ful employment of this kind of word-music, the author of *Maud* stands entirely unrivalled, as, in its general form of severe dramatic uni-personality, the poem itself is absolutely unique.

But *Maud* is moral, as well as passionate and musical. The drama has a purpose towards which its successive scenes steadily conduct. This purpose is so finely conceived, and so subtlely enunciated, that it grows insensibly on the reader, until in the final movement of the action, he finds himself thoroughly possessed with it, although quite unable to determine when and how its perception was first caught. In this again consummate skill is shown. . . .

*   *   *

. . . And now at length the fervently desired hour has come, and passed. The confident lover has told his love to Maud, and has received from her lips the welcome assurance that he is accepted, and his spirit is consequently filled with satisfaction and calm content. The verses in which this consummation of joy is described, will in the future stand amongst the grandest and most enduring efforts of poetry. Every stanza in the scene is in itself an elaborate and finished work. There is not a single line which does not bear the closest scrutiny, both on the ground of form and sense.

But on this very account these stanzas are beyond the reach of careless and cursory readers. They are marked by the highest and subtlest qualities of the Laureate's genius, and are, indeed, especially illustrative of the one leading characteristic of Tennysonian poetry, which is *intellectual elaboration*. Every image which Mr. Tennyson receives from external nature, or conjures up from the mysterious recesses of his fancy, he retains in his mental alembic, subjecting it again and again to the processes of reflective analysis, until he has at last extracted a material, that is capable of being moulded into a form of severe perfection. It is only this ultimate result of refined and patient labour that he ever presents before the world. He is almost painfully alive to the truth that one perfect and forcible line is of more value than any length of common-place versification,—and it is his object to be the high artist, rather than the facile and prolific versifier. It is his long and leal allegiance to this principle that has given him his wonderful mastery over words. The epithets that he employs are to his mind as clear-cut and definite as regards meaning, as Maud's face is in the matter of the 'least little delicate curve of the aquiline nose'. But out of all this comes one consequence which appears to excite a considerable degree of astonishment, but which ought not to do so. It is this. Mr. Tennyson cannot be a *popular poet* in the ordinary and familiar sense of the term. The people does not yet comprehend precision of language. Nine-tenths of the words it employs, it actually does not know the *precise* meaning of. Carelessness and confusion of phraseology are predominant characteristics of the language of every-day life, and as yet popular education is doing next to nothing to remedy this defect. How then is it possible that a popular mind, thus trained, should be capable of comprehending at a glance, the condensed and finished meanings, which high genius has only been able to compass, after prolonged reflection and effort? The most worthy utterances of Mr. Tennyson's muse are objects that demand assiduous and close study, and not playthings that may be taken up for the amusement of a few leisure moments. But, on this account, Mr. Tennyson's public, notwithstanding its being occasionally a turbulent and somewhat ungracious one at first, is and will be also an ever enlarging one, waxing in appreciation and enthusiasm as its comprehension is widened, and its faculties are strengthened, by the exercise which he provides for its intellect and imagination. The Laureate consciously or unconsciously is even more a teacher than he is a singer; his songs are nearly all lessons in one sense or another. The exquisite but subtle stanzas, which are now im-

mediately under notice, are appealed to, as affording ample proof of the
accuracy of these views.

The immediate object of the 18th section or scene of the drama is
the exposition of the calming influence of love, upon an excitable
nature, before morose and cynical from circumstance. It exhibits the
morbid spirit of the recluse at length restored to health by the medicine
that has been appointed by the Great Physician of the Universe, for the
accomplishment of such healing. It is, as will be presently obvious, the
culminating point of the drama; the wave-crest to which the swell of
satisfied sympathies and affections has at last raised the newly acquired
happiness of the reclaimed and convalescent cynic. In it the purpose
of the poet, which was in the earlier passages revealed only in partial
and transient glimpses, at length stands fully declared and clear.

The one feature that dwells, soul-like, within the delicious lines of
these subtle stanzas—the all-pervading inspiration of their richly-
varied movements—is the sustained sense of absolute content and calm.
There is joyous rapture within them everywhere, but the rapture is still
and deep. The very first line is, in its smooth, long measure, the audible
symbol of perfect rest—

> I have led her home, my love, my only friend.

This is followed by the abrupt and fervid exclamation, so truthful in its
exaggerative earnestness—

> There is none like her, none.

The next thought that arises is naturally suggested by the physical
sensation which the now assured and satisfied lover experiences—

> And never yet so warmly ran my blood
> And sweetly, on and on,
> Calming itself to the long-wish'd-for end,

Here, the physical result of exalted emotion, the quickened movement
of the blood, and the glow of increased warmth necessarily produced
by it, are very beautifully made the concomitants of the spiritual state.
The augmented flow of mental life, and the more rapid coursing of the
blood-current, act and re-act upon each other. But both run on with
an energy that 'calms itself to the long-wished-for end'. The stream is
in neither case a turbulent and tumultuous one. It is 'Amazonian' in
mass and volume. It moves with a steady sweep, whose force is the
result of quantity and abundance, and not of mere transient impulse.
It runs '*full to the banks*, close on the promised good'. In the next stanza,

the fond thought that so expressively sums up the good fortune of
the soliloquizer, again breaks forth into utterance—

None like her, none.

This renewed allusion to the peerlessness of his love, leads to an appropriate illustration of the peerless one's power over him—

> Just now the dry-tongued laurels' pattering talk
> Seem'd her light foot along the garden walk,
> And *shook my heart* to think she comes once more;

It is by no means surprising that the rustling of the stiff laurel leaves in
the wind should suggest this fancy, for is not all nature for him now
filled in its every form and sound with the one image? The mere
thought that she might possibly be returning is in itself electrical to
nerves strung as his are. It shook his heart. The sound, however, is
only the rustling of the laurels. She does not return—

> But even then I heard her close the door,

and the consequence, so natural under the circumstances, ensues—

> *The gates of Heaven are closed*, and she is gone.

Once again, as if for the very abundance of joy that is found in the
pleasant utterance, he repeats—

> There is none like her, none.

But this triumphant assertion of her excellence has now acquired such
force from repetition, that it can no longer rest where it did before.
She is now the peerless of all futurity, as well as of the present.

> There is none like her, none.
> Nor *will be* when our summers have deceased.

The happy lover is standing, as he indulges this jubilant reverie, near to
the cedar that grows by the hall; the same, it will be remembered, that
is already associated with Maud by the ballad, 'gallant and gay'; and
suddenly its branches are stirred by a passing breeze. His excited ear
catches the gentle murmur, and in words that are as exquisite to the
sense, as their meaning is to the understanding, he says—

> O, art thou sighing for Lebanon
> In the long breeze that streams to thy delicious East,
> Sighing for Lebanon,
> Dark cedar,

The soft murmur of the steady western breeze comes to him as if it were a sigh from the tree expressing its sympathy with his state. The 'gates of heaven' have but recently closed for him, and the cedar too, like himself, must be yearning for some absent good,—for the slopes, perchance, of its native Lebanon. But why should the cedar yearn for Lebanon, when its lot has been cast in such auspicious environments?

> Sighing for Lebanon,
> Dark cedar, tho' thy limbs have here increased,
> Upon a pastoral slope as fair,
> And looking to the South, and fed
> With honey'd rain and delicate air,

In all this his own condition, during the temporary absence of Maud, is finely imaged—as is rendered apparent by the next lines, wherein he thus continues his address to the cedar—

> And haunted by the starry head
> Of *her whose gentle will has changed my fate,*
> And made my life a perfumed altar-flame;

The first idea of a similitude between his own state and the cedar's, glides into a fancy that there is a yet more intimate bond uniting them together. She who has been so great a good to himself, must have been felt as a blessing by the favourite cedar too; and the noble tree must have delighted in her, as its ancestral cedars of the garden of Eden did in her primeval mother, Eve, when *they* covered *her,* looking 'snow-limb'd' in the contrast, with their dark shadows—

> And over whom thy darkness must have spread
> With such delight as theirs of old, thy great
> Forefathers of the thornless garden, there
> Shadowing the snow-limb'd Eve from whom she came.

The cedar tree having thus so sympathetic an aspect for him, in his present mood, he throws himself down in the deepening twilight beneath its branches—

> Here will I lie, while these long branches sway,

Immediately his glance lights upon the brilliant stars twinkling through the foliage, and in pursuance of the harmonizing and amicable spirit that is now so actively astir within him, he invites them too to become partners in his joy—

> And you fair stars that crown a happy day
> Go in and out as if at merry play,

But he who lies beneath the twinkling of these merry playmates, is no longer so wretched as he used to be of old, when he looked up at them and wished he had been born to the fate of a day labourer, rather than to the privileges of a higher culture and intelligence. 'Here will I lie',

> Who am no more so all forlorn,
> As when it seem'd far better to be born
> To labour and the mattock-harden'd hand,
> Than nursed at ease

Those stars in the old astrology were powers that ruled over, and sympathized with, the destinies of man, but the intellectual culture to which he has been born, in the stead of uncultured ignorance, has replaced these views by the sadder astrology of modern astronomy, which shows that the celestial bodies follow their own courses, and have nothing to do with human affairs—

> And brought to understand
> A sad astrology, *the boundless plan*
> That makes you tyrants in your iron skies,
> *Innumerable, pitiless, passionless eyes,*
> *Cold fires.*

The science of the present age has proved that the fields through which the sidereal hosts are scattered, are infinite, or unbounded within the wonderful extent to which the senses and researches of philosophical enquiry have been able to reach,—that in these boundless spaces, the celestial orbs are without number,—and that they are also placed with such impassable gulfs of millions upon millions of miles intervening between them and the earth, that no available influence can flow from them to the terrestrial sphere, to which consequently they are but 'pitiless, passionless eyes'. But they are not only pitiless, passionless eyes; they are also *'cold fires'*. What a wonderful embodiment there is in this designation of the very essence, physically speaking, of star existence. Stars are *flame of the very highest intensity*, dazzling to the human sight even when compressed by distance into a point of unmeasureable dimensions; but this flame is so very far away, that not even the slightest vestige of its warmth has ever touched the human sense. One thing, however, there is that even these 'cold fires' can brand into man's mental perception, although they cannot warm his corporeal frame. So stupendously far off are they, and so enormously vast in themselves, that the initiated observers of the 'boundless plan' are almost stunned with their own reflections, when they attempt to compare it with the infinitesimal proportions of terrestrial being.

> Cold fires, yet with power *to burn and brand*
> His nothingness into man.

With something like a defiant joy he continues to these cold, pitiless tyrants of the iron immensity—

> But now shine on, and what care I,
> Who in this stormy gulf have found a pearl

And then an illustration of the mighty energy he has discovered in love, is added, which, in the matter of sublimity, is quite akin to the sidereal imagery immediately preceding.

> have found a pearl
> The *countercharm of space and hollow sky,*

This recently acquired pearl is alone sufficient to counteract the sense of the drear immensity which the new and sad astrology had disclosed. The awful thought of measureless space and empty sky is now made more than tolerable through the discovery of a charm more potent than its awfulness. In the last lines of this stanza, coupled with the mention of the countercharm that he has found in the stormy gulf of the world, there is a conscious confession of the intensity with which the 'cruel madness of love' has now laid its grasp upon him,—

> And *do accept my madness*, and would die
> To save from some slight shame one simple girl.

Having said that he would die for Maud's sake, he follows the suggestion of the new idea in two separate directions—first, he would die, because there may be more vitality for love in the holier and better existence that lies beyond the grave—

> Would die; for sullen-seeming Death *may give*
> *More life to Love* than is or ever was
> In our low world,——

But even this low world is no longer contemptible to him—he cannot now even vilify it with an epithet, without immediately entering his own protest against himself—

> In our low world, where yet *'tis sweet to live.*

He then proceeds to dilate still further upon the sweetness, and characterizes it by a negative phrase, that is far more forcible than any positive description could have been, in giving a notion of the profundity of his joy—

> Let no one ask me how it came to pass;
> It seems that I am happy,

and this happiness is one of such inherent energy and strength, it is able to scatter itself as an intensity of colour even over external natural objects;

> It seems that I am happy, that to me
> *A livelier emerald twinkles in the grass,*
> *A purer sapphire melts into the sea.*

He now again returns to the idea of death, from which he had digressed through the train of associations contained in the close of the preceding stanza, and this time it is to explain that it is not really death he desires, but a newer and better life. He would live to a higher purpose, and fulfil the great object and duty of human existence by struggling to attain strength and moral advancement in a manful conflict waged against evil and wrong—

> Not die; but live a life of truest breath,
> And teach true life to fight with mortal wrongs.

Here, then, is again a distinct and precise avowal of the grand central idea that is involved in this drama,—the holy and energizing power of love over the human intellect and heart. The moping and querulous *misanthrope* is here exhibited to contemplation, after he has suffered the baptism of this influence and been transformed by it into *a man*, yearn- to perform the man's part in the appointed conflict of responsible and rational being,—that conflict, through and by which, moral and intellectual strength can alone be obtained.

It now occurs to him that it is strange the idea of death should have intruded upon this moment of high and ecstatic vitality. Why should love carry with it an association apparently so antagonistic?

> O, why should Love, like men in drinking-songs,
> Spice his fair banquet with the dust of death?

There is only one oracle which can answer *for him* this question. He recognizes but one authority in the matter, and to that authority he turns in his perplexity—

> Make answer, Maud my bliss,
> Maud made my Maud by that long lover's kiss,
> Life of my life, wilt thou not answer this?

She does answer it, by an intimation that is conveyed through the inmost recesses of his own reflective soul—and her answer is to the effect that the dark thread of Death is entwined amid the brighter strands, that make the cord of life—its Admiralty mark, so to speak— for a purpose of high beneficence.

> *The dusky strand of Death inwoven here*
> *With dear Love's tie, makes Love himself more dear.*

Who is there, whose own experience has not somewhere an echo for this charmingly expressed truth? Does not the sense, that those who are dearest, may be snatched for awhile from the sight at any moment, and taken from the sphere of sensual existence, make everyone feel most acutely how dear those loved ones are? The mere recognition of the possibility of death renders those who are the objects of the affections infinitely more dear.

The hero's sensibilities have grown so excitable while he has followed the course of his happy reveries, that now even common and familiar sounds are suspected of having some direct relation with the incidents of the day—

> Is that enchanted moan *only* the swell
> Of the long waves that roll in yonder bay?

And here the striking of the clock in the house chimes in upon the murmur of the distant sea, marking the length of time he has lain in his happy dream beneath the cedar—

> And hark the clock within, the silver knell
> Of twelve sweet hours

It is midnight. But this midnight is the knell of hours that have been *bridal or fresh in the history of his joy*, and that have past, and yet not past, because their influences over him will endure whilst he lives—

> Of twelve sweet hours that past in bridal white,
> And died to live, long as my pulses play;

The midnight chime reminds him that Maud is now sleeping—

> But now by this my love has closed her sight
> And given False Death her hand,

He is sure, however, that her sleep is not forgetfulness; with him she is dreaming of the happy occurrences that have just taken place—

> And given False Death her hand, and stol'n away
> To dreamful wastes where footless fancies *dwell*
> *Among the fragments of the golden day.*

Yet, since in that dream-land there are strange fancies as well as pleasant memories, with the tenderness of anxious love he adds,—

> May nothing there her maiden grace affright!

By this time his own long-continued excitement is passing into mental languor, he hails this as a new proof of intimate sympathy connecting his being with hers,—and takes the opportunity to say good night:—

> Dear heart, I feel with thee the drowsy spell.
> My bride to be, my evermore delight,
> My own heart's heart and ownest own, farewell.

The 'good night' may now, however, be coupled with a glad assurance,—

> It is but for a little space I go:

Raising himself from his recumbent posture, and perhaps coming out from beneath the branches of the cedar, his eye again falls on the shining stars, now very brilliant in the midnight sky, and he renews his address to them:—

> And ye meanwhile far over moor and fell
> Beat to the noiseless music of the night!

But he is surprised to perceive their changed and softened aspect, since the period when to him they were only cold fires and pitiless eyes— a yet newer astrology has once again replaced that sad one of the intellect, and the pitiless eyes have become glowing and soft.

> Has our whole earth *gone nearer to the glow*
> *Of your soft splendours* that you look so bright?

Whether it be so with the whole earth or not, he at least has approached towards heaven,—

> *I* have climbed nearer out of lonely Hell.

No other name could express what loneliness seems to him in contrast with his newly acquired companionship. But his union with the stars has now grown as intimate as it was before with the cedar, so that he proceeds to ask their 'soft splendours' to beat responsively to the pulses of his own life-stream:—

> Beat, happy stars, timing with things below,
> Beat with my heart more blest than heart can tell,

And then, when his joy is strained to the highest, it just trenches upon the confines of sadness and sorrow, for one passing moment:—

> Blest, *but for some dark undercurrent woe*
> That seems to draw—

His first bright day of joy ought not, however, to be closed by a shadow; he, therefore, drives away the presentiment, and repels the augury.

> but it shall not be so:
> Let all be well, be well.

Such is the fragment of poetry which one of the innumerable, pitiless, passionless, nameless critics has characterized as 'a splendid piece of versification, but deficient in melody and passion, and much too artificial for the situation'. To that critic it may well be believed this splendid piece of versification was deficient in one other quality too— namely, meaning of any kind. In charity it must be hoped that such was the case. These stanzas are really found to be replete with the sweetest melody, and filled by passion strong as the deep ocean in its almost unfathomable depths, if an intellect equal to their appreciation, and of patient and unprejudiced habits of investigation, is but brought to their perusal. They are exquisite in the wondrous delicacy with which they express the profound emotions of a sensitive poet-mind new-born to happiness out of a chaos of wretchedness and misery. They are exquisite for the natural way in which the high thoughts and emotions introduced are made to suggest one another, so that changes which are in themselves the most abrupt, nevertheless, are marked to the reader as probable in the extreme. They are exquisite, beyond all things, in tenderness of sentiment, in combined force and grace of diction, and in that variation of rhythmical flow which swells and contracts, like the rise and fall of a melody issuing from the living strings of a passionate human heart. . . .

*   *   *

. . . In this final scene, the moral, as well as the incidents of the drama, is rounded to its end. This moral, it will be remembered, has been already indicated on more than one occasion. It is comprised in the statement that *the proper function of love is the ennobling and energizing of the human soul*. After the full blossoming of his joy, intense suffering and severe trial enveloped the hero of the poem, but the spirit that had once been imbued with earnest and holy affection, was carried, by the supporting influence pourtrayed in the successive scenes of the drama, safe through the terrific ordeals, and has now at length emerged from them, scathed but chastened. Neither disappointment nor sorrow, neither anguish nor madness, could altogether quench the pure fire. The chastened man yearns for the consummation of his union with her who has been parted from him for a time; but he now knows that such consummation can only be effected through earnest and manful effort on his own part, and accepts the grand necessity of the fate to which he has been born. Henceforth he will mingle with mankind, and not shun them; he will labour to amend faults that he perceives, and not rail at them; he will give the remainder of his life to healthy action, and not to morbid dreams. From this time forth he will forget to preach and learn to fight, and his fight shall be one continuous effort to right the wrong. Soon after these insights have been realized, it happens that a powerful and generous people prepares a mighty armament to do battle against the oppressor. This seems to him to be the very embodiment of his own desire, and, rushing to the armed rendezvous, he mingles his voice in the glorious battle cry that is there upraised, in unison with the hope that has now become to him the breath of life.

In the fine opening stanzas of the mono-drama, opportunity was taken to allude to the diverse ways in which the spirit of war works in the events of social life during the so-called periods of peace. The hero having alluded to his suspicion that his own father was virtually murdered through a friend's commercial treachery and greed for gold, proceeds to ask whether the spirit of the first murderer, the fratricidal Cain, does not show itself quite as much in the daily sacrifice of innumerable victims to the lust for gain, as in the death of the war-slain citizen, who has poured forth his heart's blood on his own warm hearth. Although in these days mind has effected wonderful things, there are, nevertheless, strange anomalies mixed with its conquests. The pickpocket thrusts his hand into his neighbour's purse. The tradesman cheats his customer, and lies to hide the fraud. The food of the poor, scant bread earned at the cost of painful toil, is adulterated by poison. The midnight burglar is only stayed from breaking in upon unsuspicious sleep by arms. Even parents, for the consideration of a paltry burial fee, have been known to quench the new lives they had kindled. And the tyrant-mammon of the factory rejoices, though the lives of countless children have gone to rear his fortunes. Are these the symptoms of peace? By no means. They are symptoms of war, which is a

civil war, and that too of the vilest kind, because in it no redeeming
trait of magnanimity can ever, by any possibility, be found; and because it is masked, and never declares itself honestly for what it is, by
the flash of the sword. Why—open and 'loud war, by land and by sea',
with its battles and shaking thrones, fell and fearful as it is, would be
grand in comparison with it. If such arose, those very 'smooth-faced
rogues' who now cheat with the yardwand, would leap forth, and
stirred by some manly impulse, strike in defence of the worthy and the
true, and be turned perchance from greedy knaves into heroes gallant
and brave.

Critical sagacity has not blushed to avow that it has discovered in
these desultory, though unquestionably pertinent aspirations of the
morbid recluse, the expression of Mr. Tennyson's belief that a state of
warfare would serve to prevent millers from putting chalk and alum,
and plaster in their flour, and grocers from mixing chicory with their
coffee. This discovery is among the note-worthy illustrations of the
vagaries into which men may fall when impelled by the sense that they
must furnish some kind of explanation of matters that are unfortunately
beyond the range of their comprehension, or that they must effect
some narrow and conventional object prescribed for them beforehand
by their employers. The simple meaning which lurks within these
passages, is obviously, that sad as open and declared war is, it has in it
those touches of moral grandeur which make its horrors tolerable in
comparison with the more dreadful social, and domestic hostilities,
which seethe continuously in the dense populations of over-crowded
lands, and set man against man, and brother against brother, causing
base selfishness and cruelty to take the place of high principle and
worthy aim.

It is in strict accordance with these views, that in the last scene of the
drama the convalescent madman and reclaimed cynic hails the advent
of actual war, and rejoices over the tearing of the cobweb, woven
across the cannon's throat, and which is now to 'shake its threaded'
dew-drop 'tears in the wind no more'. It is because he knows open war
in a just cause to be better than the debased condition of simulated
peace, where murder and rapine lurk in disguise, that he is led to
connect his own hope for the future, with the promise that is held out
to mankind in the coming struggle. . . .

17. Tennyson gives a reading of *Maud*

Hallam Tennyson, *Alfred Lord Tennyson: A Memoir. By his Son* (1897), ed. 1899, pp. 334–6.

Emily Ritchie reported of Tennyson that 'nothing was more memorable than to hear him read his poetry. The roll of his great voice acted sometimes almost like an incantation, so that when it was a new poem he was reading, the power of realizing its actual nature was subordinated to the wonder at the sound of the tones' (Hallam Tennyson, *op. cit.*, p. 490).

I shall never forget his last reading[1] of *Maud*, on August 24th, 1892. He was sitting in his high-backed chair, fronting a southern window which looks over the groves and yellow cornfields of Sussex towards the long line of South Downs that stretches from Arundel to Hastings (his high-domed Rembrandt-like head outlined against the sunset-clouds seen through the western window). His voice, low and calm in everyday life, capable of delicate and manifold inflection, but with 'organ-tones' of great power and range, thoroughly brought out the drama of the poem. You were at once put in sympathy with the hero. As he said himself, 'This poem is a little *Hamlet*', the history of a morbid poetic soul, under the blighting influence of a recklessly speculative age. He is the heir of madness, an egotist with the makings of a cynic, raised to sanity by a pure and holy love which elevates his whole nature, passing from the height of triumph to the lowest depth of misery, driven into madness by the loss of her whom he has loved, and, when he has at length passed through the fiery furnace, and has recovered his reason, giving himself up to work for the good of mankind through the unselfishness born of his great passion. My father pointed out that even Nature at first presented herself to the man in sad visions.

And the flying gold of the ruin'd woodlands drove thro' the air.

[1] He owned that 'Some of the passages are hard to read because they have to be taken in one breath and require good lungs.'

The 'blood-red heath' too is an exaggeration of colour; and his suspicion that all the world is against him is as true to his nature as the mood when he is 'fantastically merry'. 'The peculiarity of this poem,' my father added, 'is that different phases of passion in one person take the place of different characters.'

The passion in the first Canto was given by my father in a sort of rushing recitative through the long sweeping lines of satire and invective against the greed for money, and of horror at the consequences of the war of the hearth.

Then comes the first sight of Maud, and 'visions of the night', and in Canto IV. a longing for calm, the reaction after a mood of bitterness, and yearning for

> A philosopher's life in the quiet woodland ways.

But the clarion call of the 'voice by the cedar tree' singing

> A passionate ballad gallant and gay,

awakens a love in the heart which revolutionizes and inspires the whole life. In Canto XI. my father expressed the longing for love in

> O let the solid ground
> Not fail beneath my feet:

in Canto XVII. the exultation of love, knowing that it is returned:

> Go not, happy day,
> From the shining fields.

But this blessedness is so intense that it borders on sadness, and my father's voice would break down when he came to

> I have led her home, my love, my only friend.
> There is none like her, none.

Joy culminates in 'Come into the garden, Maud', and my father's eyes, which were through the other love-passages veiled by his drooping lids, would suddenly flash as he looked up and spoke these words, the passion in his voice deepening in the last words of the stanza.

> She is coming, my own, my sweet;
>   Were it ever so airy a tread,
> My heart would hear her and beat,
>   Were it earth in an earthy bed;
> My dust would hear her and beat,
>   Had I lain for a century dead;
> Would start and tremble under her feet,
>   And blossom in purple and red.

Then we heard after the duel the terrible wail of agony and despair in

> The fault was mine,

and the depth of forlorn misery in

> Courage, poor heart of stone!

when the man feels that he is going mad, both read with slow solemnity: then the delirious madness of

> O me, why have they not buried me deep enough?

The lyrics in *Maud* which my father himself liked best were

> I have led her home,

and
> O that 'twere possible,

and
> Courage, poor heart of stone!

About the mad-scene one of the best-known doctors for the insane wrote that it was 'the most faithful representation of madness since Shakespeare'.

It is notable that two such appreciative critics as Mr. Gladstone and Dr. Van Dyke wholly misapprehended the meaning of *Maud* until they heard my father read it, and that they both then publicly recanted their first criticisms. 'No one but a noble-minded man would have done that', my father would say of Mr. Gladstone. Dr. Van Dyke's recantation he did not live to read.

18. W. Bagehot on

the *Idylls of the King* [1859]

Walter Bagehot, unsigned review, *National Review* (October 1859), ix. 368–94.

Bagehot (1826–77), economist and banker, became an editor of the *National* in 1855 and contributed a good deal of literary criticism to it. Early in the latter half of the present review, he speaks of Tennyson's 'Grandmother's Apology'; he was evidently thinking of 'The Grandmother'.

It is a hardship on quarterly reviewers that good books should be published at the beginning of a quarter. Before the next number of the Review appears, they are scarcely new books at all. Everything which need be, or ought to be, perhaps everything which can be said, has been said. Doubtless the best remarks are forestalled. Yet what is to be done? A critical journal, which hopes to influence the taste of its time, must not omit to notice any remarkable books. When they are so attractive as the *Idylls of the King*, what critic can neglect a chance of reviewing them? Although, therefore, the last poem of Mr. Tennyson has already been some time before the public, and much has already been written about it, we must devote a few words to the delineation of its peculiarities.

The *Idylls of the King* is, we think, more popular with the general public than with Mr. Tennyson's straiter disciples. It is the characteristic—in some cases it is the calamity—of every great and peculiar poet, to create for himself a school of readers. Wordsworth did so during the first twenty years of the century. For the whole of that time, and perhaps for some years longer, his works could scarcely be said to belong to general English literature: the multitude did not read them. Some of the acutest of those who gave away reputation in those days laughed at them. But a secret worship was all the while forming itself; a sect accumulated. If you read the reviews of that time, you will find that the Wordsworthians were considered a kind of Quakers in literature, that rejected finery, disliked ornate art, and preferred a 'thee and thou' simplicity in poetry. Some of the defects of Wordsworth's poems may be in part traced to the narrowing influence of this species of readers. Even the greatest artist thinks sometimes of his peculiar public. The more solitary his life is, the more he broods on it. The more rejected he is by the multitude, the more he thinks of his few disciples. It is scarcely conceivable that such a habit should not narrow the mind and straiten the sympathies. The class of persons who are the first to take up a very peculiar writer, are themselves commonly somewhat peculiar. 'I am not sure of missionaries,' said some one; 'but I detest converts.' The first believers in anything are rarely good critics of it. The first enthusiasts for a great poet are heedless in their faith; a fault in their idol is like a fault in themselves: they have to defend him in discussion, and in consequence they come to admire the most those parts of his poems which are attacked most frequently: they have a logical theory in defence of them, and are attached to the instances that show its ingenuity and that exemplify its nature: in short, they admire, not what is best in the great writer, but what is most characteristic of him; they incite him to display his eccentricities and to develop his peculiarities. 'Beware of thy friends,' says the oriental proverb; 'for affection is but the flattery of the soul.' Many of Wordsworth's best poems would have been better if he had been more on his guard against the misleading influence of a sectarian sympathy. A few years ago Mr. Tennyson was in a rather similar position. We should not like to specify the date of his ratified acceptance by the public at large; but it is indisputable that at one time he was not so accepted. Everybody admires Tennyson now; but to admire him fifteen years or so ago, was to be a 'Tennysonian'. We know what the *Quarterly* said of his first volume, and the feeling there indicated lingered a long time in many quarters. He has now vanquished it; but an observant eye may still detect in literary, and still more in semi-literary society, several differences in taste and in feeling between the few disciples of the early school and the numerous race of new admirers.

Perhaps the first Tennysonians were not among the wisest of men,—at least they were not taken from the class which is apt to be the wisest. The early poetry of Mr. Tennyson—and the same may be said of nearly all the poetry of Shelley and Keats—labours under the defect that it is written, almost professedly, for young people—especially young men—

of rather heated imaginations. All poetry, or almost all poetry, finds its way more easily to the brains of young men, who are at once intellectual and excitable, than to those of men of any other kind. Persons engaged in life have rarely leisure for imaginative enjoyment: the briefs, the sums, the politics intervene. Slowly, even in the case of young men, does the influence of a new poet enter into the mind; you hear the snatch of a stanza here; you see an extract in a periodical; you get the book and read it; you are pleased with it, but you do not know whether the feeling will last. It is the habitual pleasure that such works give which alone is the exact criterion of their excellence. But what number of occupied men read new poetry habitually? What number of them really surrender their minds to the long task of gradually conceiving new forms of imagery, to the even more delicate task of detecting the healthiness or unhealthiness of unfamiliar states of feeling? Almost all poetry, in consequence, is addressed more to young men than to others. But the early poetry of Tennyson, and of the other poets we have named, is addressed to that class even more peculiarly. In the greatest poets, in Shakespeare and in Homer, there is a great deal besides poetry. There are broad descriptions of character, dramatic scenes, eloquence, argument, a deep knowledge of manly and busy life. These interest readers who are no longer young; they refer to the world in which almost all of us have to act; they reflect with the strong light of genius the scenes of life in which the mass of men live and move. By the aid of these extraneous elements, the poetry of these great writers reaches and impresses those who would never be attracted by it in itself, or take the pains to understand it if it had been presented to them alone. Shelley and Keats, on the other hand, have presented their poetry to the world in its pure essence; they have not added—we scarcely know whether they would have been able to add—the more worldly and terrestrial elements; probably their range in the use of these would have been but limited; at any rate, they have not tried —parts of Shelley's *Cenci* perhaps excepted—to use them; they have been content to rely on imaginatively expressed sentiment, and sentiment-exciting imagery; in short, on that which in its more subtle sense we call poetry, exclusively and wholly. In consequence, their works have had a great influence on young men; they retain a hold on many mature men only because they are associated with their youth; they delineate

> Such sights as youthful poets dream
> On summer eves by haunted stream:

and young men, who were not poets, have eagerly read them, have fondly learned them, and have long remembered them.—A good deal of this description applies to the writings of Tennyson,—some years ago we should have said that almost the whole of it was applicable to him. His audience formerly consisted entirely of young men of cultivated tastes and susceptible imaginations; and it was so because his poetry contained most of the elements which are suitable to such persons in a country like England, and an age such as this is. But whatever be the cause,—whether or not our analysis of the ingredients in Mr. Tennyson's poetry which attracted young men of this kind be correct or otherwise,—the fact that it did so attract them, and that it attracted but few others with great force, is very certain. His public was limited and peculiar; it was almost as much so as Wordsworth's was at an earlier time.

When Mr. Tennyson published *Maud*, we feared that the influence of this class of admirers was deteriorating his powers. The subject was calculated to call out the unhealthier sort of youthful imaginations; and his treatment of it, so far from lessening the danger, seemed studiously selected to increase it. The hero of *Maud* is a young man who lives very much out of the world, who has no definite duties or intelligible occupations, who hates society because he is bound by no social ties and is conscious of no social courage. This young gentleman sees a young lady who is rich, and whose father has an unpleasant association with his own father, who was a bankrupt. He has all manner of feelings about the young lady, and she is partial to him; but there is a difficulty about their interviews. As he is poor and she is wealthy, they do not meet in common society; and a stolen visit in her garden ends, if we understand the matter, in his killing her brother. After this he leads a wandering life, and expresses his sentiments. Such a story is evidently very likely to bring into prominence the exaggerated feelings and distorted notions which we call unhealthy. The feelings of a young man who has nothing to do, and tries to do nothing; who is very poor, and regrets that he is not very rich; who is in love, and cannot speak to the lady he loves; who knows he cannot marry her, but notwithstanding wanders vaguely about her,—are sure to be unhealthy. Solitude, social mortification, wounded feeling, are the strongest sources of mental malaria; and all of these are here crowded together, and are conceived to act at once. Such a representation, therefore, if it was to be true, must be partially tinctured with unhealthiness. This was inevitable; and it was inevitable, too, that this taint should be rather agreeable than otherwise to many of the poet's warmest admirers. The Tennysonians, as we have said, were young men; and youth is the season of semi-diseased feeling. Keats, who knew much about such matters, remarked this. 'The imagination,' he said, 'of a man is healthy, and the imagination of a boy is healthy; but between' there is an uncertain time, when the fancy is restless, the principles are unfixed, the sentiments waver, and the highest feelings have not acquired consistency. Upon young men in such a frame of mind a delineation like that of the hero of *Maud*, adorned, as it was, with rare fragments of beautiful imagery, and abiding snatches of the sweetest music, could not but be attractive, and could not but be dangerous. It seemed to be the realised ideal of their hopes, of their hearts, of themselves; it half consecrated their characteristic defects, it confirmed their hope that their eccentricities were excellencies. Such a danger could not be avoided; but Mr. Tennyson, so far from trying to shun it, seemed intentionally to choose to aggravate it. He seemed to sympathize with the feverish railings, the moody nonsense, the very entangled philosophy, which he put into the mouth of his hero. There were some odd invectives against peace, against industry, against making your livelihood, which seemed by no means to be dramatic exhibitions of represented character, but, on the contrary, confidential expositions of the poet's own belief. He not only depicted the natural sentiments of an inactive, inexperienced, and neglected young man, but seemed to agree with them. He sympathised with moody longings; he was not severe on melancholy vanity; he rather encouraged a general disaffection to the universe. He appeared not only to have written, but to have accepted the 'Gospel according to the Unappreciated'. The most charitable reader could scarcely help fancying, that in describing an irritable confusion of fancy and a diseased moodiness of feeling, the poet for the time imbibed a certain taint of those defects.

The *Idylls of the King* suggest to us a peculiar doubt. Was not Mr. Tennyson, after all, laughing at his admirers? *Did* he believe in *Maud*, though he seemed to say he did? We do not know; but at all events we have now a poem not only of a different, but of the very opposite kind. Every line of it is defined with the delicate grace of a very composed genius; shows the trace of a very mature judgment; will bear the scrutiny of the most choice and detective taste. The feelings are natural, the thoughts such as people in life have or might have. The situations, though in a certain sense unnatural, have, we believe, a peculiar artistic propriety. There is a completeness in the whole.

For when the Roman left us, and their law
Relax'd its hold upon us, and the ways
Were fill'd with rapine, here and there a deed
Of prowess done redress'd a random wrong.
But I was first of all the kings who drew
The knighthood-errant of this realm and all
The realms together under me, their Head,
In that fair Order of my Table Round,
A glorious company, the flower of men,
To serve as model for the mighty world,
And be the fair beginning of a time.

The general public will like this, but scarcely the youthful admirers of broken art and incomplete beauties who accepted *Maud* with great delight. The world we know is opposed to earnest enthusiasts and fond disciples, and Mr. Tennyson has sided with the world.

We think that it is no chance which has made several of our poets dream of a poem on King Arthur. The story of that monarch became *par excellence the* legend of chivalry. Nothing, indeed, can be much stranger than that it should have done so. There is no evidence that such a king ever existed; and the fact has very long been questioned. Caxton, who first printed *La Mort d'Arthure* in English, relates a conversation which he either had, or feigned himself to have had, with a lover of chivalric literature, who advised the printing: 'To whom,' he says, 'I answered that dyvers men hold opinion that there was no such Arthur, and that all such books as been made of him, been but fayned and fables, because that some chronicles make of him no mention, nor remember him nothing nor of his knyhts.' And the argument in reply would hardly satisfy Sir G. C. Lewis or Mr. Grote. 'First, ye may see his sepulture in the monasterye of Glastynburye;' and next, his name, 'Patricius Arthurus, Britanniæ, Galliæ, Germaniæ, Daciæ, imperator,' on Saint Edward's shrine in Westminster Abbey; also, 'Gauvayn's skull and Cradok's mantel', at Dover; 'at Winchester, the round table; and in other places, Launcelotte's sword, and many other things.' It was a touching theory of ancient credulity, that relics prove the existence of the hero to whom it is said that they belonged. The scrupulous modern doctrine, as we know, is that they must first *prove themselves*. Even when we are certain that the hero existed, it must likewise be shown by connected links of evidence that the alleged relics—the sword or the skull—ever belonged to him. However, most people in former ages believed otherwise; 'the bricks' continued 'to testify' not only to the existence of the bricklayer, but also to his name and his lineage; the non-existent King Arthur was accepted as the hero of chivalry, the model of its excellence, and the incarnation of its virtues. Yet even admitting his existence, the conception of him was peculiarly fanciful. If Arthur ever existed, he was a British king, who resisted the northern invaders. Knighthood was the undesigned development of the feudal system—of that system which the northern conquerors of modern Europe invented, and imposed on its half-romanised inhabitants. Even in legendary history, which is naturally the most singular of histories, scarcely anything is more singular than that the hero of knighthood, the traditional model of chivalric virtues, should have been a romanised Briton, whose very name seems to have come from Britanny; whose whole character, if he had been a real person, must have been cast in a very different mould; whose exploits were alleged to have been performed over the northern hordes, but for whose victory chivalry would never have existed; who could never have comprehended the graces assigned to him, who would have lamented the barrenness of his victories, and grieved at the downfall of his race. Yet such was the case. It did not matter that the hero of the conquerors was of the race of the conquered. A literature was required to be the expression of the chivalric imagination; minstrels sang it; chroniclers wrote it. And when the conditions of knightly life were passing away with the decay of the feudal institutions, its ideal was prized more. The feeling that all trace of it was departing, that its possibility was ceasing, that a new world of tamer life and fainter features was coming in, gave to the literary embodiments of the chivalrous ideal a saddened charm, a melancholy refinement, which they had not in themselves. It is not easy to read *The History of King Arthur* now, yet it was once a treasured volume; and the French book from which it was translated was, as was natural in 'knightly France', treasured still more.

Yet when we come to examine the chivalric romance, we shall find that, though dull and tedious in its actual form, it contains many elements of great artistic value; that, though it can never again be popular itself, something more than accident has attracted our poets to it. Leibnitz spoke of the mediæval philosophy as the least agreeable of out-of-door heaps; but he added, 'there is gold in it'. We will not dare to imitate the grave coarseness of the philosophic style; but we will say, that it was the real gold of a genuine poetic interest which has attracted Milton and Dryden, and now another poet, to mediæval romance.

The value of the subject lies, if we may be allowed the expression, in its supernaturalness. Poets are frequently advised to make choice of modern subjects: it is said that ancient ones are worn out; that all which can correctly be said of them has been said; that a new world, with ardent life, and tender grace, and bold energy, is around us; that in it we should seek the topics of our art, and especially the themes of our poetry. Yet the practice of our poets does not as yet conform itself much to the teaching of this criticism. They seem to have, or to believe they have, a restraining instinct which disinclines them to act on the exhortation; they undoubtedly have an impelling tendency which incites them to select their subjects from the older world. One of our poets has said, in answer to the critics, 'a great action' is a great action anywhere; surely it is as good if it happened in former ages as if it had happened yesterday. And unquestionably this is so; yet it only amounts, after all, to a claim of equality for the older poetic subjects, it does not justify the distinct preference which the practice of poets seems to give to them.

We believe the reason of that preference to be, that in describing the ancient life it is easy to select, and it is admissible to exaggerate. The chivalrous legend is in itself both a selection and an exaggeration. A few parts of life are chosen out of many, and those few are heightened in colour and augmented in size. *Ivanhoe* is an illustration of this which everyone can understand. Scott was fond of the old chivalric life, and he told stories of it as a sagacious man of this modern world would tell them. He describes it as, in the first place, a fighting period; and in the next place, a falling-in-love period. We rise from the romance with the idea that some centuries ago there were black horses, and large lances, knights in armour, and beautiful ladies: and that there was little else. These elements of life are already selected in the traditional imagination; in speaking of those times we gratify a preconceived idea in speaking of these elements and of these only. We need not apologize for our choice; on the contrary, we should jar upon latent anticipations if we extended our range, or if we chose differently. If King Arthur existed, there were peasants in his time, and these peasants had wives, and these wives had children, and these children had measles; but no one wishes to hear of the peasants, the wives, or the babies, but of Queen Guinevere and Lancelot, of the king himself, and all the 'Table Round'. In the modern world it is different, everything runs into everything else; every detail suggests an approximate detail; every fact another fact. We see this in the appropriate description of modern life, the modern novel. No form of art has perhaps ever existed in which the detail of ordinary existence has been used with such copiousness,— in crude hands doubtless with absurd prolixity, but in the hands of the greater artists—in those, for instance, of Mr. Thackeray—with a sort of defined abundance, and the restrained tact of measured fertility. 'The novelist,' our satirist tells us, 'knows everything;' and he certainly knows all the little facts, the trivial details, the 'knives and forks' of ordinary life. But how few of these details are fit for poetry! how few of them are consistent with its sustained tone! how few would not jar upon its characteristic associations! how many would mar its effect! We are not, we own, of any formal school in poetry; we do not, as certain French critics, object to the 'mouse stirring' of the dramatist. We only mean to say, that all the facts of a life with which we are familiar have a hundred associations—that in sustained and high poetry any one of these might have an unintended influence and a disenchanting effect. In ancient life such details are few, and those few have been sifted by a sort of legendary tradition; by the testing imagination of ages of story-tellers and story-hearers.

We have said that the traditional conception of the age of mediæval chivalry is that of a fighting period, and of a falling-in-love period. If we consider the peculiar nature of these pursuits, and the peculiar mode in which we are accustomed to believe that they then existed, we shall understand their artistic value. It will be conceded that these two pursuits present human nature in what to most people is its most interesting aspect. How many people read the account of a war when it is brought to them in the newspaper, who read nothing else there! how few in proportion care for a debate in parliament, the great labours of the Chancellor of the Exchequer, or the ordinary administration of peaceful existence! Still more of love-stories we need not speak; it does not need critical ink to prove that *they* are perused. All kinds of war and all kinds of love are for ever attractive. But if we consider the form in which these pursuits appear in the chivalric legend, it will be found to be in both cases that which is most striking to the unsophisticated imagination. Without having recourse needlessly to deep metaphysics, it may be said that the imagination is more strongly impressed by strong qualities and strong passions that are vividly displayed, than by less intense elements less vividly displayed. Now the love-making in the time of chivalry was not the matter of detail that it is now—women lived in comparative seclusion; their intercourse with men was rare, was not very familiar, and was scarcely at all intellectual. Under these circumstances falling in love at first sight was rather rational than otherwise. It came under the precept, 'use your opportunities'. Unless you became enamoured at a first view, you might never be so,—you might never get a second. Intellectual calculation would therefore not forbid the practice, and there was much else to encourage it; wherever ladies are much secluded, it will always be common enough. Mr. Meadows has an anecdote in his book on China, which is, he says, authentic.

'A Chinese, who had experienced bitter disenchantments in marriage, and suffered grievously through women in many other ways,—and who, in consequence, considered them simply as unmitigated sources of trouble and mischief,—retired with his infant son to the peaks of a mountain range in Kwei chow, to a spot quite inaccessible for little-footed Chinese women; through whom he was resolved that his son should never experience similar miseries. He trained up the youth to worship the gods, and stand in awe and abhorrence of devils; but he never mentioned woman to him, and always descended the mountains alone to buy food. The infirmities of age, however, at length compelled him to take the young man with him, to carry the heavy bag of rice. But he very reasonably argued: "I shall always accompany my son, and take care that if he does see a woman by chance, he shall never speak to one; he is very obedient; he has never heard of women; he does not know what they are; and as he has lived in that way for twenty years already, he is, of course, now pretty safe."

'As they were, on the first occasion, leaving the market-town together, the son suddenly stopped short, and, pointing to three approaching objects, inquired: "Father, what are these things? Look! look! what are they?" The father hastily answered with the peremptory order: "Turn away your head: they are devils." The son, in some alarm, instantly turned away from things so bad, and which were gazing at his motions with surprise from under their fans. He walked to the mountain top in silence, ate no supper, and from that day lost his appetite and was afflicted with melancholy. For some time his anxious and puzzled parent could get no satisfactory answer to his inquiries; but at length the poor young man burst out, almost crying from an inexplicable pain, "Oh, father, that tallest devil! that tallest devil, father!"

'He had idealised the first objective reality he met with, and had "fallen deeply in love at first sight".'

We need not stay to prove that such a mode of becoming enamoured is more striking to the imagination than our quieter modern mode. The suddenness, the violence, the painfulness, of the olden mode are evidently impressive.—Something of the same qualities may be observed in the antique mode of fighting. The interest in modern military operations is curiously divided. The scene is this: We have an intellectual general, calculating, arranging, combining, taxing all the forces of a superior intellect, skilful in tactics, abounding in ingenuity; we have likewise a body of soldiery, excelling in daring, quick in attack, steady in defence, organised into a machine. Here are two sources of interest, the mind and the fighting: but the mind does not fight; and that which fights is hardly mind. The general is removed from the conflict, and the regiments which he sends do not come home to our fancies as human beings; they seem rather to be implements and organisations. We can scarcely realise the complex combat. Our interest in it, even in as far as we imagine it, is lost in the multitude of the combatants, and the scientific framework which the devising mind has planned out for them. We never see, we never hope to see, a mind, which is great both in itself and in its position, which is the leading mind of the scene,—in real danger, confronting evident perils, over-coming visible foes. In old times it was otherwise. The characters, the real prominent characters of a fiction, can be made to fight. We know how Richard I. fights in *Ivanhoe*. Dr. Johnson, in the *Life of Addison*, has scoffed at the old style of describing battles, in which Marlborough was made to win Blenheim by his personal prowess, and he and Eugene were supposed to contend with the French marshals hand to hand. His literal mind was shocked at the unreality of the delineation; he saw its untruth, and could not but laugh at its impossibility: but he has not marked, and probably did not see, that in early times, and as long as it was true, this delineation had the merit of concentrating the interest derived from intellect and the interest derived from courage in a single spot; and that no more faithful representation of a modern battle, except in most exceptional cases, does or can do so.

These illustrations are far from exhausting the subject; but they are enough for our purpose. They show, we think, that the events of the chivalric legend are better adapted to sustained and prolonged poetry than the events of recent times and of the present day; and that they are so because they abound much less in dangerous detail, are confined to selected events and chosen characters, show us human passions in a more vivid form, present human actions in a more easily intelligible shape, give us a sort of large-hand copy of life which it is comparatively easy to understand and imitate.

Mr. Tennyson has in the *Idylls* used these elements of the chivalric legend with instinctive felicity and dexterity. The tale of Prince Geraint, as the first Idyll might be called, is, in its main incidents, as pure a tale of chivalry as could be conceived. His love of Enid at first sight; his single combat with her cousin, who keeps her out of her inheritance; the general plentifulness of banditti, and his conquests over them,—are all features belonging essentially to that kind of story. It would be needless criticism to show that the poet has made a great deal of them, that the narrative is very clear and very flowing, that the choice of the events is very skilful; every reader must have perceived these excellencies.

It is more necessary to point out what the careful art of the poet disguises—that he has avoided the greatest danger of such a theme. The danger of a topic abounding in romantic and extraordinary events is, that its treatment may have a sort of glare. The first miracle we meet petrifies us, the next only astonishes, the third tires, and the fourth bores. The perpetual stimulus of such events as those which we have shown to be particularly characteristic of the chivalric legend would become wearisomely tedious, if a relieving element were not introduced in order to prevent it. Mr. Tennyson has found us such an element. He has managed to introduce to us, incidentally and without effort, many pictures of the quieter parts of human nature. He has fully availed himself of the license which his subject gives him. He never goes into any detail of life, which cannot be made attractive, which may have disenchanting associations, which may touch with a prosaic breath the accomplished exquisiteness of his art. But no mistaken hesitation, none of the over-caution which a less practised artist would have felt, has restrained him from using to the utmost the entire range of that part of life which he can make attractive. We have spoken of the first Idyll, as in its story one of the most purely chivalric of the four. Yet even in this there are several relieving elements. There is scarcely anything to be imagined of higher excellence in this kind than the character of Yniol and his wife. Yniol is an old lord who has lost his property, whose followers have deserted him, and who lives in povery at an old castle upon sufferance. He thus describes how his nephew ejected him, and what are the feelings with which he contemplates his life:

[Quotes 'The Marriage of Geraint', ll. 449–73:

' "And since the proud man . . .
. . . endure it all most patiently." ']

The quiet contemplative character, which suffers so many calamities
in rude times, and which is often so puzzled to find out why it has
experienced them, is a most suitable shading element to relieve the
mind from always admiring great knights who strike hard, who throw
immense lances, and who can kill anyone they wish. The feminine
reflections—if such they can be called—of Yniol's wife, on the changes
of her fortune, are equally appropriate, and quite as true to nature:

[Quotes 'The Marriage of Geraint', ll. 705–22:

' "For I myself unwillingly . . .
. . . fairer in new clothes than old." ']

The whole story of the dress, of which this is a part, is a very delicate
instance of relieving and softening skill; but we have no room to make
any more remarks upon it.

Mr. Tennyson has, however, introduced another element into the
description of the chivalric state of society, which, though in some sense
it relieves it, does not so well harmonise with it. As we have observed,
he avails himself of the peculiar manner—the sudden manner—of
falling in love, characteristic of that society. In the first Idyll, Geraint
falls in love with Enid on the first evening of their acquaintance; he
proposes for her at once, fights a tournament, and is accepted the next
morning. In the third Idyll we have the reverse history: a young lady
named Elaine falls in love at once with the great Sir Lancelot; but as
he does not like her as well as the Queen, she is not accepted. These
are love affairs very characteristic of a state of society when women were
seen but rarely, and even when seen were but little spoken to; but side
by side with them in the Idyll there are other scenes indicative of a
great familiarity between them and men, full of intellectual friction
between the two, showing on both sides the nice and critical knowledge of our civilised world. It seems hardly fair that a writer should
insist on the good side of both species of life; upon being permitted
to use the sudden love which arises from not knowing women, and the
love-tinged intercourse of thought and fancy which is the result of
knowing them, together and at once. The nature of the story seems
to have led Mr. Tennyson into this complication. The reign of Arthur,
as is well known, was believed to have been for many years clouded,

and at length terminated, by the unlawful affection of his Queen
Guinevere for Sir Lancelot, the greatest and most renowned of his
courtiers. This is evidently a very delicate topic for art to handle.
King Arthur and Sir Lancelot are both to be made interesting: the
Queen, of

> imperial-moulded form,
> And beauty such as never woman wore,

is to be made interesting likewise. A great deal of intellectual detail
is necessary for this end; many slight touches of delicate insight must
conduce to it; a hundred pencillings of nice art must be accumulated
to effect it. If the subject was to be treated for modern readers, some
additions to the bareness of old romance and legend were indispensable;
and even a critic could hardly object to them. But Mr. Tennyson has
gone further. There being a Queen at court who was not immaculate,
he has thought it proper that there should be ladies about her who are
no better. 'Vivien', the young lady who gives her name to the second
Idyll, is more fitted for the court of Louis Quinze than for that of the
saintly king of chivalry. The delineation speaks for itself:

[Quotes 'Merlin and Vivien', ll. 150–86:

'For once, when Arthur . . .
. . . and so the seasons went.']

There is undoubtedly much that is not modern in Merlin's character,
or rather in his occupation, for he is a faint kind of being; but the
enchanter who has a charm of 'woven paces and of waving hands',
and who has read lines of lore which no other person can read, does
not belong to the drawing-room. His pursuits, at any rate, do not.

[Quotes 'Merlin and Vivien', ll. 665–88:

' "*Thou* read the book . . .
. . . ye dream they babble of you." ']

But however removed from us Merlin's character may be, that of
Vivien in its essence rather belongs to an over-civilised and satirical,
than to an uncultivated and romantic time. It rather mars our enjoyment of the new book of chivalry, to have a character so discordant
with its idea placed in such prominence, and drawn out in such
development.

A similar charge cannot, however, be justly brought against the main story of the poem. The contrast of character between King Arthur and Sir Lancelot is one of those which exists in some degree in all ages, but which the exciting circumstances of an unsettled time necessarily tend to bring out and exaggerate. In our last Number we had occasion, in writing on another subject, to draw out at some length the delineation of the two kinds of *goodness* which have long been contrasted, and always seem likely to be contrasted, in the world,—the ascetic and the sensuous. The characteristic of the latter is to be sensitive to everything in this world, tempted by every stimulus, exposed to every passion; the characteristic of the former is to be repelled from the ordinary pleasures of the world, to be above them, to feel a warning instinct against them. In the course of life the fate of the ascetic character is to be absorbed in a somewhat chill ideal; that of the sensuous character is to purchase a fascinating richness of earthly experience by a serious number of grave errors. We had some difficulty formerly in illustrating the distinction between the two characters at once clearly and expressively, but we should have had no such difficulty if Mr. Tennyson had published his new poem a little earlier. The character of Arthur, absorbed in the ideal conception of a chivalrous monarchy, is the very type of the highest abstract or ascetic character; that of Lancelot, the great knight of many exploits and full-lipped enjoyment, whom Guinevere prefers, is the type of the sensuous and sensitive. The Queen's painting of the contrast is true both to nature and to the female idea of nature.

[Quotes 'Guinevere', ll. 371–404:

   ' "For what is true repentance . . .
   Not like my Lancelot." ']

We need not observe upon the moral tact of making the Queen see Lancelot first; it was necessary as an artistic palliation for her. It would have been scarcely pleasant to think of her without it.

There can be no doubt that Mr. Tennyson has judged wisely in telling the story of Arthur and Guinevere in a series of tales rather than in a single connected epic. The peculiar and painful nature of that story requires, in a singular degree, the continual use of relieving elements; and yet it is of the first importance that no one of these elements should assume an undue prominence, or be more interesting than the story itself. If other interesting characters had been introduced into the main plot of a continuous poem, the latter effect would have been nearly inevitable. The imagination cannot rest with satisfaction either on Guinevere's relation to Arthur or on her relation to Lancelot. In each there is a disagreeable and disenchanting something. If a competing interest had been introduced into the central plot, it could hardly fail to be intrinsically pleasanter, and might have distracted the attention intended from the chosen theme. The form which the poet has adopted—that of a set of stories, with continual allusion to a latent thread—prevents this result, and also gives the requisite shading to the painful subject. There is a continued succession of relieving interests; but there is none which can compete with the central one, or be compared with it.

We have said enough of the merits of this poem to entitle us to say what ought to be said against it. We have not, indeed, a long list of defects to set forth. On the contrary, we think we perceive only one of real importance; and it is very probable that many critics will think us quite wrong as to that one. It appears to us that the *Idylls* are defective in dramatic power. Madame de Staël said that Coleridge was admirable in monologue, but quite incapable of dialogue. Something analogous may perhaps be said of Mr. Tennyson. His imagination seems to fix itself on a particular person in a particular situation; and he pours out, with ease and abundance, with delicacy and exactness, all which is suitable to that person in that situation. This was so with 'Ulysses' in former years; it is so in his 'Grandmother's Apology', published the other day. Unnumbered instances of it may be found in the *Idylls*. But the power of writing a soliloquy is very different from that of writing a conversation; so different, indeed, that the person who is most likely to wish to write one, is most likely not to wish to write the other. Dialogue requires a very changing imagination, ready to move with ease from the mental position of one mind to the mental position of another, quick with the various language suited to either. Soliloquy—prolonged soliloquy, at any rate—requires a very steady imagination, steadily accumulating, slowly realising the exact position of a single person. The glancing mind will tend to one sort of composition; the meditative, solitary, and heavy mind to the other. All Mr. Tennyson's poems show more of the latter tendency than of the first. His genius gives the notion of a slow depositing instinct; day by day, as the hours pass, the delicate sand falls into beautiful forms—in stillness, in peace, in brooding. You fancy Shakespeare writing quick, the hasty dialogue of the parties passing quickly through his brain: we have no such idea of our great contemporary poet. He keeps his verses in his head: a meditative and scrupulous Muse is prayed to

> Let him write his random lines
> Ere they be half forgotten,
> Nor add or alter many times
> Till all be ripe and rotten.

The lightly-flowing dialogue is not so written. The lightly-moving imagination which is necessary to its composition gallops quicker, has a more varied tread, alters its point of view more frequently. If we look into the various dialogues of these *Idylls*, we shall not only observe that the tendency to monologue is great, and is greatest at the most striking points and telling situations, but also be struck with what is nearly the same phenomenon in another form—the remarkable similarity of the conversational powers of all the various personages. It is not only that a peculiar kind of language, a sort of a dialect of sentimental chivalry, pervades the whole,—this is quite in keeping with the design, and is perhaps essential to the perfect effect of such a book; but the similarity seems to go deeper: each dramatic personage is fully endowed with the expressive capacities of Mr. Tennyson's imagination; each one has them all, and consequently they are all on a level; no one has a superiority. No fact can more exactly and instructively define the precise difference between a genuine dramatic expression and the superficially analogous, but really different, art of delineative soliloquy. In the latter, it is right that the state of feeling to be expressed should be expressed with all the poet's power: we are representing the man's notion of himself; we take the liberty to say for him what he could never say; we translate into similes and phrases the half thoughts and floating feelings which he never could for a moment have expressed in that way, or probably in any other way. But in the genuine drama we are delineating a scene with more than one actor, and we are to state an imaginary dialogue. The mode in which people express themselves is an essential fact of that dialogue. The degree in which people can express themselves is one of the most dramatic parts of their characters; it is therefore contrary to all the principles of art to give to each character the same command, especially if it be a singular command over very imaginative language. The state of the supposed speaker's mind is no doubt brought out by that mode more effectually than by any other; but the effect of the scene—of the speaking mind which can delineate itself, and of the dumb mind which cannot—is altogether impaired, for the striking contrast is destroyed.

The only other defect with which the *Idylls* are, we think, to be charged, is not so much a positive defect in the poetry itself, as rather a negative deficiency in it when compared with other poems of Mr. Tennyson's that we have known for many years. A certain subtlety seems to pervade some of the latter; and it is in part ascribable to the subtlety of thought, and is greatly heightened by a peculiar subtlety of expression. There are lines in some of the older poems for which perhaps every one has

A pleasurable feeling of blind love.

We know what they express: they *do* express it to us: they dwell in our memories; they haunt us with their echo. Yet, if we try to analyse them, their charm is gone. Is the meaning expressed? Did Mr. Tennyson really mean this?—is there not this ambiguity? Might he not have intended something else? We can conceive a foreign critic, thoroughly acquainted with our language for almost all other purposes, to be quite incapable of seeing the merit of some of the more characteristic of these poems, from a want of those early floating and mysterious associations with language, in the instinctive and delicate use of which that charm consists. We have known literal-minded English persons, who preferred the plainer phraseology—the 'commin print', as Lisbeth would have called it—of every-day rhymers. And, in some sense, their preference was correct. All that they could perceive was more perfect in the entirely valueless rhyme than in the entirely invaluable. The logical structure is better; it would construe better into other words, or into a foreign language: and this the literal critics perceive. The hovering air of power and beauty which the words really have, they do not perceive. If you were to suggest the existence they would smile. We believe that of this subtle sort of beauty, there is less in the *Idylls* than in Mr. Tennyson's earlier poetry. Perhaps they have not been in our hands long enough for us to judge. These super-logical beauties, if we may so say, are those which require the longest time to perceive, and the most perfect familiarity to appreciate. Still we do think so. We think there are few passages, considering the length of the poems, which will have years hence that inexplicable and magical power over our minds which some of Mr. Tennyson's old lines have. Perhaps the subject may have something to do with it. The sentiments in these poems are simpler than his sentiments used to be; they are not 'clothed in white samite, mystic, wonderful'. The thoughts are broader and plainer. The old mystic grace of language may, therefore, not have been so much used, only because it was no longer so much needed.

Every poem of Mr. Tennyson's must suggest the inquiry, what is the place which he occupies in the series of our poets? This poem must do so most of all; because, as we have explained, it removes some of the doubts which his warmest admirers formerly felt as to the limits of the range of his genius. It shows that he has the skill to adapt, the instinctive taste and self-restraint to preserve a continued interest of considerable length. Architectonic power the long-worded critics used to say he had not; but we have now discovered that he has it. The puzzling question returns, Where is Mr. Tennyson to be placed in the rank of our poets? We know that he has genius; but is that genius great or small, when compared with others like it?

It is most natural to compare him with Keats and Shelley. The kind of readers he addresses is, as we observed, the same: a sort of intellectual sentiment pervades his works as well as theirs: the superficial resemblances of the works of all the three are many. But, on the other hand, Mr. Tennyson is deficient in the most marked peculiarity which Shelley and Keats have in common. Both of these poets are singularly gifted with a sustained faculty of lyrical expression. They seem hurried into song; and, what is more, kept there when they have been hurried there. Shelley's 'Skylark' is the most familiar example of this. A rather young musician was once asked, what was Jenny Lind's charm in singing. 'Oh,' he replied, 'she went up so high, and staid up high so long.' There is something of this sustainment at a great height in all Shelley's lyrics. His strains are profuse. He is ever soaring; and whilst soaring, ever singing. Keats, it is true, did not ascend to so extreme an elevation. He did not belong to the upper air. He had no abstract labour, no haunting speculations, no attenuated thoughts. He was the poet of the obvious beauty of the world. His genius was of the earth— of the autumn earth—rich and mellow; and it was lavish. He did not carry his art high or deep; he neither enlightens our eyes much, nor expands our ears much; but pleases our fancies with a prolonged strain of simple rich melody. He does not pause, or stay, or hesitate. His genius is continuous; the flow of it is as obvious at the best moments as the excellence, and at inferior moments is more so. Mr. Tennyson, on the other hand, has no tendencies of this kind. He broods, as we have said. There are undoubtedly several beautiful songs in his writings, —several in which the sentiment cleaves to the words, and cannot even in our memories be divorced from them. But their beauty is not continuous. A few lines fasten upon us with an imperious and overmastering charm; but the whole composition, as a whole, has not much value. The run of it, as far as it has a run, expresses nothing. The genius of Mr. Tennyson is delineative; it muses and meditates; it describes moods, feelings, and objects of imagination; but it does not rush on to pour out passion, or express overwhelming emotion.

In the special lyrical impulse, therefore, we think it indisputable that Mr. Tennyson is inferior both to Keats and to Shelley. To Shelley he is moreover evidently inferior in general intensity of mind. This intense power of conception is, indeed, the most striking of all Shelley's peculiarities. There is something nervously exciting about his way of writing, even on simple subjects. He takes them up so vividly into his brain that they seem to make it quiver, and that of a sensitive reader at times quivers in sympathy. The subjects are no doubt often abstract; too abstract, perhaps, occasionally for art. But that only makes the result more singular. That an excitable mind should be stimulated by the strong interest of the facts of the world, by the phenomena of life, by the expectation of death, is what we should expect. It is intelligible to our understanding, and in obvious accordance with our experience. But that this extreme excitement should be caused in the poet's mind very often, and in the reader's mind sometimes, by the abstractions of singular tenuity, is what few would expect. So, however, it is. The mind of Shelley seems always to work in a kind of pure rare ether, clearer, sharper, more eager than the ordinary air. The reader feels that he is on a kind of mountainous elevation, and perhaps he feels vivified by it: at times almost all persons do so, but at times also they are chilled at its cold, and half-frightened at the lifelessness and singularity. It is characteristic of Shelley that he was obliged to abandon one of his favourite speculations, 'dizzy from thrilling horror'. Of all this abstract intensity Mr. Tennyson has not a particle. He is never very eager about anything, and he is certainly not overanxious about phantoms and abstractions. In some respects this deficiency may not have injured his writings: it has rather contributed to his popularity. The English mind, which, like its great philosophers, likes to work upon 'stuff', is more pleased with genial chivalric pictures than with chiselled phantoms and intense lyrics. Still, a critic who appreciates Shelley at all, will probably feel that he has a degree of inner power, of telling mental efficiency, which Mr. Tennyson does not equal. Horrible as the *Cenci* must ever be, it shows an eager and firmer grasp of mind—a greater tension of the imagination—than the *Idylls*.

Over Keats, however, Mr. Tennyson may perhaps claim a general superiority. We are, indeed, making a comparison which is scarcely fair; Keats died when he was still very young. His genius was immature; and his education, except the superficial musing education he gave himself, was very imperfect. Mr. Tennyson has lived till his genius is fully ripe, and he has gathered in the fruits of his century. No one can read his poems without feeling this: some of his readers have probably felt it painfully. Twenty years ago, when there was an idea in the high places of criticism that he was a silly and affected writer, many ignorant persons thought they were showing their knowledge in laughing at a language which nevertheless was both most emphatic and most accurate. The amount of thought which is held in solution,—if we may be pardoned so scientific a metaphor,—in Mr. Tennyson's poetry, is very great. If you come to his poems a hundred times, it is very probable that you will even to the end find there some new allusion, some recondite trace of high-bred thought, which you had not seen before. His reflections are often not new; he would not advance for himself perhaps, his just admirers, we are sure, would not claim for him, the fame of an absolutely original thinker. But he indicates the possession of a kind of faculty which in an age of intellect and cultivation is just as important, possibly is even more important, than the power of first-hand discovery. He is a first-rate *realiser*; and realisation is a test of truth. Out of the infinite thoughts, discoveries, and speculations which are scattered, more or less perfectly, through society, certain minds have a knack of taking up and making their own that which is true, and healthy, and valuable; and they reject the rest. It is often not by a very strict analysis or explicit logical statement that such minds arrive at their conclusions. They are continually thinking the subjects in question over: they have the details of them in their minds: they have a floating picture of endless particulars about them in their imaginations. In consequence, by musing over a true doctrine, they see that it is true: it fits their picture, adapts itself to it, forms at once a framework for it. On the contrary, they find that a false tenet does not suit the facts which they have in their minds: they muse over it, find out its unsuitability, and think no more of it. The belief of these remarkably sane and remarkably meditative persons about the facts to which they devote their own understandings is one of the best criteria of truth in this world. It is the discriminating winnow of civilisation, which receives the real corn of the true discoverer, and leaves the vexing chaff of the more pompous science to be forgotten and pass away. This kind of meditative tact and slow selective judgment Mr. Tennyson possesses in a very great measure; and there is nothing of which Keats was so entirely destitute. It does not, perhaps, occur to you while reading him that he is deficient in it. It belongs to an order of merit completely out of his way. It is the reflective gift of a mature man: Keats's best gifts are those of an impulsive, original, and refined boy. But if we compare—as in some degree we cannot help doing—the indications of general mind which are scattered through the three writers, we shall think, perhaps, that in these Mr. Tennyson excels Keats, even remembering the latter's early death, and, in consequence, giving him all fair credit for the possibilities of subsequent development; just as we found before that the intellectual balance seemed, when similarly adjusted, to incline against Mr. Tennyson, and in favour of Shelley.

Some one has said that Tennyson was a drawing-room Wordsworth. There is no deep felicity or instruction in the phrase, but it has some superficial appropriateness. Wordsworth's works have no claim to be in the drawing-room: they have the hill-side and the library, and those places are enough for them. Wordsworth, as we know, dealt with two subjects, and with two subjects only,—the simple elemental passions, 'the pangs by which the generations are prepared', and in which they live and breathe and move; and secondly, the spiritual conception of nature, which implies that the universe is, in its beauties and its changes, but the expression of an inherent and animating spirit. Neither of these subjects suits the drawing-room. The simple passions are there carefully covered over; nature is out-of-doors. Mr. Tennyson, however, has given some accounts of the more refined and secondary passions in Wordsworth's intense manner; and if he does not give the exact sketches of external nature, or preach any gospel concerning it, he gives us a mental reflex of it, and a Lotus-eater's view of what it ought to be, and what it is rather a shame on the whole that it is not, which are not inadmissible in a luxurious drawing-room. A little of the spirit of Wordsworth, thus modified, may be traced in Mr. Tennyson; and perhaps this is the only marked trace of a recent writer that can be found in his writings. If we were to be asked as before, whether Mr. Wordsworth or Mr. Tennyson were the superior in general imaginative power, we think we should say that the latter was the superior, but that Wordsworth had achieved a greater task than he has as yet achieved, with inferior powers. The mind of Wordsworth was singularly narrow; his range peculiarly limited; the object he proposed to himself unusually distinct. He has given to us a complete embodiment of the two classes of subjects which he has treated of: perhaps it would be impossible to imagine one of them—the peculiar aspect of outward nature which we mentioned—to be better delineated; certainly as yet, we apprehend, it is not delineated nearly so well any where else. Although we should be inclined to believe that Mr. Tennyson's works indicate greater powers, we do not think that they evince so much concentrated efficiency, that they leave any single result upon the mind which is at once so high and so definite.

If we were asked, as we shall be asked, why we think Mr. Tennyson to have greater powers than Wordsworth, we would venture to allege two reasons. In the first place, Mr. Tennyson has a power of making fun. No one can claim that, of all powers, for Wordsworth, it is certain: no human being more entirely destitute of humour is perhaps discoverable anywhere in literature, or possibly even in society. Not a tinge of it seems ever to have influenced him. He had, through life, the narrow sincerity of the special missionary; but he had not, what is all but incompatible with it, the restraining tact of the man of the world, which teaches that all things and all gospels are only now and then in season; that it is absurd always to be teaching a single doctrine; that it is not wise to fatigue oneself by trying to interest others in that which it is perfectly certain they will not be interested in. The world of 'cakes and ale', indisputably, is not that of Wordsworth. There are quite sufficient indications that Mr. Tennyson appreciates it. Secondly, it may be said that, far more completely than Wordsworth, and far more completely than any other recent poet, Mr. Tennyson has conceived in his mind, and has delineated in his works, a general picture of human life. He certainly does not give us the whole of it, there is a considerable portion which he scarcely touches; but an acute eye can observe that he sees more than he says; and even judging exclusively and rigidly from what is said, the amount of life which Mr. Tennyson has delineated, even in these *Idylls* only, far surpasses in extent and range that which Wordsworth has described. Wordsworth's range is so narrow, and the extent of life and thought which these *Idylls* go over, slight as is their seeming structure, is so great, that perhaps no one will question this conclusion. Some may, however, deny its sufficiency; they may suggest that it does not prove our conclusion. In Shelley's case, it may be said that we allowed a certain defined intensity to have a higher imaginative value than a more diffused fertility and a less concentrated art; why is not Wordsworth entitled to share the benefit of this doctrine also? The plea is very specious, but we are not inclined to think that it is sound. Shelley has shown in a single direction, or in a few directions, an immense general power of imagination and mind. We may not pause to prove this: it is in the nature of allusive criticism to be dogmatic; we must appeal to the memory of our readers. On the other hand, we think, by a certain doggedness of nature, by high resolution, and even, in a certain sense, by an extreme limitation of mind, Wordsworth, with far less of imagination, was able in special directions to execute most admirable works. But the power displayed is, in a great degree, that of character rather than of imagination. He put all his mind into a single task, and he did it. Wordsworth's best works are the saved-up excellencies of a rather barren nature; those of Shelley are the rapid productions of a very fertile one. When we are speaking of mere intellectual and imaginative power, we run, therefore, no risk of contradiction in ranking Mr. Tennyson at a higher place than Wordsworth, notwithstanding that we have adjudged him to be inferior in the same quality to Shelley.

Perhaps we can, after this discussion, fix, at least approximately and incompletely, Mr. Tennyson's position in the hierarchy of our poets. We think that the poets of this century of whom we have been speaking,—and Coleridge may be added to the number,—may be, in a certain sense, classed together as the intellectualised poets. We do not, of course, mean that there ever was a great poet who was destitute of great intellect, or who did not show that intellect distinctly in his poems. But the poets of whom we speak show that intellect in a further and special sense. We are all conscious of the difference between talking to an educated man and to an uneducated. The difference by no means is, that the educated man talks better; that he either says better things, or says them in a more vigorous way. Possibly uneducated persons, as a rule, talk more expressively, and send whatever meaning they have farther into the hearer's mind; perhaps their meaning on the subjects which they have in common with educated men, is not very much inferior. Still there is a subtle charm about the conversation of the educated which that of other persons has not. That charm consists in the constant presence and constant trace of a cultivated intellect. The words are used with a certain distinct precision; a distinguishing tact of intellect is indicated by that which is said; a discriminating felicity is shown in the mode in which it is said. The charm of cultivated expression is like the charm of a cultivated manner; it is easy and yet cautious, natural and yet improved, ready and yet restrained. The fascination of a cultivated intellect in literature is the same. It is more easy to describe its absence, perhaps, than its presence. The style of Shakespeare, for example, wants entirely this peculiar charm. He had the manifold experience, the cheerful practicality, the easy felicity of the uneducated man; but he had not the measured abundance, the self-restraining fertility, which the very highest writer may be conceived to have. There is no subtle discretion in his words: there is the nice tact of native instinct; there is not the less necessary, but yet attractive, precision of an earnest and anxious education. Perhaps it will be admitted that the writers we have mentioned—Shelley, Coleridge, Keats, Wordsworth, and Tennyson—may all be called, as far as our own literature is concerned, in a peculiar sense the intellectualised poets. Milton indeed would, in positive knowledge, be superior to any of them, and to many of them put together, but he is an exceptional poet in English literature, to be classed apart, and seldom to be spoken of in contrast or comparison with any other; and even he, from a want of natural subtlety of mind, does not perhaps show us, in the midst of his amazing knowledge, the most acute and discriminating intellectuality. But if we except Milton, these poets may almost certainly be classed apart: and if they are to be so, we have indicated the place which Mr. Tennyson holds in this class in relation to all of them save Coleridge. A real estimate of the latter is not to be expected of us at the end of an article, and as a parenthesis in the estimate of another poet. He will long be a problem to the critics, and a puzzle to the psychologists. But, so far as the general powers of mind shown in his poems are concerned,—and this is the only aspect of his genius which we are at present considering,—we need have no hesitation in saying that they are much inferior to those shown in the poems of our greatest contemporary poet. Their great excellence is, in truth, almost confined to their singular power in the expression of one single idea. Both 'Christabel' and the 'Ancient Mariner' are substantially developments of the same conception; they delineate almost exclusively the power which the supernatural has, when it is thrust among the detail of the natural. This idea is worked out with astonishing completeness; but it is left to stand alone. There are no characters, no picture of life at large, no extraordinary thoughts, to be found in these poems; their metre and their strangeness are their charm. After what has been said, we need not prove at large that such an exclusive concentration upon such an idea proves that these poems are inferior, or rather indicate inferior imaginative genius to that of Tennyson. The range of the art is infinitely less; and the peculiar idea, which is naturally impressive, and in comparison with others easy to develop, hardly affords scope for the clear exhibition of a very creative genius, even if there were not other circumstances which would lead us to doubt whether Coleridge, rich and various as were his mental gifts, was possessed of that one. On the whole, we may pause in the tedium of our comparative dissertation. We may conclude, that in the series of our intellectualised poets Mr. Tennyson is to be ranked as inferior in the general power of the poetic imagination to Shelley, and to Shelley only;—and if this be true, the establishment of it is a contribution to criticism quite sufficient for a single article.

19. W. E. Gladstone on the *Idylls of the King [1859]* and Earlier Works

William Ewart Gladstone, from an unsigned review, *Quarterly Review* (October 1859), cvi. 454-85.

Gladstone (1809-98), the great Liberal orator, statesman and Prime Minister, revised this essay for inclusion in his *Gleanings of Past Years* (1879), ii. He introduced nearly one hundred changes, most of them with a view to polishing the expression, but some with a view to making the essay even more favourable to its subject. Tennyson already thought it one of the ablest reviews of his *Idylls* (Hallam Tennyson, *op. cit.*, pp. 250, 373). The cuts made in it for present purposes do not significantly affect Gladstone's discussion of Tennyson.

Mr. Tennyson published his first volume, under the title of *Poems chiefly Lyrical*, in 1830, and his second, with the name simply of *Poems*, in 1833. In 1842 he reappeared before the world in two volumes, partly made up from the *débris* of his earlier pieces; and from this time forward he came into the enjoyment of a popularity at once great, growing, and select. With a manly resolution, which gave promise of the rare excellence he was progressively to attain, he had at this time amputated altogether from the collection about one-half of the contents of his earliest work, with some considerable portion of the second; he had almost rewritten or carefully corrected other important pieces, and had added a volume of new compositions.

The later handiwork showed a great advance upon the earlier; as, indeed, 1833 had shown upon 1830. From the very first, however, he had been noteworthy in performance as well as in promise, and it was plain that, whatever else might happen, at least neglect was not to be his lot. But in the natural heat of youth he had at the outset certainly mixed up some trivial with a greater number of worthy productions, and had shown an impatience of criticism by which, however excusable, he was sure to be himself the chief sufferer. His higher gifts, too, were of that quality which, by the changeless law of nature, cannot ripen fast; and there was, accordingly, some portion both of obscurity and of crudity in the results of his youthful labours. Men of slighter materials would have come more quickly to their maturity, and might have given less occasion not only for cavil but for animadversion. It was yet more creditable to him, than it could be even to the just among his critics, that he should, and while yet young, have applied himself with so resolute a hand to the work of castigation. He thus gave a remarkable proof alike of his reverence for his art, of his insight into its powers, of the superiority he had acquired to all the more commonplace illusions of self-love, and perhaps of his presaging consciousness that the great, if they mean to fulfil the measure of their greatness, should always be fastidious against themselves.

It would be superfluous to enter upon any general criticism of this collection, which was examined when still recent in this Review, and a large portion of which is established in the familiar recollection and favour of the public. We may, however, say that what may be termed at large the classical idea (though it is not that of Troas nor of the Homeric period) has, perhaps, never been grasped with greater force and justice than in 'Œnone', nor exhibited in a form of more consummate polish. 'Ulysses' is likewise a highly finished poem; but it is open to the remark that it exhibits (so to speak) a corner-view of a character which was in itself a *cosmos*. Never has political philosophy been wedded to the poetic form more happily than in the three short pieces on England and her institutions, unhappily without title, and only to be cited, like writs of law and papal bulls, by their first words. Even among the rejected pieces there are specimens of a deep metaphysical insight; and this power reappears with an increasing growth of ethical and social wisdom in 'Locksley Hall' and elsewhere. The Wordsworthian poem of 'Dora' is admirable in its kind. From the firmness of its drawing, and the depth and singular purity of its colour, 'Godiva' stood, if we judge aright, as at once a great performance and a great pledge. But, above all, the fragmentary piece on the Death of Arthur was a fit prelude to that lordly music which is now sounding in our ears. If we pass onward from these volumes, it is only because space forbids a further enumeration.

The Princess was published in 1847. The author has termed it 'a medley': why, we know not. It approaches more nearly to the character of a regular drama, with the stage directions written into verse, than any other of his works, and it is composed consecutively throughout on the basis of one idea. It exhibits an effort to amalgamate the place and function of woman with that of man, and the failure of that effort, which duly winds up with the surrender and marriage of the fairest and chief enthusiast. It may be doubted whether the idea is one well suited to exhibition in a quasi-dramatic form. Certainly the mode of embodying it, so far as it is dramatic, is not successful; for here again the persons are little better than mere *personæ*. They are *media*, and weak *media*, for the conveyance of the ideas. The poem is, nevertheless, one of high interest, on account of the force, purity, and nobleness of the main streams of thought, which are clothed in language full of all Mr. Tennyson's excellences; and also because it marks the earliest effort of his mind in the direction of his latest and greatest achievements.

It will not be difficult to establish the first proposition by citations. Who can read the following speech of 'Lady Psyche' without a conversion for the moment, despite the slight interferences it involves with the fundamental laws of creation, to the whole scheme of feminine and social transformation?—

[Quotes *The Princess*, ii. 167–78:

    'At last
. . . the blood of the world." ']

After exhibiting the bane in a form so winning, we must at once present the antidote. Upon the catastrophe of the enterprise—in the manner of which Mr. Tennyson does not go to work like an ingenious playwright—then forthwith—

Love in the sacred halls
Held carnival at will, and flying struck
With showers of random sweet on maid and man.

And at last we are duly brought to the true philosophy of the case:—

[Quotes *The Princess*, vii. 274–305:

    ' "For woman is not . . .
Life." ']

The word 'animal' jars at first hearing; but, without doubt, Mr. Tennyson uses it, as Dante does in '*O animal grazioso e benigno*', to convey simply the idea of life, and as capable of reaching upwards to the highest created life.

With passages like these still upon the mind and ear, and likewise having in view many others in the *Princess* and elsewhere, we may confidently assert it as one of Mr. Tennyson's brightest distinctions that he is now what from the very first he strove to be, and what when he wrote 'Godiva' he gave ample promise of becoming—the poet of woman. We do not mean, nor do we know, that his hold over women as his readers is greater than his command or influence over men; but that he has studied, sounded, painted woman in form, in motion, in character, in office, in capability, with rare devotion, power and skill; and the poet who best achieves this end does also most and best for man.

In 1850 Mr. Tennyson gave to the world, under the title of *In Memoriam*, perhaps the richest oblation ever offered by the affection of friendship at the tomb of the departed. The memory of Arthur Henry Hallam, who died suddenly in 1833, at the age of twenty-two, will doubtless live chiefly in connection with this volume; but he is well known to have been one who, if the term of his days had been prolonged, would have needed no aid from a friendly hand, would have built for himself an enduring monument, and would have bequeathed to his country a name in all likelihood greater than that of his very distinguished father. There was no one among those who were blessed with his friendship, nay, as we see, not even Mr. Tennyson, who did not feel at once bound closely to him by commanding affection, and left far behind by the rapid, full, and rich development of his ever-searching mind; by his

> All comprehensive tenderness,
> All subtilising intellect.

It would be easy to show what, in the varied forms of human excellence, he might, had life been granted him, have accomplished; much more difficult to point the finger and to say, 'This he never could have done'. Enough remains from among his early efforts to accredit whatever mournful witness may now be borne of him. But what can be a nobler tribute than this, that for seventeen years after his death a poet, fast rising towards the lofty summits of his art, found that young fading image the richest source of his inspiration, and of thoughts that gave him buoyancy for a flight such as he had not hitherto attained?

It would be very difficult to convey a just idea of this volume either by narrative or by quotation. In the series of monodies or meditations which compose it, and which follow in long series without weariness or sameness, the poet never moves away a step from the grave of his friend, but, while circling round it, has always a new point of view. Strength of love, depth of grief, aching sense of loss, have driven him forth as it were on a quest of consolation, and he asks it of nature, thought, religion, in a hundred forms which a rich and varied imagination continually suggests, but all of them connected by one central point, the recollection of the dead. This work he prosecutes, not in vain effeminate complaint, but in manly recognition of the fruit and profit even of baffled love, in noble suggestions of the future, in heart-soothing and heart-chastening thoughts of what the dead was and of what he is, and of what one who has been, and therefore still is, in near contact with him is bound to be. The whole movement of the poem is between the mourner and the mourned: it may be called one long soliloquy; but it has this mark of greatness, that, though the singer is himself a large part of the subject, it never degenerates into egotism—for he speaks typically on behalf of humanity at large, and in his own name, like Dante on his mystic journey, teaches deep lessons of life and conscience to us all.

We subjoin one or two specimens, which have many rivals, but are among those most directly ministering to the purpose of the volume:—

[Quotes *In Memoriam*, cix:

'Heart affluence in discursive talk . . .
Nor let thy wisdom make me wise.'

and cxxx:

'Thy voice is on the rolling air . . .
I shall not lose thee, tho' I die.']

The high colour of the portrait in the first of these pieces, and the absorbing and pervading power assigned to the friendship in the second, may seem strained to such as have to take the subject of them upon trust. But we believe that the surviving friends would with one voice assert that Mr. Tennyson is fully warranted in the rare elevation of his strain by the extraordinary endowments of his original.

By the time *In Memoriam* had sunk into the public mind, Mr. Tennyson had taken his rank as our first then living poet. Over the fresh hearts and understandings of the young, notwithstanding his obscurities, his metaphysics, his contempt of gewgaws, he had established an extraordinary sway. We ourselves, with some thousands of other spectators, saw him receive in that noble structure of Wren, the theatre of Oxford, the decoration of D.C.L., which we perceive he always wears on his title-page. Among his colleagues in the honour were Sir De Lacy Evans and Sir John Burgoyne, fresh from the stirring exploits of the Crimea; but even patriotism, at the fever heat of war, could not command a more fervent enthusiasm for the old and gallant warriors than was evoked by the presence of Mr. Tennyson.

In the year 1855 Mr. Tennyson proceeded to publish his *Maud*, the least popular, and probably the least worthy of popularity, among his more considerable works. A somewhat heavy dreaminess, and a great deal of obscurity, hang about this poem; and the effort required to dispel the darkness of the general scheme is not repaid when we discover what it hides. The main thread of *Maud* seems to be this:—A love once accepted, then disappointed, leads to bloodshedding, and onward to madness with lucid alternations. The insanity expresses itself in the ravings of the homicide lover, who even imagines himself among the dead, in a clamour and confusion closely resembling an ill-regulated Bedlam, but which, if the description be a faithful one, would for ever deprive the grave of its title to the epithet of silent. It may be good frenzy, but we doubt its being as good poetry. Of all this there may, we admit, be an esoteric view: but we speak of the work as it offers itself to the common eye. Both Maud and the lover are too nebulous by far; and they remind us of the boneless and pulpy personages by whom, as Dr. Whewell assures us, the planet Jupiter is inhabited, if inhabited at all. But the most doubtful part of the poem is its climax. A vision of the beloved image 'spoke of a hope for the world in the coming wars', righteous wars of course, and the madman begins to receive light and comfort; but, strangely enough, it seems to be the wars, and not the image, in which the source of consolation lies.

> No more shall Commerce be all in all, and Peace
> Pipe on her pastoral hillock a languid note,
> And watch her harvest ripen, her herd increase.
> . . . a peace that was full of wrongs and shames,
> Horrible, hateful, monstrous, not to be told . . .
> For the long long canker of peace is over and done:
> And now by the side of the Black and the Baltic deep,
> And deathful grinning mouths of the fortress, flames
> The blood-red blossom of war with a heart of fire!

What interpretation are we meant to give to all this sound and fury?

We would fain have put it down as intended to be the finishing-stroke in the picture of a mania which has reached its zenith. We might call in aid of this construction more happy and refreshing passages from other poems, as when Mr. Tennyson is

> Certain, if knowledge brings the sword,
> That knowledge takes the sword away.

And again in 'The Golden Dream',—

> When shall all men's good
> Be each man's rule, and universal peace
> Lie like a shaft of light across the land?

And yet once more in a noble piece of *In Memoriam*,—

> Ring out old shapes of foul disease,
> Ring out the narrowing lust of gold;
> Ring out the thousand wars of old,
> Ring in the thousand years of peace.

But on the other hand we must recollect that very long ago, when the apparition of invasion from across the Channel had as yet spoiled no man's slumbers, Tennyson's blood was already up:—

> For the French, the Pope may shrive them . . .
> And the merry devil drive them
> Through the water and the fire.

And unhappily in the beginning of *Maud*, when still in the best use of such wits as he possesses, its hero deals largely in kindred extravagances:—

> When a Mammonite mother kills her babe for a burial fee,
> And Timour-Mammon grins on a pile of children's bones,
> Is it peace or war? better war! loud war by land and by sea,
> War with a thousand battles, and shaking a hundred thrones.

He then anticipates that, upon an enemy's attacking this country, 'the smooth-faced, snub-nosed rogue', who typifies the bulk of the British people, 'the nation of shopkeepers', as it has been emasculated and corrupted by excess of peace, will leap from his counter and till to charge the enemy; and thus it is to be reasonably hoped that we shall attain to the effectual renovation of society.

We frankly own that our divining rod does not enable us to say whether the poet intends to be in any and what degree sponsor to these sentiments, or whether he has put them forth in the exercise of his

undoubted right to make vivid and suggestive representations of even
the partial and narrow aspects of some endangered truth. This is at
best, indeed, a perilous business, for out of such fervid partial representations nearly all grave human error springs; and it should only be
pursued with caution and in season. But we do not recollect that 1855
was a season of serious danger from a mania for peace and its pursuits;
and even if it had been so, we fear that the passages we have quoted
far overpass all the bounds of moderation and good sense. . . . But we
have this solid consolation after all, that Mr. Tennyson's war poetry is
not comparable to his poetry of peace. Indeed he is not here successful
at all: the work, of a lower order than his, demands the abrupt force
and the lyric fire which do not seem to be among his varied and
brilliant gifts. We say more. Mr. Tennyson is too intimately and essentially the poet of the nineteenth century to separate himself from its
leading characteristics, the progress of physical science and a vast commercial, mechanical, and industrial development. Whatever he may say
or do in an occasional fit, he cannot long either cross or lose its sympathies; for while he elevates as well as adorns it, he is flesh of its flesh
and bone of its bone. We fondly believe it is his business to do much
towards the solution of that problem, so fearful from its magnitude,
how to harmonise this new draught of external power and activity
with the old and more mellow wine of faith, self-devotion, loyalty,
reverence, and discipline. And all that we have said is aimed, not at
Mr. Tennyson, but at a lay-figure which he has set up, and into the
mouth of which he has put words that cannot be his words.

We return to our proper task. *Maud*, if an unintelligible or even, for
Mr. Tennyson, an inferior work, is still a work which no inferior man
could have produced; nor would it be difficult to extract abundance of
lines, and even passages, obviously worthy of their author. And if
this poem would have made while alone a volume too light for his
fame, the defect is supplied by the minor pieces, some of which are
admirable. 'The Brook', with its charming interstitial soliloquy, and
the 'Letters' will, we are persuaded, always rank among Mr. Tennyson's
happy efforts; while the 'Ode on the Death of the Duke of Wellington', written from the heart and sealed by the conscience of the poet,
is worthy of that great and genuine piece of manhood, its immortal
subject.

We must touch for a moment upon what has already been mentioned as a separate subject of interest in *The Princess*. We venture to
describe it as in substance a drama, with a plot imperfectly worked and

with characters insufficiently chiselled and relieved. Its author began by presenting, and for many years continued to present, personal as well as natural pictures of individual attitude or movement; and, as in 'Œnone' and 'Godiva', he carried them to a very high pitch of perfection. But he scarcely attempted, unless in his more homely narrations, anything like grouping or combination. It now appears that for this higher effort he has been gradually accumulating and preparing his resources. In the sections of the prolonged soliloquy of *Maud* we see a crude attempt at representing combined interests and characters with heroic elevation, under the special difficulty of appearing, like Mathews, in one person only; in *The Princess* we had a happier effort, though one that still left more to be desired. Each, however, in its own stage was a preparation for an enterprise at once bolder and more mature.

We now come to the recent work of the poet—the *Idylls of the King*. The field, which Mr. Tennyson has chosen for this his recent and far greatest exploit, is one of so deep and wide-reaching an interest as to demand some previous notice of a special kind.

Lofty example in comprehensive forms is, without doubt, one of the great standing needs of our race. To this want it has been from the first one main purpose of the highest poetry to answer. The quest of Beauty leads all those who engage in it to the ideal or normal man as the summit of attainable excellence. By no arbitrary choice, but in obedience to unchanging laws, the painter and the sculptor must found their art upon the study of the human form, and must reckon its successful reproduction as their noblest and most consummate exploit. The concern of Poetry with corporal beauty is, though important, yet secondary: this art uses form as an auxiliary, as a subordinate though proper part in the delineation of mind and character, of which it is appointed to be a visible organ. But with mind and character themselves lies the highest occupation of the Muse. Homer, the patriarch of poets, has founded his two immortal works upon two of these ideal developments in Achilles and Ulysses; and has adorned them with others, such as Penelope and Helen, Hector and Diomed, every one an immortal product, though as compared with the others either less consummate or less conspicuous. Though deformed by the mire of after-tradition, all the great characters of Homer have become models and standards, each in its own kind, for what was, or was supposed to be, its distinguishing gift.

At length, after many generations and great revolutions of mind and of events, another age arrived, like, if not equal, in creative power to that of Homer. The Gospel had given to the whole life of man a real resurrection, and its second birth was followed by its second youth. This rejuvenescence was allotted to those wonderful centuries which popular ignorance confounds with the dark ages properly so called— an identification about as rational as if we were to compare the life within the womb to the life of intelligent though early childhood. Awakened to aspirations at once fresh and ancient, the mind of man took hold of the venerable ideals bequeathed to us by the Greeks as a precious part of its inheritance, and gave them again to the light, appropriated but also renewed. The old materials came forth, but not alone; for the types which human genius had formerly conceived were now submitted to the transfiguring action of a law from on high. Nature herself prompted the effort to bring the old patterns of worldly excellence and greatness—or rather the copies of those patterns still legible, though depraved, and still rich with living suggestion—into harmony with that higher Pattern, once seen by the eyes and handled by the hands of men, and faithfully delineated in the Gospels for the profit of all generations. The life of our Saviour, in its external aspect, was that of a teacher. It was in principle a model for all, but it left space and scope for adaptations to the lay life of Christians in general, such as those by whom the every-day business of the world is to be carried on. It remained for man to make his best endeavour to exhibit the great model on its terrestrial side, in its contact with the world. Here is the true source of that new and noble cycle which the middle ages have handed down to us in duality of form, but with a nearly identical substance, under the royal sceptres of Arthur in England and of Charlemagne in France.

. . . It is to this rich repository that Mr. Tennyson has resorted for his material. He has shown, as we think, rare judgment in the choice. The Arthurian Romance has every recommendation that should win its way to the homage of a great poet. It is national: it is Christian. It is also human in the largest and deepest sense; and, therefore, though highly national, it is universal; for it rests upon those depths and breadths of our nature to which all its truly great developments in all nations are alike essentially and closely related. The distance is enough for atmosphere, not too much for detail; enough for romance, not too much for sympathy. A poet of the nineteenth century, the Laureate has adopted characters, incidents, and even language in the main, instead of attempting to project them on a basis of his own in the region of illimitable fancy. But he has done much more than this. Evidently by reading and by deep meditation, as well as by sheer force of genius, he has penetrated himself down to the very core of his being, with all that is deepest and best in the spirit of the time, or the representation, with which he deals; and as others, using old materials, have been free to alter them in the sense of vulgarity or licence, so he has claimed and used the right to sever and recombine, to enlarge, retrench, and modify, for the purposes at once of a more powerful and elaborate art than his original presents, and of a yet more elevated, or at least of a far more sustained, ethical and Christian strain.

We are rather disposed to quarrel with the title of Idylls: for no diminutive (εἰδύλλιον) can be adequate to the breadth, vigour, and majesty which belong to the subjects, as well as to the execution, of the volume. The poet used the name once before; but he then applied it to pieces generally small in the scale of their delineations, whereas these, even if broken away one from the other, are yet like the disjoined figures from the pediment of the Parthenon in their dignity and force. One indeed among Mr. Tennyson's merits is, that he does not think it necessary to keep himself aloft by artificial effort, but undulates with his matter, and flies high or low as it requires. But even in the humblest parts of these poems—as where the little Novice describes the miniature sorrows and discipline of childhood—the whole receives its tone from an atmosphere which is heroic, and which, even in its extremest simplicity, by no means parts company with grandeur, or ceases to shine in the reflected light of the surrounding objects. Following the example which the poet has set us in a former volume, we would fain have been permitted, at least provisionally, to call these Idylls by the name of Books. Term them what we may, there are four of them—arranged, as we think, in an ascending scale.

The simplicity and grace of the principal character in 'Enid', with which the volume opens, touches, but does not too strongly agitate, the deeper springs of feeling. She is the beautiful daughter of Earl Yniol, who, by his refusal of a turbulent neighbour as a suitor, has drawn down upon himself the ruin of his fortunes, and is visited in his depressed condition by—

> The brave Geraint, a knight of Arthur's court,
> A tributary prince of Devon, one
> Of that great order of the Table Round.

We cannot do better than cite the passage which describes the mother's coming, on the evening of this visit, to the chamber of the maiden:—

[Quotes 'The Marriage of Geraint', ll. 514–38:

'She,
With frequent smile and nod departing . . .
And waited there for Yniol and Geraint.']

Geraint wins her against the detested cousin. They wed, and she becomes the purest gem of the court of Guinevere, her place in which is described in the beautiful exordium of the poem. An accident, slight perhaps for the weight it is made to carry, arouses his jealousy, and he tries her severely by isolation and rude offices on one of his tours; but her gentleness, purity, and patience are proof against all, and we part from the pair in a full and happy reconciliation, which is described in lines of a beauty that leaves nothing to be desired.

The treatment of Enid by her husband has appeared to some of Mr. Tennyson's readers to be unnatural. It is no doubt both in itself repulsive, and foreign to our age and country. But the brutal element in man, which now only invades the conjugal relation in cases where it is highly concentrated, was then far more widely diffused, and not yet dissociated from alternations and even habits of attachment. Something of what we now call Eastern manners at one time marked the treatment even of the women of the West. Unnatural means contrary to nature, irrespectively of time or place; but time and place explain and warrant the treatment of Enid by Geraint.

'Vivien', which follows 'Enid', is perhaps the least popular of the four Books. No pleasure, we grant, can be felt from the character either of the wily woman, between elf and fiend, or of the aged magician, whose love is allowed to travel whither none of his esteem or regard can follow it: and in reading this poem we miss the pleasure of those profound moral harmonies, with which the rest are charged. But we must not on these grounds proceed to the conclusion that the poet has in this case been untrue to his aims. For he has neither failed in power, nor has he led our sympathies astray; and if we ask why he should introduce us to those we cannot love, there is something in the reply that Poetry, the mirror of the world, cannot deal with its attractions only, but must present some of its repulsions also, and avail herself of the powerful assistance of its contrasts. The example of Homer, who allows Thersites to thrust himself upon the scene in the debate of heroes, gives a sanction to what reason and all experience teach, namely, the actual force of negatives in heightening effect; and the gentle and noble characters and beautiful combinations, which largely predominate in the other poems, stand in far clearer and bolder relief when we perceive the dark and baleful shadow of Vivien lowering from between them.

'Vivien' exhibits a well-sustained conflict between the wizard and, in another sense, the witch; on one side is the wit of woman, on the other are the endowments of the prophet and magician, at once more and less than those of nature. She has heard from him of a charm, a charm 'of woven paces, and of waving hands', which paralyses its victim for ever and without deliverance, and her object is to extract from him the knowledge of it as a proof of some return for the fervid and boundless love that she pretends. We cannot but estimate very highly the skill with which Mr. Tennyson has secured to what seemed the weaker vessel the ultimate mastery in the fight. Out of the eater comes forth meat. When she seems to lose ground with him by her slander against the Round Table which he loved, she recovers it by making him believe that she saw all other men, 'the knights, the Court, the King, dark in his light': and when in answer to her imprecation on herself a fearful thunderbolt descends and storm rages, then, nestling in his bosom, part in fear but more in craft, she overcomes the last remnant of his resolution, wins the secret she has so indefatigably wooed, and that instant uses it to close in gloom the famous career of the over-mastered sage.

In force and richness of fancy, as well as in the skill of handling, this poem is indeed remarkable even among the four; and, to bring our assertion to a test, we quote from it the description of Vivien's witchery when she makes her first approaches:—

[Quotes 'Merlin and Vivien', ll. 236–61:

'And lissome Vivien . . .
Veil'd in gray vapour',
omitting ll. 245–51.]

Nowhere could we more opportunely than at this point call attention to Mr. Tennyson's extraordinary felicity and force in the use of metaphor and simile. This gift appears to have grown with his years, alike in abundance, truth, and grace. As the showers descend from heaven to return to it in vapour, so Mr. Tennyson's loving observation of Nature, and his Muse, seem to have had a compact of reciprocity well kept on both sides. When he was young, and when 'Œnone' was first published, he almost boasted of putting a particular kind of grasshopper into Troas, which, as he told us in a note, was probably not to be found there. It is a small but yet an interesting and significant indication that, when some years after he retouched the poem, he omitted the note, and generalised the grasshopper. Whether we are right or not in taking this for a sign of the movement of his mind, there can be no doubt that his present use of figures is both the sign and the result of a reverence for Nature alike active, intelligent, and refined. Sometimes applying the metaphors of Art to Nature, he more frequently draws the materials of his analogies from her unexhausted book, and, however often he may call for some new and beautiful vehicle of illustration, she seems never to withhold an answer. With regard to this particular and very critical gift, it seems to us that he may challenge comparison with almost any poet either of ancient or modern times. We have always been accustomed to look upon Arisoto as one of the greatest among the masters of the art of metaphor and simile; and it would be easy to quote from him instances which in tenderness, grace, force, or all combined, can never be surpassed. But we have rarely seen the power subjected to a greater trial than in the passages just quoted from Mr. Tennyson, where metaphor lies by metaphor as thick as shells upon their bed; yet each individually with its outline as well drawn, its separateness as clear, its form as true to nature, and with the most full and harmonious contribution to the general effect.

The 'Maid of Astolat' is the next figure in the great procession: and this poem has deservedly won very general favour. The framework of it is adopted with less of variation than in any other case from the old romance: indeed it was hardly possible to add to the simplicity and pathos of the tale as it stands in the pages of Sir Thomas Mallory. The most important alteration which the poet has made is in the form of the request which the maiden proffers to Sir Lancelot, when she learns that she cannot be his wife: and he has made it with excellent taste and sense. But while he has preserved its general form, he has broadened and deepened its features, and lengthened those avenues which it opens into the destinies and heart of man.

The opening of the narrative is described in the heading of one of Sir Thomas Mallory's chapters:—'How Sir Lancelot rode to Astolat, and received a sleeve to bear upon his helm at the request of a maid.' He rides on to the tournament with a borrowed shield, and leaves the maid behind him, smitten with an absorbing fondness for the great warrior. We extract the scene in which her heart receives the seal indelible:—

[Quotes 'Lancelot and Elaine', ll. 241–59:

'He spoke and ceased . . .
. . . which was her doom.']

She keeps his shield, a precious token, and by it 'lives in fantasy' on the recollection of him. He wins the prize of valour as is his wont, but is wounded, and is 'brought unto an hermit for to be healed of his wound'. The maid repairs to him, and by her tender and constant nursing he is cured. Her love ever grows in intensity, and she prays to be his wife, or, when she finds that may not be, yet to remain with him, and to wait constantly upon him. This refused, she pines and dies; and her body, by her own prayer, is floated in a barge with only a steerer old and dumb, and bearing in her hand the written announcement of her fate, to King Arthur's palace. Lancelot had been grateful to her,—

> And loved her with all love, except the love
> Of man and woman when they love their best,
> Closest, and sweetest, and had died the death
> In any knightly fashion for her sake;

but the image of Guinevere abides alone, and guiltily supreme, in his great heart:—

> His honour rooted in dishonour stood,
> And faith unfaithful kept him falsely true.

The character of Lancelot was so lofty and tender, so just, brave, and true, so generous and humble, that it would indeed have been more than human, had it been unstained. It is charged with power almost to a surfeit, but all that power is effectually chastened by an extraordinary refinement, and immersed in a profound tenderness of feeling. Such a knight, who had love, compassion, and generosity enough and to spare for every living creature, could not but be deeply moved by the untimely doom encountered by the maiden for his sake; and he complies in deep sadness with her last request, conveyed by the letter in her dead hand, that he will bury her and pray for her. And so we have

> The maiden buried, not as one unknown,
> Nor meanly, but with gorgeous obsequies,
> And mass and rolling music, like a queen.

Besides being a new 'Maid's Tragedy', this Book is also a solemn prelude to that which is to follow, and which we are inclined to consider as marking the highest point which the poetry of our age has reached. The sleeve which Lancelot bears in his disguise arouses the jealousy of Queen Guinevere; and the play of this passion, before it is mournfully extinguished by the catastrophe of the maiden, affords us many glimpses of the interior of her deeply impassioned and powerful nature; while the dark shadows of their coming repentance begin to cross between him and his idol.

In 'Guinevere', as in all the others, Mr. Tennyson gives us liberally of his power in the opening passage; like one who knows that he has ample strength in reserve, and need not guard against disappointments from subsequent decline:—

> Queen Guinevere had fled the court; and sate
> There in the holy house at Amesbury,
> Weeping; none with her save a little maid,
> A novice: one low light betwixt them burned,
> Blurred by the creeping mist; for all abroad,
> Beneath a moon unseen albeit at full,
> The white mist, like a face-cloth to the face,
> Clung to the dead earth, and the land was still.

Sir Modred, keen to sow discord in the hope to rise by it to the throne, and the deadly enemy of Lancelot, had long laboured to detect the unlawful loves of that prince of knights and Guinevere. An instinct of apprehension, which poisoned her life after an indication of his purpose, taught the Queen he would succeed. A last meeting is appointed, that they may take a long farewell. That night betrays them; and she, repelling Lancelot's proposal (one hardly in keeping, we think, with what the romance records of his feelings) to carry her to his dominions, takes sanctuary at Amesbury without making known her name.

The childlike simplicity of the novice draws her out; and we have a prolonged conversation between them sustained with masterly skill and of the deepest interest, the maiden always artlessly and unconsciously but surely touching on the tenderest place in a sore memory and heart. The solemn and fateful strain of the poem is for a moment relieved by a passage where, with vigorous play of fancy and a just use of the preternatural, the merry life of the court and realm of Arthur, before guilt had come to taint it, is described. It purports to be a descrip-

tion by the novice of her own father's journey to attend the inauguration of the Table. We give its closing stage, which describes the
banquet:—

[Quotes 'Guinevere', ll. 258–68:

> 'And when at last he came . . .
> . . . the coming of the sinful Queen.']

These allusions at length reach their climax in a burst of passion from
the Queen, which subsides into a reverie of matchless beauty:—

[Quotes 'Guinevere', ll. 370–406:

> 'But help me, Heaven . . .
> . . . an armed warrior to the doors',
> omitting ll. 389–97.]

It is the King: he draws near:—

> Prone from off her seat she fell,
> And grovelled with her face against the floor:
> There with her milk-white arms and shadowy hair
> She made her face a darkness from the King;
> And in the darkness[1] heard his armed feet
> Pause by her; then came silence, then a voice
> Monotonous and hollow, like a ghost's,
> Denouncing judgment, but, though changed, the King's.

Then follow two most noble speeches of the King. They are indeed
hard to describe. They are of a lofty, almost an awful severity; and yet
a severity justified by the transcendent elevation which the poet has
given to the character of Arthur. Of the old romances, Lancelot, as a
sun with spots, is the hero and the favourite: and Arthur, though good,
just, and wise, if he has not the precise descents of Lancelot's character,
does not attain either to its elevation or to its breadth of scope. Mr.
Tennyson has departed from this order. He has encouraged if not
enjoined us to conceive of Arthur as a warrior no less irresistible than
Lancelot, as even perfect in purity, and as in all other respects more

---

[1] We would not interrupt the perusal of such passages with minute criticism; but just
as with the occasional insertion of weak and expletive words, we do not understand the
principle or aim of certain repetitions of which we seem to have here a double instance in
the word *face* and in the word *darkness*; more observable in the latter case, because while
the term is repeated the sense seems to be changed. We would distinguish as broadly as
possible between repetitions like these, and others which we have noticed farther on, and
which may be called repetitions of emphasis.

comprehensive, solid, and profound. But we must not quarrel with an exercise of the prerogative of genius which has altered the relative stations of the two in the main by raising the one much more than by lowering the other, and which has presented us with so invaluable a result. We know not where to look in history or in letters for a nobler and more overpowering conception of man as he might be than in the Arthur of this volume. Wherever he appears, it is as the great pillar of the moral order, and the resplendent top of human excellence: but even he only reaches to his climax in these two wonderful speeches. They will not bear mutilation: they must be read, and pondered, to be known; but we will extract the conclusion:—

[Quotes 'Guinevere', ll. 555–80:

 ' "My love thro' flesh . . .
 . . . his hands, that blest.']

He departs. She watches him from the window as he mounts, his dragon-crest gleaming in the mist; and with a face 'which then was as an angel's', enjoins the nuns 'to guard and foster her for evermore'. When he had himself

> become as mist
> Before her, moving ghost-like to his doom,

then she bursts out in a passionate apostrophe of that profound penitence, from which the air of nobleness will not depart, and of recalled and revived affection. As the nuns gather round, her strain rises higher still. But we must digress for a moment.

Mr. Tennyson practises largely, and with an extraordinary skill and power, the art of designed and limited repetitions. They bear a considerable resemblance to those Homeric *formulæ* which have been so usefully remarked by Colonel Mure—not the formulæ of constant recurrence, which tell us who spoke and who answered, but those which are connected with pointing moral effects, and with ulterior purpose. These repetitions tend at once to give more definite impressions of character, and to make firmer and closer the whole tissue of the poem. Thus, in the last speech of Guinevere, she echoes back, with other ideas and expressions, the sentiment of Arthur's affection, which becomes in her mouth sublime:—

> I must not scorn myself: he loves me still:
> Let no one dream but that he loves me still.

She prays admission among the nuns, that she may follow the pious and peaceful tenor of their life:—

> And so wear out in almsdeed and in prayer
> The sombre close of that voluptuous day
> Which wrought the ruin of my lord the King.

And it is but a debt of justice to the Guinevere of the romancers to observe, that she loses considerably by the marked transposition which Mr. Tennyson has effected in the order of greatness between Lancelot and Arthur. With him there is an original error in her estimate, independently of the breach of a positive and sacred obligation. She prefers the inferior man; and this preference implies a rooted ethical defect in her nature. In the romance of Sir T. Mallory the preference she gives to Lancelot would have been signally just, had she been free to choose. For Lancelot is of an indescribable grandeur; but the limit of Arthur's character is thus shown in certain words that he uses, and that Lancelot never could have spoken. 'Much more I am sorrier for my good knight's loss than for the loss of my queen; for queens might I have enough, but such a fellowship of good knights shall never be together in no company.'

We began with the exordium of this great work: we must not withhold the conclusion. We left her praying admission to the convent:—

> She said. They took her to themselves; and she,
> Still hoping, fearing, 'is it yet too late?'
> Dwelt with them, till in time their Abbess died.
> Then she, for her good deeds and her pure life,
> And for the power of ministration in her,
> And likewise for the high rank she had borne,
> Was chosen Abbess: there, an Abbess, lived
> For three brief years; and there, an Abbess, pass'd
> To where beyond these voices there is peace.

No one, we are persuaded, can read this poem without feeling, when it ends, what may be termed the pangs of vacancy—of that void in heart and mind for want of its continuance of which we are conscious when some noble strain of music ceases, when some great work of Raphael passes from the view, when we lose sight of some spot connected with high associations, or when some transcendent character upon the page of history disappears, and the withdrawal of it is like the withdrawal of the vital air. We have followed the 'Guinevere' of Mr. Tennyson through its detail, and have extracted largely from its pages, and yet have not a hope of having conveyed an idea of what it really is; still we have thought that in this way we should do it the least injustice, and we are also convinced that even what we have shown will tend to rouse an appetite, and that any of our readers, who may not yet have been also Mr. Tennyson's, will become more eager to learn and admire it at first hand.

We have no doubt that Mr. Tennyson has carefully considered how far his subject is capable of fulfilling the conditions of an epic structure. The history of Arthur is not an epic as it stands, but neither was the Cyclic song, of which the greatest of all epics, the *Iliad*, handles a part. The poem of Ariosto is scarcely an epic, nor is that of Bojardo; but is not this because each is too promiscuous and crowded in its brilliant phantasmagoria to conform to the severe laws of that lofty and inexorable class of poem? Though the Arthurian romance be no epic, it does not follow that no epic can be made from out of it. It is grounded in certain leading characters, men and women, conceived upon models of extraordinary grandeur; and as the Laureate has evidently grasped the genuine law which makes man and not the acts of man the base of epic song, we should not be surprised were he hereafter to realise the great achievement towards which he seems to be feeling his way. There is a moral unity and a living relationship between the four poems before us, and the first effort of 1842 as a fifth, which, though some considerable part of their contents would necessarily rank as episode, establishes the first and most essential condition of their cohesion. The achievement of Vivien bears directly on the state of Arthur by withdrawing his chief councillor—the brain, as Lancelot was the right arm, of his court; the love of Elaine is directly associated with the final catastrophe of the passion of Lancelot for Guinevere. Enid lies somewhat further off the path, nor is it for profane feet to intrude into the sanctuary, for reviewers to advise poets in these high matters; but while we presume nothing, we do not despair of seeing Mr. Tennyson achieve on the basis he has chosen the structure of a full-formed epic.

In any case we have a cheerful hope that, if he continues to advance upon himself as he has advanced heretofore, nay, if he can keep the level he has gained, such a work will be the greatest, and by far the greatest poetical creation, that, whether in our own or in foreign poetry, the nineteenth century has produced. In the face of all critics, the Laureate of England has now reached a position which at once imposes and instils respect. They are self-constituted; but he has won his way through the long dedication of his manful energies, accepted and crowned by deliberate, and, we rejoice to think, by continually growing, public favour. He has after all, and it is not the least nor lowest item in his praise, been the severest of his own critics, and has not been too proud either to learn or to unlearn in the work of maturing his genius and building up his fame.

From his very first appearance he has had the form and fashion of a true poet: the insight into beauty, the perception of harmony, the faculty of suggestion, the eye both in the physical and moral world for motion, light, and colour, the sympathetic and close observation of nature, the dominance of the constructive faculty, and that rare gift the thorough mastery and loving use of his native tongue. Many of us, the common crowd, made of the common clay, may be lovers of Nature, some as sincere or even as ardent as Mr. Tennyson; but it does not follow that even these favoured few possess the privilege that he enjoys. To them she speaks through vague and indeterminate impressions: for him she has a voice of the most delicate articulation; all her images to him are clear and definite, and he translates them for us into that language of suggestion, emphasis, and refined analogy which links the manifold to the simple and the infinite to the finite. He accomplishes for us what we should in vain attempt for ourselves, enables the puny hand to lay hold on what is vast, and brings even coarseness of grasp into a real contact with what is subtle and ethereal. His turn for metaphysical analysis is closely associated with a deep ethical insight: and many of his verses form sayings of so high a class that we trust they are destined to form a permanent part of the household-words of England.

Considering the quantity of power that Mr. Tennyson can make available, it is a great proof of self-discipline that he is not given to a wanton or tyrannous use of it. An extraordinary master of diction, he has confined himself to its severe and simple forms. In establishing this rule of practice his natural gift has evidently been aided by the fine English of the old romances, and we might count upon the fingers the cases in which he has lately deviated into the employment of any stilted phrase, or given sanction to a word not of the best fabric. Profuse in the power of graphic[1] representation, he has chastened some of his earlier groups of imagery, which were occasionally overloaded with particulars; and in his later works, as has been well remarked, he has shown himself thoroughly aware that in poetry half is greater than the

[1] We use the word in what we conceive to be its only legitimate meaning; namely, after the manner and with the effect of painting. It signifies the *quid*, not the *quale*.

whole. That the chastity of style he has attained is not from exhaustion of power may easily be shown. No poet has evinced a more despotic mastery over intractable materials, or has been more successful in clothing what is common with the dignity of his art. The Downs are not the best subjects in the world for verse; but they will be remembered with and by his descriptive line in the *Idylls*—

Far o'er the long backs of the bushless downs.

How becoming is the appearance of what we familiarly term the 'clod' in *The Princess*!

Nor those horn-handed breakers of the glebe.

Of all imaginable subjects, mathematics might seem the most hopeless to make mention of in verse; but they are with him

The hard-grained Muses of the cube and square.

Thus at a single stroke he gives us an image alike simple, true, and poetical to boot, because suited to its place and object in his verse, like the heavy Caryatides well placed in architecture. After this, we may less esteem the feat by which in 'Godiva' he describes the clock striking mid-day:—

All at once,
With twelve great shocks of sound, the shameless noon
Was clashed and hammered from a hundred towers.

But even the contents of a pigeon-pie are not beneath his notice, nor yet beyond his powers of embellishment, in 'Audley Court':—

A pasty, costly made,
Where quail and pigeon, lark and leveret lay
Like fossils of the rock, with golden yolks
Imbedded and injellied.

What excites more surprise is that he can, without any offence against good taste, venture to deal with these contents even after they have entered the mouth of the eater ('Enid'):—

The brawny spearman let his cheek
Bulge with the unswallowed piece, and turning, stared.

The delicate insight of fine taste appears to show him with wonderful precision up to what point his art can control and compel his materials, and from what point the materials are in hopeless rebellion and must be let alone. So in *The Princess* we are introduced to—

> Eight daughters of the plough, stronger than men,
> Huge women *blowzed* with health, and wind, and rain,
> And labour.

It was absolutely necessary for him to heighten, nay, to coarsen, the description of these masses of animated beef, who formed the standing army of the woman-commonwealth. Few would have obeyed this law without violating another; but Mr. Tennyson saw that the verb was admissible, while the adjective would have been intolerable.

In 1842 his purging process made it evident that he did not mean to allow his faults or weaknesses to stint the growth and mar the exhibition of his genius. When he published *In Memoriam* in 1850, all readers were conscious of the progressive widening and strengthening, but, above all, deepening of his mind. We cannot hesitate to mark the present volume as exhibiting another forward and upward stride, and that perhaps the greatest of all, in his career. If we are required to show cause for this opinion under any special head, we would at once point to that which is, after all, the first among the poet's gifts—the gift of conceiving and representing human character.

Mr. Tennyson's Arthurian essays continually suggest to us comparisons not so much with any one poet as a whole, but rather with many or most of the highest poets. The music and the just and pure modulation of his verse carry us back not only to the fine ear of Shelley, but to Milton and to Shakespeare: and his powers of fancy and of expression have produced passages which, if they are excelled by that one transcendent and ethereal poet of our nation whom we have last named, yet could have been produced by no other English minstrel. Our author has a right to regard his own blank verse as highly characteristic and original: but yet Milton has contributed to its formation, and occasionally there is a striking resemblance in turn and diction, while Mr. Tennyson is the more idiomatic of the two. The chastity and moral elevation of this volume, its essential and profound though not didactic Christianity, are such as perhaps cannot be matched throughout the circle of English literature in conjunction with an equal power: and such as to recall a pattern which we know not whether Mr. Tennyson has studied, the celestial strain of Dante.[1] This is the more remarkable,

---

[1] It is no reproach to say that neither Dante nor Homer could have been studied by Mr. Tennyson at the time—a very early period of his life—when he wrote the lines which are allotted to them respectively in 'The Palace of Art'.

because he has had to tread upon ground which must have been slippery for any foot but his. We are far from knowing that either Lancelot or Guinevere would have been safe even for mature readers, were it not for the instinctive purity of his mind and the high skill of his management. We do know that in other times they have had their noble victims, whose names have become immortal as their own.

> Noi leggevamo un giorno per diletto
> Di Lancilotto, e come amor lo strinse.

> ★　　　★　　　★

> Galeotto fu il libro, e chi lo scrisse.[1]

How difficult it is to sustain the elevation of such a subject, may be seen in the well-meant and long popular *Jane Shore* of Rowe. How easily this very theme may be vulgarised, is shown in the *Chevaliers de la Table Ronde* of M. Creuzé de Lesser, who nevertheless has aimed at a peculiar delicacy of treatment.

But the grand poetical quality in which this volume gives to its author a new rank and standing is the dramatic power: the power of drawing character and of representing action. These faculties have not been precocious in Mr. Tennyson: but what is more material, they have come out in great force. He has always been fond of personal delineations, from Claribel and Lilian down to his Ida, his Psyche, and his Maud; but they have been of shadowy quality, doubtful as to flesh and blood, and with eyes having little or no speculation in them. But he is far greater and far better when he has, as he now has, a good raw material ready to his hand, than when he draws only on the airy or chaotic regions of what Carlyle calls unconditioned possibility. He is made not so much to convert the moor into the field, as the field into the rich and gorgeous garden. The imperfect *nisus* which might be remarked in some former works has at length reached the fulness of dramatic energy: in the *Idylls* we have nothing vague or dreamy to complain of: everything lives and moves, in the royal strength of nature: the fire of Prometheus has fairly caught the clay: each figure stands clear, broad, and sharp before us, as if it had sky for its background: and this of small as well as great, for even the 'little novice' is projected on the canvas with the utmost truth and vigour, and with that admirable effect in heightening the great figure of Guinevere, which Patroclus produces for the character of Achilles, and (as some

---

[1] 'Inferno', c. V., v. 127.

will have it) the modest structure of Saint Margaret's for the giant proportions of Westminster Abbey. And this, we repeat, is the crowning gift of the poet: the power of conceiving and representing man.

We do not believe that a Milton—or, in other words, the writer of a *Paradise Lost*—could ever be so great as a Shakespeare or a Homer, because (setting aside all other questions) his chief characters are neither human, nor can they be legitimately founded upon humanity; and, moreover, what he has to represent of man is, by the very law of its being, limited in scale and development. Here at least the saying is a true one: *Antiquitas sæculi, juventus mundi*; rendered by our poet in 'The Day-dream',

> For we are ancients of the earth,
> And in the morning of the times.

The Adam and Eve of Paradise exhibit to us the first inception of our race; and neither then, nor after their first sad lesson, could they furnish those materials for representation, which their descendants have accumulated in the school of their incessant and many-coloured, but on the whole too gloomy, experience. To the long chapters of that experience every generation of man makes its own addition. Again we ask the aid of Mr. Tennyson in 'Locksley Hall':—

> Yet I doubt not through the ages one increasing purpose runs,
> And the thoughts of men are widened with the process of the suns.

The substitution of law for force has indeed altered the relations of the strong and the weak; the hardening or cooling down of political institutions and social traditions, the fixed and legal track instead of the open pathless field, have removed or neutralised many of those occasions and passages of life, which were formerly the schools of individual character. The genius of mechanism has vied, in the arts both of peace and war, with the strong hand, and has well-nigh robbed it of its place. But let us not be deceived by that smoothness of superficies, which the social prospect offers to the distant eye. Nearness dispels the illusion; life is still as full of deep, of ecstatic, of harrowing interests as it ever was. The heart of man still beats and bounds, exults and suffers, from causes which are only less salient and conspicuous because they are more mixed and diversified. It still undergoes every phase of emotion, and even, as seems probable, with a susceptibility which has increased and is increasing, and which has its index and outer form in the growing delicacy and complexities of the nervous system. Does any one believe that ever at any time there was a greater number of deaths referable to that comprehensive cause a broken heart? Let none fear that this age, or any coming one, will extinguish the material of poetry. The more reasonable apprehension might be lest it should sap the vital force necessary to handle that material, and mould it into appropriate forms. To those especially, who cherish any such apprehension, we recommend the perusal of this volume. Of it we will say without fear, what we would not dare to say of any other recent work; that of itself it raises the character and the hopes of the age and the country which have produced it, and that its author, by his own single strength, has made a sensible addition to the permanent wealth of mankind.

20. M. Arnold on Tennyson's Simplicity

Matthew Arnold, from *Last Words on Translating Homer* (1862).

Arnold (1822–88) was Professor of Poetry at Oxford from 1857 to 1867. The passage quoted here occurs about three-quarters of the way through one of his Oxford lectures. He is examining the suggestion that Tennysonian blank verse is plain enough in thought and simple enough in expression to serve for an English version of Homer.

... When Mr. Spedding talks of a plainness of thought 'like Homer's', of a plainness of speech 'like Homer's', and says that he finds these constantly in Mr. Tennyson's poetry, I answer that these I do not find there at all. Mr. Tennyson is a most distinguished and charming poet; but the very essential characteristic of his poetry is, it seems to me, an extreme subtlety and curious elaborateness of thought, an extreme subtlety and curious elaborateness of expression. In the best and most characteristic productions of his genius, these characteristics are most prominent. They are marked characteristics, as we have seen, of the Elizabethan poets; they are marked, though not the essential, characteristics of Shakspeare himself. Under the influences of the nineteenth century, under wholly new conditions of thought and culture, they manifest themselves in Mr. Tennyson's poetry in a wholly new way. But they are still there. The essential bent of his poetry is towards such expressions as—

> Now lies the Earth all Danaë to the stars;
>
>   O'er the sun's bright eye
> Drew the vast eyelid of an inky cloud;
>
> When the cairned mountain was a shadow, sunned
> The world to peace again;
>
> The fresh young captains flashed their glittering teeth,
> The huge bush-bearded barons heaved and blew;

He bared the knotted column of his throat,
The massive square of his heroic breast,
And arms on which the standing muscle sloped
As slopes a wild brook o'er a little stone,
Running too vehemently to break upon it.

And this way of speaking is the least *plain*, the most *un-Homeric*, which can possibly be conceived. Homer presents his thought to you just as it wells from the source of his mind: Mr. Tennyson carefully distils his thought before he will part with it. Hence comes, in the expression of the thought, a heightened and elaborate air. In Homer's poetry it is all natural thoughts in natural words; in Mr. Tennyson's poetry it is all distilled thoughts in distilled words. Exactly this heightening and elaboration may be observed in Mr. Spedding's

While the steeds *mouthed their corn aloof,*

(an expression which might have been Mr. Tennyson's) on which I have already commented; and to one who is penetrated with a sense of the real simplicity of Homer, this subtle sophistication of the thought is, I think, very perceptible even in such lines as these,—

And drunk delight of battle with my peers,
Far on the ringing plains of windy Troy,—

which I have seen quoted as perfectly Homeric. Perfect simplicity can be obtained only by a genius of which perfect simplicity is an essential characteristic.

So true is this, that when a genius essentially subtle, or a genius which, from whatever cause, is in its essence not truly and broadly simple, determines to be perfectly plain, determines not to admit a shade of subtlety or curiosity into its expression, it cannot even then attain real simplicity; it can only attain a semblance of simplicity.[1] French criticism, richer in its vocabulary than ours, has invented a useful word to distinguish this semblance (often very beautiful and valuable) from the real quality. The real quality it calls *simplicité*, the semblance *simplesse*. The one is natural simplicity, the other is artificial simplicity. What is called simplicity in the productions of a genius essentially not simple, is, in truth, *simplesse*. The two are distinguishable

---

[1] I speak of poetic genius as employing itself upon narrative or dramatic poetry,—poetry in which the poet has to go out of himself and to create. In lyrical poetry, in the direct expression of personal feeling, the most subtle genius may, under the momentary pressure of passion, express itself simply. Even here, however, the native tendency will generally be discernible.

from one another the moment they appear in company. For instance, let us take the opening of the narrative in Wordsworth's 'Michael':—

> Upon the forest-side in Grasmere Vale
> There dwelt a shepherd, Michael was his name;
> An old man, stout of heart, and strong of limb.
> His bodily frame had been from youth to age
> Of an unusual strength; his mind was keen,
> Intense, and frugal, apt for all affairs;
> And in his shepherd's calling he was prompt
> And watchful more than ordinary men.

Now let us take the opening of the narrative in Mr. Tennyson's 'Dora':—

> With Farmer Allan at the farm abode
> William and Dora. William was his son,
> And she his niece. He often looked at them,
> And often thought, 'I'll make them man and wife.'

The simplicity of the first of these passages is *simplicité*; that of the second, *simplesse*. Let us take the end of the same two poems; first, of 'Michael':—

> The cottage which was named the Evening Star
> Is gone,—the ploughshare has been through the ground
> On which it stood; great changes have been wrought
> In all the neighbourhood: yet the oak is left
> That grew beside their door: and the remains
> Of the unfinished sheepfold may be seen
> Beside the boisterous brook of Green-head Ghyll.

And now, of 'Dora':—

> So those four abode
> Within one house together; and as years
> Went forward, Mary took another mate:
> But Dora lived unmarried till her death.

A heedless critic may call both of these passages simple if he will. Simple, in a certain sense, they both are; but between the simplicity of the two there is all the difference that there is between the simplicity of Homer and the simplicity of Moschus. . . .

21. H. A. Taine on

Tennyson as the poet of Victorian England

Hippolyte A. Taine, from 'Poetry—Tennyson', *History of English Literature* (trans. H. van Laun, 1871), ii. 518–41.

Taine (1828–93) had originally published his *Histoire de la Littérature Anglaise* in 1863–4. In it, he presents writers as the products of race, milieu, and moment. His chapter on Tennyson ends with the pages that follow.

. . . The favourite poet of a nation, it seems, is he whose works a man, setting out on a journey, prefers to put into his pocket. Now-a-days it would be Tennyson in England, and Alfred de Musset in France. The two publics differ: so do their modes of life, their reading, and their pleasures. Let us try to describe them; we shall better understand the flowers if we see them in the garden.

Here we are at Newhaven or at Dover, and we glide over the rails looking on either side. On both hands fly past country-houses; they exist everywhere in England, on the margin of lakes, on the edge of the bays, on the summit of the hill, in every picturesque point of view. They are the chosen abodes; London is but a business-place; men of the world live, amuse themselves, visit each other, in the country. How well ordered and pretty is this house! If near it there was some old edifice, abbey, or castle, it has been preserved. The new building has been suited to the old; even if detached and modern, it does not lack style; gable-ends, mullions, broad-windows, turrets perched at every corner, have a Gothic air in their newness. Even this cottage, modest as it is, suited to people with a very good income, is pleasant to see with its pointed roofs, its porch, its bright brown bricks, all covered with ivy. Doubtless grandeur is generally wanting; in these days the men who mould opinion are no longer great lords, but rich gentlemen, well brought up, and landholders; it is pleasantness which appeals to them.

But how they understand the word! All round the house is a lawn fresh and smooth as velvet, rolled every morning. In front, great rhododendrons form a bright thicket in which murmur swarms of bees; festoons of exotics creep and curve over the short grass; honey-suckles clamber up the trees; hundreds of roses, drooping over the windows, shed their rain of petals on the paths. Fine elms, yew-trees, great oaks, jealously tended, everywhere combine their leafage or rear their heads. Trees have been brought from Australia and China to adorn the thickets with the elegance or the singularity of their foreign shapes; the copper-beech stretches over the delicate verdure the shadow of its dark metallic-hued foliage. How delicious is the freshness of this verdure! How it glistens, and how it abounds in wild flowers brightened by the sun! What care, what cleanliness, how everything is arranged, kept up, refined, for the comfort of the senses and the pleasure of the eyes! If there is a slope, streams have been devised with little islets in the glen, peopled with tufts of roses; ducks of select breed swim in the pools, where the water-lilies display their satin stars. Fat oxen lie in the grass, sheep as white as if fresh from the washing, all kinds of happy and model animals, fit to delight the eyes of an amateur and a master. We return to the house, and before entering I look upon the view; decidedly the love of Englishmen for the country is innate; how comfortable it will be from that parlour window to look upon the setting sun, and the broad network of sunlight spread across the woods! And how cunningly they have disposed the house, so that the landscape may be seen at distance between the hills, and at hand between the trees! We enter. How nicely everything is got up, and how commodious! The least wants have been foreseen, provided for; there is nothing which is not correct and perfect; we imagine that all the objects have received a prize, or at least honourable mention, at some industrial exhibition. And the attendance of the servants is as good as the objects; cleanliness is not more scrupulous in Holland; Englishmen have, in proportion, three times as many servants as Frenchmen; not too many for the minute details of the service. The domestic machine acts without interruption, without shock, without hindrance; every wheel has its movement and its place, and the comfort which it dispenses falls on the mouth like honeydew, as true and as exquisite as the sugar of a model refinery when quite purified.

We converse with our host. We very soon find that his mind and soul have always been well balanced. When he left college he found his career shaped out for him; no need for him to revolt against the Church, which is half rational; nor against the Constitution, which is nobly liberal: the faith and law presented to him are good, useful, moral, liberal enough to maintain and employ all diversities of sincere minds. He became attached to them, he loves them, he has received from them the whole system of his practical and speculative ideas; he does not waver, he no longer doubts, he knows what he ought to believe and to do. He is not carried away by theories, dulled by sloth, checked by contradictions. Elsewhere youth is like a stagnant or scattering water; here there is a fine old channel which receives and directs to a useful and sure end the stream of its activities and passions. He acts, works, rules. He is married, has tenants, is a magistrate, becomes a politician. He improves and rules his parish, his estate, and his family. He founds societies, speaks at meetings, superintends schools, dispenses justice, introduces improvements; he employs his reading, his travels, his connections, his fortune, and his rank, to lead his neighbours and dependants amicably to some work which profits themselves and the public. He is influential and respected. He has the pleasures of self-esteem and the satisfaction of conscience. He knows that he has authority, and that he uses it loyally, for the good of others. And this healthy state of mind is supported by a wholesome life. His mind is beyond doubt cultivated and occupied; he is well-informed, knows several languages, has travelled, is fond of all precise information; he is kept by his newspaper conversant with all new ideas and discoveries. But, at the same time, he loves and practises all bodily exercises. He rides, takes long walks, hunts, yachts, follows closely and by himself all the details of breeding and agriculture; he lives in the open air, he withstands the encroachments of a sedentary life, which always elsewhere leads the modern man to agitation of the brain, weakness of the muscles, and excitement of the nerves. Such is this elegant and common-sense society, refined in comfort, regular in conduct, whose dilettante tastes and moral principles confine it within a sort of flowery border, and prevent it from having its attention diverted.

Does any poet suit such a society better than Tennyson? Without being a pedant, he is moral; he may be read in the family circle by night; he does not rebel against society and life; he speaks of God and the soul, nobly, tenderly, without ecclesiastical prejudice; there is no need to reproach him like Lord Byron; he has no violent and abrupt words, excessive and scandalous sentiments; he will pervert nobody. We shall not be troubled when we close the book; we may listen when we quit him, without contrast, to the grave voice of the master of the house, who repeats the evening prayers before the kneeling servants. And yet, when we quit him, we keep a smile of pleasure on our lips. The traveller, the lover of archæology, has been pleased by the imitations of foreign and antique sentiments. The sportsman, the lover of the country, has relished the little country scenes and the rich rural pictures. The ladies have been charmed by his portraits of women; they are so exquisite and pure! He has laid such delicate blushes on those lovely cheeks! He has depicted so well the changing expression of those proud or candid eyes! They like him because they feel that he likes them. More, he honours them, and rises in his nobility to the height of their purity. Young girls weep in listening to him; certainly when, a while ago, we heard the legend of 'Elaine' or 'Enid' read, we saw the fair heads drooping under the flowers which adorned them, and white shoulders heaving with furtive emotion. And how delicate was this emotion! He has not rudely trenched upon truth and passion. He has risen to the height of noble and tender sentiments. He has gleaned from all nature and all history what was most lofty and amiable. He has chosen his ideas, chiselled his words, equalled by his artifices, successes, and diversity of his style, the pleasantness and perfection of social elegance in the midst of which we read him. His poetry is like one of those gilt and painted stands in which flowers of the country and exotics mingle in artful harmony their stalks and foliage, their clusters and cups, their scents and hues. It seems made expressly for these wealthy, cultivated, free business men, heirs of the ancient nobility, new leaders of a new England. It is part of their luxury as of their morality; it is an eloquent confirmation of their principles, and a precious article of their drawing-room furniture.

We return to Calais, and travel towards Paris, without pausing on the road. There are on the way plenty of noblemen's castles, and houses of rich men of business. But we do not find amongst them, as in England, the thinking elegant world, which, by the refinement of its tastes and the superiority of its mind, becomes the guide of the nation and the arbiter of the beautiful. There are two peoples in France: the provinces and Paris; the one dining, sleeping, yawning, listening; the other thinking, daring, watching, and speaking: the first drawn by the second, as a snail by a butterfly, alternately amused and disturbed by the whims and the audacity of its guide. It is this guide we must look upon! Let us enter Paris! What a strange spectacle! It is evening, the streets are aflame, a luminous dust covers the busy noisy crowd, which jostles, elbows, crushes, and swarms in front of the theatres, behind the windows of the cafés. Have you remarked how all these faces are wrinkled, frowning, or pale; how anxious are their looks, how nervous their gestures? A violent brightness falls on these shining heads; most are bald before thirty. To find pleasure here, they must have plenty of excitement: the dust of the boulevard settles on the ice which they are eating; the smell of the gas and the steam of the pavement, the perspiration left on the walls dried up by the fever of a Parisian day, 'the human air full of impure rattle'—this is what they cheerfully breathe. They are crammed round their little marble tables, persecuted by the glaring light, the shouts of the waiters, the jumble of mixed talk, the monotonous motion of gloomy walkers, the flutter of loitering courtesans moving anxiously in the shadow. Doubtless their homes are unpleasing, or they would not change them for these bagmen's delights. We climb four flights, and find ourselves in a polished, gilded room, adorned with stuccoed ornaments, plaster statuettes, new furniture of old oak, with every kind of pretty knick-knack on the mantlepieces and the whatnots. 'It makes a good show'; you can give a good reception to envious friends and people of standing. It is an advertisement, nothing more; we pass half an hour there agreeably, and that is all. You will never make more than a house of call out of it; it is low in the ceiling, close, inconvenient, rented by the year, dirty in six months, serving to display a fictitious luxury. All the enjoyments of these people are factitious, and, as it were, snatched hurriedly; they have in them something unhealthy and irritating. They are like the cookery of their restaurants, the splendour of their cafés, the gaiety of their theatres. They want them too quick, too lively, too manifold. They have not cultivated them patiently, and culled them moderately; they have forced them on an artificial and heating soil; they grasp them in haste. They are refined and greedy; they need every day a stock of coloured words, broad anecdotes, biting railleries, new truths, varied ideas. They soon get bored, and cannot endure tedium, They amuse themselves with all their might, and find that they are hardly amused. They exaggerate their work and their expense, their wants and their efforts. The accumulation of sensations and fatigue stretches their nervous machine to excess, and their polish of social gaiety chips off twenty times a day, displaying a basis of suffering and ardour.

But how fine they are, and how free is their mind! How this incessant rubbing has sharpened them! How ready they are to grasp and comprehend everything! How apt this studied and manifold culture has made them to feel and relish tendernesses and sadnesses, unknown to their fathers, deep feelings, strange and sublime, which hitherto seemed foreign to their race! This great city is cosmopolitan; here all ideas may be born; no barrier checks the mind; the vast field of thought opens before them without a beaten or prescribed track. Use neither hinders nor guides them; an official Government and Church rid them of the care of leading the nation: the two powers are submitted to, as we submit to the beadle or the policeman, patiently and with chaff; they are looked upon as a play. In short, the world here seems but a melodrama, a subject of criticism and argument. And be sure that criticism and argument have full scope. An Englishman entering on life, finds to all great questions an answer ready made. A Frenchman entering on life finds to all great questions simply suggested doubts. In this conflict of opinions he must create a faith for himself, and, being mostly unable to do it, he remains open to every uncertainty, and therefore to every curiosity and to every pain. In this gulf, which is like a vast sea, dreams, theories, fancies, intemperate, poetic and sickly desires, collect and chase each other like clouds. If in this tumult of moving forms we seek some solid work to prepare a foundation for future opinions, we find only the slowly-rising edifices of the sciences, which here and there obscurely, like submarine polypes, construct of imperceptible coral the basis on which the belief of the human race is to rest.

Such is the world for which Alfred de Musset wrote: in Paris he must be read. Read? We all know him by heart. He is dead, and it seems as if we daily hear him speak. A conversation among artists, as they jest in a studio, a beautiful young girl leaning over her box at the theatre, a street washed by the rain, making the black pavement shine, a fresh smiling morning in the woods of Fontainebleau, everything brings him before us, as if he were alive again. Was there ever a more vibrating and genuine accent? This man, at least, has never lied. He has only said what he felt, and he has said it, as he felt it. He thought aloud. He made the confession of every man. He was not admired, but loved; he was more than a poet, he was a man. Every one found in him his own feelings, the most transient, the most familiar; he did not restrain himself, he gave himself to all; he had the last virtues which remain to us, generosity and sincerity. And he had the most precious gift which can seduce an old civilisation, youth. As he said, 'that hot youth, a tree with a rough bark, which covers all with its shadow, prospect and path'. With what fire did he hurl onward love, jealousy, the thirst of pleasure, all the impetuous passions which rise with virgin blood from the depths of a young heart, and how did he make them clash together!

Has any one felt them more deeply? He was too full of them, he gave himself up to them, was intoxicated with them. He rushed through life, like an eager racehorse in the country, whom the scent of plants and the splendid novelty of the vast heavens urge, breast foremost, in its mad career, which shatters all before him, and himself as well. He desired too much; he wished strongly and greedily to taste life in one draught, thoroughly; he did not glean or taste it; he tore it off like a bunch of grapes, pressed it, crushed it, twisted it; and he remains with stained hands, as thirsty as before.[1] Then broke forth sobs which found an echo in all hearts. What! so young, and already so wearied! So many precious gifts, so fine a mind, so delicate a tact, so rich and mobile a fancy, so precocious a glory, such a sudden blossom of beauty and genius, and yet anguish, disgust, tears, and cries! What a mixture! With the same attitude he adores and curses. Eternal illusion, invincible experience, keep side by side in him to fight and tear him. He became old, and remained young; he is a poet, and he is a sceptic. The Muse and her peaceful beauty, Nature and her immortal freshness, Love and his happy smile, all the swarm of divine visions barely passed before his eyes, when we see approaching, with curses and sarcasms, all the spectres of debauchery and death. He is as a man in a festive scene, who drinks from a carven cup, standing up, in front, amidst applause and triumphal music, his eyes laughing, his heart full of joy, heated and excited by the generous wine descending in his breast, whom suddenly we see growing pale; there was poison in the cup; he falls, and the death-rattle is in his throat; his convulsed feet beat upon the silken carpet, and all the terrified guests look on. This is what we felt on the day when the most beloved, the most brilliant amongst us, suddenly quivered from an unseen attack, and was struck down, with the death-rattle in his throat, amid the lying splendours and gaieties of our banquet.

Well! such as he was, we love him for ever: we cannot listen to another; beside him, all seem cold or false. We leave at midnight the theatre in which he had heard Malibran, and we enter the gloomy *rue des Moulins*, where, on a hired bed, his Rolla came to sleep and die. The lamps cast flickering rays on the slippery pavement. Restless shadows march past the doors, and trail along their dress of draggled silk to meet the passers-by. The windows are fastened; here and there a

---

[1] 'O médiocrité! celui qui pour tout bien
T'apporte à ce tripot dégoûtant de la vie
Est bien poltron au jeu s'il ne dit: Tout ou rien.'

light pierces through a half-closed shutter, and shows a dead dahlia on the edge of a window-sill. Tomorrow an organ will grind before these panes, and the wan clouds will leave their droppings on these dirty walls. From this wretched place came the most impassioned of his poems! These vilenesses and vulgarities of the stews and the lodging-house caused this divine eloquence to flow! it was these which at such a moment gathered in this bruised heart all the splendours of nature and history, to make them spring up in sparkling jets, and shine under the most glowing poetic sun that ever rose! We feel pity; we think of that other poet, away there in the Isle of Wight, who amuses himself by dressing up lost epics. How happy he is amongst his fine books, his friends, his honeysuckles and roses! No matter. De Musset, in this very spot, in this filth and misery, rose higher. From the heights of his doubt and despair, he saw the infinite, as we see the sea from a storm-beaten promontory. Religions, their glory and their decay, the human race, its pangs and its destiny, all that is sublime in the world, appeared there to him in a flash of lightning. He felt, at least this once in his life, the inner tempest of deep sensations, giant-dreams, and intense voluptuousness, whose desire enabled him to live, and whose lack forced him to die. He was no mere dilettante; he was not content to taste and enjoy; he left his mark on human thought; he told the world what was man, love, truth, happiness. He suffered, but he invented; he fainted, but he produced. He tore from his entrails with despair the idea which he had conceived, and showed it to the eyes of all, bloody but alive. That is harder and lovelier than to go fondling and gazing upon the ideas of others. There is in the world but one work worthy of a man, the production of a truth, to which we devote ourselves, and in which we believe. The people who have listened to Tennyson are better than our aristocracy of townsfolk and bohemians; but I prefer Alfred de Musset to Tennyson.

22. G. M. Hopkins on Parnassian

Gerard Manley Hopkins, from a letter of 10th September 1864, *Further Letters of Gerard Manley Hopkins* (ed. C. C. Abbott, 1938), pp. 68–76.

Hopkins (1844–89) was still a student at Oxford at the time of writing.

... I think then the language of verse may be divided into three kinds. The first and highest is poetry proper, the language of inspiration. The word inspiration need cause no difficulty. I mean by it a mood of great, abnormal in fact, mental acuteness, either energetic or receptive, according as the thoughts which arise in it seem generated by a stress and action of the brain, or to strike into it unasked. This mood arises from various causes, physical generally, as good health or state of the air or, prosaic as it is, length of time after a meal. But I need not go into this; all that it is needful to mark is, that the poetry of inspiration can only be written in this mood of mind, even if it only last a minute, by poets themselves. Everybody of course has like moods, but not being poets what they then produce is not poetry. The second kind I call *Parnassian*. It can only be spoken by poets, but is not in the highest sense poetry. It does not require the mood of mind in which the poetry of inspiration is written. It is spoken *on and from the level* of a poet's mind, not, as in the other case, when the inspiration which is the gift of genius, raises him above himself. For I think it is the case with genius that it is not when quiescent so very much above mediocrity as the difference between the two might lead us to think, but that it has the power and privilege of rising from that level to a height utterly far from mediocrity: in other words that its greatness is *that it can be* so great. You will understand. *Parnassian* then is that language which genius speaks as fitted to its exaltation, and place among other genius, but does not sing (I have been betrayed into the whole hog of a metaphor) in its flights. Great men, poets I mean, have each their own dialect as it were of Parnassian, formed generally as they go on writing, and at last,—this is the point to be marked,—they can see things in this Parnassian way and describe them in this Parnassian tongue, without further effort of inspiration. In a poet's particular kind of Parnassian lies most of his style, of his manner, of his mannerism if you like. But I must not go farther without giving you instances of Parnassian. I shall take one from Tennyson, and from 'Enoch Arden', from a passage much quoted already and which will be no doubt often quoted, the description of Enoch's tropical island.

> The mountain wooded to the peak, the lawns
> And winding glades high up like ways to Heaven,
> The slender coco's drooping crown of plumes,
> The lightning flash of insect and of bird,
> The lustre of the long convolvuluses
> That coil'd around the stately stems, and ran
> Ev'n to the limit of the land, the glows
> And glories of the broad belt of the world,
> All these he saw.

Now it is a mark of Parnassian that one could conceive oneself writing it if one were the poet. Do not say that *if* you were Shakespear you can imagine yourself writing *Hamlet,* because that is just what I think you can*not* conceive. In a fine piece of inspiration every beauty takes you as it were by surprise, not of course that you did not think the writer could be so great, for that is not it,—indeed I think it is a mistake to speak of people admiring Shakespear more and more as they live, for when the judgment is ripe and you have read a good deal of any writer including his best things, and carefully, then, I think, however high the place you give him, that you must have rated him equally with his merits however great they be; so that all after admiration cannot increase but keep alive this estimate, make his greatness stare into your eyes and din it into your ears, as it were, but not make it greater,—but to go on with the broken sentence, every fresh beauty could not in any way be predicted or accounted for by what one has already read. But in Parnassian pieces you feel that if you were the poet you could have gone on as he has done, you see yourself doing it, only with the difference that if you actually try you find you cannot write his Parnassian. Well now to turn to the piece above. The glades being 'like ways to Heaven' is, I think, a new thought, it is an inspiration. Not so the next line, that is pure Parnassian. If you examine it the words are choice and the description is beautiful and unexceptionable, but it does not *touch* you. The next is more Parnassian still. In the next lines I think the picture of the convolvuluses does touch; but only the picture: the words are Parnassian. It is a very good instance, for the lines are undoubtedly beautiful, but yet I could scarcely point any-where to anything more idiomatically Parnassian, to anything which I more clearly see myself writing *qua* Tennyson, than the words

> The glows
> And glories of the broad belt of the world.

What Parnassian is you will now understand, but I must make some more remarks on it. I believe that when a poet palls on us it is because of his Parnassian. We seem to have found out his secret. Now in fact we have not found out more than this, that when he is not inspired and in his flights, his poetry does run in an intelligibly laid down path. Well, it is notorious that Shakespear does not pall, and this is because he uses, I believe, so little Parnassian. He does use some, but little. Now judging from my own experience I should say no author palls so much as Wordsworth; this is because he writes such an 'intolerable deal of' Parnassian.

If with a critical eye and in a critical appreciative mood you read a poem by an unknown author or an anonymous poem by a known, but not at once recognizable, author, and he is a real poet, then you will pronounce him so at once, and the poem will seem truly inspired, though afterwards, when you know the author, you will be able to distinguish his inspirations from his Parnassian, and will perhaps think the very piece which struck you so much at first mere Parnassian. You know well how deadened, as it were, the critical faculties become at times, when all good poetry alike loses its clear ring and its charm; while in other moods they are so enlivened that things that have long lost their freshness strike you with their original definiteness and piquant beauty.

I think one had got into the way of thinking, or had not got out of the way of thinking, that Tennyson was always new, *touching*, beyond other poets, not pressed with human ailments, never using Parnassian. So at least I used to think. Now one sees he uses Parnassian; he is, one must see it, what we used to call Tennysonian. But the discovery of this must not make too much difference. When puzzled by one's doubts it is well to turn to a passage like this. Surely your maturest judgment will never be fooled out of saying that this is divine, terribly beautiful—the stanza of *In Memoriam* beginning with the quatrain

> O Hesper o'er the buried sun,
> And ready thou to die with him,
> Thou watchest all things ever dim
> And dimmer, and a glory done.

I quote from memory. Inconsequent conclusion: Shakespear is and must be utterly the greatest of poets.

Just to end what I was saying about poetry. There is a higher sort of Parnassian which I call *Castalian*, or it may be thought the lowest kind of inspiration. Beautiful poems may be written wholly in it. Its peculiarity is that though you can hardly conceive yourself having written in it, if in the poet's place, yet it is too characteristic of the poet, too so-and-so-all-over-ish, to be quite inspiration. E.g.

> Yet despair
> Touches me not, though pensive as a bird
> Whose vernal coverts winter hath laid bare.

This is from Wordsworth, beautiful, but rather too essentially Wordsworthian, too persistently his way of looking at things. The third kind is merely the language of verse as distinct from that of prose, Delphic, the tongue of the Sacred *Plain*, I may call it, used in common by poet and poetaster. Poetry when spoken is spoken in it, but to speak it is not necessarily to speak poetry. I may add there is also *Olympian*. This is the language of strange masculine genius which suddenly, as it were, forces its way into the domain of poetry, without naturally having a right there. Milman's poetry is of this kind I think, and Rossetti's 'Blessèd Damozel'. But unusual poetry has a tendency to seem so at first. . . .

23. W. Bagehot on

Enoch Arden [1864]

Walter Bagehot, from 'Wordsworth, Tennyson, and Browning; or, Pure, Ornate, and Grotesque Art in English Poetry' (unsigned article), *National Review* (November 1864), N.S. i. 27–66.

. . . There should be a word in the language of literary art to express what the word 'picturesque' expresses for the fine arts. *Picturesque* means fit to be put into a picture; we want a word *literatesque*, 'fit to be put into a book'.

. . . The word 'literatesque', would mean, if we possessed it, that perfect combination in the *subject-matter* of literature, which suits the *art* of literature. We often meet people, and say of them, sometimes meaning well and sometimes ill, 'How well so-and-so would do in a book!' Such people are by no means the best people; but they are the most effective people—the most rememberable people. Frequently, when we first know them, we like them because they explain to us so much of our experience; we have known many people 'like that', in one way or another, but we did not seem to understand them; they were nothing to us, for their traits were indistinct; we forgot them, for they *hitched* on to nothing, and we could not classify them; but when we see the *type* of the genus, at once we seem to comprehend its character; the inferior specimens are explained by the perfect embodiment; the approximations are definable when we know the ideal to which they draw near. There are an infinite number of classes of human beings, but in each of these classes there is a distinctive type which, if we could expand it out in words, would define the class. We cannot expand it in formal terms any more than a landscape, or a species of landscapes; but we have an art, an art of words, which can draw it. Travellers and others often bring home, in addition to their long journals—which, though so living to them, are so dead, so inanimate, so undescriptive to all else—a pen-and-ink sketch, rudely done, very likely, but which, perhaps, even the more for the blots and strokes, gives a distinct notion, an emphatic image, to all who see it. They say at once, *now* we know the sort of thing. The sketch has *hit* the mind. True literature does the same. It describes sorts, varieties, and permutations, by delineating the type of each sort, the ideal of each variety, the central, the marking trait of each permutation. . . .

The great divisions of poetry, and of all other literary art, arise from the different modes in which these *types*—these characteristic men, these characteristic feelings—may be variously described. There are three principal modes which we shall attempt to describe—the *pure*, which is sometimes, but not very wisely, called the classical; the *ornate*, which is also unwisely called romantic; and the *grotesque*, which might be called the mediæval. We will describe the nature of these a little. Criticism, we know, must be brief—not, like poetry, because its charm is too intense to be sustained—but on the contrary, because its interest is too weak to be prolonged; but elementary criticism, if an evil, is a necessary evil; a little while spent among the simple principles of art is the first condition, the absolute pre-requisite, for surely apprehending and wisely judging the complete embodiments and miscellaneous forms of actual literature.

The definition of *pure* literature is that it describes the type in its simplicity; we mean, with the exact amount of accessory circumstance which is necessary to bring it before the mind in finished perfection, and *no more* than that amount. The *type* needs some accessories from its nature—a picturesque landscape does not consist wholly of picturesque features. There is a setting of surroundings—as the Americans would say, of *fixings*—without which the reality is not itself. By a traditional mode of speech, as soon as we see a picture in which a complete effect is produced by detail so rare and so harmonised as to escape us, we say how 'classical'. The whole which is to be seen appears at once and through the detail, but the detail itself is not seen: we do not think of that which gives us the idea; we are absorbed in the idea itself. Just so in literature, the pure art is that which works with the fewest strokes; the fewest, that is, for its purpose, for its aim is to call up and bring home to men an idea, a form, a character; and if that idea be twisted, that form be involved, that character perplexed, many strokes of literary art will be needful. Pure art does not mutilate its object; it represents it as fully as is possible with the slightest effort which is possible: it shrinks from no needful circumstances, as little as it inserts any which are

needless. The precise peculiarity is not merely that no incidental circumstance is inserted which does not tell on the main design:—no art is
fit to be called *art* which permits a stroke to be put in without an
object;—but that only the minimum of such circumstance is inserted
at all. The form is sometimes said to be bare, the accessories are sometimes said to be invisible, because the appendages are so choice that the
shape only is perceived.

The English literature undoubtedly contains much impure literature;
impure in its style, if not in its meaning: but it also contains one great,
one nearly perfect, model of the pure style in the literary expression of
typical *sentiment*; and one not perfect, but gigantic and close approxima-
tion to perfection, in the pure delineation of objective character. Wordsworth, perhaps, comes as near to choice purity of style in sentiment as
is possible; Milton, with exceptions and conditions to be explained,
approaches perfection by the strenuous purity with which he depicts
character. . . .

The extreme opposite to this pure art is what may be called ornate
art. This species of art aims also at giving a delineation of the typical
idea in its perfection and its fulness, but it aims at so doing in a manner
most different. It wishes to surround the type with the greatest number
of circumstances which it will *bear*. It works not by choice and selection,
but by accumulation and aggregation. The idea is not, as in the pure
style, presented with the least clothing which it will endure, but with
the richest and most involved clothing that it will admit.

We are fortunate in not having to hunt out of past literature an
illustrative specimen of the ornate style. Mr. Tennyson has just given
one, admirable in itself, and most characteristic of the defects and the
merits of this style. The story of 'Enoch Arden', as he has enhanced and
presented it, is a rich and splendid composite of imagery and illustration. Yet how simple that story is in itself. A sailor who sells fish, breaks
his leg, gets dismal, gives up selling fish, goes to sea, is wrecked on a
desert island, stays there some years, on his return finds his wife
married to a miller, speaks to a landlady on the subject, and dies. Told
in the pure and simple, the unadorned and classical style, this story
would not have taken three pages, but Mr. Tennyson has been able to
make it the principal, the largest, tale in his new volume. He has done
so only by giving to every event and incident in the volume an accompanying commentary. He tells a great deal about the torrid zone which
a rough sailor like Enoch Arden certainly would not have perceived;
and he gives to the fishing village, to which all the characters belong, a

softness and a fascination which such villages scarcely possess in reality.
  The description of the tropical island, on which the sailor is thrown,
is an absolute model of adorned art:—

[Quotes 'Enoch Arden', ll. 568–95:

  'The mountain wooded . . .
  . . . but no sail.']

No expressive circumstance can be added to this description, no
enchancing detail suggested. A much less happy instance is the description of Enoch's life before he sailed:—

[Quotes 'Enoch Arden', ll. 91–100:

  'While Enoch was abroad on wrathful seas . . .
  Whose Friday fare was Enoch's ministering.']

So much has not often been made of selling fish.
  The essence of ornate art is in this manner to accumulate round the
typical object, everything which can be said about it, every associated
thought that can be connected with it, without impairing the essence
of the delineation.
  The first defect which strikes a student of ornate art—the first which
arrests the mere reader of it—is what is called a want of simplicity.
Nothing is described as it is, everything has about it an atmosphere of
something else. The combined and associated thoughts, though they
set off and heighten particular ideas and aspects of the central and
typical conception, yet complicate it: a simple thing—'a daisy by the
river's brim'—is never left by itself, something else is put with it;
something not more connected with it than 'lion-whelp' and the
'peacock yew-tree' are with the 'fresh fish for sale' that Enoch carries
past them. Even in the highest cases, ornate art leaves upon a cultured
and delicate taste the conviction that it is not the highest art, that it is
somehow excessive and overrich, that it is not chaste in itself or chasten-
ing to the mind that sees it—that it is in an unexplained manner
unsatisfactory, 'a thing in which we feel there is some hidden
want!'
  That want is a want of 'definition'. We must all know landscapes,
river landscapes especially, which are in the highest sense beautiful,
which when we first see them give us a delicate pleasure; which in
some—and these the best cases—give even a gentle sense of surprise
that such things should be so beautiful, and yet when we come to

live in them, to spend even a few hours in them, we seem stifled and oppressed. On the other hand, there are people to whom the sea-shore is a companion, an exhilaration; and not so much for the brawl of the shore as for the *limited* vastness, the finite infinite, of the ocean as they see it. Such people often come home braced and nerved, and if they spoke out the truth, would have only to say 'We have seen the horizon line'; if they were let alone, indeed, they would gaze on it hour after hour, so great to them is the fascination, so full the sustaining calm, which they gain from that union of form and greatness. To a very inferior extent, but still, perhaps, to an extent which most people understand better, a common arch will have the same effect. A bridge completes a river landscape; if of the old and many-arched sort, it regulates by a long series of defined forms the vague outline of wood and river which before had nothing to measure it; if of the new scientific sort, it introduces still more strictly a geometrical element; it stiffens the scenery which was before too soft, too delicate, too vegetable. Just such is the effect of pure style in literary art. It calms by conciseness; while the ornate style leaves on the mind a mist of beauty, an excess of fascination, a complication of charm, the pure style leaves behind it the simple, defined, measured idea, as it is, and by itself. That which is chaste chastens; there is a poised energy—a state half thrill, and half tranquillity—which pure art gives; which no other can give; a pleasure justified as well as felt; an ennobled satisfaction at what ought to satisfy us, and must ennoble us.

Ornate art is to pure art what a painted statue is to an unpainted. It is impossible to deny that a touch of colour *does* bring out certain parts, does convey certain expressions, does heighten certain features, but it leaves on the work as a whole, a want, as we say, 'of something'; a want of that inseparable chasteness which clings to simple sculpture, an impairing predominance of alluring details which impairs our satisfaction with our own satisfaction; which makes us doubt whether a higher being than ourselves will be satisfied even though we are so. In the very same manner, though the *rouge* of ornate literature excites our eye, it also impairs our confidence.

Mr. Arnold has justly observed that this self-justifying, self-*proving* purity of style is commoner in ancient literature than in modern literature, and also that Shakespeare is not a great or an unmixed example of it. No one can say that he is. His works are full of undergrowth, are full of complexity, are not models of style; except by a miracle nothing in the Elizabethan could be a model of style; the restraining taste of that age was feebler and more mistaken than that of any other equally great age. Shakespeare's mind so teemed with creation that he required the most just, most forcible, most constant restraint from without. He most needed to be guided of poets, and he was the least and worst guided. As a whole, no one can call his works finished models of the pure style, or of any style. But he has many passages of the most pure style, passages which could be easily cited if space served. And we must remember that the task which Shakespeare undertook was the most difficult which any poet has ever attempted, and that it is a task in which after a million efforts every other poet has failed. The Elizabethan drama—as Shakespeare has immortalised it—undertakes to delineate in five acts, under stage restrictions, and in mere dialogue, a whole list of *dramatis personæ*, a set of characters enough for a modern novel, and with the distinctness of a modern novel. Shakespeare is not content to give two or three great characters in solitude and in dignity, like the classical dramatists; he wishes to give a whole *party* of characters in the play of life, and according to the nature of each. He would 'hold the mirror up to nature', not to catch a monarch in a tragic posture, but a whole group of characters engaged in many actions, intent on many purposes, thinking many thoughts . . . The severest art must have allowed many details, much overflowing circumstance, to a poet who undertook to describe what almost defies description. Pure art would have *commanded* him to use details lavishly, for only by a multiplicity of such could the required effect have been at all produced. Shakespeare could accomplish it, for his mind was a *spring*, an inexhaustible fountain of human nature; and it is no wonder that being compelled by the task of his time to let the fulness of his nature overflow, he sometimes let it overflow too much, and covered with erroneous conceits and super-fluous images, characters and conceptions which would have been far more justly, far more effectually, delineated with conciseness and simplicity. But there is an infinity of pure art *in* Shakespeare although there is a great deal else also.

It will be said, if ornate art be, as you say, an inferior species of art, why should it ever be used? If pure art be the best sort of art, why should it not always be used?

The reason is this: literary art, as we just now explained, is concerned with literatesque characters in literatesque situations; and the *best* art is concerned with the *most* literatesque characters in the *most* literatesque situations. Such are the subjects of pure art; it embodies with the fewest touches, and under the most select and choice circumstances, the highest conceptions; but it does not follow that only the best subjects are to be treated by art, and then only in the very best way. Human nature could not endure such a critical commandment as that, and it would be an erroneous criticism which gave it. *Any* literatesque character may be described in literature under *any* circumstances which exhibit its literatesqueness.

The essence of pure art consists in its describing what is as it is, and this is very well for what can bear it; but there are many inferior things which will not bear it, and which nevertheless ought to be described in books. A certain kind of literature deals with illusions, and this kind of literature has given a colouring to the name romantic. A man of rare genius, and even of poetical genius, has gone so far as to make these illusions the true subject of poetry—almost the sole subject.

'Without,' says Father Newman, of one of his characters, 'being himself a poet, he was in the season of poetry, in the sweet spring-time, when the year is most beautiful, because it is new. Novelty was beauty to a heart so open and cheerful as his; not only because it was novelty, and had its proper charm as such, but because when we first see things, we see them in a gay confusion, which is a principal element of the poetical. As time goes on, and we number and sort and measure things,—as we gain views,—we advance towards philosophy and truth, but we recede from poetry.

'When we ourselves were young, we once on a time walked on a hot summer-day from Oxford to Newington—a dull road, as any one who has gone it knows; yet it was new to us; and we protest to you, reader, believe it or not, laugh or not, as you will, to us it seemed on that occasion quite touchingly beautiful; and a soft melancholy came over us, of which the shadows fall even now, when we look back upon that dusty, weary journey. And why? because every object which met us was unknown and full of mystery. A tree or two in the distance seemed the beginning of a great wood, or park, stretching endlessly; a hill implied a vale beyond, with that vale's history; the by-lanes, with their green hedges, wound on and van-ished, yet were not lost to the imagination. Such was our first journey; but when we had gone it several times, the mind refused to act, the scene ceased to enchant, stern reality alone remained; and we thought it one of the most tiresome, odious roads we ever had occasion to traverse.'

That is to say, that the function of the poet is to introduce a 'gay confusion', a rich medley which does not exist in the actual world—which perhaps could not exist in any world—but which would seem pretty if it did exist. Everyone who reads 'Enoch Arden' will perceive that this notion of all poetry is exactly applicable to this one poem. Whatever be made of Enoch's, 'Ocean spoil in ocean-smelling osier', of the 'portal-warding lion-whelp', and the 'peacock yew-tree', everyone knows that in himself Enoch could not have been charming. People who sell fish about the country (and this is what he did, though Mr. Tennyson won't speak out, and wraps it up) never are beautiful. As Enoch was and must be coarse, in itself the poem must depend for its charm on a 'gay confusion'—on a splendid accumulation of impossible accessories.

Mr. Tennyson knows this better than many of us—he knows the country world; he has proved it that no one living knows it better; he has painted with pure art—with art which describes what is a race perhaps more refined, more delicate, more conscientious, than the sailor—the 'Northern Farmer', and we all know what a splendid, what a living thing, he has made of it. He could, if he only would, have given us the ideal sailor in like manner—the ideal of the natural sailor, we mean—the characteristic present man as he lives and is. But this he has not chosen. He has endeavoured to describe an exceptional sailor, at an exceptionally refined port, performing a graceful act, an act of relinquishment. And with this task before him, his profound taste taught him that ornate art was a necessary medium—was the sole effectual instrument—for his purpose. It was necessary for him, if possible, to abstract the mind from reality, to induce us *not* to conceive or think of sailors as they are while we are reading of his sailors, but to think of what a person who did not know might fancy sailors to be. A casual traveller on the seashore, with the sensitive mood and the romantic imagination Mr. Newman has described, might fancy, would fancy, a seafaring village to be like that. Accordingly, Mr. Tennyson has made it his aim to call off the stress of fancy from real life, to occupy it otherwise, to bury it with pretty accessories; to engage it on the 'peacock yew-tree', and the 'portal-warding lion-whelp'. Nothing, too, can be more splendid than the description of the tropics as Mr. Tennyson delineates them, but a sailor would not have felt the tropics in that manner. The beauties of nature would not have so much occupied him. He would have known little of the scarlet shafts of sunrise and nothing of the long convolvuluses. As in *Robinson Crusoe*, his own petty contrivances and his small ailments would have been the principal subject to him. 'For three years,' he might have said, 'my back was bad, and then I put two pegs into a piece of drift-wood and so made a chair, and after that it pleased God to send me a chill.' In real life his piety would scarcely have gone beyond that.

It will indeed be said, that though the sailor had no words for, and even no explicit consciousness of, the splendid details of the torrid zone, yet that he had, notwithstanding, a dim latent inexpressible conception of them: though he could not speak of them or describe them, yet they were much to him. And doubtless such is the case. Rude people are impressed by what is beautiful—deeply impressed—though they could not describe what they see, or what they feel. But what is absurd in Mr. Tennyson's description—absurd when we abstract it from the gorgeous additions and ornaments with which Mr Tennyson distracts us—is that his hero feels nothing else but these great splendours. We hear nothing of the physical ailments, the rough devices, the low superstitions, which really would have been the *first* things, the favourite and principal occupations of his mind. Just so, when he gets home he *may* have had such fine sentiments, though it is odd, and he *may* have spoken of them to his landlady, though that is odder still,—but it is incredible that his whole mind should be made up of fine sentiment. Beside those sweet feelings, if he had them, there must have been many more obvious, more prosaic, and some perhaps more healthy. Mr. Tennyson has shown a profound judgment in distracting us as he does. He has given us a classic delineation of the 'Northern Farmer' with no ornament at all—as bare a thing as can be—because he then wanted to describe a true type of real men: he has given us a sailor crowded all over with ornament and illustration, because he then wanted to describe an unreal type of fancied men,—not sailors as they are, but sailors as they might be wished.

Another prominent element in 'Enoch Arden' is yet more suitable to, yet more requires the aid of, ornate art. Mr. Tennyson undertook to deal with *half belief*. The presentiments which Annie feels are exactly of that sort which everybody has felt, and which everyone has half believed—which hardly anyone has more than half believed. Almost everyone, it has been said, would be angry if anyone else reported that he believed in ghosts; yet hardly anyone, when thinking by himself, wholly disbelieves them. Just so, such presentiments as Mr. Tennyson depicts, impress the inner mind so much that the outer mind—the rational understanding—hardly likes to consider them nicely or to discuss them sceptically. For these dubious themes an ornate or complex style is needful. Classical art speaks out what it has to say plainly and simply. Pure style cannot hesitate; it describes in concisest outline

Romantics meant in doubt about a "religious" perhaps

what is, as it is. If a poet really believes in presentiments, he can speak out in pure style. . . . But if a poet is not sure whether presentiments are true or not true; if he wishes to leave his readers in doubt; if he wishes an atmosphere of indistinct illusion and of moving shadow, he must use the romantic style, the style of miscellaneous adjunct, the style 'which shirks, not meets' your intellect, the style, which as you are scrutinising, disappears.

Nor is this all, or even the principal lesson, which 'Enoch Arden' may suggest to us of the use of ornate art. That art is the appropriate art for an *unpleasing type*. Many of the characters of real life, if brought distinctly, prominently, and plainly before the mind as they really are, if shown in their inner nature, their actual essence, are doubtless very unpleasant. They would be horrid to meet and horrid to think of. We fear it must be owned that Enoch Arden is this kind of person. A dirty sailor who did *not* go home to his wife is not an agreeable being: a varnish must be put on him to make him shine. It is true that he acts rightly; that he is very good. But such is human nature that it finds a little tameness in mere morality. Mere virtue belongs to a charity school-girl, and has a taint of the catechism. All of us feel this, though most of us are too timid, too scrupulous, too anxious about the virtue of others, to speak out. We are ashamed of our nature in this respect, but it is not the less our nature. And if we look deeper into the matter, there are many reasons why we should not be ashamed of it. The soul of man, and as we necessarily believe, of beings greater than man, has many parts beside its moral part. It has an intellectual part, an artistic part, even a religious part, in which mere morals have no share. In Shakespeare or Goethe, even in Newton or Archimedes, there is much which will not be cut down to the shape of the commandments. They have thoughts, feelings, hopes—immortal thoughts and hopes— which have influenced the life of men, and the souls of men, ever since their age, but which the 'whole duty of man', the ethical compendium, does not recognise. Nothing is more unpleasant than a virtuous person with a mean mind. A highly developed moral nature joined to an undeveloped intellectual nature, an undeveloped artistic nature, and a very limited religious nature, is of necessity repulsive. It represents a bit of human nature—a good bit, of course, but a bit only—in disproportionate, unnatural, and revolting prominence; and therefore, unless an artist use delicate care, we are offended. The dismal act of a squalid man needed many condiments to make it pleasant, and therefore Mr. Tennyson was right to mix them subtly and to use them freely.

A mere act of self-denial can indeed scarcely be pleasant upon paper. An heroic struggle with an external adversary, even though it end in a defeat, may easily be made attractive. Human nature likes to see itself look grand, and it looks grand when it is making a brave struggle with foreign foes. But it does not look grand when it is divided against itself. An excellent person striving with temptation is a very admirable being in reality, but he is not a pleasant being in description. We hope he will win and overcome his temptation, but we feel that he would be a more interesting being, a higher being, if he had not felt that temptation so much. The poet must make the struggle great in order to make the self-denial virtuous, and if the struggle be too great, we are apt to feel some mixture of contempt. The internal metaphysics of a divided nature are but an inferior subject for art, and if they are to be made attractive, much else must be combined with them. If the excellence of *Hamlet* had depended on the ethical qualities of Hamlet, it would not have been the masterpiece of our literature. He acts virtuously of course, and kills the people he ought to kill, but Shakespeare knew that such goodness would not much interest the pit. He made him a handsome prince, and a puzzling meditative character; these secular qualities relieve his moral excellence, and so he becomes 'nice'. In proportion as an artist has to deal with types essentially imperfect, he must disguise their imperfections; he must accumulate around them as many first-rate accessories as may make his readers forget that they are themselves second-rate. The sudden *millionaires* of the present day hope to disguise their social defects by buying old places, and hiding among aristocratic furniture; just so, a great artist who has to deal with characters artistically imperfect, will use an ornate style, will fit them into a scene where there is much else to look at.

For these reasons ornate art is within the limits as legitimate as pure art. It does what pure art could not do. The very excellence of pure art confines its employment. Precisely because it gives the best things by themselves and exactly as they are, it fails when it is necessary to describe inferior things among other things, with a list of enhancements and a crowd of accompaniments that in reality do not belong to it. Illusion, half belief, unpleasant types, imperfect types, are as much the proper sphere of ornate art, as an inferior landscape is the proper sphere for the true efficacy of moonlight. A really great landscape needs sunlight and bears sunlight; but moonlight is an equaliser of beauties; it gives a romantic unreality to what will not stand the bare truth. And just so does romantic art.

There is, however, a third kind of art which differs from these on the point in which they most resemble one another. Ornate art and pure art have this in common, that they paint the types of literature in as good perfection as they can. Ornate art, indeed, uses undue disguises and unreal enhancements; it does not confine itself to the best types; on the contrary it is its office to make the best of imperfect types and lame approximations; but ornate art, as much as pure art, catches its subject in the best light it can, takes the most developed aspect of it which it can find, and throws upon it the most congruous colours it can use. But grotesque art does just the contrary. It takes the type, so to say, *in difficulties.* It gives a representation of it in its minimum development, amid the circumstances least favourable to it, just while it is struggling with obstacles, just where it is encumbered with incongruities. It deals, to use the language of science, not with normal types but with abnormal specimens; to use the language of old philosophy, not with what nature is striving to be, but with what by some lapse she has happened to become.

This art works by contrast. It enables you to see, it makes you see, the perfect type by painting the opposite deviation. It shows you what ought to be by what ought not to be; when complete, it reminds you of the perfect image by showing you the distorted and imperfect image. Of this art we possess in the present generation one prolific master. Mr. Browning is an artist working by incongruity. . . .

24. A. Austin revalues Tennyson

Alfred Austin, 'Mr. Tennyson', *The Poetry of the Period* (1870), pp. 1-37.

Austin (1835-1913) was a minor poet who became Laureate in 1896. His essay on Tennyson first appeared anonymously in *Temple Bar* (May 1869), xxvi. 179-94. Revising it for his book, Austin made a few dozen minor changes: he removed traces of its original publication in a periodical, he tightened up some of his formulations, and he modified one or two excessively forensic passages. He also added the first two footnotes.

If one were to enter a modern drawing-room filled with the average polite society of the day, and then and there were to pluck up courage to declare that Mr. Tennyson has no sound pretensions to be called a great poet, and will of a certainty not be esteemed such by an un-biassed posterity, I suppose he would not create more astonishment, or be regarded more unanimously as a heretic, than would another who in a company of *savans* expressed his doubts as to the law of gravitation, or a third who, before a committee of orthodox divines, exposed his utter disbelief in the inspiration of the Scriptures. Yet that, and nothing less, is the opinion to be expounded in the ensuing pages, with a confi-dence equal to that I feel upon any subject I could name—a confidence not the growth of yesterday, but of long, deliberate, and ever-deepen-ing conviction. It is indeed high time that somebody should speak out what is, to my knowledge, distinctly in the minds of an independent few, and, I have reason to suspect, hazily in the minds of the servile many. The age in which we live is, in the formation of opinion, if not absolutely in the expression of it, such an oppressive one, the con-ventional sense of the majority so overpowers the critical sense of the discriminating minority, that when an opinion has, in the phraseology of the day, once 'turned the corner' and got itself accepted by a preponderance of voices, it is almost hopeless to think of reversing it. So hopeless is it that, as a rule, no one ever expends his energy in the attempt; or, if he does, his spoken or written efforts are relegated to the obscure pages of some neglected publication, which either expires of its eccentricity, or obtains a licence of vitality by surrendering its independence of judgment, and proclaiming in a still more extravagant key the sentiments it began by struggling to stem. So has it been by the national estimate formed of Mr. Tennyson. It would not be easy to name the precise moment at which it was settled once and for all that he is a great poet, though I am inclined to think that the period might be marked by the publication of the *Idylls of the King*. The point, however, is not one of very great importance, except as showing—as I shall have occasion to point out farther on—that his fame has steadily increased precisely as his genuine poetical power has steadily waned. What I wish to emphasize at present is, that his being a great poet is now regarded as an established fact. It is esteemed to be beyond the reach of criticism, and the vulgar suppose that nobody for a moment dreams of challenging it. I am going not only to challenge it, but to deny it altogether, and to implore the age, whilst there yet is time, to save itself by a seasonable recantation from the posthumous ridicule and contempt in which a conventional persistence in an untenable opinion of permanent interest will necessarily involve it.

We are so perniciously given in these days to extravagance of all sorts, and notably to extravagance of language—so frivolously addicted to excessive censure and unmeasured laudation—that all sense of accuracy seems to be deserting us. Ten years ago, anything that pleased, from a bonnet to an epic, was 'charming'. Five years ago, it was 'so charming'. Now it is 'too charming'. I mention these phrases as illustrative, and as proving the stringent necessity of calling the reader's attention to what it is exactly that is asserted, and what it is exactly that is denied. My proposition is, that Mr. Tennyson is not a great poet, unquestionably not a poet of the first rank, all but unquestionably not a poet of the second rank, and probably—though no contemporary perhaps can settle that—not even at the head of poets of the third rank, among whom he must ultimately take his place. The prevailing or universally expressed opinion on the subject is, that he is a great poet, a very great poet, perhaps as great a poet as ever lived, the latchet of whose shoe Dryden would not be worthy to tie; greater than Scott, greater than Shelley, greater than Keats, greater than Wordsworth, greater than Byron—yes, ever so much greater than Byron—certainly as great as Milton or Spenser, and only not quite named in the same breath with Shakespeare, because the self-same mingled academical and drawing-room conventionality, which places him in a sphere preposterously beyond his real deserts, allows nobody to be *par aut secundus* to our mighty dramatist. I do not mean to say that in the second instance conventionality, and sound criticism are not at one; but if the latter had not succeeded in compelling the adherence of the former already, and before Mr. Tennyson's claims had been mooted, I entertain no doubt whatever that even Shakespeare's superiority would not have been safe against the ignorant intrusion into his society by the Poet Laureate's worshippers of their paraded idol. But short of Shakespeare, it is certain there is no English bard with whom they do not presume continually to compare him, and almost invariably to the disadvantage of the mighty dead. This is the opinion I challenge and denounce—the opinion that will make posterity shriek with laughter and flout us with scorn.

Nobody, I presume, will contest the statement that no man can make himself a great poet by writing a large quantity of mediocre poetry, or a certain quantity of unsurpassable excellence in expression. Otherwise two men of very different merit, Blackmore and Gray, would both be great poets. Just as in Roman Catholic theology no amount of venial sins will constitute one mortal one, so according to the canons of poetry no amount of pretty, beautiful, tender, elegant, thoughtful verse, can constitute its author a mighty singer. If Mr. Tennyson be a great poet, where is his great subject greatly sung? Where is his *Hamlet*, his *Lear*, his *Faëry Queen*, his *Paradise Lost*, his *Prometheus Unbound*, his *Cenci*, his *Cain*, his *Manfred*, his *Childe Harold*, —ay, his *Endymion*, or his *Marmion*? He had his great subject once, and once only, and, in vulgar parlance, he 'funked' it. What has he made of his 'Flos Regum Arthurus'? Four[1] exquisite cabinet pictures; but that is all. You prefer cabinet pictures? Be it so. But neither four, nor forty, nor four hundred of them, constitute a *magnum opus*, or their producer a mighty artificer, or in any sense the peer of one who is. If 'King Arthur' and the 'Table Round' could not, under favourable circumstances, be woven into the substance of a really great poem, never was the subject that could. No doubt Mr. Tennyson is as well aware of that fact as anybody; and the consciousness of it governed him in his original selection of it. He kept revolving it for years, in the fond hope

---

[1] Now extended to eight.

that a due poetic treatment of it would make his laurelled head strike the stars; but eventually he had to own that he was unequal to the glorious task. The subject was too much for him. *Non ex quovis ligno fit Mercurius.* The stuff of a great poet was not in him; and he confessed as much—perhaps not quite consciously, but still, we may be sure, with a pang of mortification, when he abandoned a lofty but illusory aim, and contented himself with executing four charming and highly finished fragments or driblets, in the shape of 'Enid', 'Elaine', 'Vivien', and 'Guinevere'. Never was there a poet with such sound judgment and good common sense as Mr. Tennyson. He takes, and has always taken, his own measure far more accurately than his silly and immoderate admirers. He has never yet attempted anything beyond his reach; and the consequence is, he has never conspicuously failed. But is it not he himself who reminds us that

He is all fault who hath no fault at all?

The same holds good of the small poet, whom unwise voices want to proclaim great. There is no really great poet that has not written unmitigated nonsense, perpetrated notable fiascos—that does not, in a word, abound with faults. Where are Mr. Tennyson's faults? He has only one—the fault of not being great enough to commit any. He has what Mr. Carlyle has so happily described as 'the completeness of a limited mind'. He never stumbles, for he never runs. He never flags, because he never soars. He never rises into air too rarefied for him, as Shelley does—air so light and fine that even wings do not there support him. He knows what he can do, and he does it. It is delicate, subtle, pathetic, sometimes even solemn; it is anything else you like; but it is never great.

It is not the purpose of this present paper to note what Mr. Tennyson is, but rather what he is not. Yet the second point cannot well be established without the first being, to a certain degree, entertained. His first little volume of poems, published in 1830, could not by any possibility, even in the worst and most uncritical of times, have made a poetical reputation; and, whatever folks now affect to think of them, they were thought very little of when they first appeared. Byron had been dead only six years—we fear he would have poked shocking fun at them, with their Adelines, Madelines, and Lilians, had he been alive—and the generation that had fed on his strong meat was not prepared all of a sudden to smack its lips over food for babes. Yet there was genuine poetry in one or two of them—of course of a rather small sort, and though happy twists of expression were more noticeable in them than any more substantial quality. But, besides betokening in the author an airy fancy and a rare delicacy of touch, they prompted the expectation of something better than themselves. That something better—very decidedly better—came two years later. There was still a rather namby-pamby 'sweet pale Margaret', recalling the Madelines and Adelines of the previous volume; but there were likewise the 'Dream of Fair Women', the 'Palace of Art', 'Œnone', and the 'Lotos-Eaters'; and what was more important to most people, and is to this day, there were in it 'New Year's Eve', the 'Miller's Daughter', and 'Lady Clara Vere de Vere'. There could be no doubt in any reasonable mind that the author was a poet, and a poet of no mean order. Ten years passed away; and in 1842 came the 'Talking Oak', 'Locksley Hall', and those blank verse English Idylls which sounded the key-note of nearly all Mr. Tennyson's latest and more extensive poetic labours. He has added no fresh poetic laurels, *in kind*, to his brow since that date. As far as quality is concerned, there are to be found in those first three volumes, now published as one under the simple name of *Poems*, types of everything he has since written, and types equal to anything that has followed. I am not forgetting *Maud*[1]—the weakest and worst, despite its several beauties, of Mr. Tennyson's works—nor *In Memoriam*, in the opinion of many people, though certainly not in mine, his strongest and best. *Maud* is a *pot pourri* of his various manners, each of which is plainly discernible in some one page or other of the *Poems*. The key of *In Memoriam* was first struck in the verses beginning, 'You ask me why, though ill at ease', published in 1832. But I take 1842 as the climacteric. No higher note has been struck by Mr. Tennyson since, and by far his best notes have since then wholly deserted him. It is pretty certain that no posterity, however distant, will allow the 'Talking Oak', or 'Locksley Hall' to die; but the English Idylls, if they survive far into the next century, will survive in an academical sense only, as Thomson's *Seasons*, or Young's *Night Thoughts* do now. *In*

---

[1] In an article written by a distinguished French critic in the *Revue des Deux Mondes*, February 15, 1869, entitled 'Un Retour vers Byron', occurs the following passage: 'Aujourd'hui même les admirables passages de Byron contre la guerre n'ont rien perdu de leur puissance. Aujourd'hui *Maud* est à peu près oublié; on est toujours transporté des chaudes peintures de la prise d'Ismaïl. La vérité seule est durable, et Byron l'a rencontrée.' These remarks are by M. Louis Etienne; but if the reader wishes to know what the impartial 'foreign friend' thinks of Mr. Tennyson, let him read M. Taine. In fact, Mr. Tennyson is only an English poet, and never will be anything more. That is another note of his comparative inferiority.

Memoriam will assuredly be handed over to the dust as soon as a generation arises which has come to its senses, or even to a tolerable notion of what it is aiming at, in religious and spiritual thought. Passages no doubt will be saved, as they will from *Maud*, and from the *Idylls of the King*, but their very survival will doom the text from which they are selected to practical oblivion. As for *The Princess*, such is even already its fate. Its pretty little songs and a well-known passage at the close of the poem are being perpetually quoted, only to prove what a trivial impression, if any, has been created in the general mind by its other innumerable pages. All of them alike are already manifestly destined to be, *as complete poems*, to dumb forgetfulness a prey; and all of them for the same reason—their length, though by no means excessive when poems of any pretension are spoken of, is so conspicuously greater than their excellence. Their weight is too much for their momentum, and consequently they will fall short and soon. If you want to be heard afar off, you must shout, not loud or long, but *high*. Mr. Tennyson's poetical pitch is not high enough—he cannot make it high enough—and the inevitable consequence is that posterity will not hear him, save in little snatches or breaks of voice, as it still hears Cowley or Falconer.

Still if it could be shown that Mr. Tennyson—though he has written no single great work, no one poem sufficiently sublime in conception and execution to defy the destructiveness of Time—has given frequent or even occasional utterance to really great poetical thoughts, or to poetical images really sublime, it might perhaps be impossible, and it would certainly be churlish, to refuse him the title, by courtesy at least, of a great poet. It is true that single-speech Hamilton does not usually figure in the list of English orators, nor is Earl Russell regarded as a famous epigrammatist, because he once made the exceedingly happy remark that proverbs are the wisdom of many and the wit of one. Nevertheless, though I could not waive the important point on which I have been insisting, I would not press it, if sublimity of idea could be indicated as ever and anon rising out of the usually tame and scarcely undulating level of Mr. Tennyson's compositions. But, with an intimate acquaintance with everything he has written, and after long and deliberate reflection and search, I have no hesitation in saying that, in the whole range of his poetry, there is not to be found even a solitary instance of a sublime thought sublimely expressed. In really great poets —in Shakespeare, Byron, Shelley—such thoughts crowd upon us thick and fast—pelt us, in fact, with their prodigal frequency. They smite us, stun us, take away our breath, make us bow our heads and wonder, fancying that we have seen over into the other world—had a glimpse of the supernatural, a flash of the Eternal. But Mr. Tennyson! He is sweet, tender, touching, polished—his is the *perpolita oratio*—a gentleman, a scholarly writer, a more highly-finished oneself, so to speak, but never the man 'who has seen Hell', or any of the non-visible things of the universe. He is not even the *gran maestro*, of whom anybody can say

> . . . da cui io tolsi
> Lo bello stile che m' ha fatto onore.

Many have imitated him, it is true, and most successfully; but who has gained special honour by it? Names need not be mentioned; anybody can suggest them for himself; but his metrical disciples have been so numerous, have copied their original so amazingly well, and their excellence in this respect has been the subject of such general remark, that Mr. Tennyson has thereby been betrayed into one of the few undignified acts of his singularly self-respecting and honourable life. Unwisely stung by the observation that his works were objectionably easy of imitation, he has retorted in some stupid little verses to the effect that all can grow the flower now that they have got the seed, which came originally from his garden. The conceit is pretty, and quite in the author's style; but used as an argument, for which it is intended, it is not only sophistical—it is damning to the person that employs it. Let us accept the metaphor, and use it in this further inquiry: Who has grown Shakespearean flowers of poesy?—flowers such as Byron's, that he did not cultivate, but coaxed, like Spring, with a smile, or drew, like hot Summer, with the warmth of imperious passion, from the mountain side?—flowers such as Shelley has scattered broadcast through his pages?—flowers such as he himself speaks of in language whose very syllables distil the wild-honied poetry of no fabled Hymettus?—flowers such as

> Daisies, those pale arcturi of the earth,
> The constellated flower that never sets?

or such as

> . . . the tender harebell, at whose birth
> The sod scarce heaved?

Who has got the seed of these, and grown their duplicates? Who has imitated any of these three? No one, and for the simple reason that nobody can. Mr. Tennyson does well to speak of 'his garden'. There it is! His flowers of poesy are flowers of the garden—a beautiful, exquisite, tasteful, sweet-smelling, brightly-glittering garden, but—a garden. And gardens and all that they produce are essentially imitable. There may be only one Sir Joseph Paxton and only one Chatsworth, but their imitators run them hard. Similarly, Mr. Tennyson's may still be the best as it was the first garden of its sort, and he deserves, like Paxton and Chatsworth, the honour due and invariably rendered to precursors. But it is of the very essence of truly great poetry that it can neither be invented, cultivated, nor copied. It grows of itself in a certain soil, and it will grow in no other, let metrical floriculturists labour as deftly as ever they will. It is an affair, not of grafting, crossing, fertilizing, or of ordinary reproduction at all, but of spontaneous generation, or what we call such in default of knowledge whence this strange, fitful, efflorescent foliage comes. The birds drop it, the winds bring it, the heavens rain it, the mist and the storm-clouds carry it about. It germinates in the rays of the sun, in the beams of the watery moon, in the secrecy and shroud of unfathomable darkness. It comes of the breath of God. Let there be light! And, lo! there is light and a poet! It has nothing to do with gardens and garden seeds, trim parterres, new variations, and watering-pots. There lies the whole difference between great poets and poets that are not great—between Mr. Tennyson and the Di Majores. And as there is a difference between them not only intensely of degree, but even of kind, so is there a difference in their doom. Garden poetry, besides being imitable, is variable, and subject to fashion, whim, caprice. Now Dutch gardening is in vogue, as it was when Pope[1] wrote. Now Italian gardening is all the rage, as it was when Cowper trimly moralized. Now English landscape-gardening ousts both, and Mr. Tennyson comes to the front. But Shakespeare, Byron, Shelley, have nothing to do with gardens and gardening. Their concern is with the permanent aspects of Nature—human nature included; with the sea, the sky, the mountains, the far-stretching landscape, stormy winds that fulfil His Word, the planets, the intolerable thunder, grim murder, vaulting ambition, mad revenge, earthquakes, and Promethean discontent. These are enduring. No fashion can change the waves and waters, no mode move the mountains, no alteration of taste obliterate the stars. These are always the self-same, and their years shall not fail. So are their singers. Where are the gardens of Sallust?

[1] Pope, however, like Lucretius, has made his peace with posterity, and saved himself from all peril of oblivion, by writing a great ethical poem—a possession for ever—the *Essay on Man*.

Where the fountains of Mæcenas? Where the terraces and laurelled walks of Hadrian?

> Cypress and ivy, weed and wallflower grown
> Matted and massed together.

These survive, and would still survive, even if the ruins on which they feed had been consumed. The Sabine hills are there, so are the Alban, so is the Campagna. You can kill neither the gods nor Nature, nor the inspired voices that are divinely commissioned to speak of them to their fellows. But mere man and his tricks and fancies, his little comedies and lesser tragedies; his fashions, poses, and conceits; his Adelines, Madelines, and Enoch Ardens, well enough for their little day, necessarily pass away, and with them the gentle, elegant, but ephemeral creatures that have twittered about them on the particular guitar of the period.

The more one considers this garden metaphor and all that it suggests, the more applicable it ever seems to be to Mr. Tennyson as a poet, and the more satisfactorily explanatory of his exact poetical position, and its relation to that occupied by those with whom he has been so unwisely, and indeed sillily, compared. Let me quote a beautiful passage from the 'Gardener's Daughter', to my thinking the best of his Idylls:—

> Not wholly in the busy world, nor quite
> Beyond it, blooms the garden that I love.
> News from the humming city comes to it
> In sound of funeral or of marriage bells;
> And, sitting muffled in dark leaves, you hear
> The windy clanging of the minster clock;
> Although between it and the garden lies
> A league of grass, washed by a slow broad stream,
> That, stirred with languid pulses of the oar,
> Waves all its lazy lilies,[1] and creeps on,
> Barge-laden, to three arches of a bridge
> Crown'd with the minster-towers.
> > The fields between
> Are dewy-dresh, browsed by deep-uddered kine,
> And all about the large lime feathers low,
> The lime a summer home of murmurous wings.[2]

You like that vastly! It is one of your favourite passages! So it is with me—especially because it is so intensely Tennysonian, and marks

[1] A bit of plagiarism from Shelley, by the way.
[2] Again, copied from Keats, and spoiled in the copying.

in a definite manner his powers, his mission—in a word, his sweep. I will illustrate and enlarge on my meaning in a moment. But let me first ask, *à propos* of your admiring the above passage so warmly, in what sense it is you admire it, and to what extent? You like it immensely! But what do you *think of it*? Do you seriously think it equal to, or worthy to be named in the same poetical breath with the thunderstorm in the Jura in *Childe Harold*, the description of Waterloo, the long-sustained wail over the 'lone mother of dead Empires, the Niobe of Nations', the address, as of an equal, to the Ocean? equal to or fit to be mentioned in the same poetical breath with the best-known quotations from *Lear, Measure for Measure, Henry the Fourth, A Midsummer Night's Dream*, or with the most glittering passages from *Alastor*, the *Lament for Adonais*, the *Revolt of Islam*, or the *Prometheus Unbound*? Do you think *that*? No, but you like it better; it comes home to you more; you care more for it? Be it so. Perhaps, too, you prefer the canter of your mamma's steady nag to the long stride and tremendous bound of your father's thoroughbred? But which, after all, is the better horse of the two? We dare say you prefer Zephyrus to Eurus; but which is the stronger, grander wind? The first is smoother, softer, and more in harmony with your mood. That is quite conceivable. But what is your mood? An amiable, elegant, refined one, truly and obviously. But an heroic one?—a sublime one?—a great one? Scarcely. Yet it cannot be supposed that, because you are so constituted as to have a personal preference for the less, you do not know the difference between the less and the greater, and mistake the one for the other. Like Mr. Tennyson, by all means; it would be the height of stupidity and intolerance to try to prevent your doing so. All that is asked is, that you should confess you think a great deal more of poets whom you care to read a good deal less. To refuse that much would imply only obstinacy or dullness, and place you among your favourite poet's 'purblind race of miserable men', who 'take true for false, or false for true'.

But quitting the ground of mere individual predilection, which, as we have seen, goes for absolutely nothing in a correct estimate of the relative grandeur of poets, let us revert to our quotation, and scrutinize it as it illustrates what I have termed the 'sweep' of its author. I have said that it is intensely Tennysonian. It is the poet speaking not so much from his heart as from his whole nature:—

> Not wholly in the busy world, nor quite
> Beyond it, blooms the garden that I love.

What a mine of confession and suggestiveness there is in those two lines, when we come to consider and accurately measure the genius of their author! From the fulness of the heart the mouth speaketh, and his heart is partly in the city and partly in the fields. He is too much of a poet to be enamoured of Rotten Row or Piccadilly, or to be able to exclaim, 'Give *me* the sunny side of Pall Mall'; but he is not enough of a poet, not exclusively such, so as to be able to exclaim:—

> With me,
> High mountains are a feeling, but the hum
> Of human cities torture.

It is a different lyre that strikes out that discontented note. Mr. Tennyson avows that he loves 'news from the humming city', and does not like to get too far away from it. And when he does, where does he wish to find himself? Among the mountains? Anywhere but there! I do not remember a single earnest allusion to high mountains in the whole of his poems. They are not with him a feeling. They are too much for him. If he confronted them, he feels instinctively they would silence him. Wordsworth, the sublime and holy, awed by them, yet competent, like Moses, to bring down from them to the vulgar world the lessons they command in fire of sunset or thunder of storm, fled to them as companions, not without sense of dread, but imperiously drawn to their tops by inspiration and worship:—

> The sounding cataract
> Haunted me like a passion: the tall rock,
> The mountain, and the deep and gloomy wood,
> Their colours and their forms, were then to me
> An appetite; a feeling and a love
> That had no need of a remoter charm,
> By thought supplied, nor any interest
> Unborrowed from the eye.

Again, in *The Excursion*, the same lofty voice smites our ears as with tidings from that land of 'light that never was on sea or shore':—

> The solid frame of earth
> And ocean's liquid mass in gladness lay
> Beneath him. Far and wide the clouds were touched,
> And in their silent faces could be read
> Unutterable love. *Sound needed none,*
> *Nor any sense of joy.*

No need of 'news from the humming city'. No need of 'sound of funeral or of marriage bells'. No need of 'the windy clanging of the minster clock':—

> Sound needed none,
> Nor any sense of joy; his spirit drank
> The spectacle: sensation, soul, and form
> All melted into him; they swallowed up
> His animal being; in them did he live,
> And by them did he live; they were his life.
> In such access of mind, in such high hour
> Of visitation from the living God,
> Thought was not; in enjoyment it expired.

I have preferred to quote from Wordsworth, because it would be a bold thing to insist, despite the unsurpassed sublimity of these passages, that he is, taken all in all, a poet of the very highest order, and because it never enters the vulgar mind to suppose that he is a far greater poet than Mr. Tennyson. I wish Mr. Moxon would tell us what proportion there is between his sale, during the last twenty-five years, of the works of the two men. The figures would show the estimation in which they are held, respectively, by the critical crowds of the age. But I defy Mr. Tennyson's admirers to quote anything from his works fit for one moment to be compared as sublime—in other words, as great poetry—with the lines just printed; and there are many more of them equally sublime in the two particular passages from which they are taken. The challenge is of course unanswerable, or can be answered only by Mr. Tennyson's preference for

> A league of grass, washed by a slow broad stream,
> That, stirred with languid pulses of the oar,
> Waves all its lazy lilies, and creeps on,
> Barge-laden, to three arches of a bridge
> Crown'd with the minster-towers.

Who does not feel that we have dropped to a lower key—from 'sounding cataracts' to 'languid pulses of the oar'—from storm-winds to zephyrs—from thunder-fugues to 'clanging clocks'? I have nothing to say against it. It is exceedingly pretty, soothing, elegant; but it is not grand. It is the poetry of the drawing-room, not the music of the Spheres.

Nor will it avail to plead that Wordsworth goes on to confess

That time is past,
And all its aching joys are now no more,
And all its dizzy raptures.
... I have learned
To look on Nature not as in the hour
Of thoughtless youth; but hearing oftentimes
The still sad music of humanity.

For the lines that follow show what was the real change that had come
over him, enabling him oftentimes to hear this still sad music of humanity. No man is a great poet who does not hear it, and who confines
himself to singing of Nature alone. It is the poet's loftiest mission to
blend the two, but to blend them in so subtle a manner that the mystery
of the one deepens the mystery of the other, and makes them almost
interchangeable; to produce, in fact, that

Sense sublime
Of something far more deeply interfused,

of which Wordsworth speaks in the selfsame passage. Mr. Tennyson
knows nothing of this. He writes 'of funeral and of marriage bells',
as novelists do, and he writes of 'a vapour from the margin, blackening
over heath and holt', as poets of a certain order do; but even these he
does not contrive to commingle in such a way as to bring before us the
everlasting puzzle of the sympathy, and yet conflict, of Humanity with
Nature.

Drug thy memories, lest thou learn it, lest thy heart be
    put to proof,
In the dead unhappy night, and when the rain is on the
    roof,

is his nearest approach to it that I can recall; and this, though an exceedingly happy touch, has in it no element of real grandeur or sublime
pathos. What is it compared to Byron's touch about Spring-coming,

With all her joyous birds upon the wing,
I turned from all she brought to those she could not bring.

Here we have Man, Nature, and the Perpetual Mystery face to face; no
shrinking on any side, and the poet giving adequate voice and expression
to all:—

Not that I love Man less, but Nature more,
From these our interviews, in which I steal
From what I may be, or have been before,
To mingle with the Universe, and feel
What I can not express, yet cannot all conceal.

It is in such passages as these that we are lifted up, just as we are in
Shakespeare's magnificent lines:—

> To be embodied in the viewless winds,
> And blown with restless violence round about
> The pendent world:

and are made to feel that even we, like the wizard hands that thus for a
moment exalt us, are, as Shelley says, 'made one with Nature'. But
what mighty pinions are required for such empyrean flights as these!
In one of Lacordaire's most magnificent sermons, preached upon the
text, 'Go and convert all nations', he winds up an impassioned passage
concerning apostolic zeal and the missionary spirit, by exclaiming, 'Go
across the mountains and the seas! Go, but go straight! Go, as the eagles
go, and the angels!' Poets should, and great poets do, go in such a
fashion. They go—like the eagles! They mount, ride on the storm, scale
the ether, calm or disturbed, and stare at the sun. They go—like the
angels! You cannot shut them out of heaven. You cannot exclude them
from the deepest fathoms of the sea. For them, however it may be with
kings, there is no 'Thus far, and no farther' . . . 'I have loved thee,
ocean . . . I am, as it were, a child of thee . . . I lay my hand upon thy
mane . . . Thou dost bound beneath me, as a steed that knows its rider.'
What splendid familiarity!—familiarity like that which enabled
Shakespeare too to write:—

> . . . I have bedimm'd
> The noontide sun, call'd forth the mutinous winds,
> And 'twixt the green sea and the azur'd vault
> Set roaring war: to the dread rattling thunder
> Have I given fire, and rifted Jove's stout oak
> With his own bolt: the strong-bas'd promontory
> Have I made shake; and by the spurs pluck'd up
> The pine and cedar . . .
> By my so potent art.

Ay, there it is! 'By my so potent art.' If we could imagine Shakespeare, Byron, and even Wordsworth, meeting in the Elysian Fields,
can we doubt that the 'one touch of nature', common, as we have
briefly shown, to all three, would make them kin, and force them to
recognize each other as master-minds? But Mr. Tennyson! I fear Shakespeare would consider he had too much of the 'pouncet-box' about
him. They would relegate him to 'the garden that he loves', and regard
him as one who, like his own 'slow broad stream', is stirred only with

languid pulses. His muse is dainty and delicious, but it is not daring and defiant. It is Pegasus, and Pegasus with four very decent legs, small, elegant head, right well groomed, and with an uncommonly good mane and tail; but it is Pegasus without wings. It would be cruel to apply to him Lacordaire's splendid image. Alas! he is no eagle. As I have said, he never soars. He twitters under our roof, sweeps and skims round and round our ponds, is musical in the branches of our trees, plumes himself on the edges of our fountains, builds himself a warm nest under our gables and even in our hearts, 'cheeps', to use his own words, 'twenty million loves', feeds out of our hand, eyes us askance, struts along our lawns, and flutters in and out among our flowery parterres—does all, in fact, that welcome, semi-domesticated swallows, linnets, and musical bullfinches do; but there it ends. He is no 'scorner of the ground'. He never leaves us to plunge among the far-off precipitous crags, to commune with embryonic tempests, to travel with the planets, and then swoop down divinely laden with messages hard yet not altogether impossible to understand. We love him, because he is ours. We love him, because, like the garden he himself loves, he is 'not wholly in the busy world, nor quite beyond it'.

In other words, he thinks with us of this particular day, feels with us of this day, and is the exponent of such poetical feelings as in this day we are capable of. But as far as poetry is concerned we and our day are not great, but little, and he shares our littleness with us. It is not our fault, some may perhaps think it is not even our misfortune, that such greatness as the present age achieves, or can achieve, does not lie in the poetical, but in a wholly opposite direction. The age is scientific or it is nothing. Now science and all its processes, its aims and its methods alike, are antagonistic to poetry, and its aims and methods. The scope of science, as far as literature is concerned, is demonstration, and its machinery must be strict reasoning of some sort. The scope of poetry is the embodiment of emotion, and its vehicle and means must be of an unreasoning, and sometimes even of an unreasonable character. Greater contrast, indeed more absolute conflict, could not well be imagined. Mr. Tennyson has been the complete sport of this conflict; with what results anybody who is well acquainted with his works and has this key to guide him may soon perceive for himself. He is alternately the poet pure and simple, singing true songs, sweet or sad, as it happens; or the poet crossed by the man of scientific thought and intelligence, trying to weld together two things that are essentially antagonistic, and producing a species of metrical emulsion that people with only poetical instincts feel not to be poetry, and people with only scientific insight know not to be science, but which people with lingering poetical tastes and growing scientific proclivities combined would like to make serve both for poetry and science. Men with a strong poetical turn of mind, but with not so decided and obstinate a bias for being poets as Mr. Tennyson, give up the struggle, consciously or unconsciously, and become—like Professor Tyndall or Mr. Disraeli —philosophers or politicians. Men, on the contrary, with the same turn, but with a still more decided, obstinate, and exclusive poetical nature and temperament than Mr. Tennyson, squander their lives in trying to attain the impossible, exhaust themselves in poetical spasms, and illustrate Alexander Smith's simile:—

> O Poesy! thou art a rock;
> I, a weak wave, would break on thee, and die.

I could name one or two living men who have achieved considerable notoriety by their volumes of verse, whom it would be easy to imagine being, in an age more favourable to the achievement, poets of the very highest order. I feel sure that Mr. Tennyson could never have been that in any age, and probably never in any age a greater poet than he has proved himself in this. Yet, to the impartial mind, there can be no doubt that, as far as work done goes, the one or two men to whom I allude are very much his inferiors. And it is no paradox to say that their natural superiority to him is the very cause of their inferiority. Success, and even merit, as far as we can judge it, is the composite result of the agent and his conditions; and if the larger and grander agent be more out of harmony with the conditions under which he works than the smaller agent, it is not only possible, but almost certain, that the latter will produce more valuable work. To put an extreme but conclusive case. If Shakespeare had been living now, would he have been as great a poet as Mr. Tennyson is? I entertain little doubt that he would not, and I have serious doubt whether he would have been known as a poet at all worth speaking of. A pigmy can live and breathe in a place and atmosphere in which a giant could not move for want of room, or speak for want of air. Let us reverse the case. If Mr. Tennyson had been born in the Elizabethan era, should we ever have heard of him? Perhaps; but at most as the author of some courtly masques.

The truth is, the present age, taken in the lump, likes Mr. Tennyson's poetry, as any, and every age, has liked its particular poet, because he speaks its mind for it far more efficiently than anybody else. Consequently it likes and enjoys him better than Scott, better than Shelley, better than Byron, better than Milton, and—whatever it may now and then pretend to the contrary, out of sham and conventional deference —it likes and enjoys him better than Shakespeare. It reads him more, and gets more satisfaction out of reading him. But, as I said before, liking and enjoyment of a poet are no test of that poet's greatness. There are men of sound intellect and sense who infinitely prefer Horace to Homer, and women of exquisite sentiment who infinitely prefer Mrs. Hemans to Mrs. Barrett Browning. It so happens, however, that the serious critic can put himself outside folks' various likings and preferences. He is not bound by the average tastes of his time. All literature is open to him, and he approaches the measurement of any new poetical claimant with the standard left by the productions of bygone centuries. He does not ask men to give up their newly-found idol, the cherished poetical god of their narrow domestic hearth; but he does and must insist that they shall not mistake him for a celestial, and most of all that they shall not thoughtlessly or presumptuously call him Jove. If they do, he must produce his god-measurer, and reduce their little divinity to his true proportions.

It is natural enough that the age, having got in Mr. Tennyson a poet that it vastly likes, should want to persuade itself that he is a a great poet. Self-love impels it to nourish the delusion. Nobody will deny that ours is a particularly vainglorious age; and, being such, it would be painful to it to confess that it has not produced a first-rate specimen of what it has hitherto been the universal creed to believe the highest mental type of humanity—viz., a really great poet. How do we note the past ages? We speak of the age of Homer, the age of Dante, the age of Shakespeare. Can anybody in his senses imagine posterity speaking of our age as the age of Tennyson? Posterity will be too kind to do anything so sardonic. It will speak of it as the age of Railways, the age of Destructive Criticism, or the age of Penny Papers. In some way or other it will try to distinguish us. But the age of Tennyson! The notion is, of course, preposterous. If, then, this age of ours does not wish to cease to pride itself upon its achievements, and cannot make up its mind to lay aside its vaingloriousness, let it strive to persuade itself that great poetry is by no means the best and highest outcome of human genius. Let it turn round and assert that the Submarine Telegraph is grander than *Lear*, the Pneumatic Dispatch grander than *Comus*, Great Exhibitions grander than the *Tragedies of Æschylus*, and the halfpenny *Echo* a greater triumph for man than the fourth canto of *Childe Harold*. It is an intelligible position; I do not say it is an indefensible one, though I confess I would rather not have to defend it. But, at any rate, let it either do that, and justify its vaingloriousness and conceit of superiority over all its predecessors by pointing to something in which it has unquestionably and immeasurably surpassed them, or let it stick to the old doctrine that a great poet is the crown and summit of an age's glory, and meekly confess that, though it has done its best, it has failed to produce one. But let it not make itself a laughing-stock to an irreverent posterity by piquing itself on what it has not got. We laugh at the contemporaries of Hayley. Do we want to be laughed at by our grandchildren? Mr. Tennyson is much more of a poet than Hayley, no doubt; but then Hayley was never belauded as Mr. Tennyson is by us. There is yet time to revise and recall our hasty and extravagant praises; and Mr. Tennyson's merits are so obvious and so considerable that, when we have plucked off all the false feathers in which we have bedecked him, some very beautiful plumage will remain. But our attempts to glorify ourselves by over-exalting him can do no possible good to anybody; and if we persist in this ridiculous course, it will only ensure our being scoffed at by less partial times as a parcel of indiscriminating dunces.

25. J. T. Knowles on
the *Idylls*

James Thomas Knowles, letter to the editor, *Spectator*
(1st January 1870), xliii. 15–17.

Knowles (1831–1908) repeated much of this letter in 'The
Meaning of Mr. Tennyson's "King Arthur" ', *Contemporary
Review* (May 1873), xxi. 938–48, an article which contains
a reply to Swinburne (No. 26). Tennyson praised the
letter in the words quoted in the Introduction to the present
volume. But later he came to feel that it 'explained some
things too allegorically, although there is an allegorical or
perhaps rather a parabolic drift in the poem' (Hallam
Tennyson, *op. cit*, p. 523).

Knowles, architect and editor, made Tennyson's
acquaintance in 1866. In 1877, he founded the *Nineteenth
Century*, his main editorial principle being 'signed writing'
by eminent persons; Tennyson contributed a prefatory
sonnet to the first number.

TENNYSON'S ARTHURIAN POEM
[TO THE EDITOR OF THE *Spectator*.]

SIR,—Your excellent review of Mr. Tennyson's Arthurian *Idylls* refers to
one aspect of them which has never yet received much critical attention,
and on which I should greatly like to add a few words to your own.

The fine and wholesome moral breeze which always seems to blow
about the higher realms of Art comes to us fresh as ever from this great
poem, and more acceptably than ever just now. A constant worship of
Purity, and a constant reprobation of Impurity as the rock on which
the noble projects of the 'blameless king' are wrecked, appear throughout upon the surface of the story.

But besides this, there doubtless does run through it all a sort of under-tone of symbolism, which, while it never interferes with the clear *melody* of the poem, or perverts it into that most tedious of riddles a formal allegory, gives a profound *harmony* to its music and a prophetic strain to its intention most worthy of a great spiritual Bard.

King Arthur, as he has always been treated by Mr. Tennyson, stands obviously for no mere individual prince or hero, but for the 'King within us'—our highest nature, by whatsoever name it may be called—conscience; spirit; the moral soul; the religious sense; the noble resolve. His story and adventures become the story of the battle and pre-eminence of the soul and of the perpetual warfare between the spirit and the flesh.

For so exalting him there is abundant warrant in the language of many old compilers, by whom 'all human perfection was collected in Arthur'; as where, for instance, one says,—'The old world knows not his peer, nor will the future show us his equal,—he alone towers over all other kings, better than the past ones, and greater than those that are to be'; or another, 'In short, God has not made, since Adam was, the man more perfect than Arthur'.

How and why Arthur ever grew to so ideal a height we need not now inquire, it is sufficient here to note the fact, and that Mr. Tennyson is archæologically justified thereby in making him the type of the soul on earth, from its mysterious coming to its mysterious and deathless going.

In the *Idylls of the King*, the soul comes first before us as a conqueror in a waste and desert land groaning under mere brute power. Its history before then is dark with doubt and mystery, and the questions about its origin and authority form the main subject of the introductory poem. Many, themselves the basest, hold it to be base-born, and rage against its rule,—

> And since his ways are sweet,
> And theirs are bestial, hold him less than man;
> And there be those who deem him more than man,
> And dream he dropt from heaven.

Of those who recognize its claim, some, as the hoary chamberlain, accept it on the word of wizards who have written all about it in a sacred book which, doubtless, some day will become intelligible. Others, as Ulfius, and Brastias, standing for common-place men with common-place views, are satisfied to think the soul comes as the body does, or not to think at all about it. Others, again, as Bedivere, with warmer hearts, feel there is mystery, where to the careless all is plain, yet seek among the dark ways of excessive natural passion for the key, and drift towards the scandalous accordingly. Then comes the simple touching tenderness of the woman's discovery of conscience and its influence given by Queen Bellicent in the story of her childhood; and this, again, is supplemented and contrasted by the doctrine of the wise men and philosophers put into Merlin's mouth. His 'riddling triplets' anger the woman, but are a wonderful summary of the way, part-earnest, part-ironical, and all-pathetic, in which great wit confronts the problem of the soul.

The inscrutableness of its origin being thus signified, we see next the recognition of its supremacy, and its first act of kinghood,—the inspiration of the best and bravest near it with a common enthusiasm for Right. The founding of the Order of the Round Table coincides with the solemn crowning of the soul. Conscience, acknowledged and throned as king, binds at once all the best of human powers together into one brotherhood, and that brotherhood to itself by vows so strait and high,

> That when they rose knighted from kneeling, some
> Were pale as at the passing of a ghost,
> Some flush'd, and others dazed, as one who wakes
> Half blinded at the coming of a light.

At that supreme coronation-moment, the Spirit is surrounded and cheered on by all the powers and influences which can ever help it—earthly servants and allies and heavenly powers and tokens—the knights, to signify the strength of the body; Merlin, to signify the strength of intellect; the Lady of the Lake, who stands for the Church, and gives the soul its sharpest and most splendid earthly weapon; and, above all, three fair and mystic Queens, 'tall, with bright sweet faces', robed in the living colours sacred to love and faith and hope, which flow upon them from the image of our Lord above. These, surely, stand for those immortal virtues which only will abide 'when all that seems shall suffer shock', and leaning upon which alone, the Soul, when all else falls from it, shall go towards the golden gates of the new and brighter morning.

As the first and introductory idyll thus seems to indicate the coming and the recognition of the soul, so the ensuing idylls of the 'Round Table' show how its influence fares—waxes or wanes—in the great battle of life. Through all of these we see the body and its passions gain continually greater sway, till in the end the Spirit's earthly work is thwarted and defeated by the flesh. Its immortality alone remains to it, and, with this, a deathless hope.

From the story of 'Geraint and Enid', where the first gust of poisoning passion bows for a time with base suspicion, yet passes, and leaves pure a great and simple heart, we are led through 'Merlin and Vivien', where, early in the storm, we see great wit and genius succumb,—and through 'Lancelot and Elaine', where the piteous early death of innocence and hope results from it,—to 'The Holy Grail', where we find religion itself under the stress of it, and despite the earnest efforts of the soul, blown into mere fantastic shapes of superstition. It would be difficult to find a nobler and manlier apology for pure and sane and practical religion, fit for mighty men, than the verdict of the King at the end of this wonderful poem.

In 'Pelleas and Ettarre' the storm of corruption culminates, whirling the sweet waters of young love and faith (the very life-spring of the world) out from their proper channels, sweeping them into mist, and casting them in hail upon the land. A scarcely-concealed harlot here rides splendid to the Court, and is crowned Queen of Beauty in the lists; the lust of the flesh is all but paramount. Then comes in 'Guinevere' the final lightning stroke, and all the fabric of the earthly life falls smitten into dust, leaving to the soul a broken heart for company, and a conviction that if in this world only it had hope, it were of all things most miserable.

Thus ends the 'Round Table', and the story of the life-long labour of the Soul. No reason appears why yet further idylls should not be added to it, yet further illustrating the manifold temptations of the flesh, and absorbing all the rest of the more striking Arthur legends.

There remains but the passing of the soul 'from the great deep to the great deep', and this is the subject of the closing idyll. Here the 'last dim, weird battle', fought out in densest mist, stands for a picture of all human death, and paints its awfulness and confusion. The soul alone, enduring beyond the end wherein all else is swallowed up, sees the mist clear at last, and finds those three crowned virtues, 'abiding' true and fast, and waiting to convey it to its rest. Character, upheld and formed by these, is the immortal outcome of mortal life. They wail with it awhile in sympathy for the failure of its earthly plans; but at the very last of all are heard to change their sorrow into songs of joy, and departing, 'vanish into light'.

Such or suchlike seems to be the high significance and under-meaning of this noble poem,—a meaning worthy of the exquisite expression which conveys it and of the wealth of beauty and imagery which enfolds it.

But nothing is more remarkable than the way in which so much symbolic truth is given without the slightest forcing of the current of the narrative itself. Indeed, so subtle are the touches and so consummately refined the art employed, that quite possibly many readers may hold there is no parable at all intended. It is most interesting, for instance, to note the thread of realism which is preserved throughout, and which, whether intentionally or not, serves the double purpose of entirely screening any such symbolic under-meaning from all who do not care to seek it, and also of accounting naturally for all the supernatural adventures and beliefs recorded in the story itself.

Thus, in 'The Holy Grail', the various apparitions of the mystic vessel are explicable by passing meteors or sudden lightning flashes seen in a season of great tempests and thunderstorms,—first acting on the hysterical exaltation of an enthusiastic nun, and then, by contagion from her faith, upon the imaginations of a few kindred natures.

Again, in the 'Coming of Arthur', the marvellous story of his birth, as told by Bleys, might simply have been founded on a shipwreck when the sea was phosphorescent, and when all hands suddenly perished save one infant who was washed ashore.

Or, again, in the same poem, the three mystic Queens at the Coronation—who become, in one sense, so all-important in their meaning—derive their import in the eyes of Bellicent simply from the accident of coloured beams of light falling upon them from a stained-glass window.

May I, in conclusion of this too-long letter, say how happily characteristic of their English author, and their English theme seems to me the manner in which these *Idylls of the King* have become a complete poem? It brings to mind the method of our old cathedral-builders. Round some early shrine, too precious to be moved, were gathered bit by bit a nave and aisles, then rich side chapels, then the great image-crowded portals, then a more noble chancel, then, perhaps, the towers, all in fulfilment of some general plan made long ago, but each produced and added as occasion urged or natural opportunity arose. As such buildings always seem rather to have *grown* than been *constructed*, and have the wealth of interest, and beauty, and variety which makes Canterbury Cathedral, for instance, far more poetical than St. Paul's,—so with these *Idylls*. Bit by bit the poem and its sacred purport have grown continually more and more connected and impressive. Had Mr. Tennyson sat down in early youth to write the symbolic epic of King Arthur which he then projected, his 'Morte d'Arthur' is enough to show how fine a work might have resulted. But, for once, at any rate, the interposing critics did art good service, for they deferred till the experience of life had given him, as it were, many lives, a poem which could not have been produced without wide acquaintanceship with the world and human nature. We should never otherwise have had the parable 'full of voices' which we now fortunately possess.—I am, Sir, &c., J.T.K.

26. A. C. Swinburne on

the *Idylls*

Algernon Charles Swinburne, from *Under the Microscope* (1872).

In this pungent little book, Swinburne (1837–1909) replies to 'The Fleshly School of Poetry', a pseudonymous attack on the Pre-Raphaelites by Robert Buchanan (1841–1901), published in the *Contemporary* in 1871. Swinburne's comments on the *Idylls* occur on pp. 34–42 of his essay and are incidental to the main line of his argument.

. . . The enemies of Tennyson . . . are the men who find in his collection of Arthurian idyls,—the Morte d'Albert as it might perhaps be more properly called, after the princely type to which (as he tells us with just pride) the poet has been fortunate enough to make his central figure so successfully conform,—an epic poem of profound and exalted morality. Upon this moral question I shall take leave to intercalate a few words. . . . It seems to me that the moral tone of the Arthurian story has been on the whole lowered and degraded by Mr. Tennyson's mode of treatment. Wishing to make his central figure the noble and perfect symbol of an ideal man, he has removed not merely the excuse but the explanation of the fatal and tragic loves of Launcelot and Guenevere. The hinge of the whole legend of the Round Table, from its first glory to its final fall, is the incestuous birth of Mordred from the connexion of Arthur with his half-sister, unknowing and unknown; as surely as the hinge of the *Oresteia* from first to last is the sacrifice at Aulis. From the immolation of Iphigenia springs the wrath of Clytæmnestra, with all its train of evils ensuing; from the sin of Arthur's youth proceeds the ruin of his reign and realm through the falsehood of his wife, a wife unloving and unloved. Remove in either case the plea which leaves the heroine less sinned against indeed than sinning, but yet not too base for tragic compassion and interest, and there remains merely the presentation of a vulgar adulteress. . . . Mr. Tennyson has lowered the note and deformed the outline of the Arthurian story, by reducing Arthur to the level of a wittol, Guenevere to the level of a woman of intrigue, and Launcelot to the level of a 'co-respondent'. Treated as he has treated it, the story is rather a case for the divorce-court than for poetry. . . . Adultery must be tragic and exceptional to afford stuff for art to work upon; and the debased preference of Mr. Tennyson's heroine for a lover so much beneath her noble and faithful husband is as mean an instance as any day can show in its newspaper reports of a common woman's common sin. In the old story, the king, with the doom denounced in the beginning by Merlin hanging over all his toils and triumphs as a tragic shadow, stands apart in no undignified patience to await the end in its own good time of all his work and glory, with no eye for the pain and passion of the woman who sits beside him as queen rather than as wife. Such a figure is not unfit for the centre of a tragic action; it is neither ignoble nor inconceivable; but the besotted blindness of Mr. Tennyson's 'blameless king' to the treason of a woman who has had the first and last of his love and the whole devotion of his blameless life is nothing more or less than pitiful and ridiculous. All the studious care and exquisite eloquence of the poet can throw no genuine halo round the sprouting brows of a royal husband who remains to the very last the one man in his kingdom insensible of his disgrace. The unclean taunt of the hateful Vivien is simply the expression in vile language of an undeniable truth; such a man as this king is indeed hardly 'man at all'; either fool or coward he must surely be. Thus it is that by the very excision of what may have seemed in his eyes a moral blemish Mr. Tennyson has blemished the whole story; by the very exaltation of his hero as something more than man he has left him in the end something less. The keystone of the whole building is removed, and in place of a tragic house of song where even sin had all the dignity and beauty that sin can retain, and without which it can afford no fit material for tragedy, we find an incongruous edifice of tradition and invention where even virtue is made to seem either imbecile or vile. The story as it stood of old had in it something almost of Hellenic dignity and significance; in it as in the great Greek legends we could trace from a seemingly small root of evil the birth and growth of a calamitous fate, not sent by mere malevolence of heaven, yet in its awful weight and mystery of darkness apparently out of all due retributive proportion to the careless sin or folly of presumptuous weakness which first incurred its infliction; so that by mere hasty resistance and return of violence for violence a noble man may unwittingly bring on himself and all his house the curse denounced on parricide, by mere casual indulgence of light love and passing wantonness a hero king may unknowingly bring on himself and all his kingdom the doom imposed on incest. This presence and imminence of Ate inevitable as invisible throughout the tragic course of action can alone confer on such a story the proper significance and the necessary dignity; without it the action would want meaning and the passion would want nobility; with it, we may hear in the high funereal homily which concludes as with dirge-music the great old book of Sir Thomas Mallory some echo not utterly unworthy of that supreme lament of wondering and wailing spirits—

$$\pi\hat{o}\hat{\imath}\ \delta\hat{\eta}\tau\alpha\ \kappa\rho\alpha\nu\hat{\epsilon}\hat{\imath},\ \pi\hat{o}\hat{\imath}\ \kappa\alpha\tau\alpha\lambda\acute{\eta}\xi\epsilon\iota$$
$$\mu\epsilon\tau\alpha\kappa\omega\mu\iota\sigma\theta\grave{\epsilon}\nu\ \mu\acute{\epsilon}\nu\omicron\varsigma\ \check{\alpha}\tau\eta\varsigma;$$

The fatal consequence or corollary of this original flaw in his scheme is that the modern poet has been obliged to degrade all the other figures of the legend in order to bring them into due harmony with the degraded figures of Arthur and Guenevere. The courteous and loyal Gawain of the old romancers, already deformed and maligned in the version of Mallory himself, is here a vulgar traitor; the benignant Lady of the Lake, foster-mother of Launcelot, redeemer and comforter of Pelleas, becomes the very vilest figure in all that cycle of more or less symbolic agents and patients which Mr. Tennyson has set revolving round the figure of his central wittol. I certainly do not share the objection of the virtuous journalist to the presentation in art of an unchaste woman; but I certainly desire that the creature presented should retain some trace of human or if need be of devilish dignity. The Vivien of Mr. Tennyson's idyl seems to me, to speak frankly, about the most base and repulsive person ever set forth in serious literature. Her impurity is actually eclipsed by her incredible and incomparable vulgarity—('O ay,' said Vivien, 'that were likely too'). She is such a sordid creature as plucks men passing by the sleeve. I am of course aware that this figure appears the very type and model of a beautiful and fearful temptress of the flesh, the very embodied and ennobled ideal of danger and desire, in the chaster eyes of the virtuous journalist who grows sick with horror and disgust at the license of other French and English writers; but I have yet to find the French or English contemporary poem containing a passage that can be matched against the loathsome dialogue in which Merlin and Vivien discuss the nightly transgressions against chastity, within doors and without, of the various knights of Arthur's court. I do not remember that any modern poet whose fame has been assailed on the score of sensual immorality—say for instance the author of *Mademoiselle de Maupin* or the author of the *Fleurs du Mal*—has ever devoted an elaborate poem to describing the erotic fluctuations and vacillations of a dotard under the moral and physical manipulation of a prostitute. The conversation of Vivien is exactly described in the poet's own phrase—it is 'as the poached filth that floods the middle street'. Nothing like it can be cited from the verse which embodies other poetic personations of unchaste women. From the Cleopatra of Shakespeare and the Dalilah of Milton to the Phraxanor of Wells, a figure worthy to be ranked not far in design below the highest of theirs, we may pass without fear of finding any such pollution. Those heroines of sin are evil, but noble in their evil way; it is the utterly ignoble quality of Vivien which makes her so unspeakably repulsive and unfit for artistic treatment. 'Smiling saucily,' she is simply a subject for the police-court. . . .

27. E. Dowden on

Tennyson as the poet of Law

Edward Dowden, from 'Mr Tennyson and Mr Browning',
Studies in Literature 1789–1877 (1878), ed. 1882, pp. 191–239.

Dowden (1843–1913), the well-known Shakespearean
scholar, dates his essay '1867'; but his references to *Queen
Mary* (1875) and *Harold* (1876) show that he had brought it
up to date before publishing it in his volume of 1878. The
discussion of Tennyson printed here occupies section ii
(pp. 195–211) of it; in section iii, Dowden goes on to say
that Browning 'vividly feels the importance, the greatness
and beauty of passions and enthusiasms, and that his
imagination is comparatively unimpressed by the presence
of law and its operations' (p. 211).

. . . Let us start in our study,—a partial study made from a single point
of view,—with what may be an assumption for the present, but an
assumption which will lead to its own verification. Let us start by saying
that Mr. Tennyson has a strong sense of the dignity and efficiency of
law,—of *law* understood in its widest meaning. Energy nobly con-
trolled, an ordered activity delight his imagination. Violence, extravagance, immoderate force, the swerving from appointed ends, revolt,—
these are with Mr. Tennyson the supreme manifestations of evil.

Under what aspect is the relation of the world and man to God
represented in the poems of Mr. Tennyson? Surely,—it will be said,—
one who feels so strongly the presence of law in the physical world,
and who recognises so fully the struggle in the moral nature of man
between impulse and duty, assigning to conscience a paramount
authority, has the materials from which arises naturally a vivid feeling
of what is called the personal relation of God to his creatures. A little
reflection will show that this is not so. It is quite possible to admit in
one's thoughts and feelings the existence of a physical order of the

material world, and a moral order of the spiritual world, and yet to enter slightly into those intimate relations of the affections with a Divine Being which present him in the tenderest way as a Father,—as a highest Friend. Fichte, the sublime idealist, was withheld from seeing God by no obtruding veil of a material universe. Fichte, if any man ever did, recognised the moral order of the world. But Fichte—living indeed the blessed life in God,—yet annihilated for thought his own personality and that of God, in the infinity of this moral order. No: it is not law but will that reveals will; it is not our strength but our weakness that cries out for the invisible Helper and Divine Comrade; it is not our obedience but our aspiration, our joy, our anguish; it is the passion of self-surrender, the grief that makes desolate, the solitary rapture which demands a partaker of its excess, the high delight which must save itself from as deep dejection by a passing over into gratitude.

Accordingly, although we find the idea of God entering largely into the poems of Mr. Tennyson, there is little recognition of special contact of the soul with the Divine Being in any supernatural ways of quiet or of ecstasy. There is, on the contrary, a disposition to rest in the orderly manifestation of God, as the supreme Law-giver, and even to identify him with his presentation of himself, in the physical and moral order of the universe. And if this precludes all spiritual rapture, that 'glorious folly, that heavenly madness, wherein true wisdom is acquired',[1] it preserves the mind from despair or any deep dejection; unless, indeed, the faith in this order itself give way, when in the universal chaos, no will capable of bringing restoration being present, a confusion of mind, a moral obscurity greater than any other, must arise.

Wordsworth in some of his solitary trances of thought really entered into the frame of mind which the mystic knows as union or as ecstacy, when thought expires in enjoyment, when the mind is blessedness and love, when 'the waters of grace have risen up to the neck of the soul, so that it can neither advance nor retreat'. With Mr. Tennyson the mystic is always the visionary, who suffers from an over-excitable fancy. The nobler aspects of the mystical religious spirit, are unrepresented in his poetry. St. Simeon upon his pillar is chiefly of interest, as affording an opportunity for studying the phenomena of morbid theopathetic emotion. We find nowhere among the persons of his imagination a Teresa, uniting as she did in so eminent a degree an administrative genius, a genius for action with the genius of exalted piety. The feeble Confessor beholds visions; but Harold strikes ringing

[1] S. Teresa, Life, ch. xvi.

blows upon the helms of his country's enemies. Harold is no virgin, no confessor, no seer, no saint, but a loyal, plain, strong-thewed, truth-loving son of England, who can cherish a woman, and rule a people, and mightily wield a battle-axe. In the *Idylls* when the Grail passes before the assembled knights, where is the king? He is absent, actively resisting evil, harrying the bandits' den; and as he returns, it is with alarm that he perceives the ominous tokens left by the sacred thing:—

> Lo there! the roofs
> Of our great hall are rolled in thunder smoke!
> Pray heaven, they be not smitten by the bolt.

The Grail is a sign to maim the great order which Arthur has reared. The mystical glories which the knights pursue are 'wandering fires'. If Galahad beheld the vision, it was because Galahad was already un-meet for earth, worthy to be a king, not in this sad yet noble city of men, but in some far-off spiritual city.

[Quotes 'The Holy Grail', ll. 884–98:

' "And spake I not too truly . . .
. . . crown him otherwhere." ']

The Round Table is dissolved, the work of Arthur is brought to an end, because two passions have overthrown the order of the realm, which it has been the task of the loyal, steadfast and wise king to create, —first, the sensual passion of Lancelot and Guinevere; secondly, the spiritual passion hardly less fatal, which leaped forth when the disastrous quest was avowed. Only that above all order of human institution, a higher order abides, we might well suppose that chaos must come again; but it is not so:—

> The old order changeth giving place to new,
> And God fulfils himself in many ways.

Thus, as has been already remarked, Mr. Tennyson's sense of a bene-ficient unfolding in our life of a divine purpose, lifts him through and over the common dejections of men. With his own friend, it is as with his ideal king; he will not mourn for any overmuch. The fame which he predicted to his friend is quenched by an early death; but he will not despair:—

> The fame is quench'd that I foresaw,
> The head hath missed an earthly wreath;
> I curse not nature, no, nor death;
> For nothing is that errs from law.

Even the thought of the foul corruption of the grave becomes support-able, when it is conceived as a part of the change which permits the spirit to have its portion in the self-evolving process of the higher life:—

> Eternal process moving on,
>   From state to state the spirit walks;
>   And these are but the shatter'd stalks,
> Or ruin'd chrysalis of one.

It is only when the doubt of a beneficient order of the world cannot be put away—it is only when nature (as discovered by the investigations of geology), seems ruthless alike to the individual and the species, 'red in tooth and claw with ravine', it is only then that the voice of the mourner grows wild, and it appears to him that his grief has lost its sanctity and wrongs the quiet of the dead.

Mr. Tennyson finds law present throughout all nature, but there is no part of nature in which he dwells with so much satisfaction upon its presence as in human society. No one so largely as Mr. Tennyson, has represented in art the new thoughts and feelings, which form the impassioned side of the modern conception of progress. His imagination is for ever haunted by 'the vision of the world, and all the wonder that would be'. But the hopes and aspirations of Mr. Tennyson are not those of the radical or movement character. He is in all his poems conservative as well as liberal. It may be worth while to illustrate the feeling of Shelley, in contrast with that of Mr. Tennyson, with reference to this idea of progress. In the year 1819 Shelley believed that England had touched almost the lowest point of social and political degradation:

> An old, mad, blind, despised, and dying king,—
> Princes, the dregs of their dull race, who flow
> Through public scorn, mud from a muddy spring,—
> Rulers, who neither see, nor feel, nor know,
> But leech-like to their fainting country cling,
> Till they drop, blind in blood, without a blow,—
> A people starv'd and stabb'd in the untilled field,—
> An army which liberticide and prey
> Make as a two-edged sword to all who wield,—
> Golden and sanguine laws which tempt and slay,—
> Religion Christless, Godless,—a book sealed,
> A Senate—time's worst statute unrepealed.—

Such laws, such rulers, such a people Shelley found in his England of half a century since. Did he therefore despair, or if he hoped was the

object of his hope some better life of man in some distant future? No:
all these things

> Are graves, from which a glorious Phantom may
> Burst, to illumine our tempestuous day.

The regeneration of society, as conceived by Shelley, was to appear
suddenly, splendidly shining with the freshness and glory of a dream;
as the result of some bright, brief national struggle; as the consequence
of the apparition of some pure being, at once a poet and a prophet,
before whose voice huge tyrannies and cruel hypocrisies must needs go
down, as piled-up clouds go down ruined and rent before a swift, pure
wind; in some way or another which involves a catastrophe, rather
than according to the constantly operating processes of nature.

Now Mr. Tennyson's conception of progress, which he has drawn
from his moral and intellectual environment, and which accords with
his own moral temper, is widely different. No idea perhaps occupies a
place in his poems so central as that of the progress of the race. This it
is which lifts out of his idle dejection and selfish dreaming the speaker
in 'Locksley Hall';

> Not in vain the distance beacons. Forward, forward let us
>   range,
> Let the great world spin for ever down the ringing grooves
>   of change.

This it is which suggests an apology for the fantasies of 'The Day-
Dream'. This it is which arms the tempted with a weapon of defence,
and the tempter with a deadlier weapon of attack in 'The Two Voices'.
This it is of which Leonard writes, and at which old James girds in
'The Golden Year'. This it is which gives a broad basis of meditative
thought to the Idyll that tells of the passing of Arthur, and renders it
something more than a glorious fable. This it is which is the sweetness
of 'The Poet's Song', making the wild swan pause, and the lark drop
from heaven to earth. This it is which forms the closing prophecy of
The Princess, the full confession of the poet's faith. This it is which is
heard in the final chords of the *In Memoriam*, changing the music from
a minor to a major key. And the same doctrine is taught from the
opposite side in 'The Vision of Sin', in which the most grievous disaster
which comes upon the base and sensual heart is represented as hopelessness with reference to the purpose and the progress of the life of
man:

> Fill the can and fill the cup,
> All the windy ways of men
> Are but dust that rises up
> And is lightly laid again.[1]

But in all these poems throughout which the idea of progress is so variously expressed, and brought into relation with moods of mind so diverse, the progress of mankind is uniformly represented as the evolution and self-realisation of a law; it is represented as taking place gradually and slowly, and its consummation is placed in a remote future. We 'hear the roll of the ages'; the 'increasing purpose' runs through centuries; it is 'with the process of the suns' that the thoughts of men are widened. It is when our sleep should have been prolonged through many decades and quinquenniads that we might wake to reap the flower and quintessence of change:

> For we are Ancients of the earth,
> And in the morning of the times.

It is because millenniums will not bring the advance of knowledge near its term that the tempted soul in 'The Two Voices' feels how wretched a thing it must be to watch the increase of intellectual light during the poor thirty or forty years of a life-time. It is 'in long years' that the sexes shall attain to the fulness of their mighty growth, until at last, man and woman

> Upon the skirts of Time
> Sit side by side, full-summ'd in all their powers,
> Dispensing harvest, sowing the To-be,

> *   *   *

> Then comes the statelier Eden back to man:
> Then reign the world's great bridals, chaste and calm;
> Then springs the crowning race of humankind.
> May these things be!

And the highest augury telling of this 'crowning race' is drawn from those who already having moved upward through the lower phases of being become precursors and pledges of the gracious children of the future:

> For all we thought and loved and did,
> And hoped, and suffer'd, is but seed
> Of what in them is flower and fruit;

---

[1] So in the *In Memoriam* when the 'light is low' and the heart is sick, Time appears not as a wise master-builder, but as a 'maniac, scattering dust'.

Whereof the man, that with me trod
This planet, was a noble type
Appearing ere the times were ripe,
That friend of mine who lives in God,

That God, which ever lives and loves,
One God, one law, one element,
And one far-off divine event,
To which the whole creation moves.

The great hall which Merlin built for Arthur, is girded by four zones of symbolic sculpture; in the lowest zone, beasts are slaying men; in the second, men are slaying beasts;

And on the third are warriors, perfect men,
And on the fourth are men with growing wings.

To work out the beast is the effort of long ages; to attain to be 'a perfect man' is for those who shall follow us afar off; to soar with wings is for the crowning race of the remotest future.

Apart from the growth of the individual that golden age to which the poet looks forward, the coming of which he sees shine in the distance, is characterized, as he imagines it, chiefly by a great development of knowledge, especially of scientific knowledge; this first; and, secondly, by the universal presence of political order and freedom, national and international, secured by a vast and glorious federation. It is quite of a piece with Mr. Tennyson's feeling for law, that his imagination should be much impressed by the successes of science, and that its promises should correspond with his hopes. The crowning race will be a company

Of those that, eye to eye, shall look
On knowledge; under whose command
Is Earth and Earth's, and in their hand
Is Nature like an open book.

Were we to sleep the hundred years, our joy would be to wake

On science grown to more,
On secrets of the brain, the stars.

It is the promises and achievements of science which restore sanity to the distraught lover of 'Locksley Hall'. In *The Princess* the sport half-science of galvanic batteries, model steam-engines, clock-work steamers and fire-balloons, suggest the thought of a future of adult knowledge:

This fine old world of ours is but a child
Yet in the go-cart. Patience! Give it time
To learn its limbs: there is a hand that guides.

But Mr. Tennyson's dream of the future is not more haunted by
visionary discoveries and revelations of science than by the phantoms
of great political organizations. That will be a time

When the war-drum throbs no longer, and the battle flags are
furl'd
In the Parliament of men, the Federation of the world.

A time in which

Phantoms of other forms of rule,
New Majesties of mighty states

will appear, made real at length; a time in which the years will bring
to being

The vast Republics that may grow,
The Federations and the Powers;
Titanic forces taking birth.

These days and works of the crowning race are, however, far beyond
our grasp; and the knowledge of this, with the faith that the progress
of mankind is the expression of a slowly self-revealing law, puts a
check upon certain of our hopes and strivings. He who is possessed by
this faith will look for no speedy regeneration of men in the social or
political sphere, and can but imperfectly sympathise with those enthusiastic hearts whose expectations, nourished by their ardours and desires,
are eager and would forestall futurity. Mr. Tennyson's justness of
mind in a measure forsakes him, when he has to speak of political
movements into which passion in its uncalculating form has entered
as a main motive power. Yet passion of this type is the right and
appropriate power for the uses of certain times and seasons. It is by
ventures of faith in politics that mountains are removed. The Tory
member's elder son estimates the political movements of France in an
insular spirit which, it may be surmised, has in it something of Mr.
Tennyson's own feeling:—

Whiff! there comes a sudden heat,
The gravest citizen seems to lose his head,
The king is scared, the soldier will not fight,
The little boys begin to shoot and stab.

Yet to France more than to England the enslaved nations have turned their faces when they have striven to rend their bonds. It is hardly from Mr. Tennyson that we shall learn how a heroic failure may be worth as much to the world as a distinguished success. It is another poet who has written thus:—

> When liberty goes out of a place it is not the first to go, nor the
>   second or third to go,
> It waits for all the rest to go—it is the last.
> When there are no more memories of heroes and martyrs,
> And when all life, and all the souls of men and women are dis-
>   charged from any part of the earth,
> Then only shall liberty, or the idea of liberty, be discharged from
>   that part of the earth,
> And the infidel come into full possession.

Mr. Tennyson's ideal for every country is England, and that is a blunder in politics:

> A land of settled government,
>   A land of just and old renown,
>   Where Freedom slowly broadens down
> From precedent to precedent.

That is an admirable verse; but it is nobler to make than to follow precedents; and great emotions, passionate thought, audacities of virtue quickly create a history and tradition of precedents in the lives alike of individuals and of nations. Mr. Tennyson loves freedom, but she must assume an English costume before he can recognize her; the freedom which he loves is

> That sober freedom out of which there springs
> Our loyal passion to our temperate kings.

She is

> Freedom in her royal seat
> Of England, not the schoolboy heat—
> The blind hysterics of the Celt.

He cannot squander a well-balanced British sympathy on hearts that love not wisely but too well:—

> Love thou thy land with love far brought
>   From out the storied Past, and used
>   Within the Present, but transfused
> Through future time by power of thought.

What Mr. Tennyson has written will indeed lead persons of a certain type of character in their true direction; for those of a different type it will for ever remain futile and false. 'Reason', Vauvenargues has said, 'deceives us more often than does nature.' 'If passion advises more boldly than reflection, it is because passion gives greater power to carry out its advice.' 'To do great things, one must live as if one could never die.' England can celebrate a golden wedding with Freedom, and gather children about her knees; let there be a full and deep rejoicing. But why forbid the more unmeasured joy of the lover of Freedom who has dreamed of her and has fought for her, and who now is glad because he has once seen her, and may die for her?

Mr. Tennyson's political doctrine is in entire agreement with his ideal of human character. As the exemplar of all nations is that one in which highest wisdom is united with complete self-government, so the ideal man is he whose life is led to sovereign power by self-know-ledge resulting in self-control, and self-control growing perfect in self-reverence. The golden fruit which Herè prays for, promising power, which Aphrodite prays for, promising pleasure, belongs of right to Pallas alone, who promises no other sovereignty, no other joy than those that come by the freedom of perfect service,—

> To live by law,
> Acting the law we live by without fear.

Mr. Tennyson has had occasion to write two remarkable poetical *éloges*—one on the late Prince Consort, the other on the great Duke. In both, the characters are drawn with fine discrimination, but in both, the crowning virtue of the dead is declared to have been the virtue of obedience, that of self-subjugation to the law of duty. In both the same lesson is taught, that he who toils along the upward path of painful right-doing

> Shall find the toppling crags of Duty scaled
> Are close upon the shining table-lands
> To which our God Himself is moon and sun.

Even Love 'takes part against himself' to be at one with Duty, who is 'loved of Love'. Through strenuous self-mastery, through the strong holding of passion in its leash, Enoch Arden attains the sad happiness of strong heroic souls. But it is not only as fortitude and endurance that Mr. Tennyson conceives the virtue of noble obedience; it flames up into a chivalric ardour in the passionate loyalty of the Six Hundred riders at Balaclava; and Cranmer redeems his life from the dishonour of fear, of faltering and of treason, by the last gallantry of a soldierlike obedience to the death:

> He pass'd out smiling, and he walk'd upright;
> His eye was like a soldier's, whom the general
> He looks to, and he leans on as his God,
> Hath rated for some backwardness, and bidd'n him
> Charge one against a thousand, and the man
> Hurls his soil'd life against the pikes and dies.

Self-reverence, self-knowledge, self-control, the recognition of a divine order and of one's own place in that order, faithful adhesion to the law of one's highest life,—these are the elements from which is formed the ideal human character. What is the central point in the ethical import of the Arthurian story as told by Mr. Tennyson? It is the assertion that the highest type of manhood is set forth in the poet's ideal king, and that the worthiest work of man is work such as his. And what is Arthur? The blameless monarch, who 'reverenced his conscience as a king'; unseduced from his appointed path by the temptations of sense or the wandering fires of religious mysticism; throughout the most passionate scene of the poem 'sublime in self-repression':—

> I wanted warmth and colour, which I found
> In Lancelot,—now I see thee what thou art,
> Thou art the highest, and most human too,
> Not Lancelot, not another.

Arthur's task has been to drive back the heathen, to quell disorder and violence, to bind the wills of his knights to righteousness in a perfect law of liberty. It is true that Arthur's task is left half done. While he rides forth to silence the riot of the Red Knight and his ruffian band, in his own court are held those 'lawless jousts', and Tristram sings in the ears of that small, sad cynic, Dagonet, his licentious song:

> Free love—free field—we love but while we may.

And thus were it not that a divine order overrules our efforts, our successes, and our failures, we must needs believe that the realm is once more reeling back into the beast.

Disorder of thoughts, of feelings and of will is, with Mr. Tennyson, the evil of evils, the pain of pains. The Princess would transcend, through the temptation of a false ideal, her true sphere of womanhood; even this noblest form of disobedience to law entails loss and sorrow; she is happy only when she resumes her worthier place through the wisdom of love. In 'Lucretius' the man who had so highly striven for light and calm, for 'the sober majesties of settled, sweet Epicurean life', is swept by a fierce tempest in his blood back into chaos; there is but one way of deliverance, but one way of entering again under the reign of law,—to surrender his being once more to Nature, that she may anew dash together the atoms which make him man, in order that as flower, or beast, or fish, or bird, or man, they may again move through her cycles; and so Lucretius roughly woos the passionless bride, Tranquillity. And may we not sum up the substance of Mr. Tennyson's personal confessions in *In Memoriam*, by saying that they are the record of the growth through sorrow of the firmer mind, which becomes one with law at length apparent through the chaos of sorrow; which counts it crime 'to mourn for any overmuch'; which turns its burden into gain, and for which those truths that never can be proved, and that had been lost in the first wild shock of grief, are regained by 'faith that comes of self-control'. . . .

28. G. M. Hopkins on

the *Idylls*

Gerard Manley Hopkins, from a letter of 27th February 1879, *Correspondence of Gerard Manley Hopkins and Richard Watson Dixon* (ed. C. C. Abbott, 1935), pp. 20–26.

The 'other drama', to which Hopkins refers in the last sentence quoted here, is *Harold* (1876).

... You call Tennyson 'a great outsider'; you mean, I think, to the soul of poetry. I feel what you mean, though it grieves me to hear him depreciated, as of late years has often been done. Come what may he will be one of our greatest poets. To me his poetry appears 'chryselephantine'; always of precious mental material and each verse a work of art, no botchy places, not only so but no half wrought or low-toned ones, no drab, no brown-holland; but the form, though fine, not the perfect artist's form, not equal to the material. When the inspiration is genuine, arising from personal feeling, as in *In Memoriam*, a divine work, he is at his best, or when he is rhyming pure and simple imagination, without afterthought, as in the 'Lady of Shalott', 'Sir Galahad', the 'Dream of Fair Women', or 'Palace of Art'. But the want of perfect form in the imagination comes damagingly out when he undertakes longer works of fancy, as his Idylls: they are unreal in motive and incorrect, uncanonical so to say, in detail and keepings. He shd. have called them *Charades from the Middle Ages* (dedicated by permission to H. R. H. etc). The Galahad of one of the later ones is quite a fantastic charade-playing trumpery Galahad, merely playing the fool over Christian heroism. Each scene is a triumph of language and of bright picturesque, but just like a charade—where real lace and good silks and real jewelry are used, because the actors are private persons and wealthy, but it is acting all the same and not only so but the make-up has less pretence of correct keeping than at Drury Lane. His opinions too are

334

not original, often not independent even, and they sink into vulgarity: not only 'Locksley Hall' but *Maud* is an ungentlemanly row and 'Aylmer's Field' is an ungentlemanly row and *The Princess* is an ungentlemanly row. To be sure this gives him vogue, popularity, but not that sort of ascendancy Goethe had or even Burns, scoundrel as the first was, not to say the second; but then they spoke out the real human rakishness of their hearts and everybody recognised the really beating, though rascal, vein. And in his rhetorical pieces he is at his worst, as the 'Lord of Burleigh' and 'Lady Clara Vere de Vere' (downright haberdasher). But for all this he is a glorious poet and all he does is chryselephantine. Though by the by I owe him a grudge for *Queen Mary*, written to please the mob, and for that other drama where a portent of a man in flaxen locks and ring-mail mouths rationalism 'to torment us before the time'. . . .

29. A. C. Swinburne replies to Taine (No. 21)

Algernon Charles Swinburne, from 'Tennyson and Musset', *Miscellanies* (1886), pp. 219–59.

Most of Swinburne's discussion of Musset has been omitted from the text given here. The 'then uncrowned assassin' mentioned towards the end of the essay was the future Emperor Napoleon III. He seized power by a *coup d'état* in 1851 and exchanged visits with Queen Victoria in 1855.

When the history of poetry in this age shall be written by the critical chroniclers of the next, one thing will of necessity be noted as distinctive of its latter years: the singular and splendid persistence of genius and prolongation of working power in the greatest of those great writers who were born in the infancy or in the adolescence of the nineteenth century. Its eighty-first year bestowed on us not only a new poem from the hand of its mightiest master, but also a volume which did more than sustain—which actually magnified and heightened —the fame of Wordsworth's successor as poet laureate of England. It is no rare or strange experience for an admirer of noble work to feel deeply the inadequacy of language to express the depth and translate the fervour of admiration: and never assuredly was any poor penman of the humblest order more inwardly conscious of such impotence in his words to sustain the weight of their intention, than was the present writer of his inability to cast into any shape of articulate speech the impression and the emotion produced by the first reading of Tennyson's 'Rizpah'. To him it seemed then that never since the very beginning of all poetry were the twin passions of terror and pity more divinely done into deathless words or set to more perfect and profound magnificence of music; never more inseparably fused and harmonized into more absolute and sublime identity: that the poet never lived on earth whose glory would not be heightened by the attribution of this poem to his hand: that thousands of readers for centuries to come would be

336

moved by it to trembling and to tears. I did not, even then, forget the fact that prediction of this kind was proverbially futile: but it should also be remembered that art has her certainties no less absolute than those of science: and that this was one of them the judgment which could hesitate to affirm must surely, I thought,—so strong was the instant impression of tragic pity and terror—be either cancerous with malevolence or paralytic with stupidity. Some indeed may probably be found to object that pity is here strained and racked into actual and intolerable anguish—that terror here darkens and condenses into sheer physical pain and horror: and, doubtless, of no contemporary writer can it be so truly said—nor can it be said more truly of any writer in time past—that he has 'created a new shudder'; a pang of piercing and dreadful compassion which cleaves as it were the very core of 'the spirit of sense' in sunder. But here is one more proof—and a proof beyond all price and beyond all question—that passion and imagination are justified of all their children. Were it not so, the very crowning glory of this most pathetic and terrible poem would be frightful rather than terrible, and unbearable rather than pathetic. As it is, those four central and consummating lines, unspeakably pitiful and unutterably beautiful, are made endurable, and therefore in some deeper sense delightful, by sheer force of genius alone. They cannot be separately transcribed—wrenched out of their natural framework, or torn off the stem of thorns on which they set the topmost crown of tear-drenched and passion-coloured blossom. But six words of them—the six last words, 'they had moved in my side'—give perfect proof once more of the deep truth that great poets are bisexual; male and female at once, motherly not less than fatherly in their instincts towards little children; from the day when Homer put Astyanax into the arms of Hector to the day when Hugo found the sweetest of all cradle-songs on the lips of the death-stricken Fantine. And among all these not one—not even Victor Hugo's very self—has ever touched the very deepest and finest chord on the lyre of the human spirit with a diviner power, a more godlike strength of tenderness, than Tennyson has touched it here. Nothing more piteous, more passionate, more adorable for intensity of beauty, was ever before this wrought by human cunning into the likeness of such words as words are powerless to praise.

Two consequences, each of some little importance to students of poetry, though to a writer of Lord Tennyson's rank and station they may be personally indifferent and insignificant enough, should follow on the appearance of such a poem as this. First, there must be an end for ever on all hands to the once debateable question whether the author can properly be called in the strictest sense a great poet, or whether his admirers should be content with the application to their master of such commendatory epithets as 'a fine, a gracious, an exquisite poet'. If after a thousand years all trace of all his poems had vanished from all human record, save only these eighty-six verses of 'Rizpah', proof positive and ample and overflowing would be left in the survival of these that in the author of this single poem a truly great poet had been born. And secondly there must be an end, for ever and a day beyond at least, of a question which once was even more hotly debateable than this: the long contested question of poetic precedence between Alfred Tennyson and Alfred de Musset. Four lines of 'Rizpah', placed in one scale of the balance of judgment, would send all the loveliest verse of Musset flying up in the other, to kick the beam and vanish. Of passion such as this he knew no more than he knew of such execution. He was about as capable of either as of writing *Ratbert*, *The Cenci*, or *King Lear*.

. . . The message or the legacy of Musset to his country and his kind, apart from the manner of its delivery or the grace of its presentation, scarcely seems to me on the whole so precious in itself, or so worthy of a great national poet, that the English flag flying on board the Laureate's ship of song must needs be lowered to salute it at the challenge of M. Taine. If I proceed to inquire, on the other hand, into the positive worth and actual weight of Lord Tennyson's message, taken equally apart from the method of its delivery, it must not and I trust it will not be supposed by any candid reader that I wish to play the odious part of devil's advocate. So much I hope may be premised without fear of self-accusation by dint of self-excuse. And against the most forcible charges of the foreign champion, strong of wrist and skilful of fence as he is, it would not be difficult to bring an answer or to make an appeal on grounds less personal or provincial than I have often seen assumed by the professional admirers of Lord Tennyson. His assailant gave proof that as far as daring is concerned his motto might be Strafford's word, 'Thorough', when he struck with the sharp point of his lance 'the spotless shield' which bears inscribed the words *In Memoriam*. His impeachment of Lord Tennyson's great monumental poem as the cold and correct work of a 'perfectly gentlemanlike' mourner, who never can forget to behave himself respectably and carry his grief like a gentleman conscious of spectators, may be classed for perfection of infelicity with Jeffrey's selection of the finest lines in Wordsworth's finest ode for especially contemptuous assault on the simple charge of sheer nonsense. Had he reserved his attack for the pretentiously un-pretentious philosophy of the book, we might not so assuredly have felt that his hand had lost its cunning. Lord Tennyson is so ostentatious of his modesty, so unsparing in his reserve, so incessant and obtrusive in his disclaimer of all ambition to rank as a thinker or a teacher, while returning again and yet again to the charge as an ethical apostle or a sentimental theosophist, that we are almost reminded of the philosopher whose vociferous laudation of the dumb, and ear-splitting inculcation of silence, might seem to all half-deafened hearers enough to 'crack his lungs, and split his brazen pipe'—if possibly such a thing might have been possible. I trust it may be held allowable and compatible with loyalty to observe that it is hardly reasonable to touch repeatedly and with obvious earnestness on the gravest and the deepest questions of life and death, of human affection and mortal bereavement—to pour forth page upon page of passionate speculation, of love and fear and hope and doubt and belief, and then to turn round on the student to whose sympathy the book—if there be any reason whatever for its existence or publication—must surely be supposed to appeal, with the surely astonishing protest that it does not pretend to grapple with the questions on which it harps and the mysteries of which it treats. The fitfulness of a mourner's mood will hardly be held as a sufficient excuse to justify or to reconcile such incompatible incoherences of meditation and profession. To say that these effusions of natural sorrow make no pretence, and would be worthy of contempt if they pretended, to solve or satisfy men's doubts—and then to renew the appearance of an incessant or even a fitful endeavour after some such satisfaction or solution—is surely so incongruous as to sound almost insincere. But the possession of a book so wholly noble and so profoundly beautiful in itself is more precious than the most coherent essay towards the solution of any less insoluble problem. It would be cruel to set over against it for comparison any sample of the bitter or the sweet futilities of Musset, from the date of his 'Vœux Stériles' to the date of his not much fruitfuller 'Espoir en Dieu'.

Towards the Morte d'Albert, or Idylls of the Prince Consort, I should almost equally regret to seem desirous of playing the aforesaid part of devil's advocate. The most mealy-mouthed critic or the most honey-tongued flatterer of Lord Tennyson cannot pretend or profess a more cordial and thankful admiration than I have always felt for the exquisite magnificence of style, the splendid flashes of episodical illumination, with which those poems are vivified or adorned. But when they are presented to us as a great moral and poetic whole, the flower at once of all epics and all ethics—

Cette promotion me laisse un peu rêveur.

I do not think much of Alfred de Musset as a shepherd of souls or a moral philosopher: but I should feel very sincere pity for a generation which felt itself obliged to fall back upon the alternative ideal here proposed to it by Alfred Tennyson. A writer in a contemporary review dropped once an observation on this matter which struck me as so scientifically remarkable that I made a note of it for possible future service. A more patient or methodical man would have transcribed the passage at length; but the gist of it I believe that I set down correctly enough for any needful purpose. It was to this impressive and instructive effect: that is to say, that certain pitiful weaklings of no specified kind, who find themselves in the surely very pitiable condition of aspirants after an impossible experience of passions and emotions which real men possess, and begin by subduing, but from which these unclassified unfortunates are shut out by congenital imperfection or deficiency in fullness of nature, have wilfully and maliciously impeached the master-work of Lord Tennyson on the charge—of all charges upon earth—that its moral tone was over highly pitched. We live and learn in this world: there never was a truer saying. But I should myself, I must needs confess, as soon have expected to hear that the Memoirs of Casanova or the *Adventures of Faublas* had ever been attacked on the score of too exalted a morality. Among all poems of serious pretentions in that line, it had appeared to the infirmity of my judgment that this latest epic of King Arthur took the very lowest view of virtue, set up the very poorest and most pitiful standard of duty or of heroism for woman or for man. To abstain from talking scandal or listening to it is a moral principle which I sincerely wish were more practically popular than it is: and ever since the first edition of *The Princess*, wherein there shot up a long eruption of blazing eloquence, extinguished or suppressed in later issues of the poem, on that sin of 'narrowest neighbourhoods—where gossip breeds and seethes and festers in provincial sloth', Lord Tennyson has missed few opportunities of denouncing it with emphatic if not virulent iteration. But the lesson of abstinence from promiscuous tattle can hardly be considered by itself as 'the law and the gospel'. And whatever else there is of sound doctrine in Lord Tennyson's *Idylls* was preached more simply and not less earnestly in the grand old compilation of Sir Thomas Mallory. But, says the

Laureate, it is not Mallory's King Arthur, nor yet Geoffrey's King Arthur, that I have desired to reproduce: on the contrary, it is 'scarce other than' Prince Albert. And in that case, of course, there is no more room for discussion. All I can say is that most assuredly I never heard 'these Idylls' attacked on any moral ground but this: that the tone of divine or human doctrine preached and of womanly or manly character exalted in them, directly or indirectly, was poor, mean, paltry, petty, almost base; so utterly insufficient as to be little short of ignoble: that it is anything but a sign of moral elevation to be so constantly preoccupied by speculations on possible contact with 'smut' and contamination from 'swine': that Byron for one and Musset for another have been violently reviled and virtuously condemned on the charge of handling subjects very much less offensive than the stimulation and seduction of torpid and reluctant senility by the cajoleries and caresses of a lissom Vivien: that the tone of the original 'eleventh book', once 'picked from the fire', and now most incongruously incorporated with an incompatible mass of new matter, was incomparably higher, finer, manlier, than the Albertine ideal of later days. There the great dying king had been made to say, in words which 'give a very echo to the seat' where conscience is enthroned,

I have lived my life, and that which I have done
May He within himself make pure!

If this be taken as the last natural expression of a gallant, honest, kindly, faulty creature like the hero of old Mallory, it strikes home at once to a man's heart. If it be taken as the last deliberate snuffle of 'the blameless king', it strikes us in a different fashion. We feel that even at Almesbury, when denouncing the fallen Guinevere in such magnificent language that the reader is content and indeed thankful to take the manliness and propriety of such an address for granted, this blameless being had not attained to the very perfection of pretence—a flight beyond his preceding pretence of perfection.

The real and radical flaw in the splendid structure of the *Idylls* is not to be found either in the antiquity of the fabulous groundwork or in the modern touches which certainly were not needed, and if needed would not have been adequate, to redeem any worthy recast of so noble an original from the charge of nothingness. The fallacy which obtrudes itself throughout, the false note which incessantly jars on the mind's ear, results from the incongruity of materials which are radically incapable of combination or coherence. Between the various Arthurs of different national legends there is little more in common than the name. It is essentially impossible to construct a human figure by the process of selection from the incompatible types of irreconcilable ideals. All that the utmost ingenuity of eclecticism can do has been demonstrated by Lord Tennyson in his elaborate endeavour after the perfection of this process; and the result is to impress upon us a complete and irreversible conviction of its absolute hopelessness. Had a poet determined to realize the Horatian ideal of artistic monstrosity, he could hardly have set about it more ingeniously than by copying one feature from the *Mabinogion* and the next from the *Morte d'Arthur*. So far from giving us 'Geoffrey's' type or 'Mallory's' type, he can hardly be said to have given us a recognizable likeness of Prince Albert; who, if neither a wholly gigantic nor altogether a divine personage, was at least, one would imagine, a human figure. But the spectre of his laureate's own ideal knight, neither Welsh nor French, but a compound of 'Guallia and Gaul, soul-curer and body-curer', sir priest and sir knight, Mallory and Geoffrey, old style and middle style and new style, makes the reader bethink himself what might or might not be the result if some poet of similar aim and aspiration were to handle the tale of Troy, for instance, as Lord Tennyson has handled the Arthurian romance. The half godlike Achilles of Homer is one in name and nothing else with the all brutish Achilles of Shakespeare; the romantic Arthur of the various volumes condensed by Mallory into his English compilation—incoherent itself and incongruous in its earlier parts, but so nobly consistent, so profoundly harmonious in its close—has hardly more in common with the half impalpable hero of British myth or tradition. And I cannot but think that no very promising task would be undertaken by a poet who should set before himself the design of harmonizing in one fancy portrait, of reconciling in one typic figure, the features of Achilles as they appear in the *Iliad* with the features of Achilles as they appear in *Troilus and Cressida*.

I cannot say that Lord Tennyson's lifelong tone about women and their shortcomings has ever commended itself to my poor mind as the note of a very pure or high one. There is always a latent if not a patent propensity in many of his very lovers to scold and whine after a fashion which makes even Alfred de Musset seem by comparison a model or a type of manliness. His Enids and Edith Aylmers are much below the ideal mark of Wordsworth, who has never, I believe, been considered a specially greater master in that kind: but his 'little Letties' were apparently made mean and thin of nature to match their pitifully poor-

spirited suitors. It cannot respectfully be supposed that Lord Tennyson
is unaware of the paltry currishness and mean-spirited malice displayed
in verse too dainty for such base uses by the plaintively spiteful mani-
kins, with the thinnest whey of sour milk in their poor fretful veins,
whom he brings forward to vent upon some fickle or too discerning
mistress the vain and languid venom of their contemptible contempt.
But why on earth a man of high genius and high spirit, a poet and a
patriot, should be so fond of harping on such an untuneful string as this,
is a question which will always vex the souls and discomfit the sympathies of his readers. And some of these will perhaps consider it a
just retribution for this habit, and others perhaps as a different symptom
of the same infirmity, that with all his elaborate graces of language he
should never once have come within a thousand leagues of the pure and
perfect grace, unfettered and unforced, which even in the doleful days
of his decadence the better genius of Musset could infuse into the
laughingly tender undertone of his adorably delicate and magically
musical verses improvised for a young lady in a hood like a monk's
cowl. It would be too cruel to bid any reader set these for comparison
beside such things as the 'Wrens' or the 'Ringlet' of Lord Tennyson in
evidence how exquisitely good or bad such fanciful effusions at their
worst or at their best may be.

I have just touched in passing on a point in which the incomparable
superiority of the English poet is not more evident than it is infinite.
But, with all due admiration for the genuine patriotism of his 'ballad
of the fleet' and 'Defence of Lucknow', I must be permitted to observe
that his general tone of thought and utterance on large questions of
contemporary national history is such as might with admirable propriety find such expression as it finds at the close of *The Princess* from
the lips, not even of 'the Tory member', but of the Tory member's
undergraduate son—supposing that young gentleman to be other for
the nonce than a socialist. There is a strain, so to speak, as of beardless
bluster about it, which could by no possible ingenuity have been so
rendered as to suggest a more appropriate mouthpiece. It has the shrill
unmistakable accent, not of a provincial deputy, but of a provincial
schoolboy. And this fact, it would seem, was revealed to Lord Tennyson
himself, of all men on earth, by some freak of the same humorous if
malicious fairy who disclosed to him the not less amusing truth, and
induced him to publish it, with a face of unmoved gravity, to the
nation and the world, that whenever he said 'King Arthur' he meant
Prince Albert. No satirist could have ventured on either stroke of

sarcasm. So it was from the beginning (1830), so it is, and so it will be, for all momentary protest or incongruous pretence to the contrary. In a sonnet addressed to Victor Hugo, Lord Tennyson, with rather singular and rather more than questionable taste, informed the master poet of his age that he was said not to love England. No doubt, as I have elsewhere found occasion to remark, he did not love England as he loved his mother France and his foster-mother Spain; and against certain phases of modern English policy, as against certain shades of modern English character, Hugo did undoubtedly think fit once and again to utter a frank and friendly word of protest. But such a tone as Lord Tennyson's almost invariable tone towards France is simply inconceivable as coming from Victor Hugo with reference to any great nation in the world. Now this sort of strident anti-Gallican cackle was all very well, if even then it was not very wise, in the days of Nelson. But in our piping times of peace it is purely ludicrous to hear a martial shepherd of idyllic habits thus chirping defiance and fluting disparagement of the world beyond his sheep-cote. Besides the two fine sonnets of his youth and his age on Poland and Montenegro, he has uttered little if anything on public matters that I can remember as worth remembering except the two spirited and stalwart songs of 'Hands all round' and 'Britons, guard your own', which rang out a manful response of disgust and horror at the news of a crime unequalled in the cowardly vileness of its complicated atrocity since the model massacre of St. Bartholomew. Not as yet had the blameless Albert—under the spell of a Palmerstonian Merlin?—led forth—we will not say his Guinevere—to clasp the thievish hand of a then uncrowned assassin. If Lord Tennyson has no personal or official reason for wishing to suppress the record and stifle the recollection of work which in every sense does him honour, some of us may venture to think that these verses would better bear reprinting than many which are allowed to keep their place on his list. As it is, he can hardly wonder if they should be 'mercilessly pirated'.

On the crowning question of metre much might be said on both sides in praise and in dispraise of Musset and of Tennyson alike. At the best of their good work, the world can show no sweeter musicians of truer touch on the keys of language than are they. At their worst, the world as certainly can show none worse. The rocks on which either vessel is ever likely to split lie in exactly opposite directions. The Englishman is too hard to satisfy: the Frenchman was too easily pleased. Musset, I should venture to guess, was born with a decidedly finer ear than Tennyson's; but, as a punster might express himself, he let that ear run hopelessly to seed, and ultimately left it to rot out of sheer indolence. Coleridge, on the other hand, very greatly understated the case in saying that he could hardly scan some of the Laureate's earlier verses. There are whole poems of Lord Tennyson's first period which are no more properly to be called metrical than the more shapeless and monstrous parts of Walt Whitman; which are lineally derived as to their form—if form that can be called where form is none—from the vilest example set by Cowley, when English verse was first infected and convulsed by the detestable duncery of sham Pindarics. At times, of course, his song was then as sweet as ever it has sounded since; but he could never make sure of singing right for more than a few minutes or stanzas. The strenuous drill though which since then he has felt it necessary to put himself has done all that hard labour can do to rectify this congenital complaint: by dint of stocks and backboard he has taught himself a more graceful and upright carriage. For the shambling rhyme and the flaccid facility of Musset's verse at its weakest, he too evidently had not self-respect enough, nor care enough for the duties of his art, to go through a similar process of laborious cure. So much the lower is his rank, and so much the worse it is for his memory. That it would be well worth Lord Tennyson's while to make his yet girlish Muse undergo this physical course of discipline must from the first have been obvious to all who could appreciate the heavenly beauty of her higher early notes. He never has written anything of more potent perfection, of more haunting and overpowering charm, than the divine lament of which the central note is a gentler echo[1] to the Duchess of Malfi's exceeding bitter cry:—

> O that it were possible we might
> But hold some two days' conference with the dead!
> From them I should learn something I am sure
> I never shall learn here.

Even with the sound of Webster's more intense and passionate verse rekindled in the ear of our memory, we can take softer pleasure in the tender note of Lord Tennyson's.

[1] A most unlucky sycophant of the Laureate's was once pleased to observe, with unquestionable accuracy, that it is ridiculous to infer the fact of imitation or reminiscence from the fact that Lord Tennyson's poem happens to begin with the same four or five words as the speech of Webster's heroine. Whence it would appear that the ardent admirer of a well-known poem, and the gratuitous champion of its author against a perfectly inoffensive charge of conscious or unconscious recollection or derivation from a famous passage in the master-work of a mightier predecessor, may never have read as far as the fifteenth line of the poem in question.

It may not be the highest imaginable sign of poetic power or native inspiration that a man should be able to grind a beauty out of a deformity or carve a defect into a perfection; but whatever may be the comparative worth of this peculiar faculty, no poet surely ever had it in a higher degree or cultivated it with more patient and strenuous industry than Lord Tennyson. Idler men, or men less qualified and disposed to expend such length of time and energy of patience on the composition and modification, the rearrangement and recision and reissue, of a single verse or copy of verses, can only look on at such a course of labour with amused or admiring astonishment, and a certain doubt whether the linnets, to whose method of singing Lord Tennyson compares his own, do really go through the training of such a musical gymnasium before they come forth qualified to sing. But for one thing, and that a thing of great price, this hard-working poet had never any need to work hard. Whatever the early imperfection of his ear, no man was ever born with a truer and more perfect eye. During fifty years he has never given us a book without unquestionable evidence of this. Among his many claims and credentials as a poet, there is none more unimpeachable or more clear. Nor can any kind of study be more helpful or delightful to the naturally elect student of poetry than that which traces through the work of any poet the vein of colour or of sentiment derived from his earliest or deepest impressions of nature. Because the earliest are usually the deepest of these, it would be a false conclusion—hateful as an unfilled can—to infer that they must be so always. By far the strongest and most significant impressions of 'naked nature'—of sea and shore, and stars and winds, and all forces and all features of all these—that we find engraved upon the page and engrained into the imagination of Victor Hugo, may be dated from the dawn of his fifty-first year—the first of eighteen patient and indignant years of dauntless and glorious exile. The splendours and the terrors, the rapture and the rage, the passion and the subtlety of the most dangerous of all seas known to seamen, and surely the loveliest as well as the deadliest of them all, passed all into 'the thunder and the sunshine' of his verse, and made of the greatest living poet a tenfold greater poet than ever he had been before. So that those who believe all heaven and all earth, all evil and all good, to exist only or mainly for the sake of the singer and the songs he may make of them, are bound to suppose that the great first cause and ultimate reason or pretext for the existence of Napoleon III, was the necessity that occasion should be given and means supplied for the production and the perfection of the greatest work possible to the godlike hand of Victor Hugo. And certainly some such excuse or apology would appear to be required by the conscience of humanity from a conscious and rational First Cause.

The influence and impression of outward and visible nature on the spirit and the work of Tennyson may not less confidently be inferred from comparison of his studies after the life with the life itself of the nature to which he was a native. Many years ago, as I have always remembered, on the appearance of the first four *Idylls of the King*, one of the greatest painters now living pointed out to me, with a brief word of rapturous admiration, the wonderful breadth of beauty and the perfect force of truth in a single verse of 'Elaine'—

And white sails flying on the yellow sea.

I could not but feel conscious at once of its charm, and of the equally certain fact that I, though cradled and reared beside the sea, had never seen anything like that. But on the first bright day I ever spent on the eastern coast of England I saw the truth of this touch at once, and recognized once more with admiring delight the subtle and sure fidelity of that happy and studious hand. There, on the dull yellow foamless floor of dense discoloured sea, so thick with clotted sand that the water looked massive and solid as the shore, the white sails flashed whiter against it and along it as they fled: and I knew once more the truth of what I never had doubted—that the eye and the hand of Tennyson may always be trusted, at once and alike, to see and to express the truth. But he must have learnt the more splendid lesson of the terrors and the glories of the Channel before he caught the finest image ever given in his verse—the likeness of a wave 'green-glimmering' from its summit—

with all
Its stormy crests that smoke against the skies.

Assuredly there will be found no touch like that in all the work of Musset. It has all the faithful subtlety of Shelley's, and all the heavenly majesty of Milton's. Only Victor Hugo himself can make words lighten and thunder like these. . . .

30. Walt Whitman thanks Tennyson

Walt Whitman, 'A Word about Tennyson', *The Critic*
(1st January 1887), vii. 1–2.

Whitman (1819–92), though not the public figure that
Tennyson was, had by this time gained wide acceptance
as the national poet of America.

Beautiful as the song was, the original 'Locksley Hall' of half a century
ago was essentially morbid, heart-broken, finding fault with everything,
especially the fact of money's being made (as it ever must be, and
perhaps should be) the paramount matter in worldly affairs.

Every door is barr'd with gold, and opens but to golden keys.

First, a father, having fallen in battle, his child (the singer)

Was left a trampled orphan, and a selfish uncle's ward.

Of course love ensues. The woman in the chant or monologue proves
a false one; and as far as appears the ideal of woman, in the poet's
reflections, is a false one, at any rate for America. Woman is *not* 'the
lesser man'. (The heart is not the brain.) The best of the piece of fifty
years since is its concluding line:

For the mighty wind arises roaring seaward and I go.

Then for this current 1886–7, a just-out sequel, which (as an apparently
authentic summary says) 'reviews the life of mankind during the past
sixty years, and comes to the conclusion that its boasted progress is of
doubtful credit to the world in general and to England in particular.
A cynical vein of denunciation of democratic opinions and aspirations
runs throughout the poem, in marked contrast with the spirit of the
poet's youth.' Among the most striking lines of this sequel are the
following:

Envy wears the mask of love, and, laughing sober fact to scorn,
Cries to weakest as to strongest, 'Ye are equals, equal-born.'
Equal-born! Oh yes, if yonder hill be level with the flat.
Charm us, orator, till the lion look no larger than the cat;
Till the cat, through that mirage of overheated language, loom
Larger than the lion—Demos end in working its own doom.

★　　　★　　　★

Tumble nature heel over head, and, yelling with the yelling street,
Set the feet above the brain and swear the brain is in the feet.
Bring the old Dark Ages back, without the faith, without the hope
Beneath the State, the Church, the throne, and roll their ruins
down the slope.

I should say that all this is a legitimate consequence of the tone and
convictions of the earlier standards and points of view. Then some
reflections, down to the hard-pan of this sort of thing.

The course of progressive politics (democracy) is so certain and
resistless, not only in America but in Europe, that we can well afford
the warning calls, threats, checks, neutralizings, in imaginative literature, or any department, of such deep-sounding and high-soaring
voices as Carlyle's and Tennyson's. Nay, the blindness, excesses, of the
prevalent tendency—the dangers of the urgent trends of our times—in
my opinion, need such voices almost more than any. I should, too,
call it a signal instance of democratic humanity's luck that it has such
enemies to contend with—so candid, so fervid, so heroic. But why do
I say enemy? Upon the whole is not Tennyson—and was not Carlyle
(like an honest and stern physician)—the true friend of our age?

Let me assume to pass verdict, or perhaps momentary judgment,
for the United States on this poet—a removed and distant position
giving some advantages over a nigh one. What is Tennyson's service
to his race, times, and especially to America? First, I should say, his
personal character. He is not to be mentioned as a rugged, evolutionary,
aboriginal force—but (and a great lesson is in it) he has been consistent
throughout with the native, personal, healthy, patriotic spinal element
and promptings of himself. His moral line is local and conventional,
but it is vital and genuine. He reflects the upper-crust of his time, its
pale cast of thought—even its *ennui*. Then the simile of my friend John
Burroughs is entirely true, 'his glove is a glove of silk, but the hand is
a hand of iron'. He shows how one can be a royal laureate, quite
elegant and 'aristocratic', and a little queer and affected, and at the same
time perfectly manly and natural. As to his non-democracy, it fits him
well, and I like him the better for it. I guess we all like to have (I am
sure I do) some one who presents those sides of a thought, or possibility,
different from our own—different, and yet with a sort of home-likeness
—a tartness and contradiction offsetting the theory as we view it, and
construed from tastes and proclivities not at all our own.

To me, Tennyson shows more than any poet I know (perhaps has been a warning to me) how much there is in finest verbalism. There is such a latent charm in mere words, cunning collocutions, and in the voice ringing them, which he has caught and brought out, beyond all others—as in the line,

And hollow, hollow, hollow, all delight,

in 'The Passing of Arthur', and evidenced in 'The Lady of Shalott', 'The Deserted House', and many other pieces. Among the best (I often linger over them again and again) are 'Lucretius', 'The Lotos-Eaters', and 'The Northern Farmer'. His mannerism is great, but it is a noble and welcome mannerism. His very best work, to me, is contained in the books of *The Idylls of the King*, all of them, and all that has grown out of them. Though indeed we could spare nothing of Tennyson, however small or however peculiar—not 'Break, Break', nor 'Flower in the Crannied Wall' nor the old, eternally-told passion of 'Edward Gray':

Love may come and love may go,
And fly like a bird from tree to tree
But I will love no more, no more
Till Ellen Adair come back to me.

Yes, Alfred Tennyson's is a superb character, and will help give illustriousness, through the long roll of time, to our Nineteenth Century. In its bunch of orbic names, shining like a constellation of stars, his will be one of the brightest. His very faults, doubts, swervings, doublings upon himself, have been typical of our age. We are like the voyagers of a ship, casting off for new seas, distant shores. We would still dwell in the old suffocating and dead haunts, remembering and magnifying their pleasant experiences only, and more than once impelled to jump ashore before it is too late, and stay where our fathers stayed, and live as they lived.

Maybe I am non-literary and non-decorous (let me at least be human, and pay part of my debt) in this word about Tennyson. I want him to realize that here is a great and ardent Nation that absorbs his songs, and has a respect and affection for him personally, as almost for no other foreigner. I want this word to go to the old man at Farringford as conveying no more than the simple truth; and that truth (a little Christmas gift) no slight one either. I have written impromptu, and shall let it all go at that. The readers of more than fifty millions of people in the New World not only owe to him some of their most agreeable and harmless and healthy hours, but he has entered into the formative influences of character here, not only in the Atlantic cities, but inland and far West, out in Missouri, in Kansas, and away in Oregon, in farmer's house and miner's cabin.

Best thanks, anyhow, to Alfred Tennyson—thanks and appreciation in America's name.

31. R. H. Hutton surveys Tennyson's work and replies to Swinburne

Richard Holt Hutton, 'Tennyson', *Literary Essays* (1888), pp. 361–436.

Hutton (1826–97), theologian, journalist, and man of letters, was joint-editor and part-proprietor of the *Spectator* from 1861. The 'J.T.K.' whom he mentions in the course of his reply to Swinburne was James Thomas Knowles (No. 25). Hutton was writing before Tennyson gave the *Idylls* their final shape by publishing 'Balin and Balan' (1885) and dividing 'Enid' into two poems, 'The Marriage of Geraint' and 'Geraint and Enid' (1886).

Lord Tennyson was an artist even before he was a poet; in other words, the eye for beauty, grace, and harmony of effect was even more emphatically one of his original gifts than the voice for poetical utterance itself. This probably it is which makes his very earliest pieces appear so full of effort, and sometimes even so full of affectation. They were elaborate attempts to embody what he *saw*, before the natural voice of the poet had come to him. Coleridge remarks, in his 'Table Talk', that Tennyson had begun to write poetry before he knew what metre was. The remark applied, of course, only to his very earliest publication; and of that it was, I think, true, odd as it now reads in relation to one of the greatest masters of metre, both simple and sonorous, that the English language has ever known. It is interesting as showing how laborious and full of effort his early verse sounded to one of the finest judges of English verse, and so confirming the suspicion that this great poet's vision of beauty had ripened earlier than his poetic faculty for shaping that vision into words. I think it is possible to trace not only a pre-poetic period in his art—the period of the Orianas, Owls, Mermans, etc.—a period in which the poem on 'Recollections of the Arabian Nights' seems to me the only one of real interest, and that is a poem expressive of the luxurious sense of a gorgeous inward picture-gallery—but to date the period at which the soul was 'infused' into his poetry, and the brilliant external pictures became the dwelling-places of germinating poetic thoughts creating their own music. The Roman Catholics have, I believe, a doctrine that at a certain stage in the growth of the embryo body the soul is 'infused' into it, and from that stage it shapes and moulds all the structures of the body with a view to their subserviency to a moral and spiritual growth. Apply that analogy to Tennyson's poems, and the period before 1832 is the period before his vivid pictures had a soul in them, and consequently before they had a music of their own. He himself has told us very finely in one of his newer poems, when describing the building of Arthur's great capital,—which, like Ilium, was rumoured to have been built to a divine music,—how the highest works of the human spirit are created:—

> For an ye heard a music, like enow
> They are building still, seeing the city is built
> To music, therefore never built at all,
> And therefore built for ever.

There was no such music in Tennyson's earliest verses, but he himself has all but told us when the period in which his productiveness was due more to the 'lust of the eye' than to any true poetic gift, ceased. Curiously enough, the first poem where there is any trace of those musings on the legends of the Round Table to which he has directed so much of his maturest genius, is also a confession that the poet was sick of the magic mirror of fancy and its picture-shadows, and was turning away from them to the poetry of human life. 'The Lady of Shalott', the first poem of those published in the autumn of 1832—the same sad year which laid the foundation of Tennyson's most perfect, if not his greatest poem, *In Memoriam*—has for its real subject the emptiness of the life of fancy, however rich and brilliant, the utter satiety which compels any true imaginative nature to break through the spell which entrances it in an unreal world or visionary joys. The Lady of Shalott— a variation on Elaine—gazing in her magic mirror, sees a faithful picture of all that passes by her solitary isle, and copies it in the web she weaves:—

> There she weaves by night and day
> A magic web with colours gay.
> She has heard a whisper say,
> A curse is on her if she stay

> To look down to Camelot.
> She knows not what the curse may be,
> And so she weaveth steadily,
> And little other care hath she,
> The Lady of Shalott.

The curse, of course, is that she shall be involved in mortal passions, and suffer the fate of mortals, if she looks away from the shadow to the reality. Nevertheless, the time comes when she braves the curse:—

> But in her web she still delights
> To weave the mirror's magic sights,
> For often through the silent nights
> A funeral, with plumes and lights,
>   And music, went to Camelot:
> Or when the moon was overhead,
> Came two young lovers lately wed:
> 'I am half sick of shadows,' said
>   The Lady of Shalott.

And probably it was the vision of a 'funeral', at least as much as that other vision which made the fairy Lady of Shalott more than half sick of shadows, that first led the author of this beautiful little poem into his true poetic work.

But even after the embryo period is past, even when Tennyson's poems are uniformly moulded by an 'infused' soul, one not unfrequently notices the excess of the faculty of vision over the governing conception which moulds the vision, so that I think he is almost always most successful when his poem begins in a thought or a feeling rather than from a picture or a narrative, for then the thought or feeling dominates and controls his otherwise too lavish fancy. 'Ulysses' and 'Tithonus' are far superior to 'Œnone', exquisite as the pictorial workmanship of 'Œnone' is; 'The Palace of Art' is finer than 'The Dream of Fair Women'; 'The Death of Lucretius', painful as the subject is, than 'Enoch Arden' or 'Aylmer's Field'; and, for the same reason, In Memoriam is perhaps an even more perfect whole than the poem of greatest scope, and in some respects the noblest of his imaginative efforts, the great Arthurian epic which he completed so much later. Whenever Tennyson's pictorial fancy has had it in any degree in its power to run away with the guiding and controlling mind, the richness of the workmanship has to some extent overgrown the spiritual principle of his poems.

I suppose it is in some respects this lavish strength of what may be called the bodily element in poetry, as distinguished from the spiritual life and germ of it, which has given Lord Tennyson at once his delight in great variety and richness of materials, and his profound reverence for the principle of spiritual order which can alone impress unity and purpose on the tropical luxuriance of natural gifts. It is obvious, for instance, that even in relation to natural scenery, what his poetical faculty delights in most are rich, luxuriant landscapes in which either Nature or man has accumulated a lavish variety of effects. There is nothing of Wordsworth's passion for the bare, wild scenery of the rugged North in his poems. For one picture of wild and barren grandeur like the first of the two following in 'The Palace of Art', there are at least fifty variations on the last, in his various poems:—

> And one, a foreground black with stones and slags,
> Beyond, a line of heights, and higher
> All barr'd with long white cloud the scornful crags,
> And highest, snow and fire.

> And one, an English home—gray twilight pour'd
> On dewy pastures, dewy trees,
> Softer than sleep—all things in order stored,
> A haunt of ancient Peace.

It is in the scenery of the mill, the garden, the chase, the down, the rich pastures, the harvest-field, the palace pleasure-grounds, the Lord of Burleigh's fair domains, the luxuriant sylvan beauty bearing testimony to the careful hand of man, 'the summer crisp with shining woods', that Tennyson most delights. If he strays to rarer scenes it is almost always in search of richer and more luxuriant loveliness, like the tropical splendours of 'Enoch Arden' and the enervating skies which cheated the Lotus-Eaters of their longing for home. There is always complexity in the beauty which fascinates Lord Tennyson most.

And with the love of complexity comes, as a matter of course, in a born artist the love of the ordering faculty which can give unity and harmony to complexity of detail. Measure and order are for Tennyson of the very essence of beauty. His strong fascination for the Arthurian legends results no doubt from the mixture, in the moral materials of the age of chivalry, of exuberant stateliness and rich polish with the imperious need for spiritual order to control the dangerous elements of the period. His Arthurian epic is a great attempt to depict the infusion of a soul into a chaos of stately passions. Even in relation to modern politics you always see the same bias, a love of rich constitutional traditions welded together and ruled by wise forethought and temperate judgment. He cannot endure either spasmodic violence on the one hand, or bald simplicity on the other. What he loves is a land

> Where Freedom broadens slowly down
> From precedent to precedent.

In *In Memoriam* he goes out of his way to condemn French political anarchy—

> The schoolboy heat,
> The blind hysterics of the Celt—

and to throw scorn on the 'red fool-fury of the Seine'. Still more curious is the parenthetic question, interpolated almost angrily, in the opening of an exquisite love poem, 'Love and Duty':—

> O shall the braggart shout
> For some blind glimpse of freedom, work itself
> *Through madness, hated by the wise, to law,*
> *System, and empire?*

—as if he grudged revolutionary energy even its occasional success. Never was any cry more absurd than the cry made against *Maud* for the sympathy it was supposed to show with hysterical passion. What it *was* meant to be, and what it was, though inadequately,—the failure being due, not to sympathy with hysterics, but to the zeal with which Tennyson strove to caricature hysterics,—was an exposure of hysterics. The love of measure and order is as visible in Tennyson's pictures of character as in every other aspect of his poetry. His 'St. Simeon Stylites' is his hostile picture of the fanatic, just as his 'Ulysses' is his friendly picture of the insatiable craving for new experience, enterprise, and adventure, when under the control of a luminous reason and a self-controlled will.

And this love of measure and order in complexity shows itself even more remarkably in Lord Tennyson's leaning to the domestic, modern type of women. All his favourite women are women of a certain fixed class in social life, usually not the lowest; sometimes homely, like Alice the miller's daughter, and Rose the gardener's daughter, or Dora, or the wife of the Lord of Burleigh; sometimes women of the Drawing-room or the Palace, like Maud, Lady Flora in 'The Day-Dream', or the princess in the poem about women, or Lynette, and Enid, and Elaine, and Guinevere in *The Idylls of the King*; but always women of the quiet and domestic type (except indeed the heroine of 'The Sisters'), women whom you might meet every day in a modern home, women of the garden-flower kind rather than of the wild-flower kind. He has set even his exquisite poem on 'The Sleeping Beauty' in a drawing-room framework, *i.e.* made the 'Lady Flora' to whom it is related 'take her broidery frame and add a crimson to the quaint macaw'. In the beautiful little idyll called 'The Miller's Daughter', Mr. Tennyson even injures the rustic effect of the piece by introducing an artificial element, a song about Alice's earring and necklace, a touch which, however true it may be to life—(earrings and necklaces are just what millers' daughters would most value)—is idyllically false as destroying the simplicity of the picture, just as it might have been true to life, but would have been idyllically false, to call the heroine Juliana or Matilda, instead of Alice. The simplest and most lyrical heroines, heroines like Gretchen in *Faust* or Mignon in *Wilhelm Meister*, are hardly in Tennyson's way. He loves something of the air and manner which a fixed social status gives. His 'May Queen' has always seemed to me one of his few falsetto poems. There is art, in the sense of complex harmony, in all his greatest poems.

The simplest though hardly the most characteristic form of that art is no doubt the 'Idyll', in which Tennyson has delighted from the first; —so much so, that he has applied the term, somewhat misleadingly I think, to one of his later, and in many respects his greatest, works. The 'idyll' proper is, I suppose, a *picture* coloured by a single emotion, and intended to give a perfect illustration of that emotion. The power which makes Tennyson's idylls so unique in their beauty is, I think, his wonderful skill in creating a perfectly real and living scene,[1]—such as always might, and perhaps somewhere does, exist in external Nature,— for the theatre of the feeling he is about to embody, and yet a scene every feature of which helps to make the emotion delineated more real and vivid. For illustrations of what I mean take the idylls of 'The Miller's Daughter' and 'The Gardener's Daughter', both stories of happy first love, told in their later years by old men who had married rustic beauties. The former, however, paints a boy's first unexpected passion, which finds him a dreaming lad, and breaking upon his quiet suddenly transforms him into a man; the latter paints the passion of an artist who had long played with the feeling of love, and who had heard enough beforehand of the rustic beauty he was going to visit, to be

[1] This criticism was first made in a very fine essay on Tennyson's genius, by the late Mr. W. C. Roscoe, which will be found in his volumes of posthumous poems and essays, published by Chapman & Hall.

thrilling with hope and expectation of his destiny. Remembering this, notice the completely different key of the two poems, the simple brook-like music of the first, which seems to keep time to the mill-stream, and its cool April scenery,—the rich, full, conscious sweetness of the second, and its fragrant scents of May:—

[Quotes 'The Miller's Daughter', ll. 57–88:

'But, Alice, what an hour was that . . .
That these have never lost their light.']

That is April love in the heart of April, keeping time to the liquid rapids of the mill-weir. The vivid picture, too, of the kindly, dusty miller, with his smile that seemed 'half within and half without, and full of dealings with the world', which introduces the piece, and suggests the inequality of lot over which this boyish passion was to leap, prepares us for the sort of love—sudden, youthful, defying obstacles of station—which the bubbling mill-stream was to witness.

Now turn to the fair, rich, elaborate, and still more lovely scene, by which the reader's mind is prepared for the love-story of an artist, who, as the prelude shows, had, like St. Augustine, been eagerly loving to love (*amans amare*), and who was in his heart fully prepared for the first plunge.

[Quotes 'The Gardener's Daughter', ll. 73–95:

'And sure this orbit of the memory folds . . .
Sang loud, as though he were the bird of day.']

That is the rich gladness which prepares for the fuller and deeper passion of a mind devoted to the study of beauty and nearing the verge of an anticipated joy. Note especially the realism (which Tennyson never fails to show) in the explanation of the especial fragrance of the air,— that 'one large cloud drew downward',—so supplying the moisture that brings out the odours of the spring. Observe, too, that instead of the dancing mill-stream, we have a stream in harmony with the richer, riper passion of the conscious love of beauty:—

[Quotes 'The Gardener's Daughter', ll. 35–44:

'News from the humming city . . .
Crown'd with the minster-towers.']

Two more real scenes cannot be imagined than these. And yet how delicately their differences are fitted (whether calculated or not I cannot say) to deepen and enhance the impressions of the special shade of love which each poem delineates.

But I should quote for ever were I to illustrate as fully as might be Lord Tennyson's wonderful power of putting Nature under contribution to help him in delineating moods of feeling. It is not limited to his idylls, but is equally marvellous in his pure lyrics. Especially wonderful is this power in the illustration of the sense of loss. Not to touch *In Memoriam*, take the voice which Mr. Tennyson has found for a dumb, wistful grief in the following little lyric. No poet ever made the dumb speak so effectually:—

> Break, break, break
>   On thy cold gray stones, O Sea!
> And I would that my tongue could utter
>   The thoughts that arise in me.
>
> O well for the fisherman's boy,
>   That he shouts with his sister at play;
> O well for the sailor lad,
>   That he sings in his boat on the bay!
>
> And the stately ships go on
>   To their haven under the hill;
> But O for the touch of a vanish'd hand,
>   And the sound of a voice that is still!
>
> Break, break, break
>   At the foot of thy crags, O Sea!
> But the tender grace of a day that is dead
>   Will never come back to me!

Observe how the wash of the sea on the cold gray stones is used to prepare the mind for the feeling of helplessness with which the deeper emotions break against the hard and rigid element of human speech; how the picture is then widened out till you see the bay with children laughing on its shore, and the sailor-boy singing on its surface, and the stately ships passing on in the offing to their unseen haven, all with the view of helping us to feel the contrast between the satisfied and the unsatisfied yearnings of the human heart. Tennyson, like every true poet, has the strongest feeling of the spiritual and almost mystic character of the associations attaching to the distant sail which takes the ship on its lonely journey to an invisible port, and has more than once used it to lift the mind into the attitude of hope or trust. But then the song returns again to the helpless breaking of the sea at the foot of crags it cannot climb, not this time to express the inadequacy of human speech to express human yearnings, but the defeat of those very yearnings themselves. Thus does Lord Tennyson turn an ordinary sea-shore landscape into a means of finding a voice indescribably sweet for the dumb spirit of human loss. Another closely analogous illustration, at least as signal of the same magic power to press Nature into the service of the heart in uttering the sense of loss, will be familiar to every one who loves Tennyson's genius in that wonderful song in *The Princess* concerning the sad strange 'days that are no more', in which he likens the mingled freshness and sadness with which we contemplate them as they flash upon our memory to a mixture of the feelings with which we see the light upon an approaching sail that brings us friends from the other hemisphere, and the light upon a retreating sail which takes them away thither; for does not the memory of those days both bring and take away? does it not restore us the vivid joy of the past only to make us feel that it is vanished? No poet has ever had a greater mastery than Tennyson over the power of real things—with him they are always real, and not mere essences or abstractions—to express evanescent emotions that almost defy expression. I know no other poet, except the author of *Antony and Cleopatra* himself, who might have imagined Cleopatra's passionate cry over the corpse of Antony—

And there is nothing left remarkable beneath the visiting moon.

Lord Tennyson's power of compelling the external world to lend him a language for the noblest feelings is, however, but the instrument of a still higher faculty, the power of apprehending those feelings themselves with the vigour of a great dramatist; and though his range is not wide, they include some of the most delicate and intellectual, and some of the coarsest and most earthly. He is not a great dramatist, for his delineations move almost wholly in one plane, in the mood he has studied and writes to interpret. He can find the exactly appropriate reverie for the smarting and not very deeply wounded heart of a grandiose and somewhat bumptious lover dismissed like the rejected of Locksley Hall, for his deficiencies in wealth and station, and who does not suffer so much but that he can concern himself even then with the prospects of the race and 'the process of the suns'. Tennyson renders to perfection the random and humorous fancies of the poet under the mellowing influence of a pint of port, when the Muse

Used all her fiery will and smote
Her life into the liquor.

He can tell you how St. Simeon Stylites must have felt when the glory of his penances, mounting like fumes into his head, aided the delirium of his wandering brain to triumph over the half-dead body which had in great measure dropped away from him before he died. He can portray the intolerable restlessness of the wanderer born and bred, when, like Ulysses, he is expected to shut himself in between the narrow walls of humdrum duties. He can conceive with the subtlest power the passionate longing for death of a mortal endowed with immortality, doomed like Tithonus to outlive all life and joy, and tremble at the awful prospect of a solitary eternity of decay. Nay, he can find a language as real as the thought for the kind grandmother's wandering maternal memories, as well as for the overweening vanity of the coarse old Northern Farmer, whose only notion of duty is to serve the 'squoire' and the 'lond' with a loyal and even passionate service, and who has no patience with 'God-amoighty' for not sparing him to calve the cows and finish the 'stubbing' of Thornaby waste,—and finally for the far sordider and more selfish farmer of the new style, who worships 'proputty', especially in land, with a devout worship, and can tell his son with the most serious and earnest assurance—

Taäke my word for it, Sammy, the poor in a loomp is bad.

All this he can do with marvellous finish; but he has hardly succeeded, except in *Queen Mary* and his fine picture of Henry II in *Becket*, in drawing a character in all its variety of attitudes; and though those poems are quite fine enough to show dramatic power, they are not sufficiently characteristic of his genius to show any wealth of dramatic fancy; and indeed *Harold* must be pronounced a decided failure. Hence his genius can hardly be called dramatic, though in relation to single moods he finds an infinitely more characteristic language for their expression than Mr. Browning, who would make Tithonus, Ulysses, St. Simeon Stylites, and the Northern Farmers all talk Browningese. But admitting the partial limitation of Tennyson's genius to the interpretation of *moods*, admitting even the limited number of moods he can interpret adequately,—for he seems to fail through caricature when he attempts, as in *Maud* or 'The Vision of Sin', to express mis-anthropical moods,—yet no other poet has rivalled, in force and subtlety, the work he has thus achieved. When first published, 'The Norther Farmer (Old Style)' and 'Tithonus' stood side by side, and it is hardly possible to find specimens of wider-removed human emotions on the subject of death:—

[Quotes 'Northern Farmer, Old Style', stanzas xvi and xvii; and 'Tithonus', ll. 1–23.]

The atom of common thought that connects the two passages is the feeling expressed in both that there is a price at which life, with its sweetness lost, is not worth purchasing; and though to the Northern Farmer that price is the sacrifice of what he calls 'breaking rules' to please the doctor, *i.e.* giving up his accustomed draught of ale, and to Tithonus it is the loss of all that made up the vigour and gladness of life, incurred to save an ever-dwindling consciousness of personality stripped of all command over the old springs of happiness, still there is just enough common to the two thoughts to make the range of dialect and feeling the more startling and effective. I should certainly have supposed, till 'The Grandmother', the two 'Northern Farmers', *Queen Mary*, and *Becket* were published, that Tennyson's power of poetical interpretation extended only to the more refined, if not the more intellectual habits of mind; but that notion has been disposed of. He can furnish good grandmotherly reminiscences, or a hearty devotion to a narrow calling and a coarse obtuseness to everything beyond, with a voice at least as appropriate as he finds for that restless craving for ever new experience, and that contemptuous pity for plodding humdrum piety, which he attributes to his somewhat modernised but marvellously conceived Ulysses. But I think that while the latter class of poems belong to him, as it were, the former are the results of study, though of a study which only a poet's imagination could have harmonised into wholes so perfect. It is impossible to forget, in reading the three studies of rural character I have just referred to, that Lord Tennyson's powers of observation, though by no means rapid, are exceedingly close and tenacious, and that he has the strong apprehensive grasp of a naturalist in conjunction with the harmonising faculty of the poet. He seems to me to have studied his 'Grandmother' and his two 'Northern Farmers' much as he has studied the habits of trees and animals. He has a striking microscopic faculty on which his poetic imagination works. No poet has so many and such accurate references to the vegetable world, and yet at the same time references so thoroughly poetic. He calls dark hair

> More black than ash-buds in the front of March;

auburn hair,

> In gloss and hue the chestnut, when the shell
> Divides three-fold to show the fruit within.

He is never tired of reflecting in his poetry the physiology of flowers and trees and buds. The 'living smoke' of the yew is twice commemorated in his poems. He tells us how the sunflower, 'shining fair',

Rays round with flames her disk of seed;

observes on the blasts 'that blow the poplars white'; and, to make a long story short,—for the list of instances might be multiplied to hundreds,—in his latest *Idylls of the King*, he thus dates an early hour in the night:—

Nigh upon that hour
When the lone hern forgets his melancholy,
Lets down his other leg, and stretching, dreams
Of goodly supper in the distant pool.

It is precisely the same microscopic faculty as this applied to characteristic human habits which has produced the three wonderful studies in English vernacular life. Just as Tennyson delights to chronicle that at a given hour of the night the heron lets down his other leg and stretches himself, and as he conjectures that the heron's dreams then take a happier turn, so he delights to chronicle that an old woman with her faculties failing, when she hears of the death of her eldest-born, himself an old man, will muse on the beauty of his baby legs after this fashion:—

Willy, my beauty, my eldest-born, the flower of the flock;
Never a man could fling him, for Willy stood like a rock.
'Here's a leg for a babe of a week,' says Doctor, and he
would be bound
There was not like, that year, in twenty parishes round.

And so precisely, too, he makes the property-worshipping 'Northern Farmer' of the new style put the poor curate, whose daughter his eldest son wishes to marry, under the microscope, as if he were a kind of insect, in this contemptuous way:—

[Quotes 'Northern Farmer, New Style', stanzas vii and viii:

'Parson's lass 'ant nowt, . . .
. . . 'e married fur luvv.']

It is impossible not to see that it is much more as naturalist than as poet that Tennyson has mastered the materials for these three most remarkable poems, though without his imaginative faculty he could never have harmonised them into these wonderful wholes. When

Shakespeare gives us a character like Juliet's nurse, we feel somehow that Juliet's nurse was in him, that he needed as little study to enter into her and appropriate her as Tennyson needed to enter into the full ripe passion which breathes through 'The Gardener's Daughter' or the gusty heroics of 'Locksley Hall'. But his fine studies of those three rustics have been like the studies which the late Mr. Waterton devoted to the habits of birds, or which Mr. Frank Buckland bestows on the hippopotamuses of his heart. He has made them his own, and made them perfectly living and true; and if he had time to give to other types as large and simple, he could paint them also as faithfully and impressively. But his insight into them does not come through his sympathy with active life, as Shakespeare's did; it comes of the careful scrutinising eye of a naturalist feeding the brooding heart of a poet. And there are plenty of indications of the same kind of close microscopic power in the higher and purely spiritual sphere of Tennyson's genius. What, for instance, can be finer than the picture of the gloomy forecast of evil which haunts Merlin before his living burial?—

> So dark a forethought rolled about his brain
> As on a dull day in an ocean cave
> The blind wave feeling round his long sea-hall
> In silence.

In Memoriam is full of such magnifying-glasses for secret feelings, and doubts, and fears, and hopes, and trusts. How true and pathetic, yet how like the effect of a brooding reverie under a microscope, is the passage in which Tennyson describes his minute comparison of the path of the moonbeams in his bedroom with what he knows it must be in the chancel where the tablet to his friend is placed, and paints the half-superstitious anxiety with which he watches them while they are lighting up the letters of the name, and then passing away, leaving it in darkness till the glimmer of the dawn returns upon it! How large he makes the fear that when he follows his friend into the other world he may find himself 'a life behind' him, and doomed to follow ever at the same distance! How big seems the doubt—one that we must all of us have felt in such cases—that he is exaggerating the delight which the past companionship of his friend had caused him, that it is but 'the haze of grief' which made the 'former gladness loom so great'. Clearly there is much of the microscopic naturalist in the spiritual as well as the physical part of Tennyson's musings. Any mood, however subtle, when submitted to his eye, grows large beneath that close and minute scrutiny, and reappears on a new and magnified scale, like Plato's moral law of the individual conscience when written out large in the structure and function of the perfect State.

And yet it would be completely false to give the impression that Lord Tennyson's studies are studies in 'still' life, studies of human nature as much at rest as the fragment of a bat's wing under a microscope. There is always the movement of real life in his poems, even in passages where the movement could never show, if the movement itself, like the subject of it, were not magnified by the medium through which he makes us view it. 'Will Waterproof's Lyrical Monologue', for instance, never halts a moment at any one point, though the whole might have actually passed through the mind in a few seconds. The 'Grandmother's' and 'Northern Farmer's' reveries flow on at much the same rate they might flow at in actual life; and it is only the extreme elaboration of the picture, reminding one of some of Denner's portraits of rustic life, in which every wrinkle and every shade of colour is accurately rendered, that suggests to the reader the impression of slow movement. So, too, the scorn of Ulysses for the petty drudgery of his Ithacan household and government, his longing to be once more shooting the rapids of earthly adventure, his contemptuous satisfaction in the capacity of Telemachus to fill his place, and the great bound which his heart makes towards the sea that 'moans round with many voices', succeed each other with a movement certainly not more languid than that of Homer himself. In painting, Tennyson is so terse and compressed, that, though he never suggests the idea of swiftness,—there is too much pains spent on the individual stroke for that,—it would be simply absurd to call his manner dilatory. Indeed, his pictures often succeed each other too rapidly, without the graduation which prepares the mind for the change, so as to give a sense of effort to the reader by implying an extreme condensation in the writer. It is only in the song, or pieces closely approaching a song in structure, like 'The Brook', that his style ripples along with perfect ease and grace. If we compare the lovely modulation of 'The Brook', or the liquid notes of 'Blow, bugle, blow, set the wild echoes flying', or the delicate rapture of 'Come into the garden, Maud', with the stately compression of 'The Palace of Art' or of most of the *Idylls of the King*, we shall at once see that it is not want of motion, but rather excessive compression, which gives to so many of Tennyson's poems the air of moving through a resisting medium. There is nothing like 'still' life to be found in his poems. When he puts a half-understood emotion or a new natural fact under his poetic object-glass, it may occupy a larger space than it ever did in the poems of other poets, but that is only because the scale of life is really larger. No poet is less justly liable to the charge of making much of a little or of pottering over his poetic discoveries.

And, indeed, *In Memoriam* is the only one of Tennyson's poems of which even his most hostile critics could say that its movement is slow. Here, however, there is necessarily the brooding movement of a haunting grief, for it is of the very essence of a poem devoted to the expression of the pain, and fear, and doubt, and hope, and faith, which a great wound to the heart causes, to hover perpetually over the same theme, and to transform every seemingly foreign subject of reflection into new food for suffering or new promise of peace. Mrs. Browning, in perhaps her finest sonnet, has said that

> If to conquer love has tried,
> To conquer grief tries more, as all things prove,
> For grief indeed *is* love, and grief beside.
> Alas, I have grieved so, I'm hard to love.

And Tennyson's great poem is a comment on this text, a comment showing how much *more* grief may be than love—not only more absorbing, which it must be, not only more tasking and more urgent in pushing the sufferer on to seemingly vain and thankless efforts to vindicate his fidelity of heart, from which he sinks back exhausted into himself, for that to a great extent it must be also—but also more fruitful of strength, of courage, of hope, and of peace. St. Paul has not got much credit for poetic feeling amongst the many great poets of the Bible, and no doubt the passages in which he rises into poetry are somewhat rare; but of one of them, I suspect, we miss the beauty and force rather for want of such a mental history as that of *In Memoriam* to explain it, than from any want of pathos, depth, and singular precision of feeling in the passage itself. It would injure *In Memoriam* to give it a Biblical motto, for that would tend to classify a great modern poem in that dismal category of works known as 'Serious reading', and so to diminish its just influence; otherwise it would be hard to find a more exact and profound summary of its cycle of thought and emotion than St. Paul's reason (evidently an afterthought) for 'glorying in tribulation'— 'knowing that tribulation worketh patience, and patience experience, and experience hope; and hope maketh not ashamed, because the love of God is shed abroad in our hearts by the Holy Ghost which is given unto us'. That is a true summary of the drift of *In Memoriam*. The poet sets out with a cry of desolation, of self-pitying numbness of heart;—for the piece which now stands first of the series, and immediately follows the grand apostrophe, 'Strong Son of God, immortal Love', is evidently a poetical preface to the whole, and not even one of the first in point of time. The first apostrophe to the tree of churchyards, the funeral yew, whose roots 'are wrapped about the bones' of the dead, is a cry of life in death, a cry of horror at the prospect of death in life. And in all those which follow it, till the poet's interest begins to awaken as to the fate of the ship which was to bring home his friend's body from the Adriatic, we hear, under the various restlessly changing forms of a stunned spirit, the constant presence of the thought—

> Break, thou deep vase of chilling tears
> That grief hath shaken into frost.

Then his imagination begins to fix itself, at intervals, with the fanciful fidelity which grief always transfers from the dead to some half-living representative of the dead, on the ship that is bringing home all that remained of his friend, and some of the most beautiful reveries in the language describe how he follows all its motions as if they were the motions of his friend himself:—

> I hear the noise about thy keel;
> I hear the bell struck in the night;
> I see the cabin windows bright;
> I see the sailor at the wheel.

He flies off in reverie, on visionary wings, 'a weight of nerves without a mind' (could there be a finer expression for the acute sensation which renders thought impossible?), to meet the vessel on her way, and 'circles moaning in the air, "Is this the end? Is this the end?"' Then he tries to convince himself that he does not suffer 'in a dream'; records, what every one has felt in such cases, that if the dead should prove to be alive and express compassion and grief for the illusions that have given so much pain, nothing would seem more natural to him; he hails the vessel bearing the remains of his friend on her arrival with a gleam of thankfulness that is the first softening touch; and from that point we have gentler moods of grief alternating with the despair:—

> Ah yet, e'en yet, if this might be,
> I, falling on his faithful heart,
> Would breathing thro' his lips impart
> The life that almost dies in me;

That dies not, but endures with pain,
And slowly forms the firmer mind,
Treasuring the look it cannot find,
The words that are not heard again.

Tribulation has already worked patience.

Then, first, we meet with 'the Shadow cloak'd from head to foot, who keeps the keys of all the creeds', and the long series of poems full of searching thought, and, here and there, of gleams of returning serenity of spirit, in which the self-accusations, the self-justifications, the doubts of science, the hopes of conscience, the glimpses of God's love, alternate like the parting clouds and shining stars of a stormy November night. At last he can answer thus his own question, whether love would not survive in this life, even if it could hope for nothing beyond:—

And Love would answer with a sigh,
'The sound of that forgetful shore
Will change my sweetness more and more,
Half-dead to know that I shall die.'

O me, what profits it to put
An idle case? If Death were seen
At first as Death, Love had not been,
Or been in narrowest working shut.

And then we know that patience is already working experience, and experience hope; and hope the greater and not the less, for that vivid insight into not merely the thoughts, but the living facts that are the food of Doubt, which Tennyson has compressed into some of these noble poems. There is hardly finer reflective poetry in existence than the series of poems in which he adduces the evidence that Nature, as Nature, cares for neither individual nor type; that

She cries, 'A thousand types are gone,
I care for nothing, all shall go;

that she is utterly indifferent whether or not Man,

Who loved, who suffered countless ills,
Who battled for the True, the Just,
Be blown about the desert dust
Or sealed within the iron hills.

And when he breasts all these hostile demonstrations of science with the unconquerable though trembling faith which man's nature and

God's revelations oppose to all the vestiges of the lower creation, and ends with the cry to what he feels is 'Lord of all', and faintly trusts 'the larger hope', we cannot help confessing that 'hope maketh not ashamed', since it can face boldly even this dread array of dumb discouragements.

From this point the poet's grief passes more and more into gentle memory, contemplation, and even joy. Here and there, before the anguish dies wholly away, we have exquisite bursts of returning life and joy, like that wonderful little address to the nightingale, which seems to express the rapture at once of pain and of victory over it:—

[Quotes *In Memoriam*, lxxxviii:

> 'Wild bird, whose warble, liquid sweet . . .
> Will flash along the chords and go.']

With such alternations of joy, and an always rising note of love and faith, this great history of grief comes to a triumphant end,

> With faith that comes of self-control,
> The truths that never can be proved
> Until we close with all we loved
> And all we flow from, soul in soul,

—where, if ever in human poetry, we see the glow of that 'love of God which is shed abroad in our hearts by the Holy Ghost that is given us'. I know of no poem so great or so perfect which deals with grief at all. The higher poetry has a tendency to shun grief—submissive grief at least; for grief that bows to the stroke is of all emotions the one most depressing to the immediate store of mental vitality; and the higher poetry springs from the fullest well of life. Pain of all other kinds, including even that defiant despair which fights against God, finds ample voice in poetry; but grave and quiet anguish under the acknowledged fact of loss, anguish which does not strive to kick against the pricks, and yet does not seek to quench itself in mystic passion, has had few and fragmentary representatives in our higher poetry. Only a very strong spirit of poetry could have prevented so long a series of mournful poems as this from becoming oppressively sombre. Even as it is, it is only in one's sadder moods that one turns to this great poem; and, indeed, it is only in one or two of the latter poems of the series that it is possible for Tennyson to embody the full strength and elasticity of his poetic genius. There is a natural limitation of power and vitality imposed by the nature of the subject in this respect.

In one respect, however, I think *In Memoriam* surpasses all his other works—I mean in the exquisite tone of the pictures it contains. Elsewhere his pictures are apt to start out from the surface of his poems with colours almost too brilliant and outlines almost too strongly defined, so that one is dazzled by the detail, and the main subject of the poem is thrown into the shade. It is never so in *In Memoriam*, where the lowered key of grief and hesitating hope, results in colours as liquid in tone as the mood they illustrate. Is there in the whole range of English poetry such a picture of a summer twilight, itself drawn in the very mood of such a twilight, as this?—

[Quotes *In Memoriam*, xcv, ll. 1–16:

'By night we linger'd on the lawn . . .
Laid their dark arms about the field.']

And what a living picture of the dawn ends the same wonderful poem!—

[Quotes *In Memoriam*, xcv, ll. 49–64:

'Till now the doubtful dusk reveal'd . . .
To broaden into boundless day.']

I know no descriptive poetry that has the delicate spiritual genius of that passage, its sweet mystery, its subdued lustre, its living truth, its rapture of peace. And besides the indescribable beauty of the pictures in *In Memoriam*, in intellectual depth, especially in the truthfulness of its knowledge of the heart, and in the elasticity of soul which thrusts back the heaviest burdens by its own inherent force, this poem has never been rivalled in its kind by any English poet. Its defects are few and very slight, and mostly what I observe in all Lord Tennyson's poems. He always shows a certain tendency to over-express any morbid thought or feeling he wishes to resist, and this jars more on the ear in a poem of which the very essence is its sad self-possession and submissive pain. Thus, where he says that man tried to believe Love to be 'Creation's final law',

Tho' Nature, red in tooth and claw
With ravine, shriek'd against his creed,

the phrase sounds to me hysterical, for Nature is very much besides the teeth and claws of beasts of prey, and the 'shrieks' of her victims can hardly be fairly represented as her voice. The significance of the objection, which is undeniable, loses, I think, instead of gaining in weight, from so excited a form of expression. I feel just the same jar at the phrase twice used of sorrow, 'Sorrow with thy lying lip', which, as representing the illusions into which sorrow betrays us, sounds harsh, almost like the phrase of a scold;—yet nothing can be conceived less like the general tenor of feeling in the poem than the scolding mood. Now and then, too, there is a tone of 'effusion' beyond what a perfectly simple taste admits, as where the poet supposes that his friend might come down alive from the ship in which he was looking only for his corpse, and *'strike'* a sudden hand in mind', where 'strike' is surely too pronounced, too emphatic a word for the occasion, especially as the idea is conveyed by the word 'sudden'. But when seeming faults, so 'infinitely little' as these, are the only ones to be perceived in such a poem as this, the poem must be great, unless indeed the critic be very blind. Certainly to me it seems the most beautiful and vivid of all poems that ever grew out of a grave.

No one can criticise *In Memoriam* and *The Idylls of the King*, still less pass from the one to the other, without being conscious of the immense influence which ethical principles have had in moulding Tennyson's work as an artist, or without reflecting in some form on the charge so commonly made or implied against him, that he has injured the character of his art for the sake of the perfectly irrelevant interests of morality. No one can doubt that if a poem which is, as it asserts itself, the simple outpouring of long years of grief, has what may be called a moral teaching at all, the teaching of *In Memoriam* is that Knowledge severed from Love and Faith is 'a child and vain'; that she should know her place, which is to be second, not the first; that

> A higher hand must make her mild
> If all be not in vain; and guide
> Her footsteps, moving side by side
> With Wisdom, like the younger child.

If *In Memoriam* has a definite teaching at all, as distinguished from a lyrical burden, this is it. And no doubt it expresses a conviction which springs from the very depths of the poet's soul. Whether it injures his poetry or not must depend on two conditions. First, Is it obtruded didactically instead of merely shaping and turning his song? In other words, Does it mar the music, or is it of the essence of the music? For any one may spoil a song or a poem of any kind by incorporating with it fragments of a sermon. The second question is, 'Is it true?' For if the doctrine that Knowledge severed from Love and Faith is out of place, be incorporated into the very heart of the music, and be yet false, unmanly, enervating doctrine, I at least should admit at once that it must injure the poem, as well as the morality of the poem. Mr. Swinburne,—who, when he can lay aside petty resentments and clear his essays from the intricate inuendoes inspired by a whole host of unintelligible literary animosities, always writes with the lucid beauty of genius, though somewhat too much also with the 'high action' of complacent consciousness,—appears to think the first question alone relevant. He has declared that 'the worth of a poem has properly nothing to do with its moral meaning or design'; that 'the only absolute duty of Art is the duty she owes to herself'; that 'she is dependent on herself alone, and on nothing above or beneath'. He does not therefore *prohibit* Art from taking a moral aim, so long as the aim does not so protrude as to injure the art. But he will not admit that the character of the morality involved is even an element in the matter. Indeed, 'there is a value,' he says, 'beyond price and beyond thought, in the Lesbian music which spends itself on the record of fleshly fever and amorous malady'. Unquestionably this is not Lord Tennyson's doctrine. In verses which, had they not been in all probability written long before Mr. Swinburne was born, might have been supposed to bear some reference to his genius, the Laureate has said that the highest creative beauty, whether of the divine or of the poetic kind, must imply a moral law:—

> My own dim life should teach me this,
> That life shall live for evermore,
> Else earth is darkness at the core
> And dust and ashes all that is;
>
> This round of green, this orb of flame
> Fantastic beauty; *such as lurks*
> *In some wild Poet when he works*
> *Without a conscience or an aim.*

Nor can I conceive of any rational interpretation of the view for which Mr. Swinburne declares himself so absolutely—without, however, himself attempting to give it a rational interpretation. I doubt if he even agrees heartily with himself. He declares, for instance, against Tennyson's 'Vivien', on the ground that in depicting an unchaste woman, Art requires 'at least some trace of human, or, if need be, of devilish dignity'. Now, I do not suppose that Mr. Swinburne means to imply that all the proper subjects of Art must have dignity, either human, devilish, or of any other kind. Malvolio and Caliban are both, I suppose, fit subjects for Art, and neither of them by reason of their dignity, rather by reason of the want of it. What Mr. Swinburne meant, I suppose, was that in a figure of the type of Vivien, some trace of other dignity is needed to render the intrinsic want of womanly dignity tolerable. But if this be admitted, Mr. Swinburne's 'absolute independence of Art' is surrendered at once. Why is some vestige of dignity specially needed in the portraiture of one of Vivien's type, except because the higher taste is so intolerant of mere meanness—especially meanness of the sensual order—that when you are painting a character in this essential respect destitute of worth, you are bound to relieve the picture by portraying some trait of greatness of some other kind, greatness of passion, or intelligence, or, if it must be so, greatness of evil purpose itself? I agree with the general principle, if not with its special application to Vivien; but what does it imply? This fastidiousness of the higher taste is not an accident of the artistic temperament. We shrink from the meaner types of evil in Art, because they are less representative of our nature, because they fail to call out the deeper and more ennobling moral emotions; because, while we can despise and loathe them, we cannot dread or hate them. Well, but this is a virtual admission that Art acknowledges the supremacy of these moral emotions—in other words, of the conscience which shapes them; and, if it be so, then the poetry which makes the lower passions speak as if there were no such moral emotions at all, is worse *as poetry* for its grovelling blindness. Mr. Swinburne's 'Lesbian music which spends itself on the record of fleshly fever and amorous malady', seems to me the music of the satyr, not the music of human beings, and to be condemned by the very reasons which he assigns for condemning 'Vivien'. It is wanting in all dignity except the dignity of flame, or rather it revels in indignity, in what is the disgrace and not the honour of human nature. You might as well say that it is a fit subject for Art to paint the morbid ecstasy of cannibals over their horrid feasts, as to paint lust without love. If you are to delineate man at all, you must delineate him with his human nature, and therefore you can never really omit from any worthy picture that conscience which is its crown. I believe, myself, that Tennyson is never guilty of letting his moral purpose crop out ostentatiously so as to injure his art; indeed, I have never seen it even alleged that he is so guilty, except in relation to his picture of Arthur, of which I have presently to speak. And as I believe that his intense conviction, that Knowledge is 'the second, not the first', is true—that

Art herself must walk by the light of Love and Faith, and must not paint human nature in the monstrous and conscienceless shapes it sometimes really assumes, unless with some foil which shall make the void where the moral life should be, painfully visible,—I cannot think that in any respect Lord Tennyson has shown himself a higher artist than in the important but generally unostentatious place which the conscience takes in his greater poems.

Of course the soundness of this judgment on Tennyson as a poet must depend on the real value of the great poem called, I think with somewhat unfortunate modesty, *The Idylls of the King*. The title misled the public, and the fragmentary mode in which the poem appeared misled it the more. I confess that when the first four Idylls first appeared I did not enjoy them nearly so much as many of the Laureate's earlier poems. No one, I suppose, with any taste for poetry at all could possibly have read 'Elaine' and 'Guinevere', especially the latter, without delight. But appearing, as they did, without any notice of their fragmentary character, and with, I still think, a good deal in the first of them, 'Enid', to suggest that they were rich pictorial fancies, taken, certainly not altogether at random, but yet without any really coherent design, out of a great magazine of romantic story, there was some exuse, I think, for the hasty impression that they were four minutely finished cabinet pictures, painted of course to hang by and illustrate each other, but nevertheless with more view to the beauty of the individual effects than to their relation to each other. By the side of 'Ulysses', 'The Two Voices', and many others of Tennyson's earlier poems, I certainly thought at first the four first *Idylls* a little wanting in intellectual interest, a little too dependent on their pictorial brilliancy. But as the poem put forth new shoots in both directions, backwards and forwards, and the noble portions on 'The Coming of Arthur', 'The Holy Grail', and 'The Passing of Arthur', appeared,—poems in which the gradual growth and fall of the ideal kingdom of the spiritual chivalry were depicted,—the grandeur of the new poem began, for me at least, to eclipse in interest almost everything that Tennyson had written, and the first published Idylls themselves grew in intellectual fascination. 'The Last Tournament', and 'Gareth and Lynette', which furnished respectively almost the last and first links in the chain, except the 'Passing' and 'Coming' of Arthur themselves, seem to me to have wrought up the poet's conceptions into a far completer expression, and to have put the final touches to a very great, though not quite perfect whole. Most readers seem to find much less of grace and finish in the later than in the earlier published Idylls. As regards 'Pelleas and Ettarre' and 'The Last Tournament', this is not only true, but was necessary to the poet's purpose, which was to give the impression of rude storms, gloom, and coming ruin before the tragic close. I do not think myself that it is true at all of the other parts. The new additions to 'The Passing of Arthur'—which now embodies Tennyson's earliest as well as his latest work on this great poem—seem to me to contain the grandest lines he has ever written, lines resonant with the highest chords of spiritual yearning and bewildered trust, lines which echo and re-echo in one's imagination like the dying tones of the organ in a great cathedral's aisles. 'Gareth and Lynette', which is intended to paint the freshest period of the ideal kingdom and also to foreshadow its course, has to my ear a mingled sweetness and depth that make it far surpass 'Enid' in poetic power, and so no doubt it introduces a certain flaw into the workmanship of the whole poem, which rather declines in power as it passes from its first to its second stage and shows the origin of the evil influence which is to lay the whole fair structure in ruins. I think, too, there is a flaw of the same kind in the comparative inferiority of 'Pelleas and Ettarre' to the parts which precede and follow it. 'Pelleas and Ettarre' is not merely harsh and revolting, as 'The Last Tournament' is harsh and revolting—that it must have been: it is harsh and revolting without presenting any of the assuaging and ennobling effects of Arthur's exalting influence, without any reconciling touch such as the passionate fidelity of the fool gives to 'The Last Tournament', and also I think without sufficient grandeur even in the evil. Ettarre, at all events, is hardly a figure dignified enough for the evil part she has to play in a great tragedy. She is no greater than she is in the old story itself, where she has to play a far less important part, and where there is a foil to her wanting in Tennyson's picture.

These are the kind of artistic objections—objections of detail—to which I think Lord Tennyson's great Arthurian poem is justly liable. The design as a whole seems to me more within true poetic limits, if not nobler in itself, than anything in our epic literature; and though Tennyson does not of course bring to its execution a voice of the mighty volume of Milton's, he has not only written what is far more perfect as a work of art, though less imposing as a work of genius, than *Paradise Lost*—indeed, the former might easily be—but one which shadows forth the ideal faith of his own time—a time of at least as sincere if much less definite faith, and of far higher moral and intellectual discrimination—more adequately.

In taking his subject from the great mediæval myth of English chivalry, it was of course open to Tennyson to adopt any treatment of it which would really incorporate the higher and grander aspects of the theme, and also find an ideal unity for a number of legends in which of unity there was none. It is obvious that in dealing with the chivalric story with which strange and grand fragments of mediæval Christian mysticism are closely interwoven, it was impossible to avoid the blending of the distinct themes of ideal courage and honour, ideal love and purity, and the rapt visions of an ideal faith. This could not have been avoided. But undoubtedly these various elements might have blended in various ways; and it would have been possible, no doubt, to make the central figure of the poem one in which the highest ideal aims were crossed by the tragic consequences of a youthful sin, so that everywhere his own sin rose up against him till it brought to ruin the fair dream of his life. This is the view of the story of Arthur which Mr. Swinburne and his school maintain to be the only natural and legitimate one. And there is no doubt that the treachery which finally undermines and ruins Arthur's work is the treachery of Modred, nor that, according to the story of the old legend, Modred is Arthur's own son, the offspring of Arthur's guilty passion for one whom he did not then know to be his half-sister Bellicent. According to the old story, Merlin prophesied to him the evil destiny in store for him as the penalty of this sin, and also forbade him to take part in the search for the Holy Grail, as being rendered unworthy of it by that sin. Nor can it be denied that there are various other traces in the early part of these legends of the moral taint which Arthur's nature had thus incurred. For instance, the sword brought by the lady of the isle of Avelyon cannot be drawn by Arthur, because it can only be drawn by a knight in whom there is no hidden shame.

For the rest, the picture of Arthur as given in the old legends is exceedingly wavering and uncertain. For the most part it is the picture of a gracious and noble figure of mysterious origin and mysterious destiny,—'Rex quondam, Rexque futurus', according to the legendary inscription on his tomb,—whose nobility inspires a passion of love and fidelity in his knights, and the profoundest agony of remorse in his unfaithful queen; but also at times crafty, and at times weak, trying in the beginning of his reign, like Herod, to exterminate the infants amongst whom Merlin's lore pronounces that the cause of his own ruin and death is to be found; and yielding at the end of his reign, against his own better mind, to the bloody and vindictive counsels of his nephew Gawain in the war with Lancelot. I will venture to say that if only those legends collected by Sir Thomas Malory were to be taken as authorities (and though I do not profess a knowledge of the various other collections, it is quite clear that many of them are far more favourable to the ideal view of Arthur than Sir Thomas Malory's), and if everything they say of Arthur were put together, no coherent character at all could be constructed out of them. It would have been impossible to draw any poetical portrait of the king without the freest principle of selection. Had Tennyson taken the view which Mr. Swinburne affirms, —with a pert dogmatism quite unworthy of the exquisite English in which he writes, and the frequent flashes of genius in the substance of what he writes,—to be the only possible one; had the story of Arthur been turned into that of a kind of mediæval Œdipus, and the awful destiny which avenged his voluntary sin but involuntary incest, that of death by the hand of his own son, been made the subject of it,—there would have been no room at all for the spiritual halo which the mysterious stories of Arthur's birth and of his return from the island of his rest shed round the subject. No Greek tragedian would have dreamt of investing Œdipus with such a halo as that. This view of the story is a tragic one in the true old sense of a story purifying the heart by pity and by fear. The subject of so dread and dark a destiny may be enabled to answer Sphinx-riddles as a step to his own doom, but he cannot be one whose coming is preceded by heavenly portents, and whose passing takes place amidst the wailing of unearthly mourners, the bitter grief and remorse of faithless companions, and the mystic presage of a glorious return. It seems to me perfectly evident that Tennyson, as every true poet—Mr. Swinburne himself, for example— had to choose between the various inconsistent elements in the Arthurian legends, which of them he would keep and which he would eliminate, that it would have been simply impossible to keep the element of shame and retribution along with the element of mystic spiritual glory, and that the last is far the most characteristic and the most in keeping with the Christian mysticism of the San Grail legends, of the two. Let any one read either Sir Thomas Malory's book, or the brief, graceful, and classical compilation of the Legends of King Arthur by J. T. K., and then judge for himself whether the sin of King Arthur or his unearthly glory be the more deeply ingrained element of the two, and I suspect he will end by accepting as the overruling idea, and also as by far the better adapted for coherent treatment, the verdict of the old chroniclers, of Joseph of Exeter, for example: 'The old world knows not his peer, nor will the future show us his equal; he alone towers over all other kings, better than the past ones, and greater than those that are to be'; and again another old compiler: 'In short, God has not made, since Adam was, the man more perfect than King Arthur.'[1] It is perfectly evident that this tradition of unrivalled spiritual glory was a development of elements of the story quite inconsistent with that of his great sin and shame.

Mr. Swinburne asserts, however, that Guinevere's sin is closely implicated with Arthur's: 'From the sin of Arthur's youth proceeds the ruin of his reign and realm through the falsehood of his wife—a wife unloving and unloved.'[2] I believe this is not only without basis in the story as told by Sir Thomas Malory, but wholly inconsistent with it. So far is Guinevere from being 'unloved', that when Merlin asks Arthur, 'Is there any faire lady that yee love better than another?' he answers, 'Yea, I love Guinevere the King's daughter, Leodegrance of the land of Camelyard, which Leodegrance holdeth in his power the Table Round that yee told hee had of my father Uther. And this demosell is the most gentilest and fairest lady that I know living, or yet that I ever could find.' 'Sir,' said Merlin, 'as of her beautie and fairenesse, she is one of the fairest that live; *but an yee loved her not so well as yee doe, I would finde yee a demosell of beautie and of goodnesse that should like yee and please yee, and your heart were not set. But there as a man's heart is set, he will be loth to return.*' 'That is truth,' said Arthur;—and here not only is Arthur's passion for his queen represented as beyond resistance, but Merlin treats the want of love of Guinevere as the root of the calamities that were to come, and intimates that by a happier choice these calamities might have been avoided. And the simple truth is, that this is the whole drift of the legends, from the date of Arthur's marriage to the close. After Arthur's mysterious death, Guinevere freely takes upon herself and Lancelot the whole guilt of the ruin of Arthur's kingdom. 'Through this knight and mee all these warres were wrought, and the death of the most noble knights of the world; for through our love that we have loved together is my most noble lord slaine. . . . For as well as I have loved thee, Sir Lancelot, now mine heart will not once serve mee to see thee; for through thee and mee is the floure of kings and knights destroyed.' And her last prayer is not to see Sir Lancelot again with her bodily eyes, lest her earthly and disloyal love should return upon her, but that he should bury her beside her true lord and master, King

---

[1] I quote these from the preface to J. T. K.'s compilation.

[2] *Under the Microscope*, by Algernon Charles Swinburne, p. 37. (White, Coventry Street.)

Arthur. No one can read Sir Thomas Malory's book without being struck by the complete disappearance, as it proceeds, of all trace of remorse or shame in King Arthur, and by the weight of guilt thrown upon the passionate love of Lancelot and Guinevere. Obviously, if Tennyson was to keep to the legends which cast so mysterious a halo of spiritual glory around King Arthur, he had no choice but to ignore those which connected, Œdipus-fashion, his youthful sin with the final catastrophe.

But it has been said that Arthur's exclusion from the search for the San Grail is only intelligible on the ground of his youthful guilt. Here again, I think, Tennyson's poetic instinct proves triumphant. For in the story of it as told by Sir Thomas Malory, there is not only no trace of this, but a distinct justification of the Poet Laureate's view that Arthur looked on this search for the San Grail as almost a disloyalty to the higher though humbler task that he had set himself and his knights —of restoring order on earth; while, on the other hand, knights, who, like Sir Lancelot, are stained with far deeper and more voluntary guilt than any with which the King, even on Mr. Swinburne's view, is chargeable, are allowed to join in the search. I do not know anything happier or more true in its instinct, in English poetry, than the tone Tennyson has attributed to Arthur's reluctant assent to the search for the San Grail. It is amply justified by the old legends, and it just enables the poet to express through Arthur that spiritual distrust of signs and wonders which, while it serves to link his faith closely with modern thought, is in no way inconsistent with the chivalric character of the whole story. In Sir Thomas Malory's version, after the descent of the Holy Ghost, the vision of the holy vessel, and that Pentecostal scene in which all the knights, amid profound silence, had beheld each other invested with a higher beauty than their own, Arthur yields thanks to God 'of his grace that hee had sent them, and for the vision hee had showed them at the high feast of Pentecost', yet not only suggests no quest, but imagines none; nor is it the holiest of the knights, nor one of those who are to succeed wholly or partially in achieving it, who proposes it. It is Sir Gawain;—though Tennyson, who has accepted for other reasons a lower conception of Sir Gawain than the old chroniclers, puts the first oath into the mouth of the mystic-minded Percivale. Arthur at once expresses his displeasure in language at least fairly interpretable as implying disapprobation of the surrender of a prior earthly duty for a visionary spiritual aim. ' "Alas!" said King Arthur unto Sir Gawain, "yee have nigh slaine mee with the vow and promise

yee have made; for through you yee have bereft mee of the fairest
fellowship and the truest of knighthood that ever were seene together
in any realme of the world. For when they shall depart from hence, I
am sure that all shall never meete more in this world, for there shall
many die in the quest, and so it forethinketh [repenteth] mee a little, for
I have loved them as well as my life; wherefore it shall grieve me right
sore the separation of this fellowship, for I have had an old custome to
have them in my fellowship." ' And again, more passionately: ' "Ah,
Sir Gawain, Sir Gawain, yee have betraied mee, for never shall my
heart be amended by you, but yee will never be sorry for mee as I am
for you"; and therewith the teeres began to runne downe by his visage.
And therewith the King said: "Ah, knight, Sir Lancelot, I require thee
that thou wilt counsaile mee, for I would this quest were undone, and
it might bee".' This is not the language of one too guilty to join in the
quest himself, but of one who sincerely disapproves it, as the exchange
of a clear prior duty undertaken by his knights, for one of doubtful
obligation, though of spiritual ambition.

On the whole, I cannot help thinking that Mr. Swinburne's hostile
criticism of *The Idylls of the King* for their omission of the taint in the
king's life and character, is virtually a complaint that the poet has not
excluded the whole halo of spiritual glory from the Arthurian traditions, and substituted an old Greek tragedy for a mystic mediæval
vision. Doubtless Mr. Swinburne himself would have preferred the
former subject—the dark shadows of fate, the sensual horror, the black
remorse, and the fell retribution, which haunt a sin of passion and an
unnatural though partly involuntary crime. He has often shown an
almost ostentatious preference for artistic subjects of this specially painful
kind. But looking solely to the Arthurian legends themselves, I think
Tennyson was more than justified in taking the other view. By doing
so he has not only raised the character of his poem, but connected it
with some of the most prominent and distinctive threads in our modern
spiritual life.

To come to the poem itself,—the various links in which too few of
its readers have, I fear, as yet considered in the order in which Tennyson
means them to be ultimately studied, rather than in that in which he has
given them to the world,—what a splendour of dusk and dawn is there
not in the introductory poem, 'The Coming of Arthur'; what a veil of
lustre is drawn over the birth and origin of this mysterious king, whose
royal right is half reflected rumour flashed back from the greatness of
his subsequent deeds, and half that dim oracular testimony which always

seems to anticipate the higher orders of greatness from their earliest days! His knights believe him to be of the old royal race, the more that his tones of command 'and simple words of great authority' sink into them with a self-attesting power, so

> That when they rose, knighted from kneeling, some
> Were pale as at the passing of a ghost,
> Some flush'd, and others dazed, as one who wakes
> Half-blinded at the coming of a light.

His sister, full of a deeper loyalty and a more feminine faith, believes the rumour of a supernatural origin,—that he came with portents, borne a naked babe upon the sea, the sign of the winged dragon above him in heaven, and a lambent fire playing round him as the last and greatest of nine great waves bore him to Merlin's feet. Merlin himself, the great master of all mediæval lore, could only say of Arthur that though men might wound him, he could never die, but 'pass, again to come', declaring of him in words that haunt the mind of Guinevere when she sees him depart to return to her no more—

> From the great deep to the great deep he goes.

Leodogran's dream, when he is doubting whether Arthur's mysterious descent is truly royal, so that he may give him Guinevere for his wife, or not,—the dream in which he mingles the story of the actual wars of Arthur against the heathen with the rumours of the still struggling passions of his rebellious subjects, and yet augurs that the grandeur of the King will survive even the history of his deeds,—is a splendid embodiment of Tennyson's drift throughout the poem. Grant that a perfect king is a phantom of the human imagination, yet it is a phantom which will haunt it long after what we call the real earth shall have been dissolved:—

[Quotes 'The Coming of Arthur', ll. 424–45:

> 'She spake and King Leodogran . . .
> . . . answering yea.']

Like all true authority, that of the ideal king is hidden in mystery, but the image of his glory in the heavens survives the crumbling of his kingdom on earth. Not in painting the restless hunger of travel in his 'Ulysses', not in making us shudder at the immortal mortality of the weary 'Tithonus', has Tennyson displayed more power than in this wonderful picture of the mystery which envelops, and the inspiration which seems to attend, the exercise of spiritual authority over the wills of men,—of the spell which it lays upon them,—of the certain failure of that spell as passion and pleasure and selfish interest reassert their sway, and yet of the inevitable reassertion of its power in memory and its eternal triumph in faith.

The second of these poems, and the newest of them, 'Gareth and Lynette', is meant to paint the golden age of Arthur's reign, while as yet no germ of guilt has sprung into visible life, while the chivalry of perfect courage, perfect love, and perfect faith is still dominant, and all Arthur's knights are aiding him in redeeming the earth and the souls of men from the tyranny of brutal instincts and the lawless caprice of human self-will. Gareth is the embodiment of childlike loyalty and buoyant youthful faith, willing for any service, however seemingly ignominious, which is the service of the true King 'who makes us free', and not only willing for it, but happy and radiant in it. He is chosen for one which is representative of the aims of Arthur's whole kingdom,—to rescue her who is beset in 'Castle Perilous' by four strong but foolish and boastful knights, who resist Arthur's authority and wish to destroy the order he has founded, and who have challenged him to send his bravest and most glorious knight to encounter them, and deliver their fair captive if he may. Whom the fair captive of 'Castle Perilous' may represent, and of what fashion the knights who there confine her, Tennyson has not left us to conjecture, though the allegory must not be pushed so far as to destroy the beauty of the poetic story:—

[Quotes 'Gareth and Lynette', ll. 1163–79:

'Anon they past . . .
. . . the hermit's cave.']

In this the earliest and most joyous of the pictures of Arthur's reign, something more of symbolism is permissible, by way of illustrating the drift and bearing of the whole, than in the later poems, where sin and shame have struck their dark personal impress on the story; and nothing can be brighter and yet in its way more thrilling than the story of Gareth's fearful encounter with the Evening Star—him who with the wiry tenacity of worldly experience and indurated habit, warded off the daring enthusiasm of youth and faith,—and him who chilled the blood of all under the awful seeming of Night and Death, and yet proved to be but a blooming boy, disguised in false terrors by the stratagem of the children of Time. Of course Tennyson means that the whole aim of Arthur's Order was to deliver the spiritual captive of

'Castle Perilous' from the power of these worldlings of the flesh, and that the battle was to grow more grievous as the long day grew towards its close, though 'the passing of Arthur' at the last, fearful as it seemed, should be but the easy victory over a danger really conquered before—the passing into an isle of rest, whence in higher glory he should return again. The mixture of buoyant life with symbolism in this story of Gareth, and the delicacy with which Tennyson has used and yet quite transformed the old Arthurian story of this relief of 'Castle Perilous', seem to me to rank this poem amongst his happiest efforts.

In 'Enid', where it is the purpose of the poet to picture the infection of distrust, the contagious jealousy which the rumour of Guinevere's unfaithfulness with Lancelot spread downwards amongst the knights of Arthur, though as yet in but a comparatively incipient and conquerable stage, Tennyson's delight in picture rather overpowers his main purpose; and we approach nearer to the type of the versified novelette—the type of 'Enoch Arden' and 'Aylmer's Field'—than in any other section of the Arthurian epic. We must remember, however, that Enid is painted as especially distinguished by Guinevere's love; that it is her closeness to Guinevere which alarms Geraint on her behalf when he hears Guinevere's virtue impugned; and that it is the King's healing influence, no less than Enid's spotless purity, which restores Geraint to himself. Arthur's chivalry is already attacked from the side of purity, but the taint is not yet deep. In 'Vivien' and 'Elaine' the taint spreads. In the former, which Mr. Swinburne has assailed for vulgarity and grossness, we have certainly, in Vivien's wiles with Merlin, the picture of a true harlot worming out of that time-worn craft and intellect—which, while it is high enough to discern and serve willingly the true spiritual king, yet is not itself of moral or spiritual descent,—its secrets of power, in the very wantonness of selfish envy. She had first tried her wiles with the higher nature, with the King himself, and failed. She has heard of the sensual charm by which a living death may be brought upon the highest mind:—

> And Vivien ever sought to work the charm
> Upon the great Enchanter of the Time,
> As fancying that her glory would be great
> According to his greatness whom she quench'd.

How the great Enchanter hears the foul libels of her evil heart with loathing, and *then*, 'overtalked and overworn', yields to her allurements, tells her the charm, and becomes its victim, so robbing Arthur's kingdom of its shrewdest mind, Tennyson tells in one of his most powerful but certainly not one of his most attractive poems. Yet I cannot see that it would have been right, as Mr. Swinburne asserts, to clothe Vivien with some sort of dignity, 'human or diabolic'. Shakespeare himself never clothes with dignity, even in tragedy, characters against which he desires to excite pure loathing,—like Goneril and Regan. What is wanted is to show the power which sensual natures, partly *because* they are without dignity, may attain over the highest and most experienced intellects unprotected by something higher yet. Any addition of dignity to Vivien would have been a fault for the purposes of the picture. But I do think that Vivien's naked wickedness is insufficiently connected with the taint on Arthur's Court caused by Guinevere's and Lancelot's sin. Vivien should belong, at all events, to the last and not to the earliest period. She might be conceivable when Ettarre was the queen of beauty, and during the open shamelessness of 'The Last Tournament'. She is before her time in the period when even Guinevere's fall has only just become the scandal of the time. Vivien, the type of those who

> Inflate themselves with some insane delight
> And judge all Nature from her feet of clay,

is surely premature!

I do not suppose any one questions the exquisite beauty of the poem in which Elaine's pure first love for Lancelot, and her death on his behalf, is contrasted with the Queen's jealous and guilty passion. The lurid picture of the crowned skeleton on which Arthur trod in a moon-lit pass, long before he became king, when he broke from it that diadem all the jewels in which Lancelot was to win for the object of his guilty passion, makes a fine opening of evil augury to this contrast between guilty and innocent love, just as the passage of Elaine's corpse in the boat to Camelot makes for it a noble and tragic close. The contrast between Guinevere and Elaine, imaged in that simple and exquisite passage where the Queen flings the diamonds that Lancelot offers her into the river,—

> And down they flash'd, and smote the stream,
> *Then from the smitten surface flash'd as it were,*
> *Diamonds to meet them, and they pass'd away,*—

marks the turning point of the Arthurian story. The King's pure influence wanes, and the Queen's guilty passion grows. Sir Gawain, the type of gay and gallant pleasure-seeking, has already begun to trifle disloyally with his King's orders. And the burst of grand remorse in Lancelot, with which the poem ends, prepares the way for that morbid, self-introspective cast of thought, those fever-fits of spiritual craving and despondency, that yearning for signs and wonders, that thirst for expiation, by which the search for the Holy Grail, with its lurid enthusiasms and its apocalyptic dreams, is ushered in. 'The year of miracle' is painted, as it seems to me, with even more than Mr. Tennyson's higher kind of power. The mystic passion in it, the stormy remorse, the fitful humility, the dreamy mingling of earth and heaven, tell of the closest study of the literature of ecstasy and the rapture of the seventh heaven. The picture is heightened by the striking glimpse given us of that common-place monk with his village gossips, and his earthly cares, all glued like 'the martin's nest' to the little thorpe which lies under the monastery's walls, to whom Percivale relates it—a picture almost worthy to set by that of the 'Northern Farmers' for its realism and its force. The close of the poem, in which Arthur claims for himself spiritual visions more than all of them, and yet condemns the neglect of one plain practical duty in order to indulge these visions, one of Tennyson's finest touches, serves to mark at once the waning influence of the King, and the growing stature of the 'phantom' whom men disowned:—

[Quotes conclusion of 'The Holy Grail', starting 18 lines from the end:

' "And some among you held . . .
. . . ye have seen what ye have seen." ']

I have said I cannot greatly admire the poem which follows, 'Pelleas and Ettarre'. It has great power, and delineates the growth of a sensual chaos with terrible force, but there is no relieving element in it. Pelleas, who starts with an enthusiastic purity, deserves a better fate (which, indeed, in the old legends he obtains) than that of desperation and wild defiance of the kingdom in whose greatness he had believed. We miss altogether Arthur's presence. All is sensual anarchy, and the victory of the harlot is complete. The reader greatly needs a touch like that which ends 'The Last Tournament', where the fidelity even of a fool turns horror into true tragedy, and opens a glimpse of love behind the foul orgies of victorious lust. I think the Arthurian poem would be a more perfect whole if 'Pelleas and Ettarre' were completely omitted. 'The Last Tournament' seems to me not only to give us over again all that

'Pelleas and Ettarre' gives, but to give it in a nobler form, in less harsh and grating discords.

'Guinevere', and 'The Passing of Arthur', however, heal all wounds. The passage in which the King, while shrinking from even the touch of the Queen's hand, tells her it is his doom to love her still, and that he claims her in the eternal world as his—one of those passages on which, I believe, the taunt has been founded, that Tennyson's 'Arthur' is 'an impeccable prig',—seems to me one of the noblest and most moving in English poetry. Doubtless, in one view, all sinlessness is didactic, and therefore jarring to those who are not sinless. But Tennyson means Arthur for the impersonation of spiritual authority from the first, as he means Guinevere for the impersonation of that highest form of woman's beauty, which is the noblest embodiment of purity, and therefore shows most sadly the flaw of passionate sin. If the spirit of holiness, of mercy, of love, is priggish because it is impeccable, then, and only then, could I see the truth of that flippant charge against language such as this:

[Quotes 'Guinevere', ll. 550–80:

' "I cannot take thy hand . . .
. . . his hands that blest.']

'The Passing of Arthur', which contains some of Tennyson's earliest, and also of his latest, work, and all of it in his best and highest and most masculine strain, is a striking evidence of the singular unity of his genius. No single poem of his contains at once so much vivid colour and so much intellectual and spiritual magic. The wonderful picture of the weird and desolate hour of seeming spiritual failure, of the wounded heart, of forsaken suffering, of sinking trust, but not of failing fortitude or shrinking will, which precedes and follows the last great battle, is perhaps the highest Lord Tennyson has drawn. Nothing in all his poems gives me so strong a feeling of his power as those which contain the dream in which he seems to see the ghost of the pleasure-loving, pleasure-seeking Gawain:—

[Quotes 'The Passing of Arthur', ll. 29–49:

'Before that last weird battle in the west . . .
. . . knowing it will go along with me?" ']

The state of mind in which the spirit begins to creep against the flesh, as knowing that the period of united existence is past, and all things look spectral, while a horror descends even upon the highest courage at a prospect rendered in this case indefinitely more chill by the broken honour and sullied vows of others, and the seeming failure of the purest spiritual constancy to subdue the world to itself, is delineated as only one of the great poets of the world can delineate anything. Tennyson is never so great as when he has a mystic dread to paint, when Tithonus is shivering at the prospect of an immortal burden, or Arthur asking himself on the edge of the hereafter, whether there had been anything of true eternity in his life here. I have said that what is rich and complex, like the beauty and chivalry and faith of this great poem, always attracts the Laureate most; that his most characteristic poetry contains in it all the richest elements of artistic composition. But, perhaps, for that very reason, no other poet has painted so powerfully that mysterious thrill with which the glory of this world passes away, and leaves the nakedness of the soul behind. Percivale, with every grand and lovely vision, falling into dust at his touch, and leaving him alone, and 'wearying in a land of sand and thorns', or Arthur feeling a way

> Thro' this blind haze, which ever since I saw
> One lying in the dust at Almesbury,
> Hath folded in the passes of the world,

is alike clad in the sublimity of that deepest kind of desolation from which a vesture of rich thought and hope has suddenly been stripped away. The very grandeur of the scenery from which Arthur passes to his isle of rest, when, after the long day's battle wrapped in mist, and the grievous wound from the traitor's hand, and the one remaining knight's unfaithfulness, he is borne to the margin of the mystic water,—

> When on a sudden, lo! the level lake
> And the long glories of the winter moon,

contributes, by the rich flash of its contrast, to enhance the impression of a ghostly solitude of spirit and a trembling, halting faith. The vision of Leodogran's dream is literally fulfilled. The cloud has rolled down upon the earth, and the King, a mighty phantom, stands out in heaven —but stands out crowned, for he has lost nothing in himself of the spiritual elements of his kingdom; his courage is unshaken, his honour unsullied, his purity untarnished, and his faith, though wavering as, in the hour of deepest darkness, it wavers in the most perfect humanity, is still the life and blossom of his nature. And as Merlin's riddling prophecy rings in our ears,

> Where is he who knows?
> From the great deep to the great deep he goes,

we recognise in the drooping King, as the barge takes him slowly to his isle of rest, the image of the 'new order' almost as much as of the old—the elements of that true chivalry, in which courage, truth, purity, and faith are even more of spiritual and inward than of outward gifts, and stretch out arms of yearning towards the life beyond the veil.

If not the most perfectly finished of Tennyson's poems, *The Idylls of the King* has a grander aim and larger scope than any, and paints the waste places of the heart and the strength of the naked soul with a stronger and more nervous touch. As the rich colours of the great story fade, the air fills with low, spiritual rumours of that higher life of which the order of the Round Table is but a symbol; while Tennyson paints the stately passing of the spirit to its rest as he painted the greatness of its rising, but with added touches of mystery and beauty. The old Arthurian epic has been rendered by Tennyson significant to modern ears. In it he has found the common term between the ideas of chivalry and the ideas of an age of hesitating trust, an age of a probing intellect and of a trusting heart. The conquests and the yearnings, and the sad resolves of a spirit far too kingly to rule successfully men who only half recognise the kingly voice, have never before been delineated by a poet who can use almost all the wealth of colour belonging at once to the visible and the invisible life, with the reticent hand and sure eye of Tennyson's rich and patient and spiritual genius.

Of Tennyson's plays, whether *Queen Mary* or *Becket* or *Harold*, no one will, I think, be inclined to say that they are fully worthy of his genius. Though he has the dramatic mind, yet his mind is not by instinct dramatic. On the contrary, you see that drama is to a certain extent foreign to him, and puts the curb on his favourite modes of thought. Still *Queen Mary* is strong from end to end, which could not be said of either *Becket* or *Harold*. It is so thoroughly dramatic that it might, with an adequate cast of actors, be produced with the highest effect on the stage; and if this has not been done, it is chiefly that the number of the actors, and of the good actors required, is too great for the command of any manager. Almost all the characters who play a real part in the drama, however slightly touched, are clearly defined— Philip, whose disgust for the Queen is powerfully painted, but who remains otherwise something of a cold, cruel, and sensual shadow, being perhaps in some degree an exception. Courtenay, Earl of Devon, —the vain and flighty Catholic Plantagenet,—'this Prince of fluff and feather', as Lord Howard in speaking to Elizabeth calls him; Reginald Pole, the fair-weather Papal Legate, who shrinks alike from being persecuted and from persecuting, but is easily driven into the latter policy under fear of the former; Bishop Gardiner, with his fierce Romanising dogmatism and his English hatred of Italian interference in English concerns,—

> . . . His big baldness,
> That irritable forelock which he rubs,
> His buzzard beak, and deep incavern'd eyes;

Bonner and his moral brutality; Lord Paget, with the half-confessed Protestantism of his statesman's intellect, and yet that craving for English influence abroad which makes him support the alliance with Spain; Lord Howard, with his aristocratic Catholicism, his complete contempt for the vulgarity and ignorance of the new schismatics, and yet his thoroughly rooted antipathy to the bigotry of the sacerdotal spirit; Sir Thomas Wyatt, with his tasteful literary cravings, and the keen, audacious soldier beneath them; Sir Ralph Bagenhall, with his bold, meditative insubordination and his hopelessness of active resistance; Sir Thomas White (the Lord Mayor), with his political indecision, and his wonderful dexterity at swaying the London Guilds directly the feather's-weight has turned the scale which he is pleased to call his mind, so as to decide him on his own course; Cranmer, with his somewhat questionable faith and courage,—questionable we mean as regards historical fact, not questionable at all in Tennyson's picture,— his humility, penitence, and sweetness; and lastly, the imaginary servants and peasants, both men and women, who are made parties to the drama,—these are all drawn with a firm hand and painted with a delicate touch. But the great characters of the piece are, as of course they ought to be, Mary and her half-sister Elizabeth, whose star declines as the Catholic Queen's rises, and rises fair again as Mary's sets. Of course the portrait of Elizabeth is comparatively slight as compared with that of Mary, but though much less carefully filled-in, it is to the full as dramatic and lifelike. Moreover, as it is intended to do, it makes by contrast the chief portrait all the more striking and characteristic. Both Mary and Elizabeth have the Tudor courage in emergencies, and flashes of what may be called that dramatic magnanimity which enables them to see how best to seem superior to suspicion and fear in a moment of danger. Mary, when she met Elizabeth at Wanstead, at the moment when her own accession was still doubtful, took her rival's hand, as Tennyson's drama reminds us, called her 'sweet sister', and kissed not her alone, but all the ladies of her following, and further spoke of the Lady Jane Grey as a poor innocent child who had but obeyed her father. Elizabeth, again, could so far feel with the dead Queen, whose reign had been one long menace to her, as to half-believe in her own reluctance to succeed her, and to be absorbed for the moment, or think herself absorbed, in pity for the sad fate which had darkened steadily down to the miserable close. But while both had the Tudor instinct in emergencies, in Mary it was, as a rule, entirely subordinated to personal emotions, like her irrational passion for the Spanish prince she had never seen, her fixed hatred for the counsellors who were forward in advocating her mother's divorce, and her super-stitious craving for the blood of the enemies of the Church. On the contrary, in Elizabeth, personal feeling was, as a rule, subordinated to her strong instinct of policy, so that her personal wilfulness flashed up almost as capriciously in her as the Tudor sagacity did in Mary's less sober mind. The masterly sketch of Elizabeth which Tennyson puts into Cecil's mouth at the close of the play,—a sketch which ends it with a Shakespearian strength and pithiness that make Cranmer's somewhat hyperbolic and certainly by no means discriminating *éloge* of Elizabeth, at the close of the play of *Henry VIII* sound flat as well as flattering in the comparison,—is a key to Tennyson's drift throughout his delineation of Mary. I may be excused for giving the closing passage of the play first, on the ground that the critic who wants to point out the movement of the poet's thought in the drama to those who have not yet read it, cannot follow the gradually opening purpose of the play itself, but must make the end clear from the beginning. This is Cecil's brief picture of Elizabeth:—

> Much it is
> To be nor mad, nor bigot—have a mind—
> Nor let priests' talk, or dream of worlds to be,
> Miscolour things about her—sudden touches
> For him, or him—sunk rocks; no passionate faith—
> But—if let be—balance and compromise;
> Brave, wary, sane to the heart of her—a Tudor
> School'd by the shadow of death—a Boleyn, too,
> Glancing across the Tudor—not so well.

It is against this background, as it were, of the ideal Tudor character, that Tennyson paints, with great power and many flashes of striking detail, the breakdown of Mary's reign,—the picture of the woman who, with momentary intervals of true English feeling and true Tudor sagacity, yet sacrificed her realm to a hopeless and capricious passion which even her most devoted ecclesiastical advisers discouraged; who was, in addition, mad with bigotry; who let 'priests' talk miscolour things about her' while dreaming of worlds to be; who had a passionate prejudice which she supposed to be faith forbidding all 'balance and compromise'; who, with all her courage and self-devotion, was neither 'sane' nor 'wary'; and who, instead of having been 'schooled' by the shadow of death, had been rendered by it fierce, wild, and vindictive. The personal caprices of the Tudors were almost always dangerous and evil; it was only the power that lay in them of subordinating the personal to the national feeling on matters which most deeply affected the nation which made them great Sovereigns; and Mary Tudor either had not this power, or cast it away from her in the heat of her Spanish passion and gloomy superstition. The fitful ascendancy of these personal impulses over the political instincts which were never quite wanting to Mary is finely delineated in an early scene:—

[Quotes *Queen Mary*, I. v. 1–62:

'*Mary (kissing the miniature)*. Most goodly, kinglike . . .
. . . and kindled with the palms of Christ!']

Then comes the picture of infatuated and almost mad hope for the birth of a son in which Mary indulges, in the childish belief that that event, without any other change of character or policy, will bring her Philip's love, and restore the nation's pride in her—the self-will of the Tudor caprice clouding her brain more and more, and the cool Tudor sympathy with English policy showing itself less and less,— indeed, only when her advisers urge her to something conspicuously opposed to all the currents of national feeling, like the execution of Elizabeth, or when the open detestation felt for her proposed marriage and the perils of a great revolt call her out of herself into that world of action in which she was always most of a Tudor, and least of a brooding fanatic. One of the finest scenes in the play is the one in which the two morbid veins of Mary's nature, her religious fanaticism and the passion for Philip, including the power of persuading herself that her son is quick within her, beat with the fullest pulse of hope, and extinguish for the time all the latent sagacity of the Tudor monarch. Cardinal Pole's ingratiating professional quotation from the Song of Solomon, as he places Mary between himself and Philip, and the grim, ill-omened jokes with which he garnishes his conversation on the happy occasion of his inauguration at Lambeth, lend the additional force of a fine contrast to the fierce intensity of Mary's brooding hopes:—

[Quotes *Queen Mary*, III, ii. 38–130:

'Ah, gentle cousin . . .
Well, Madam, this new happiness of mine.']

Except the close, this is, we think, the finest portion of the play. The scene in which Pole absolves the Estates of the Kingdom assembled in Parliament for their heresy, and receives them back into the Catholic Church, the quarrel in the Council as to the revival of the statutes against Lollardism, and the scene of Mary's cold refusal to spare Cranmer even after his retractation, are scenes of a fair level of power, but tame as compared with many in the book. Especially it is not made clear why Philip takes his wife's part in urging and flattering Cardinal Pole into the policy of bitter persecution to which the Legate was opposed, and to which it seems probable that, in England at least, where he desired popularity for the sake of the political help it might bring him against his enemies abroad, Philip also was opposed. Nor does Lord Paget, who is eager for a policy of tolerance, though probably as much from sympathy with the Protestants as from pure statesmanship, give Cardinal Pole the sort of support we might have expected, or avail himself, as so shrewd a statesman would, both of the Cardinal's influence and of his own former good service in forwarding the Queen's marriage, to bring the Queen to her senses as regards the violent policy proposed. On the whole, the scene of the quarrel in the Council as to the revival of the Lollard Acts is the tamest in the play, and that in which Mary declines to spare Cranmer is, perhaps, the next to it in deficiency of colour. In that scene we should have expected signs of a fiercer struggle between the Tudor Queen, with her keen instinct for the true policy, and the Spanish fanatic, with her frantic thirst for revenge on the author of her mother's divorce, than any Tennyson gives us. With the scenes of Cranmer's martyrdom the fire of the play revives, though the view of Cranmer is, we suspect, a good deal too heroic. Yet Tennyson permits himself, as we suppose, one sarcasm at Cranmer's expense:—

> *Cranmer.* Last night, I dream'd the faggots were alight,
> And that myself was fastened to the stake,
> And found it all a visionary flame,
> Cool as the light in old decaying wood;

And then King Harry look'd from out a cloud,
And bad me have good courage; and I heard
An angel cry, 'There is more joy in heaven,'—
And after that, the trumpet of the dead.

That notion of the self-willed, bloody, and cruel King Henry, as the
ministering angel who raises the old Archbishop's courage, even though
it was only in his dreams, ought to be intended as a bitter satire on the
pliant ecclesiastic's former subservience. No whitewashing will ever
turn Henry VIII. into an angel of light, and it can hardly be doubted that
Tennyson here allows himself the only sneer at Cranmer's worldliness
and servility which the play contains. After Cranmer's withdrawal of
his retractation, there follows a dialogue between two countrywomen,
Tib and Joan, which brings out the popular feeling about Gardiner and
the burning of Cranmer, and which is admirably dramatic of its kind
—and after it the gloom of the play grows rapidly towards its tragic
end. The scene in which Mary—with her reason already on the verge
of delirium—hears of the loss of Calais, and in which her despair pours
itself forth in the one exquisite lyrical wail of the drama, is as fine as
anything in modern literature. Take this passage, for instance, where
Mary, among her ladies, picks up one of the seditious papers strewn
about the palace, which Cardinal Pole had intended but failed to remove:—

[Quotes *Queen Mary*, V. ii. 189–228:

'*Mary (seeing the paper* . . .
. . . she looks a corpse.']

Such gloom as that can hardly be said to deepen even in the final scene,
but it spreads. The reader is made to see the hatred in which the
Queen's policy is held out of doors, and the confusion which it has
introduced within.

On the whole, I think I may say that this is a play which will compare with something more than advantage with Shakespeare's *Henry
VIII*. Of course that is by no means the finest even of the historical plays
of Shakespeare, nor is it probably wholly his own,—and I only mention
it because it, too, contains a study of the good and of the evil qualities
of the Tudor character,—but then no play of any modern poet's
would be likely to rank with any of the greater plays of Shakespeare.
Certainly I should be surprised to hear that any true critic would rate
Queen Mary, whether in dramatic force or in general power, below
Henry VIII, and my own impression is that it is a decidedly finer work

of dramatic art. The morbid passions of Mary, the brief intervals of her lucid and energetic action, the gloom of her physical decay, and the despair of her moral desolation, together make up a picture which it would be impossible for any one who can enter into it ever to forget.

Becket, quite the second of Tennyson's poems in dramatic power, is not the equal of *Queen Mary*. The two main portions of the play are hardly fused together. We pass from the one play,—the play on the great ecclesiastical hero,—to the other play,—the play on the King's mistress, Fair Rosamund, whom Becket is made to save from the dagger and the cup of poison without, we suppose, any historical authority for such an achievement,—as if they were distinct compositions added together rather than blended into one. We are well aware that in the fine prologue,—one of the finest scenes in the whole,— provision is carefully made for connecting the two threads of interest. But even so the connection between the two threads seems a rather arbitrary knot. The interest of *Becket* centres somewhat more than it ought to do in Henry, and somewhat less than it ought to do in Becket. The picture which Tennyson gives us of Henry's sudden Angevine fury, and of the high imaginative statesmanship that alternated with it, is very striking, and, indeed, interests us far more deeply than the picture of the great ecclesiastical statesman to whom Henry was opposed. But even *Becket* will not add to Tennyson's reputation as a dramatic writer, for, taken as a whole, and in spite of some passages which perhaps surpass any in *Queen Mary*, it falls considerably below that fine study of the most unfortunate of the Tudors. The great poet of the nineteenth century will certainly never be regarded as a great dramatist. But that, being the great lyric poet he is, he should be so great as he is even in drama, will always be his singular distinction.

32. F. W. H. Myers

'Tennyson as Prophet'

Frederic William Henry Myers, 'Tennyson as Prophet',
Nineteenth Century (March 1889), xxv. 381–96.

Throughout the last twenty years of his life, Myers (1843–
1901), poet and essayist, was deeply interested in the phenomena of mesmerism and spiritualism. In 1882, he was one
of the founders of the Society for Psychical Research.

Of the two unnamed poets whom he characterizes near
the end of the present article, the 'singer before sunrise'
was certainly Swinburne, and the traveller 'along how
hazardous a way' was presumably D. G. Rossetti (1828–82).

And we, the poor earth's dying race, and yet
No phantoms, watching from a phantom shore,
Await the last and largest sense to make
The phantom walls of this illusion fade,
And show us that the world is wholly fair.
The Ancient Sage.

The aspect, the countenance of Lord Tennyson—best rendered in Sir J.
Millais's portrait, but faithfully given also in many a photograph—must
often have struck his admirers with a sense of surprise. It does not fit
the popular conception of him—a conception founded mainly on his
earlier work, and which presents him as a refined, an idyllic poet, the
chanter of love and friendship, the adorner of half-barbarous legends
with a garb of tender grace. The faces of other poets—of the ethereal
Shelley, the sensuous Keats, the passionate Byron, the benignant
Wordsworth—correspond well enough to our notion of what they
ought to be. But Tennyson's face expresses not delicacy but power; it
is grave even to sternness; it is formidable in the sense which it gives of
strength and wisdom won through pain.

For indeed, both in aspect and in mood of mind, there has arisen between the poet of the 'Dream of Fair Women' and the poet of 'Vastness' a change like the change between the poet of *Comus* and the poet of *Samson Agonistes*. In each case the potent nature, which in youth felt keenlier than any contemporary the world's beauty and charm, has come with age to feel with like keenness its awful majesty, the clash of unknown energies, and 'the doubtful doom of humankind'. And the persistence of Lord Tennyson's poetic gift in all its glory—a persistence scarcely rivalled since Sophocles—has afforded a channel for the emergence of forces which must always have lain deep in his nature, but which were hidden from us by the very luxuriance of the fancy and the emotion of youth.

I would speak, then, of Tennyson as a *prophet*, meaning by that term much more than a self-inspired mystic, an eloquent visionary. I know not how else to describe a service which humanity will always need. Besides the *savant*, occupied in discovering objective truth—besides the artist occupied in representing and idealising that truth—we need some voice to speak to us of those greatest, those undiscoverable things which can never be wholly known but must still less be wholly ignored or forgotten. For such a service we need something more than orator or priest; we need a sage, but a sage whose wisdom is kindled with emotion, and whose message comes to us with the authority of a great personality, winged at once and weighted by words of power.

Yet Tennyson's prophetic message has been so delicately interwoven with his metrical and literary charm, and has found, moreover, its most potent expression in poems so recent in date, that it has not often, I think, been adequately recognised, or traced with due care from its early to its later form. There need, therefore, I trust, be no presumption in an attempt—for which the writer, of course, is alone responsible— to arrange in clearer connection those weighty utterances which the exigencies of art have scattered irregularly over many pages, but which those who seek the guidance of great minds must often desire to reunite.

We have not here, indeed, a developed system whose dogmas can be arranged in logical order. Rather may the reader be disposed to say that there is no sure message; that the net result consists in hopes and possibilities which the poet himself regards as transcending proof. Alas! like the haul of living things from the deep sea, the group of dogmas which any mind brings up from the gulf of things is apt to dwindle as the plummet sinks deeper down; and we have rather to ask, 'Is there at the bottom life at all?' than to expect to find our highly organised creeds still flourishing when we have plunged far into the dark abyss.

This may sound but a cheerless saying, and the Christian reader may perhaps complain of a lack of explicit adhesion to Christian doctrine in our representative poet. But I would beg him to consider that the cause of any creed, however definite, can hardly at present be better subserved than by indirect and preliminary defences. I would remind him that the Gospel story is not now supported, in Paley's fashion, by insistence on its miracles alone, but rather and mainly by subjective arguments, by appeals to its intrinsic beauty and probability, its adaptation to the instincts and needs of men. Christianity assumes an unseen world, and then urges that the life of Christ is the fittest way in which such a world could come into contact with the world we know. The essential spirituality of the universe, in short, is the basis of religion, and it is precisely this basis which is now assailed. In former times the leading opponents of Christianity were mainly 'Deists', and admitted in some form or other a spiritual substratum for visible things. Rousseau's irreducible minimum of religion included a God and a future life. But now the position is changed. The most effective assailants of Christianity no longer take the trouble to attack, as Voltaire did, the Bible miracles in detail. They strike at the root, and begin by denying—outright or virtually—that a spiritual world, a world beyond the conceivable reach of mathematical formulæ, exists for us at all. They say with Clifford that 'no intelligences except those of men and animals have been at work in the solar system'; or, implying that the physical Cosmos is all, and massing together all possible spiritual entities under the name which most suggests superstition, they affirm that the world 'is made of ether and atoms, and there is no room for ghosts'.

Now it is evident that unless this needful preamble of any and every religion can be proved—say rather unless the existence of an unseen profounder world can be so presented as to commend itself to our best minds as the more likely hypothesis—it will be useless to insist now-a-days on the adaptation of any given religion to the needs of the soul. The better adapted it is to man, the stronger the presumption that it is a system created by man—'the guess of a worm in the dust, and the shadow of its desire'. It does not, of course, follow that even were the existence of a spiritual world demonstrated, any specific revelation of that world would be manifestly true. But at any rate *unless* such a world be in some sense believed in by the leading minds of the race, no specific revelation whatever can permanently hold its ground. If, therefore, certain readers feel that Tennyson's championship is confined mainly to what they may regard as mere elements of Natural Religion, they need not on that account value him the less as a leader of the spiritual side of human thought. The work which he does may not be that which they most desire. But at least it is work indispensably necessary, if what they most desire is ever to be done. And they may reflect also that the Laureate's great predecessor did more for a spiritual view of the universe by his 'Tintern Abbey' or his Platonic Ode than by his *Ecclesiastical Sonnets* or his pious hymn to St. Bees.

And first let us briefly consider the successive steps which mark Tennyson's gradual movement to his present position. They show, I think, an inward development coinciding with, or sometimes anticipating, the spiritual movement of the age. We may start with the 'Supposed Confessions of a Second-rate Sensitive Mind'—a juvenile work, from whose title, for present purposes, we may perhaps omit the adjectives 'supposed' and 'second-rate'. In this, the most agitated of all his poems, we find the soul urging onward

> Thro' utter dark a full-sail'd skiff,
> Unpiloted i' the echoing dance
> Of reboant whirlwinds;—

and to the question 'Why not believe, then?' we have as answer a simile of the sea which cannot slumber like a mountain tarn, or

> Draw down into his vexèd pools
> All that blue heaven which hues and paves

the tranquil inland mere. Thus far there is little that is distinctive, little beyond the common experience of widening minds. But in 'The Two Voices' we have much that will continue characteristic of Tennyson, and a range of speculation not limited by Christian tradition. Here we first encounter what may be termed his most definite conjecture, to which he returns in 'De Profundis', and in the 'Epilogue' which forms almost his latest work—namely, the old Platonic hypothesis of the multiform pre-existence of the soul. His analogy from 'trances' has received, I need not say, much reinforcement from the experimental psychology of recent years.

> It may be that no life is found,
> Which only to one engine bound
> Falls off, but cycles always round.

As old mythologies relate,
Some draught of Lethe may await
The slipping through from state to state.

As here we find in trances, men
Forget the dream that happen'd then,
Until they fall in trance again.

There can be no doubt that any hypothesis of our survival of death must logically suggest our existence before earthly birth. Since, however, this latter hypothesis is not insisted on (though neither is it denied) by Christian orthodoxy, and has no quite obvious bearing on man's hopes and fears, it has dropped out of common thought, and its occurrence in individual speculation marks a certain disengagement and earnestness of inquiry.

The next main step is represented by *In Memoriam*; and in reading *In Memoriam* it is difficult to realise that the book was written by a young man, some half-century ago; so little is there, in all its range of thought and emotion, which the newest Science can condemn or the truest Religion find lacking. So sound an instinct has led the poet to dwell on the core of religion—namely, the survival of human love and human virtue—so genuine a candour has withheld him from insisting too positively on his own hopeful belief. In spite of its sparse allusion to Christianity, *In Memoriam* has been widely accepted as a helpful companion to Christian devotion. Is not this because the Christian feels that the survival of human love and virtue—however phrased or supported—is the essence of his Gospel too? that his good news is of the survival of a consummate love and virtue, manifested with the express object of proving that love and virtue *could* survive?

It is hardly too much to say that *In Memoriam* is the only speculative book of that epoch—epoch of the 'Tractarian movement', and much similar 'up-in-the-air balloon-work'—which retains a serious interest now. Its brief cantos contain the germs of many a subsequent treatise, the indication of channels along which many a wave of opinion has flowed, down to that last 'Philosophie der Erlösung', or Gospel of a sad Redemption—

> To drop head foremost in the jaws
> Of vacant darkness, and to cease—

which tacitly or openly is possessing itself of so many a modern mind.

Yet *In Memoriam*, in spite of all its pregnancy, hardly forms a part of what I have called the prophetic message of Tennyson. He still is feeling for Wisdom; he has not reached the point from whence he can speak with confidence and power.

The first words, as I hold them, of the message are presented, with characteristic delicacy, in the form of a vision merely, and in one of the least conspicuous poems. The wife's dream in 'Sea Dreams' is an utterance of deep import—the expression of a conviction that the truth of things is good; and that the resistless force of truth, destroying one after another all ancient creeds, and reaching at last to the fair images of Virgin Mother and sinless Babe, is nevertheless an impulse in harmony with the best that those creeds contained; and sheds a mystic light on the ruined minsters, and mixes its eternal music with the blind appeals of men.

[Quotes 'Sea Dreams', ll. 201–17:

'But round the North . . .
. . . king or saint, or founder fell.']

But here the subtlest point is that the very lamentations of those who regret this ruin are themselves part and parcel of the same harmonious impulse—

Their wildest wailings never out of tune
With that sweet note

to which the ancient images are crumbling down, and the resistless wave advancing from a luminous horizon of the sea.

Where, then, are we to look for a revelation of the secret which, broadening from its far belt of light, is to overwhelm the limited and evanescent phases of human faith?

The nearest approach to a statement of creed in Tennyson's poems is to be found in a few stanzas which he read at the first meeting of the Metaphysical Society, the group of thinkers mentioned in his sonnet on the inception of the Review in which these pages appear:—

The sun, the moon, the stars, the seas, the hills and the plains,
Are not these, O Soul, the Vision of Him who reigns?

Is not the Vision He? tho' He be not that which He seems?
Dreams are true while they last, and do we not live in dreams?

Earth, these solid stars, this weight of body and limb,
Are they not sign and symbol of thy division from Him? . . .

Speak to Him thou for He hears, and Spirit with Spirit can meet—
Closer is He than breathing, and nearer than hands and feet. . . .

And the ear of man cannot hear, and the eye of man cannot see;
But if we could see and hear, this Vision—were it not He?

In the 'Higher Pantheism' of these familiar lines, the reader accustomed to the study of religions will seem to recognise that we have come to the end of the story. We have reached the end of Oriental religion, the end of Greek; we stand where stood Plotinus, fusing into a single ecstasy every spiritual emotion of that ancient world.

> But to see and to have seen that Vision is reason no longer, but more than reason, and before reason, and after reason; as also is that Vision which is seen. And perchance we should not speak of *sight*. For that which is seen—if we must needs speak of the Seer and the Seen as twain and not as one—that which is seen is not discerned by the seer nor conceived by him as a second thing; but, becoming as it were other than himself, he of himself contributeth nought, but as when one layeth centre upon centre he becometh God's and one with God. Wherefore this vision is hard to tell of. For how can a man tell of that as other than himself, which when he discerned it seemed not other, but one with himself indeed?[1]

Or take again the words of Arthur at the end of 'The Holy Grail'—the spiritually central passage, so to say, in all the *Idylls of the King*—when that king describes the visions of the night or of the day which come when earthly work is done—

> In moments when he feels he cannot die,
> And knows himself no vision to himself,
> Nor the high God a vision;—

and compare this with any one of the passages where Plotinus endeavours in halting speech to reproduce those moments of unison whose memory brightens his arid argument with oases of a lucid joy.

> And it may be that this was not vision, but some other manner of sight, ay, an ecstasy and a simplicity and a self-surrender, and a still passion of contact and of unison, when that which is within the Holy Place is discerned. . . . And falling from that sight if he arouse again the virtue in him, and perceive himself wholly adorned, he shall be lifted up once more; through Virtue looking upon Mind and through Wisdom upon very God. Thus is the life of blessed gods and of godlike men a renunciation of earthly joy, a deliverance from earthly sorrow, a flight of the One to the One.

To some such point as this, as I have said, the instinct of reverence, the emotion of holiness, must tend to lead souls to such emotions born. And in former times this mystical standpoint seemed in some sense

---

[1] Plotinus, *Enn.* vi. 10.

independent of controversy. Historical criticism on the Gospels, geological disproof of the Mosaic cosmogony, scarcely rose into that thinner air. But the assault now made is more paralysing, more fundamental. For it is based on formulæ which are in a certain sense demonstrable, and which seem to embrace the whole extent of things. The Cosmos, we now say, is a system of ether and atoms, in which the sum of matter and the sum of energy are constant quantities. And the Cosmos is the scene of universal evolution, according to unchangeable law. Hence it seems to follow that no human soul or will can add a fresh energy of its own; that there can be nothing but a ceaseless transformation of force, which would proceed in just the same way were all consciousness to be removed from the automata who fancy that they direct the currents along which they inevitably flow. It seems to follow, too, that even the highest of these automata have been brought into a momentary existence by no Heavenly Father, no providential scheme; but in the course of a larger and unconscious process, which in itself bears no relation to human happiness or virtue.

As all this begins to be dimly realised, men may be seen, like ants in a trodden ant-hill, striving restlessly to readjust their shattered conceptions. It is borne in upon them that the traditional optimism of Western races may be wholly illusory; that human life may indeed, as the East has held, be on the whole an evil, and man's choice lie between a dumb resignation and that one act of rebellion which makes at least an end. And thus, in an age little given to metaphysic, we find pessimistic systems more vigorous than any other, and the intellect of France, Russia, Germany deeply honeycombed with a tacit despair.

But though pessimism may spread among the thoughtful, it cannot possibly be the practical creed of progressive peoples. They must maintain their energy by some kind of compromise between old views and new; and the compromises which we see around us, though at war among themselves, are yet the offspring of the same need, and serve to break, at different points, the terrible transition. There is the movement which began with Broad-Churchism, and which seems now to broaden further into a devotion to Christ which altogether repudiates the Resurrection on which His first followers based His claim to be the bringer of a true Gospel rather than the most mistaken of all enthusiasts. And a few steps further from old beliefs stands that other compromise known as Positivism—a religion consisting simply in the resolute maintenance of the traditional optimistic view when the supposed facts that made for optimism have all been abandoned. Never have we come nearer to 'the grin without the cat' of the popular fairy tale than in the brilliant paradoxes with which some kindly rhetorician —himself steeped in deserved prosperity—would fain persuade us that all in this sad world is well, since Auguste Comte has demonstrated that the effect of our deeds lives after us, so that what we used to call eternal death—the cessation, in point of fact, of our own existence—may just as well be considered as eternal life of a very superior description.

But although these and similar compromises are only too open to the pessimist's attack, one may well hesitate as to whether it is right or desirable to assail them. Should we not encourage any illusion which will break the fall, and repeat in favour of these fragile substitutes the same reticence which it so long seemed well to use in criticising Christianity itself?

Such, at any rate, is not Lord Tennyson's attitude in the matter. In his view, it seems, these blanched survivals of optimism may be brushed aside without scruple. He is not afraid to set forth a naked despair as the inevitable outcome of a view of the world which omits a moral government or a human survival. A grave responsibility, which the clear-seeing poet would scarcely have undertaken, had not his own confidence in the happier interpretation been strong and assured.

His presentation of absolute hopelessness is put in the mouth of a man undergoing one of those seasons of unmerited anguish which are the real, the intimate problem with which any religion or any philosophy has to deal.

'A man and his wife, having lost faith in a God, and hope of a life to come'—so run the prefatory words to 'Despair'—'and being utterly miserable in this, resolve to end themselves by drowning. The woman is drowned, but the man rescued by a minister of the sect he had abandoned';—and to this minister he describes the reflections of that which had so nearly been his own last hour.

And first of all, and prompting to the suicidal act, was the passion of pity for himself and all mankind—the feeling that there was no hope or remedy except that last plunge into the dark.

> But pity—the Pagan held it a vice—was in her and in me,
> Helpless, taking the place of the pitying God that should be!
> Pity for all that aches in the grasp of an idiot power,
> And pity for our own selves on an earth that bore not a flower;
> Pity for all that suffers on land or in air or the deep,
> And pity for our own selves till we long'd for eternal sleep.

'It seemed to me,' says the character in which one of the ablest of our younger writers has expressed her own inward battle, 'it seemed to me as if I saw, mysteriously, a new Satan, a rebel angel of good, raising his banners against the Jehovah of Evil; a creature like Frankenstein's image, a terrible new kind of monster, more noble than its base maker.'[1] How shall a man avoid such indignant compassion as this? Let him face his own doom bravely as he may, how shall he look complacently on the anguish of others, knowing that for their forlornness there is no pity anywhere save such thin stream as he and his like can give? that there lives, perhaps, no creature wiser or more helpful than himself in the star-sown fields of heaven?

> And the stars of the limitless Universe sparkled and shone in the sky,
> Flashing with fires as of God, but we knew that their light was a lie—
> Bright as with deathless hope—but, however they sparkled and shone,
> The dark little worlds running round them were worlds of woe like our own.
> No soul in the heaven above, no soul on the earth below,
> A fiery scroll written over with lamentation and woe.

'The starry heavens without; the moral law within': with what an irony must that old formula of august hope strike on a mind like this! 'The moral law within': the inherited instincts which have made my tribe successful among its neighbour tribes, but which simply fail and have no further meaning in this my solitary extremest hour! 'The starry heavens without': appalling spectacle of aimless immensity! inconceivable possibilities of pain! vastness of a Universe which knows not of our existence and could not comprehend our prayer!

> O we poor orphans of nothing—alone on that lonely shore—
> Born of the brainless Nature who knew not that which she bore!

The man and wife bid farewell to each other as the water rises round them.

> Ah God, should we find Him, perhaps, if we died, if we died;
> We never had found Him on earth, this earth is a fatherless Hell—
> 'Dear Love, for ever and ever, for ever and ever farewell.'
> Never a cry so desolate, not since the world began,
> Never a kiss so sad, no, not since the coming of man!

A comparison of these lines with the lines in the 'Palace of Art' where Tennyson, still a young man, has painted the soul's last distress,

---

[1] *Baldwin*, by Vernon Lee, p. 124.

will show how far more awful the world-problem reflected in the poet's mind has become since that earlier day. In the 'Palace of Art' the soul which has lived for her own pleasure alone feels herself 'exilèd from eternal God', severed like a land-locked pool from the mighty movement of all things 'toward one sure goal'. It is an agony of remorse and terror, but it carries with it a germ of hope. There *is* the goal towards which the universe is striving. There *is* the eternal God. And after repentance and purgation the erring soul can hope to renew the sacred sympathies, and to rejoin the advancing host.

On the other hand the woe described in 'Despair' deepens where that other sorrow found its dawn. There is absolutely nothing to which effort can be directed, or appeal can lie. It is no longer conceivable that any soul, by any action or passion, can alter the immutable destiny which hangs blindly over all.

Yet I must not speak as if those who deem human survival a superfluous consolation had made no effort to meet such crises as that on which Tennyson dwells. I quote a well-known passage in which Clifford has depicted the 'unseen helper' who may be looked for when no other help is night.

He who, wearied or stricken in the fight with the powers of darkness, asks himself in a solitary place, 'Is it all for nothing? shall we indeed be overthrown?' he does find something which may justify that thought [of an unseen helper of men]. In such a moment of utter sincerity, when a man has bared his own soul before the immensities and the eternities, a presence in which his own poor personality is shrivelled into nothingness, arises within him, and says, as plainly as words can say, 'I am with thee, and I am greater than thou.' . . . The dim and shadowy outlines of the superhuman Deity fade slowly away from before us; and as the mist of his presence floats aside, we perceive with greater and greater clearness the shape of a yet grander and nobler figure—of Him who made all Gods and shall unmake them. From the dim dawn of history, and from the inmost depth of every soul, the face of our father Man looks out upon us with the fire of eternal youth in his eyes, and says, 'Before Jehovah was, I am!'

Yet would one not be in danger of observing that the face of this summarised or composite ancestor was of somewhat too simian a type? Might not 'the fire of youth in his eyes' suggest unpleasantly that he had called his descendants into being for reasons quite other

than a far-seeing desire that they should suffer and be strong? And if
Jehovah and all gods be his fable and his fiction, does that make him a
whit more strong to save?

> Why should we bear with an hour of torture, a moment of pain,
> If every man die for ever, if all his griefs are in vain,
> And the homeless planet at length will be wheel'd thro' the silence
>   of space,
> Motherless evermore of an ever-vanishing race,
> When the worm shall have writhed its last, and its last brother-
>   worm will have fled
> From the dead fossil skull that is left in the rocks of an earth that
>   is dead.

'What is it to me,' said Marcus Aurelius, 'to live in a world without
a Providence?' 'I live,' said Prince Bismarck in 1878, 'a life of great
activity, and occupy a lucrative post; but all this could offer me no
inducement to live one day longer, did I not believe in God and a
better future.' It is well to quote men like these when one sees the
words 'morbid' and 'unmanly', taking in the Positivist Camp the place
which the words 'dangerous' and 'unsound' have occupied so long in
orthodox polemics. It is not clear why it should be unmanly to face the
bitter as well as the sweet; to see life in a dry light, tinted neither by
the sunset rays of a vanishing Paradise, nor by the silvery moonlight of
a philosopher's dream.

In Tennyson's view, at any rate, this deliberate rejection of human
life as meaningless without a future is not the mere outcome of such
misery as that of the spokesman in 'Despair'. It forms the theme of one
of his last and most majestic personal utterances, of that poem of
'Vastness', which one may place beside the choruses in the Œdipus at
Colonus, as illustrations, the one of an old man's wisdom in all its
benignity, the other of an old man's wisdom in all its authority and
power.

The insignificance of human life, if moral evolution be for ever
checked by death, is no new theme; but it is here enforced as though
by Plato's 'spectator of all time and of all existence', with a range of
view which sees one man's death recall or prefigure, not, as Dido's,
the fall only of Tyre or Carthage, but the desolation of entire planets,
and the evanescence of unknown humanities in dispeopled fields of
Heaven. Seen with that cosmic gaze, earth's good and evil alike seem
the illusions of a day.

Many a hearth upon our dark globe sighs after many a vanish'd face,
Many a planet by many a sun may roll with the dust of a vanish'd race.

Raving politics, never at rest—as this poor earth's pale history runs—
What is it all but a trouble of ants in the gleam of a million million
  of suns?

Stately purposes, valour in battle, glorious annals of army and fleet,
Death for the right cause, death for the wrong cause, trumpets of
  victory, groans of defeat; . . .

Pain that has crawled from the corpse of Pleasure, a worm that
  writhes all day, and at night
Stirs up again in the heart of the sleeper and stings him back to the
  curse of the light; . . .

Love for the maiden crown'd with marriage, no regrets for aught
  that has been,
Household happiness, gracious children, debtless competence,
  golden mean; . . .

What is it all if we all of us end but in being our own corpse-coffins
  at last,
Swallow'd in vastness, lost in silence, drown'd in the deeps of a
  meaningless Past?

What but a murmur of gnats in the gloom, or a moment's anger of
  bees in their hive?
Peace, let it be! for I loved him, and love him for ever; the dead are
  not dead but alive.

How else than thus can we now imagine the cosmic position of man?
We have long ceased to think of him as standing on an immutable
earth, with sun and stars revolving round his central home. Nor can
we any longer fancy him, as Comte used to fancy him, housed in the
snug security of his solar system;—an unroofed and fenceless plot,
from whence every moment the irrecoverable sun-rays tremble out
into the blackness and are squandered in the gulf of heaven. We must
regard him with foresight of his end; with such comfort only as we
may find in the thought that other races, powerless as he, may have
been shaped, and may yet be shaped, from the like clash of atoms, for
the like history and the like doom. Let these cry aloud if they will
into the interstellar spaces, and call it prayer; they hear not each other,
and there is none else to hear. For in this infinity love and virtue have
no share; they are of all illusions the most fragile, derivative, evanescent;
they have no part or lodgment in the fixed reality of things.

And yet this prospect, which is slowly imposing itself as inevitable, is in reality but a conjecture like all the rest. Such, we may admit, must be the universe if it be reducible to ether and atoms alone; if life and consciousness be its efflorescence and not its substratum, and that which was from the beginning be the lowest and not the highest of all. But in truth a reduction of the Cosmos into ether and atoms is scarce more reasonable than its reduction into the four elements, air, water, earth, and fire. The ancients boldly assumed that the world was made of things which our senses can reach. The modern *savant* too often tacitly implies that the world is made of things which our *calculations* can reach. Yet this is still a disguised, a mediate anthropomorphism. There is no reason to assume that our calculations, any more than our senses, have cognisance of any large fraction of the events which are occurring even in our own region of time and space. The notion that we have now attained to a kind of outline sketch of the universe is not really consistent with the very premises on which it is based. For on those premises our view must inevitably have limits depending on nothing wider than the past needs of living organisms on this earth. We have acquired, presumably, a direct perception of such things as it has helped our ancestors most to perceive during their struggle for existence; and an indirect perception of such other things as we have been able to infer from our group of direct perceptions. But we cannot limit the entities or operations which may coexist, even in our part of the Cosmos, with those we know. The universe may be infinite in an infinite number of ways.

Thoughts like these are not formally disputed, but they are constantly ignored. In spite of the continued hints which nature gives us to enlarge our conceptions in all kinds of unlooked-for ways, the instinct of system, of a rounded and completed doctrine, is apt to be too strong for us, and a determined protest against premature synthesis is as much needed now as ever. Such protest may naturally take one of two forms. It may consist of a careful registration of residual phenomena in all directions, which the current explanations fail to include. Or it may consist—and this is the prophet's task—of imaginative appeal, impressive assertion of the need of a profounder insight and a wider purview before we quit our expectant attitude, and act as though apparent limitations were also real, or the universe fathomed in any of its dimensions by human perception and power. It is in this mood that Tennyson draws from the standing mystery of a child's birth the conception of a double, a synchronous evolution; of a past which has

slowly shaped the indwelling spirit as well as the fleshly habitation.
First comes the physical ancestry:—

> Out of the deep, my child, out of the deep,
> Where all that was to be, in all that was,
> Whirl'd for a million æons thro' the vast
> Waste dawn of multitudinous-eddying light.

For thus does the baby's structure remount to the primordial nebula;
the atoms of its hand have been volleyed for inconceivable ages through
far-off tracts of gloom, and have passed through a myriad combinations, inanimate and animate, to become the child's for a moment, and
to speed once more away.

> Out of the deep, my child, out of the deep,
> From that great deep, before our world begins,
> Whereon the Spirit of God moves as He will—
> Out of the deep, my child, out of the deep,
> From that true world within the world we see,
> Whereof our world is but the bounding shore.

For thus an invisible world may antecede the visible, and an inconceivable world the conceivable; while yet we ourselves, here and now,
are living equally in both; though our spirit be beclouded by its
'descent into generation'; which, in Plotinus' words, is 'a fall, a banish-
ment, a moulting of the wings of the soul'.

> O dear Spirit half lost
> In thine own shadow, and this fleshly sign
> That thou art thou, who wailest being born
> And banish'd into mystery, and the pain
> Of this divisible-indivisible world
> Among the numerable-innumerable
> Sun, sun, and sun, thro' finite-infinite space
> In finite-infinite time—our mortal veil
> And shattered phantom of that infinite One
> Who made thee unconceivably thyself
> Out of His whole World-self and all in all.

Is there, then, any hint of a possibility of transcending these contradictory inconceivables? of re-attaining the clearness which is blurred
and confused by the very fact of our individuation? of participating in
that profounder consciousness which, in Tennyson's view, is not the
'epiphenomenon' but the root and reality of all?

A passage in the 'Ancient Sage', known to be based upon the poet's own experience, describes some such sensation of resumption into the universal, following upon a self-induced ecstasy.

> And more, my son! for more than once when I
> Sat all alone, revolving in myself
> The word that is the symbol of myself,
> The mortal limit of the Self was loosed
> And past into the Nameless, as a cloud
> Melts into heaven. I touch'd my limbs, the limbs
> Were strange not mine—and yet no shade of doubt,
> But utter clearness, and thro' loss of Self
> The gain of such large life as match'd with ours
> Were sun to spark—unshadowable in words,
> Themselves but shadows of a shadow-world.

This passage raises in the directest form a question which becomes ever more vitally important as external systems of theology crumble away. Can ecstasy ever be a state higher than normal life, or is it always referable to delusion or disease? Now it is undoubted that the great majority of states of true ecstasy which are now observed occur in hysterical patients, as one phase of a complex attack. The temptation to rank ecstasy on much the same level with hysterical spasm or mutism is naturally irresistible. And yet, as I have urged elsewhere, this is by no means a safe conclusion. A hysterical fit indicates a lamentable instability of the nervous system. But it is by no means certain, à priori, that every symptom of that instability, without exception, will be of a degenerative kind. The nerve-storm, with its unwonted agitations, may possibly lay bare some deep-lying capacity in us which could scarcely otherwise have come to light. Recent experiments (especially in France) on both sensation and memory in certain abnormal states, have added plausibility to this view, and justify us in holding that, in spite of its frequent association with hysteria, ecstasy is not necessarily in itself a morbid symptom.

And if we can allow ourselves to look at ecstasy apart from its associations with hysteria and fanaticism—as it is presented to us, say, by Plato or Wordsworth, or, in more developed form (as we have seen), by Tennyson or Plotinus—then, assuredly, it is a phenomenon which cannot be neglected in estimating man's actual or nascent powers of arriving at a knowledge of truth. 'Great wit and madness' are both of them divergences from the common standard; but the study of genius may have as much to teach us of the mind's evolution as the study of insanity has to teach us of its decay.

And, moreover, if indeed, as Tennyson has elsewhere suggested, and as many men now believe, there exist some power of communication between human minds without sensory agency—

> Star to star vibrates light; may soul to soul
> Strike thro' some finer element of her own?—

then surely it would be in accordance with analogy that these centres of psychical perception should be immersed in a psychical *continuum*, and that their receptivity should extend to influences of larger than human scope. And if so, then the obscure intuitions which have made the vitality of one religion after another may have discerned confusedly an ultimate fact, a fact deeper than any law which man's mind can formulate, or any creed to which his heart can cling. For these things, to whatever purport, were settled long ago; they must be the great structural facts of the Cosmos, determined before our Galaxy shaped itself or souls first entered into man.

Enough, perhaps, has been said to indicate the aspect in which this great poet's teaching—in itself, no doubt, many-sided, and transcending the grasp of any single disciple—has presented itself to at least one student, who has spared no pains to follow it. As here conceived, it is a teaching which may well outlast our present confusion and struggle. For Tennyson is the prophet simply of a Spiritual Universe: the proclaimer of man's spirit as part and parcel of that Universe, and indestructible as the very root of things. And in these beliefs, though science may not prove them, there is nothing which can conflict with science; for they do but assert in the first place that the universe is infinite in more ways than our instruments can measure; in the second place that evolution, which is the law for the material universe, is the law for virtue as well. It is not on interference but on analogy, not on catastrophe but on completion, that they base the foundation of hope. More there may be—truths holier, perhaps, and happier still; but should not *these* truths, if true they be, suffice for man? Is it not enough to give majesty to the universe, purpose and dignity to life, if he can once believe that his upward effort—what he here calls virtue—shall live and persist for ever? 'Give her the glory of going on, and still to be.'

If there are some who will deem this hope insufficient, there are many more among the disciples of science who will smile at it as an unprovable dream. For my own part, too, I believe that the final answer —and this I say in no unhopeful spirit—must depend on the discoveries of Science herself. 'We are ancients of the earth'; and if there be indeed an unseen world we assuredly need not imagine that we have yet exhausted our means of discovering it. But meantime we more than ever need our prophets; and the true poet comes nearer to inspiration than any prophet to whom we can hope to listen now. Let his intuitions come to us dissolved in that fusion of thought and melody which makes the highest art we know; let flashes of a strange delight—'like sparkles in the stone avanturine'—reveal at once the beauty and the darkness of the meditations whence the song has sprung. Give us, if so it may be, the exaltation which lifts into a high community; the words which stir the pulse like passion, and wet the eyes like joy, and with the impalpable breath of an inward murmur can make a sudden glory in the deep of the heart. Give us—but who shall give it? or how in days like these shall not the oracles presently be dumb?

In Tennyson and Browning we have veritable fountain-heads of the spiritual energy of our time. 'Ranging and ringing thro' the minds of men', their words are linked in many a memory with what life has held of best. But these great poets have passed already the common term of man; and when we look to the pair whose genius might have marked them as successors, we see too clearly the effect of this 'dimness of our vexation' upon sensitive and generous souls. The 'singer before sunrise'—capable of so quick a response to all chivalrous ardours—has turned his face from the vaster problems, has given himself to literature as literature, and to poetry as art alone. And he, again, who dwelt with so ravishing a melancholy on Eld and Death, whose touch shall shrivel all human hope and joy,—he has felt that every man may well grasp with hasty eagerness at delights which so soon pass by for all, and has followed how incoherent an ideal along how hazardous a way!

It seems sometimes as though poetry, which has always been half art, half prophecy, must needs abandon her higher mission; must turn only to the bedecking of things that shall wither and the embalming of things that shall decay. She will speak, as in the *Earthly Paradise*, to listeners

> laid upon a flowery slope
> 'Twixt inaccessible cliffs and unsailed sea;

and behind all her utterance there will be an awful reticence, an unforgotten image of the end. How, then, will Tennyson's hopes and visions sound to men, when his living utterance has fallen silent, like the last oracle in the Hellenic world? I can imagine that our descendants may shun the message whose futile confidence will add poignancy to their despair. Or, on the other hand, if indeed the Cosmos make for good, and evolution be a moral as well as a material law, will men in time avail to prove it? For then they will look back on Tennyson as no belated dreamer, but as a leader who in the darkest hour of the world's thought would not despair of the destiny of man. They will look back on him as Romans looked back on that unshaken Roman who purchased at its full price the field of Cannæ, on which at that hour victorious Hannibal lay encamped with his Carthaginian host.

33. J. M. Robertson

'The Art of Tennyson'

John Mackinnon Robertson, 'The Art of Tennyson',
Essays Towards a Critical Method (1889), pp. 233–82.

Robertson (1856–1933), writer and politician, is now remembered most commonly as having been a militant free
thinker. He dates the present essay '1887'. His preference
of Tennyson to Gray as a craftsman reverses the judgment
made by James Russell Lowell (1819–91), the American
essayist and poet.

Laying down the new 'Locksley Hall' and taking up the solider volume
that contains the old; turning over the familiar leaves, noting many a
well-known strain and scanning anew some only half-remembered,
one is moved to ask some grave questions concerning the poet who
has woven all that divers-coloured web of song. It is not wonderful,
considering all he must have heard of the lofty function of the poet and
of his own lofty performance, that he should in these latter years assume
so frequently as he has done the guise of the prophet: it is not wonderful, but it becomes a little trying. For one thing, the ermine of the peer
will trail its ceremonious length below the seer's exiguous mantle; and
an ancient echo about kind hearts and coronets seems to lend itself
malignly to fantastic variations. But there are graver grounds of
question. These last outcries over human hopes and human strivings,
these raging indictments against to-day's life as compared with yesterday's, how do they ring beside some dozen of the different notes we
recall from the older music? By the last account, with its rhymed
recapitulation of the bad-blooded objurgations of gout-stricken Tory-
ism, we moderns, having 'risen from out the beast', are lapsing 'back
into the beast again', what with Atheism, Zolaism, Radicalism,
extension of the franchise, and disestablishment. That being so, we

must needs take what pensive satisfaction we can in those earlier musings of the time when, the laureate being young instead of old, and poor instead of rich in publishers' royalties, the universe so accommodatingly taught such a different lesson. And even as we con the earlier song, there rise up before us a few merely prosaic contrasts between the lyric organism and its environment. They are almost as piquant in their way as the poet's own more inspired visions of to-day. A quarter of a century or more ago, there is painful reason to believe, there was 'incest in the warrens of the poor', prostitution, impurity, murderous misery, and all the rest of it; and about those times our poet was inditing, among other things, welcomes to Alexandra, hallelujahs to the Queen, and hosannas to the Duke of Wellington *in excelsis*. One year the admiring world would have a snatch on the higher Pantheism; in another, such a product of the higher Jingoism as 'The Third of February, 1852', in which the singer is so patriotically successful in proving that the laureate of England can at a pinch beat any *poseur* of anarchic France at his own weapons of newspaper fustian and hustings braggadocio. If his lordship's career as a publicist could only be reviewed by an equally gifted *vates sacer*, in a temper something like that which has inspired his latest efforts, it might furnish a very tolerable companion-piece. The lofty and other sentiments of the young lover of the first 'Locksley Hall', with the commentary which represents the personal element in the poem to have included the vulgarly malignant vituperation by a rejected lover of a better man than himself; the chronic hysterical war-whoop of the muse which achieved the definition of 'this French God, the child of Hell, wild War'; the operose heroics over that undertaker's apotheosis, the funeral of the Duke; the general inculcation of high-mindedness, and the interludes of assiduous incense-burning before that imposing piece of upholstery, the British throne:—a prose-writing Swift, in the absence of another Tennyson, might make a very pretty picture of human imbecility out of it all. And if good is to be done in this world by unpacking our mouths with words and falling a-cursing over the teachings we cannot agree with, it ought to be somebody's business to do for the Laureate what he does with such a will for his contemporaries in general.

Alas! the situation is poignant enough without any splenetic or dithyrambic comment. We need no pessimist to point for us the moral of these murky utterances of the grey-haired singer, the sting of these acrid taunts at the high hopes of his own youth. His mere self-expression, as such, will go as far as any item in his catalogue of ills to create among the fit audience the impression he has so eagerly sought to convey; and if anything can obviate a sense of bitterness in the recipients it will be their perception of the bitterness of the poet's own self-consciousness. No critic can exult over such a demonstration of the fallacy of the inveterate habit of viewing poets as teachers with a clearer and further view of things than other men. It is no satisfaction to have such a proof that the miraculous singer can be as weak and unmagnanimous as any of those he affects to scorn, as far as they from the white light of truth, as false as they to his own ideals. Nor, when we have weighed his teaching in the balances and found it so wofully wanting, can we afford to hold him in the mere contempt in which he so lavishly enfolds his generation; for these very flaws of his are in a manner a penalty attaching to the work he has done for us. It has been half-jestingly half-sadly said that actors and some others are to be regarded as suffering in their own personalities for the sake of those they entertain; and so it is with the poet in his degree. He too must 'go here and there, and make himself a motley to the view, gore his own thoughts, sell cheap what is most dear, make old offences of affections new'. Most flattered of all the artist tribe, he must dree his weird like the rest. We say he is no authoritative teacher, but yet it is in his destiny that the impulse to teach is his highest inspiration, recognizable as such both by himself and his listeners. His song must be beautiful if it is to conquer men; yet if he seeks only beauty his search will never lead him to beauty of the highest kind; which he is doomed to attain only in striving after that moral truth which he is not fated to reach. He is part of the 'riddle of the painful earth', not its unraveller. We shall gain nothing by turning on him a lowering brow; and we shall accordingly do well to deal with the vices of Tennyson's teaching as we might deal with the vices of other poets' lives, as something to be considered apart from his art, if at all, the art being, when all is done, his net performance and our clear gain.

For Tennyson is a great artist, let him now rack his voice and his theme as he will. It must surely have been the constraint of the etiquette of criticism in regard to contemporaries that made Mr. Lowell the other year say of Gray that 'he was the greatest artist in words that Cambridge has produced'. Gray is indeed the most consummate artist, properly speaking, in English poetry down to Tennyson's time, but even Mr. Lowell may safely be defied to draw up such a case for the finished craftsman of last century as can be made out for the one of to-day. Making all due allowance for the amount of artistic cerebration that went to the doing of such work as the 'Elegy'—an allowance apt to be unfairly withheld by critics who dwell on the various sources of the material which the poet has built into his structure—Gray's performance can bear no comparison with Tennyson's, whether in point of range, power, charm, finish, or masterly ease. His best work is not more pregnant than Tennyson's best; there is much less of it; and it is always less perfectly melodious. The later singer came into a heritage of song such as the earlier had not known: he found a tradition of freshness and freedom, where the other came under a burden of scruple and formality.

In sheer devotion to art, however, Tennyson stands out even more notably from his contemporaries than did Gray; his bias being made only the more obvious by his early shortcomings. Mr. Swinburne has indicated these with, as usual, all imaginable emphasis.

There are whole poems of Lord Tennyson's first period which are no more properly to be called metrical than the more shapeless and monstrous parts of Walt Whitman; which are lineally derived as to their form—if form that can be called where form is none—from the vilest example set by Cowley, when English verse was first infected and convulsed by the detestable duncery of sham Pindarics. At times, of course, his song was then as sweet as ever it has sounded since; but he could never make sure of singing right for more than a few minutes or stanzas. The strenuous drill through which since then he has felt it necessary to put himself has done all that hard labour can do to rectify this congenital complaint; by dint of stocks and backboard he has taught himself a more graceful and upright carriage.[1]

I do not remember that Mr. Swinburne has ever thought it necessary to speak of *Queen Mab* with a judicial fervour proportionate to the above; but, allowing for the dialect, the central judgment as to Tennyson's early need and practice of drill is sufficiently well founded; Mr. Swinburne's verdict having important though verbally inadequate support in the opinions long ago independently expressed on Tennyson's metre by Coleridge and Poe,[2] of whom the first was not unfriendly

---

[1] 'Miscellanies', p. 255.

[2] There are several curious points of agreement between Coleridge and Poe in criticism. Both, for instance, had a boundless admiration for Fouqué's *Undine*, and they expressed themselves in almost identical terms. See the *Table Talk*, under date May 31st, 1830, and compare Poe's works (Ingram's ed.) iii, 388, 461; iv. 132, 369.

to Tennyson, while the second admired him intensely. Coleridge said:—

> The misfortune is that he [Tennyson] has begun to write verses with-
> out very well understanding what metre is. Even if you write in a
> well-known and approved metre, the odds are, if you are not
> a metrist yourself, that you will not write harmonious verses; but to
> deal in new metres without considering what metre means and
> requires, is preposterous. What I would, with many wishes for
> success, prescribe to Tennyson—indeed without it he can never be a
> poet in act—is to write for the next two or three years in none but
> one or two well-known and strictly defined metres, such as the
> heroic couplet, the octave stanza, or the octo-syllabic measure of the
> Allegro and Penseroso. He would, probably, thus get imbued with a
> sensation, if not a sense, of metre without knowing it, just as Eton
> boys get to write such good Latin verses(!) by conning Ovid and
> Tibullus. As it is, I can scarcely scan his verses.[1]

Poe in his essay on 'The Poetic Principle' says of Tennyson: 'In
perfect sincerity, I regard him as the noblest poet that ever lived'; but
in another passage, after expressing and elaborating a similar opinion,
he writes:

> Tennyson's shorter pieces abound in minute rhythmical lapses
> sufficient to assure me that—in common with all poets living or
> dead(!)—he has neglected to make precise investigation of the
> principles of metre; but, on the other hand, so perfect is his rhyth-
> mical instinct in general, that, like the present Viscount Canterbury,
> he seems *to see with his ear*.[2]

The closing qualification is to Poe's critical credit. After all, far too
much is made by all three censors of the faults of Tennyson's juvenile
work; metrical laxity belonging in more or less degree to the early
compositions of the great majority of poets. Tennyson's 'first period',
be it remembered, was a very youthful period indeed, and it is to this
that Coleridge's criticism must apply. He cannot have been speaking
of the poems published in 1833, the best of which show, to say the
least, as strong a sense of metre as his own; and when he animadverts
as he does on the first volume, issued in 1830, he must have been thinking of what Mr. Swinburne calls the sham Pindarics, which bulk very
largely in it. And even of these it is only fair to say that they show rather
an early proclivity to wandering measures than an incapacity for strict

[1] *Table Talk*, under date April 24th, 1833.
[2] *Marginalia*, cxcvi.

metre. There are, no doubt, metrical lapses in 'A Dirge', but 'The Sleeping Beauty' is flawless, sufficiently showing that Coleridge's *de haut en bas* suggestions were not needed. At all events, they were not taken; the young poet discarding his Pindarics, but choosing other metres than Coleridge had prescribed. What is really proved, however, by his early sowing of his wild oats and his speedy reformation, is the immense part that may be performed by careful art in the production of the very finest poetry. There is no more remarkable lesson to be learned from a comparison of Tennyson's work with Mr. Swinburne's than this, that the element of inspiration or cerebral excitement, which as it were gives flight to the poet's song, may be possessed in unfailing abundance without securing real poetic success, while a muse that is lacking on that side, to the point even of occasional serious discomfiture, may yet by stress of patient art produce a mass of work that is entirely lovely. Such at least is the fashion in which I am fain to figure to myself the explanation of the fact that Mr. Swinburne, while apparently incapable of such lapses into crass prose as are undeniably committed at times by Tennyson, yet so generally turns out what is to me but tortured verbiage, while Tennyson, despite his 'congenital infirmity'—very real in this regard—so often yields me golden song. There is, indeed, this to be said for the elder poet, that almost from the first he has grappled with artistic difficulties which the younger has from first to last avoided. There is much significance in Mr. Swinburne's attack on Mr. Arnold for taking as poetic themes ideas which are 'flat' and uninspiring. While praising Mr. Arnold's *Empedocles*—in part at least—Mr. Swinburne[1] remarks that 'elsewhere, in minor poems, Mr. Arnold . . . has now and then given signs of sweeping up dead leaves fallen from the dying tree of belief'; in objecting to which practice Mr. Swinburne ostensibly follows a French critic who appears to insist that poetry can only arise out of emotions of a positive or violent order. Further on he appears to reiterate the same doctrine thus: 'This alone I find profitless and painful in his [Mr. Arnold's] work; this occasional habit [*sic*] of harking back and loitering in mind among the sepulchres. Nothing is to be made by an artist out of scepticism, half-hearted or double-hearted doubts or creeds; nothing out of mere dejection and misty mental weather. Tempest or calm you may put to use, but hardly a flat fog.' I confess I can make nothing out of an antithesis of this kind, in which a fog is treated as something negative and a calm as something positive; and my difficulty is only deepened when Mr. Swinburne goes on to

[1] *Essays and Studies*, p. 133.

say that 'Deep-reaching doubt and "large discourse" are poetical, so is faith, so are sorrow and joy; but so are not the small troubles of spirits that nibble and quibble about beliefs living or dead; so are not those sickly moods which are warmed and weakened [*sic*] by feeding on the sullen drugs of dejection,' &c. All that can distinctly be gathered from such a deliverance is that Mr. Swinburne does not like verse that is vaguely melancholy, preferring either joy or black despair: of reasoned justification for the judgment there is none. We have no canon to enable us to distinguish even between 'deep-reaching doubt' and 'sickly moods', to say nothing of the more recondite distinction between such doubt and 'scepticism' pure and simple, or 'half-hearted or double-hearted doubts or creeds': we are simply driven to the conclusion that Mr. Swinburne, disliking the sentiment of certain verses, relieved his mind in some appropriate rhetoric which pretended to be technical criticism, but possessed no such character. Such an utterance is the more surprising as coming from a writer who, however questionable may be some of his technical judgments—notably in the case of the poetry of Mr. Rossetti—is in general so catholic in his recognition of the scope of poetic art and of the artistic values of verse. Such a criticism is fitly followed by the extravagantly unsound dictum that 'When the thought goes wrong, the verse follows after it',—as if poetry were a matter of propositions. It will never do thus to make our sympathy with or antipathy to a poet's philosophical attitude a ground for deciding that his poetry is not poetical. It is certainly not clear which of Mr. Arnold's poems Mr. Swinburne has in view, as he seems to praise in one place verses which would be thought to come under his ban in another; but, taking his hostile dicta as they stand, they are once for all refuted by Mr. Arnold's production of fine verse on the very motives interdicted. The truth is, of course, that different poetic idiosyncrasies yield different kinds of verse; that Mr. Arnold is, after all, more of a thinker than Mr. Swinburne; and that he can find a lasting dynamic quality in ideas to which Mr. Swinburne instinctively gives a wide berth. These he transmutes into poetry just because he has been profoundly impressed by them. And so, in a different way, Tennyson is capable of poetically transfiguring themes which Mr. Swinburne never thinks of handling, such as those of 'The Miller's Daughter', 'The May Queen', 'Enoch Arden', 'The Gardener's Daughter', 'The Talking Oak', 'Sea Dreams': at least, if the younger singer were to take up such motives, he would infallibly denaturalize them in order to get his due poetic elevation. When Mr. Swinburne goes about to praise anybody in prose, he raises, as a journalist said the other day, a tumulus of laudatory adjectives and substantives; and he does the same sort of thing in all his verse. Simple pregnancy is as far from him as the gift of surrounding an every-day subject with beauty by an 'imperceptible heightening' of the every-day tone. Turning over his volumes, you find a constant hankering after themes that are either antique, or mediæval, or abnormal; and when they are modern without being abnormal, there is still a constant reliance on the device of archaic diction—one of the easiest methods of being unprosaic, but perhaps also one of the surest signs of a want of the highest poetic originality. Now in Tennyson you will find in general a reaching towards modern naturalness of speech, a preference for simple constructions, similar to that shown and argued for by Words-worth; though a sense of Wordsworth's frightfully precarious fortune in applying his principle evidently caused the pupil to swerve from the rule of the master. As compared with Swinburne, he is for the most part a realist both in choice of poetic subject and in poetic style, his language having, with certain exceptions, a bias to naturalism even when he treats what would be called elevated themes; while Mr. Swinburne, as has been said, brings to bear on all his subjects alike a style of inordinate and artificial magniloquence; securing elevation indeed without fail, but leaving a critical reader fatigued and nauseated with his waste of sound and fury, and at bottom psychologically un-touched. He may move many readers by the sheer contagion of his sibylline excitement; but the piercing power of chosen and welded words, the high art of making a line so eternally living that it can in an instant, at the twentieth coming, clutch our very hearts and stir the deepest wells of unshed tears—this is beyond him, or at least is hardly attained by him once in a thousand pages. If, then, Tennyson falls at times into mere bathos and Swinburne never does, it is to be remem-bered that the former runs the extra risk by, so to speak, sailing much more closely in the wind's eye than the other; and that the latter secures his immunity by such an exclusive cultivation of the orotund as makes the bulk of his work a mere weariness of the flesh, or at best a marvel of futile fecundity, to the initiated lover of verse; raising, to take a late instance, such a pother of vocables by way of suggesting the fragile personalities of children, as to fatally recall Goldsmith's antici-pation of how Johnson would make the little fishes talk like the whales. Tennyson's very mishaps, in short, are found to involve a proof that he has by far the wider artistic range. All this being so, however, it will still hold that his excellences are emphatically the outcome of patient workmanship; that he is, as has been said, above all things an artist.

One of the prominent proofs of the constant care the Laureate has taken to perfect himself in his art is the extent to which he has suppressed the weaker work of his young days, and from time to time retouched for the better very many of his more successful performances. It is probably not generally known that out of the 154 pages of his first volume of *Poems, Chiefly Lyrical*, he afterwards withdrew from his works as much as 61 pages, or two-fifths of the book. There can be no doubt that the suppressed pieces on the whole deserved their fate, being with hardly an exception unimpressive in conception and unsuccessful in execution; though the variety of rhythmical experiment is, it should be said, sufficiently remarkable as coming from a youth of barely twenty.[1] But, as Mr. Swinburne admits, some of the successful poems in the first volume are as finely turned as anything he has done since. The 'melody' which now, as then, stands first in the collection of his poems, is practically perfect to the extent of two-thirds—the only emendation found necessary in the first two stanzas being the change of 'bee low hummeth' to 'wild bee hummeth'—though the awkward succession of dentals in the last stanza makes a feeble finish. And in the middle stanza there may be found, I think, an interesting proof of the care which the young poet was already capable of exercising in his work, though he was not yet grown circumspect enough all round. It runs, as most readers will remember:

> At eve the beetle boometh
> Athwart the thicket lone;
> At noon the wild bee hummeth
> About the mossed headstone;
> At midnight the moon cometh
> And looketh down alone.

Here the proper order of time is departed from—eve coming before noon—probably in order that the rhymes shall fall to the best advantage. I have no information on the subject, but I have an intuition that the poet at first put the third and fourth lines first and second, and then wrote, 'At eve the beetle *drummeth*'; but that, rightly deciding that 'drummeth' would spoil the whole stanza, and having no nearer sound than 'boometh' left him, he decided to put eve before noon in order to have the proper rhyme value of 'hummeth' and 'cometh', which would be in large part lost if 'boometh' came between. Similarly, in

---

[1] [Footnote gives particulars of poems published in 1830 and 1833 and dropped later.

the later poem, 'The Lotos-Eaters', one strongly suspects that it was only after some trouble that the author was content to make the first and third lines both end in 'land': he probably tried at first some such locution as 'pointed with his hand', deciding, perhaps for once a little lazily, to use 'land' twice because he could not bring in 'hand' satisfactorily. But the finest samples of the poet's 'prentice-work are, I think, the admirable poem, miscalled a song, beginning 'A spirit haunts the year's last hours'; the three stanzas of 'The Sleeping Beauty', which were later embodied in 'The Day Dream', but appeared as a separate poem in the volume of 1830; and 'Mariana'; and in these there is little alteration. The first remains unchanged, needing no improvement; and in the second there are just a few differences in the later version, as 'She lying on her couch alone' for 'The while she slumbereth alone'; 'Across' for 'Over' in the third line; and 'broider'd' for 'braided'. Its music was thus substantially perfect, well deserving the fervent praise bestowed on it by Poe. Here, and in 'Mariana', was seen that gift of close observation, the power of the 'seeing eye', so warmly commended by Mr. Swinburne; and in the short piece on 'The Kraken', too, we have the earnest of a fresh kind of achievement in our literature, that weaving of the ideas or the fancies of science into harmonious poetry without loss of the scientific outline, in respect of which Tennyson stands apart from those poets, like Shelley, who have paraphrased such ideas into allegories, as well as from those who, like Mr. Swinburne, steadfastly leave science alone.

Not, however, till the publication of the volume of 1833 could the most clear-sighted reader have seen that the new singer's endowment was really great. Within the three years he had produced a body of work which left his first collection far behind; which indeed included a greater number of short pieces destined to become classic than are to be found in any other volume of English verse, of similar size, ever published. Now it was that English readers were first charmed by the rich chords and the novel modulations of 'The Lady of Shalott'; the tender music of 'The Miller's Daughter'; the new and masterly blank-verse of 'Œnone'; the incomparable blending of form and colour in 'The Palace of Art' and 'A Dream of Fair Women'; and the absolutely unmatchable beauty of 'The Lotos-Eaters'. Here was art such as the generation of Wordsworth, Coleridge, Byron, and Shelley, had not yet seen. Art for art's sake indeed might seem to be the object of the poet's pursuit when he appended to 'The Palace of Art' footnotes explaining what his plan had been, giving specimens of excluded sections of the poem, in which he had given other views of the palace than those in the text, and intimating how hard it was to design statues in verse.[1] In 'A Dream of Fair Women' again, where, speaking of Chaucer, he tells how 'for a while *the knowledge of his art held me above the subject*', there is a material inconsistency which the poet has never remedied, much as he has retouched his earlier work, and which, there can be no doubt, he introduced and allowed to stand just because the inconsistent segment was by itself such a perfect piece of workmanship. It is the song of the daugher of Jephthah. Thus he introduces it, after the glowing picture of Cleopatra:

> Slowly my sense undazzled. Then I heard
> A noise of someone coming thro' the lawn,
> And singing clearer than the crested bird
> That claps his wings at dawn.

I hardly dare to ask myself, on this stanza, whether 'the crested bird', so admirably named whoever he be, is he that was erst hight Chanticleer; and, assuming him to be that familiar fowl, I am as loth to decide honestly whether the figure is or is not bathetic. But one thing is obtrusively plain, that the verbal music of the virgin's song, thus heralded, should be lyrically incomplex, implying by its simplicity and spontaneity of flow a vocal solo, whose charm lies in its soprano silveriness and beauty of outline. But what have we here—

> The torrent brooks of hallow'd Israel
> From craggy hollows pouring, late and soon,
> Sound all night long, in falling thro' the dell
> Far-heard beneath the moon.

> The balmy moon of blessed Israel
> Floods all the deep-blue gloom with beams divine:
> All night the splinter'd crags that wall the dell
> With spires of silver shine.

—? Harmony of the very richest kind: hardly a noun without its choicely-fitted adjective: the entire strain packed with tone and colour, stroke upon stroke and chord upon chord, till the whole throbs with music like the charmed thunder of a noble organ. Jephthah's daughter

---

[1] Since this was written, an interesting account of the development of the poem in question has appeared in the *Princeton Review* (1887 or 1888) under the title 'The Vicissitudes of a Palace'.

could hardly sing an orchestral andante! The poet knows perfectly the structure and the effect of his interlude, for he goes on:

> As one that museth where broad sunshine laves
> The lawn by some cathedral, thro' the door
> Hearing the holy organ rolling waves
> Of sound on roof and floor . . .
>   so stood I—

a rather different account from the preliminary parallel of the crested bird of dawn. The incongruity is complete; and yet I fancy we can most of us pardon it for the music's sake, though indeed it might have been averted by the simple sacrifice of the bird, and by, say, making the singer accompany herself on a stringed instrument. An artist who can give us such work is not to be quarrelled with for a trifle; and there are a hundred perfect touches in the same poem to atone for a solitary perversity. We cannot now well conceive what were the feelings of the competent readers of fifty years ago when they turned over the pages of that second volume; but it seems as if there must have been something ecstatic in the sensations of the more tasteful over such a succession of beauties as make up each of the great poems in the book.

A critic enamoured of the past has somewhere complained that our literature is poor in 'gnomic phrases' as compared with those of Greece and Rome; citing among others, if I remember rightly, a phrase of Apuleius—'inevitabiles oculos magnae Veneris', 'great Venus's inevitable eyes'—as a sample of what we cannot do; but one might cite a dozen equally fine coinages from Tennyson's second volume alone. Take 'the maiden splendours of the morning star'—not pure gold perhaps, but still a fine phrase; or 'the star-like sorrows of immortal eyes'; or 'the spacious times of great Elizabeth'—a doubtful proposition certainly, but again a mighty line; or 'brow-bound with burning gold'; or 'the tearful glimmer of the languid dawn'; or even 'those dragon eyes of anger'd Eleanor'—all out of 'A Dream of Fair Women'. So far from there being any suspicion of a lack of 'sense for metre' here, the metre and the sense, in the best lines, are perhaps more thoroughly interpenetrative than in any previous verse in the language. Let one passage be conned as proof:

> There was no motion in the dumb dead air,
>   Not any song of bird or sound of rill;
> Gross darkness of the inner sepulchre
>   Is not so deadly still

> As that wide forest. Growths of jasmine[1] turn'd
> Their humid arms festooning tree to tree,
> *And at the root thro' lush green grasses burn'd*
> *The red anemone.*

I do not think it is possible to get anything more perfectly canorous, and at the same time more simply forceful, in English poetry than these lines, especially the two last. And almost as adroit a sequence of words occurs in a descriptive stanza of a more difficult kind, though here the adroitness lapses into noticeable artifice:

> Squadrons and squares of men in brazen plates,
> Scaffolds, still sheets of water, divers woes,
> Ranges of glimmering vaults with iron grates,
> And hush'd seraglios.

The close is perfect, but 'divers woes' is a too palpable patch. How masterly, however, is this:

> 'Moreover it is written that my race
> Hew'd Ammon, hip and thigh, from Aroer
> On Arnon unto Minneth.' Here her face
> Glow'd, as I look'd at her.

> *She lock'd her lips:* she left me where I stood;
> 'Glory to God,' she sang, and past afar,
> Thridding the sombre boskage of the wood,
> Toward the morning star.

With an artist who can electrify language so, I suppose we must infer a certain touch of indolence when we find him leaving in such a poem, after all these years, two such lines as these:

> The times when I remember to have been
> Joyful and free from blame.

But against that one unredeemedly weak stroke in the 'Dream', there are to be gratefully reckoned some emendations so extensive and decisive as to make the remaining blemish seem a small thing to complain of.

It is the Rev. Mr. Fleay who, in dedicating his *Shakspere Manual* to Tennyson, declares that the Laureate, 'had he not elected to be the greatest poet of his time, might easily have become its greatest critic'. This and other praises of Tennyson's judgment in connection with

---

[1] 'Clasping jasmine' in the first edition.

Shaksperology[1] doubtless proceed upon personal knowledge; but while outsiders are not in a position to endorse such a conclusion as Mr. Fleay's—while, indeed, they will incline to gravely suspect it of extravagance—they can find data enough in the poet's revision of his own work to satisfy them that his critical power is indeed high. No poet, I believe, has rewritten so much as he; and probably none has ever retouched with anything like such perfect judgment. Wordsworth, for instance, can in no case be safely assumed to have improved his work when he altered it. His well-known but generally misquoted[2] line in the 'Elegiac Stanzas' on a picture of Peele Castle—'the light that never was on sea or land',—stood so in the first appearance of the poem in 1807; but in the edition of 1820 we have:

a gleam
Of lustre known to neither sea nor land;

and in that of 1827 the slight modification of 'the gleam, the lustre'; and as it was only in 1832 that Wordsworth had the wisdom to restore the matchless original, some non-copyright editions, as the Chandos, have the tasteless intermediate reading. In 'The Solitary Reaper', again, one line has been changed twice and another thrice, and in each case it may well be doubted whether the first form was not best. It will be found impossible to convict Tennyson of any such unprosperous second thoughts. His more important revisions are always happy, and there is no more striking achievement of the kind in our literature than the extensive emendation he has made on the first cast of 'The Lotos-Eaters'—now, to my judgment, the masterpiece of all English poetic art, strictly considered as such. A few alterations, always judicious, have been made in single lines and phrases; the line 'Full-faced above the valley stood the moon' being a substitution for 'Above the valley burned the golden moon', where the cadence made a monotony with the context which the spondee 'full-faced' dissolves; and 'Three silent pinnacles of aged snow' having taken the place of the too ambitious 'Three thunder-cloven thrones of oldest snow'. Then we have 'watch' for 'hear', before 'the *emerald-colour'd* water falling'; and 'barren peak' for 'flowery peak'; and even a finikin excision of the plural in 'eyelids still', and of the possessive in 'river's seaward flow', in accordance with

---

[1] It was he, it appears, who first suggested to Mr. Spedding that Fletcher's hand was apparent in the *Henry VIII*, and Mr. Spedding pronounced him 'a man of first-rate judgment on such a point'. See Furnivall's Introduction.

[2] Twice, for instance, by Mr. Lowell, who gives it 'land or sea' in his essay on Pope (*My Study Windows*, 6th ed. p. 283, *n.*), and in his essay on Wordsworth('Camelot' vol. of Essays, p. 208).

a view on which the poet has acted in several other cases, that a final and an initial sibilant should not come together. But the great improvement in the revised poem—in addition to the gain of the present sixth section, an exquisite piece which did not appear in the volume of 1833 —is the insertion of the noble passage from 'We have had enough of action and of motion we' to the end, in the place of forty lines of irregular and entirely boyish versification, possessing neither dignity nor adequate melody. It is nothing short of startling to compare such facile jingle as this—

> And the dark pine weeps,
> And the lithe vine creeps,
> And the heavy melon sleeps
> On the level of the shore—

with the glorious harmony of those immortal later lines in which, shifting his key and his measure, the poet so strangely and so finely rises from the perfect loveliness of the lotos-eaters' self-regarding song to a strain of intense and thrilling brilliance, pitched at as high a level of moral inspiration as the great poets of the world have ever reached. Magistral as Milton at his greatest, but subtle beyond his scope, and informed with even a richer art than his, the strain that limns the life of the Olympian Gods is one of the supreme possessions of the English tongue; and it exists for us as the amends made by the poet for an ill-planned piece of youthful composition which his mature judgment could not tolerate.

Certainly the change makes good anything that Mr. Swinburne or any of his predecessors has said on the all-importance of form and measure. The enduring beauty of 'The Lotos-Eaters' rests as a whole on its rigorous regard to metrical law; the deleted passage being one of those early experimental performances in loose-flowing verse, of which the 1833 volume furnishes another ineffectual sample in 'The Hesperides', which, a reader feels, might have been a fine poem if only the singer had resolutely bitted and reined his wandering fancy as he did in the great poems he published at the same time. For in the face of these it is clear that Mr. Swinburne's theory of a constitutional weakness of spine which only the back-board could cure, is one of the most gratuitous of that authority's rhetorical flights. We are dealing with a case in which a poet set out with an equipment of splendid artistic gifts in company with one or two vicious propensities, which last, when he saw whither they led him, he speedily and entirely discarded.

And this was but one exhibition of a capacity of artistic self-criticism which asserts itself in other ways than in the abandonment of a mistaken theory of versification. There were other errors of taste in these first poems. Thus in 'A Dream of Fair Women', in Iphigenia's account of her death, we have in the first version, which was still allowed to stand in the edition of 1842, this unpleasant and awkward passage:

> One drew a sharp knife thro' my tender throat
> Slowly,—and nothing more;

now supplanted by the every way happier lines:

> The bright death quiver'd at the victim's throat;
> Touch'd; and I knew no more.

Then, in Cleopatra's reverie on Mark Antony, in place of the two stanzas beginning, 'The man, my lover', there originally stood three, in which were these lines:

> The glories of great Julius lapse and wane
> And shrink from suns to stars—

(that cheap conceit being of course begot by the need of a rhyme to 'Mars')—

> That man of all the men I ever knew
> Most took my fancy;

> What sweet words, only made
> Less sweet by the kiss that broke 'em, liking best
> To be so richly stayed—

the last about as insufferable a piece of Elizabethanism as any modern has turned out. At the beginning of the poem, too, there originally stood four stanzas, embodying an ill-chosen figure in which 'the Poet' was vaingloriously enough presented as 'self-poised' like a man in a balloon, 'hearing apart the echoes of his fame'; the deletion of which youthfully self-sufficient prologue allows the poem to begin much more naturally and efficiently, as it now stands. Again, there is quite a multitude of alterations in 'The Lady of Shalott' since the first version, the reason for the changes being not so much inferiority of technique in that as an apparent re-conception of the theme in the poet's mind. There are, however, some curious re-arrangements of the rhymes, of which I give a few samples:

First Version.	*Present Version.*
The little isle is all inrailed,	By the margin, willow-veil'd,
With a rose-fence, and overtrailed	Slide the heavy barges trail'd
With roses; by the marge unhailed,	By slow horses; and unhail'd
The shallop flitteth silken-sailed.	The shallop flitteth silken-sail'd.
★ ★ ★ ★	★ ★ ★ ★
She lives with little joy or fear;	And moving thro' a mirror clear
Over the water, running near,	That hangs before her all the year,
The sheep-bell tinkles in her ear;	Shadows of the world appear.
Before her hangs a mirror clear,	There she sees the highway near,
Reflecting towards Camelot.	Winding down to Camelot.
And, as the mazy web she whirls,	There the river eddy whirls
★ ★ ★ ★	★ ★ ★ ★
Till her eyes were darkened wholly,	Till her blood was frozen slowly,
And her smooth face sharpened slowly.	And her eyes were darken'd wholly.

But the most decisive transformation is that made in the last stanza:

First Version	*Present Version.*
They crossed themselves, their stars they blest,	Who is this? and what is here?
Knight, minstrel, abbot, squire, and guest.	And in the lighted palace near Died the sound of royal cheer;
There lay a parchment on her breast,	And they crossed themselves for fear,
That puzzled more than all the rest,	All the knights at Camelot:
The well-fed wits at Camelot.	But Lancelot mused a little space;
'The web was woven curiously,	He said, 'She has a lovely face;
The charm is broken utterly,	God in his mercy lend her grace,
Draw near and fear not—this is I,	The Lady of Shalott.'
The Lady of Shalott.'	

The deepening and heightening of the later finish is too obvious to need comment. I can conceive, however, that some readers, following such a process of technical, or, as it might be put, mechanical elaboration, will exclaim that this is surely not the method of the true poet, the 'inspired singer' of literary tradition. Assuredly the actuality does not correspond with the myth; but it is just so much the worse for the myth. The notion of a poet as a semi-divine personage who gets his rhymes and rhythms from heaven, as it were, and whose function is to convey a superior form of truth to a world whose part it is to listen to him with reverence and allude to him as 'the Poet' with a capital P— this view of the matter is no doubt very agreeable to 'the Poet', and has naturally received much support from his own deliverances on the subject; but a more rational analysis simply sets such transcendentalism aside, and reckons up the inspired one as an artistic organism of a particular kind, whose very constitution partly incapacitates him for steadiness, solidity, or real depth of thought, but whose work it is to put such ideas as he comes by into the perfectest form he can attain. He may often think soundly and nobly, if not originally; but such wisdom and elevation will avail him little as poet if he cannot charm them into the shape of beautiful speech. And the beauty of his speech is a matter of manipulation of words, just as the painter's art is a matter of handling pigments. When he strikes such a chord of rhymes as this:

> All in the blue unclouded weather,
> Thick jewell'd shone the saddle leather,
> The helmet and the helmet-feather
> Burn'd like one burning flame together,
> As he rode down to Camelot,

any one can see that he must have reckoned up the chimes at his disposal; that it must have cost him some calculation to introduce 'leather' without being absurd; and that the whole musical effect is thus no outburst of one who 'sings because he must'—that is a professional affectation which, cherishing it as he does in common with prophets and Christian warriors and other self-esteeming personages, we must be content to forgive him—but the carefully adjusted performance of a man of culture with a delicate taste in words and cadences. And he is just as much fulfilling the poetic function when he charms us with an old-world concord like that picture of Sir Lancelot, as when he weaves a larger harmony to tell of the heartless Gods of ancient song:

> For they lie beside their nectar, and the bolts are hurled
> Far below them in the valleys, and the clouds are lightly curled
> Round their golden houses, girdled with the gleaming world.

There are only four or five rhymes to 'world', and the poet's moral lesson here must needs adopt the vocables 'curled' and 'hurled', or else 'furled' and 'whirled', or 'purled'. Is it supposed that his inspiration gave him the right words without his having to stop to think? And if his specialty is admitted thus to lie in the exquisite expression of ideas rather than in the study of human problems, how shall he rank as any more of a 'teacher' than any other thoughtful man of fair thinking power who seeks to teach his fellows in speech or printed prose? The poet's propositions, as such, if they strike the reader favourably, do so because they are of a kind already made more or less common property by non-artistic means; and to credit him with pre-eminence as a thinker for thus working in intellectual material is no more reasonable than to credit with pre-eminent mental power a painter who puts into a picture a view of life that appeals to many ordinary people who have not the power to paint. In three lines in 'The Two Voices' we have a rhymed and cadenced expression of the pathos of the grave, simple but forceful:—

> High up the vapours fold and swim:
> About him broods the twilight dim:
> The place he knew forgetteth him.

There is nothing here—no idea, that is—that has not been thought and said one way or another a thousand times: it is the utterance of a universal sentiment. But the poet chances to put it into a shape of mournful beauty, and his tercet henceforth haunts us like a profound phrase of Beethoven; and, whatever we may say about the matter, we can see perfectly well that the effect is psychologically traceable to the sheer throb of the rhythm and the climax of the consonances; that the effect, in short, is subtly æsthetic, and physiologically akin to that produced by music. And when, at the close of the early poem beginning. 'My life is full of weary days', we con the stanza—

> Then let wise Nature work her will,
>   And on my clay her darnel[1] grow;
> Come only, when the days are still,
>   *And at my headstone whisper low,*
>   *And tell me if the woodbines blow*

—we become sensible of that indescribable transmutation of mood, the working of which in us is the triumph of tragic art; but here too we shall find that it is the culminating movement of the verse in the closing lines that is the added something without which the triumph had not been.

But this very finish, as it happens, is the success it is because the poet has had the judgment to discard two other stanzas which in the first version followed that quoted; stanzas good in themselves, but constituting an anti-climax to its noiseless intensity and effortless poignancy of strain. That particular revision is one of many proofs of a gift he has in perhaps a unique degree among poetic artists—the eye for an ending. I can think of no one but Keats who had previously shown a sense of the technical importance of a 'perfect close'; and even he has not always proved himself alive to it; the last stanza of the 'Ode to a Nightingale', for instance, being a partial falling away from the level

---

[1] Originally 'darnels', which was perhaps better.

of the rest of the poem. We have, however, examples of perfect success in the 'Ode to Melancholy'; in the closing line of the sonnet on Chapman's Homer:

> Silent, upon a peak of Darien;

and in the even finer sonnet that ends

> And faithful Petrarch, gloriously crowned.

The effect here is one of cessation while still on the wing, so to speak, as compared with the so general poetic practice of conscientiously dismounting from Pegasus in order to take leave of the reader. That Tennyson had the fullest appreciation of this secret in technique would, I think, be decisively proved, if in no other way, by the fact of his retaining in his collected poems the piece entitled 'The Captain'. That is a performance at best melodramatic in conception, and quite third-rate in execution—a rhymed story which, save for a few phrases, might have been by an average workman like Whittier. But one line, the last, is admirably perfect; and it can hardly be doubted that the poet has allowed the piece to stand mainly for the sake of that.

> There the sunlit ocean tosses
> O'er them mouldering,
> And the lonely seabird crosses
> *With one waft of the wing.*

If we must needs read a rhymed moral tale—including such a line as 'Years have *wander'd by*'—to light on such a masterly touch as that, we can afford the sacrifice. The presence of the weak elements must, of course, be put to the poet's debit, with a due protest against what one feels, in his case, to be a falling short of attainable perfection. Something must indeed be set down to 'judicial blindness' in many cases of unredeemed sins in verse; as when Wordsworth, after all his anxious alterations on 'The Solitary Reaper', left unnoticed to the last the weak tautology, 'I listened motionless and still'. So we must assume that Tennyson has somehow missed seeing the metrical and other flaws in a number of the lines of 'Aylmer's Field', and the pedestrian character of a number of the phrases in *In Memoriam*, as, 'kill'd in falling from his horse', 'the noble letters of the dead', and such a *banal* attempt at serious humour as this:

> These mortal lullabies of pain
> May bind a book, may line a box,
> May serve to curl a maiden's locks.

He duly repented of the line 'She lit white steams of dazzling gas' in the first version of 'The Palace of Art', recognizing how domestic use had pre-empted past hope of elevation the illuminant in question; and perhaps there is not for every reader, what there is for some of us, a prosaic ring in the legal phrase 'portions and parcels', which has been allowed to stand in 'The Lotos-Eaters'; or a clink as of machinery in the inapposite 'dew'd with showery drops', or in the lines about the dews on waters between walls of granite 'in a gleaming pass'—the only hints of flaw that I can discover in the poem after dreaming myself to sleep with it a thousand times. But there can be few right-thinking people who have not shuddered over that unspeakable intimation at the end of 'Enoch Arden':

> And when they buried him the little port
> Had seldom seen a costlier funeral.

Here—such is human imperfection—we have perhaps Tennyson's very worst line employed as an ending. Such an offence against the common- est sanctities of song and taste, not to say syntax, can hardly be dis- missed as an artistic oversight: it must be held to point to a certain strain of commonness, of Beaconsfieldian tawdriness of sentiment, so to say, in the Laureate, which makes itself specially felt in his attitude towards the royal family, and, as Mr. Swinburne has not unjustly argued—though here the vice is less crude in its manifestations—in the morality of the *Idylls of the King*. It is a vein of clay which runs here and there through the fine gold of his art. We cannot overlook such a blemish in reckoning up his personality: it is as real as his better ele- ments. But in a critical study of his art we can do no more than resignedly or bitterly recognize it; turning with a sense of relief, in this matter of poem-endings, to the happier closes of so many of his works, getting rid of the flavour of undertaker's sentiment in a study of the perfect judgment he has shown in rounding off so many of his other things; and winding up, say, with such an artistic *bonne bouche* as the stanza, at the end of 'The Talking Oak', on that 'famous brother-oak',

> Wherein the younger Charles abode
> Till all the paths were dim,
> And far below the Roundhead rode,
> And humm'd a surly hymn.

Only less felicitous than such endings is the poet's art of lyric begin- nings, shown in so many a musical reduplication, as in 'Tears, idle tears', 'Turn, fortune, turn thy wheel', 'Low, low, breathe and blow',

'Low, my lute, breathe low, my lute', 'Sun, rain, and sun', 'Late, late, so late'—an artifice arising out of the very psychological instinct of song. Sheer bad taste, in matters of feeling, must needs spoil a poet's verse whatever be his skill; but against the few purely artistic vulgarities in Tennyson's poetry we can at least set more master-strokes of unprecedented felicity than any other man's work will yield us.

Our study has dealt thus mainly with the earlier portions of Tennyson's work, for the sufficient reason that it is in connection with that we can most closely trace the decisive workings of his artistic faculty. His later volumes were, practically, fully smelted before issue, and we can but trace in them the line of his development. A few alterations there are in these; indeed, the 'Ode on the Duke of Wellington' has been very much retouched since its first appearance; but one does not find many changes in the rest of the poet's work; the substitution of 'great world' for the original 'peoples' in the well-known line in 'Locksley Hall'—

Let the great world spin for ever down the ringing grooves
of change—

being one of the few that have much importance. *Maud*, which represents the high-water mark of the poet's lyrical achievement, has undergone almost no verbal alteration, though a number of passages have been added to the first version, as—stanzas 14, 15, and 16 in Part I, section i; numbers 4 and 6 in section x; the whole of section xix; section iii in Part II; and the closing number. These additions, it will be seen, are calculated to give greater continuity and completeness to the poem as a narrative whole—a form of improvement which the poet had not neglected in revising his earlier work. Thus 'The Miller's Daughter' has been not only very much retouched, but the stanza which now stands fourth is an addition, as are likewise those three which describe the share of the lover's mother in the episode, and the two which stand third last and second last; and the second of the two songs is a complete substitution, while the first has been altered. The total effect is to add weight and solidity to the whole; the process indeed showing that the poet altered his tale at his pleasure, but being none the less a gain. And so in 'The Palace of Art' there has been an extensive re-arrangement of the stanzas, as well as a re-casting of some, the logical scheme of the first version having evidently failed to satisfy the author on re-reading. While, however, his progress has thus not been merely one of skill in the choice and concatenation of words, but has, as was natural, involved a certain ordering and reconsidering of his general thought, the nature of the latter development will be found to negate once more the theory that a poet's special endowment or inspiration, as such, is moral or intellectual, in the sense of a prompting and a capacity to teach men truth of any kind. This at least, I should be prepared to maintain in the face of such poems as 'The Two Voices', 'The Palace of Art', taken either as a final whole or in respect of the modifications made on the first form, and *In Memoriam*. Any careful reader who will take the trouble to analyse these productions for their didactic significance will find that they only group loosely a number of quasi-philosophical reflections of a sufficiently familiar order, and that the poet has really no connected system of thought of his own. Professor Masson indeed stoutly maintains, in his book on *Recent British Philosophy*, that it is a gross oversight to exclude from such a survey as he professes to make, the names and teachings of such writers as Tennyson, the Brownings, and Clough. But we do not find that the Professor indicates what contributions the poets have actually made to philosophy, and such an omission is rather fatal to the claim. The truth is, Tennyson, like Browning, has passed with many people as a philosophical teacher because he raises philosophic questions in his verse; and it may be said for the Laureate that, with less metaphysical subtlety than his friend and rival, he contrives much the oftener to 'drop into poetry' in the course of his disquisitions. It is, I think, the Duke of Argyll who has pronounced *In Memoriam* a great storehouse of poetic thought and feeling for these generations, and in this form the claims made for that work by its admirers need not be disputed. What it does is to give us, in verse almost constantly good and often admirable in its sad dignity and grave harmony, a train of reflections such as occur to a cultured poet, in common with other men of culture whose thought is mostly coloured by feeling, in connexion with a sorely-felt bereavement. And the feeling is in general so vital and so freshly phrased that the total effect is decisively poetic; so that, fatally as fashions of 'poetic thought' tend to pass away—witness the proved mortality of *The Excursion* and *The Prelude*—we cannot well conceive that Tennyson's many-toned lament for his friend will ever take its place in the limbo of disestablished classics. None the less confidently may we maintain, however, that the means by which it will hold its place will be the artistic charm of phrase and cadence in its parts in detail, and not their philosophic import whether singly or together. And the truth of this, if it need further enforcement, will be apparent to most readers from a consideration of the merits of *Maud* in its two aspects of an ethical contention and a sustained lyric rapture. That any one in these days will defend the final political or social doctrine deducible from that poem, I shall not believe until I am definitely challenged. Even the author has shown some misgivings about his thesis; for the added closing stanza has a certain deprecating ring in comparison with what went before; and one of the few alterations in the diction of the work is in the preceding stanza, where the 'peace, that I deem'd no peace' has long substituted for the more uncompromising 'long, long canker of peace', of the first edition. The prescription to society conveyed in the final section—a prescription fitly summed up in the formula 'go to the Crimea and thou shalt be saved'—is a piece of sanguinary sentiment too crude and too puerile to be worth getting indignant over at this time of day, though it might well exasperate rational people at the time of publication. If this is to be taken as a sample of the element of inspirational value in the teaching of poets, the discussion need not go far. But just as obvious as the crudity of the teaching, to an impartial critic, is the exquisite perfection of the style of the song. To me, at least, such lines as these—

> And the cobweb woven across the cannon's throat
> Shall shake its threaded tears in the wind no more—

are as entirely admirable in point of poetic art as they are repulsive in their moral intention. To share in such an exultation we must be pestilent citizens; to miss the felicity of the expression we must be dull readers. Clearly we cannot reckon the poet a teacher.

Maud, I venture to repeat, is Tennyson's high-water mark as a lyrist or singer of passion; as 'The Lotos-Eaters' may be reckoned his masterpiece in sheer form and the loveliness of repose. And in studying the former work we are able to see the trend of Tennyson's artistic movement as it relates to and affects the development of our poetry in general. He is in his own way a realist or naturalist; that is, he has tended on the whole, in the works under review, towards naturalness of speech and away from old convention; which is the sum of the whole matter as regards the realistic spirit in any art. We shall not go far wrong in saying that the note of originality, and therefore of permanence, is mainly traceable, in the case of modern poets whom we esteem, to a faculty of saying things, however finely, more straightforwardly, more plainly, more unaffectedly, more in the fashion in which, rhyme and cadence apart, they might be said singly in prose, than did their predecessors. I need only refer to the critical gospel of Wordsworth for the first explicit statement of the theory. As to the practice, one instance can suffice; and we may take that of Poe's poem 'For Annie', where it will be found that, in respect of mere accidence or arrangement of terms and clauses, the writing goes on about as inartificially, and with about as few inversions, as would a prose statement of the same ideas; the reiterations being the chief element of difference. Now, this reaching towards freedom of verbal movement concurrently with the fullest circumspection, is strikingly apparent in *Maud*; where there is perhaps more of the air of spontaneity than in any contemporary verse, not excepting that of Mr. Browning, whose rhymes are too often far-fetched to permit of any such illusion. In this poem Tennyson has finally attained, without sacrifice of metrical coherence, that ease of cadence which he seems to have been aiming at in his early 'sham Pindarics', where the effort was too much for his hold of metre. To give the full proof would involve sampling every metre in the poem, with its extraordinary wealth of various melody, where each transition seems to be a new triumph of easeful beauty, which is yet as constantly virile as the early experiments were lax and emasculated. Just to show what entire freedom of form may be obtained in strict obedience to fundamental law, let us take one passage, which is indeed 'irregular' to the eye and the finger, but which is all the same metrically perfect to the last pulse of its flow:

[Quotes *Maud*, XVIII. iii:

'O, art thou sighing for Lebanon . . .
. . . Eve from whom she came.']

The very simple reasons why this versification is entirely delightful, while such things as 'The Hesperides' leave us wearied and uncharmed, are that, in the first place, the pace or beat is never ruptured, but throbs lullingly through the continuously varied rhyme-lengths, exactly like the tempo of music that, wedded to no meted lengths of speech, proceeds by its own rhythmic law—or, to take another instance, like the movement of a *danseuse* who carries beauty of motion far beyond the narrow limits of ordinary dancing without once giving us the idea of of jolt or hiatus; while, again, the poet has of course attained a much more perfect judgment in words and a much clearer sense of what he wants to say, and gives us a rounded period in which not a word is strained or misused, in place of the old thin-spun tissues of wilful fantasy.

But if we thus praise the supple freedom of the verse of *Maud*, I fear we are committed to a somewhat different attitude towards the *Idylls of the King* and the tragedies which the author has been producing of late years. The having previously ventured a detailed commentary[1] on *Becket* is a sufficient reason why I should not here offer more than a summary judgment on these dramatic experiments, to the effect that while the great and various mass of the poet's rhymed verse represents a constant advance in poetic technique, his work in drama has been radically unhappy, in that he has held to a worn-out form, to which he has quite failed to give any new life. He has, in fact, stuck to the old fallacy that the drama is a branch of poetry, and has in consequence sought to fuse together two literary arts which were indeed once in constant combination, but which have in this country for three hundred years been more and more differentiating; and which Tennyson has himself done a vast deal to differentiate further by the very advance he has made in one of them. The function of the dramatist in these days, it cannot be too often repeated, is not to say things finely —the poet's task—but in all seriousness to 'hold as 'twere the mirror up to nature'. Now, the mere harking back to the far-gone past for dramatic subjects instead of showing the 'body of the time his form and pressure', is in itself a sign of an unvital variety of the dramatic instinct —a habit of mind in which, instead of seizing and presenting genuine characters in whom the actor's art may become incarnate, the artist sees everything in a medium of inherited convention, and accordingly prefers instinctively to take his personages from periods over which convention has always reigned, that he may be disturbed by no air of disobedience in his puppets. It stands to reason that if verse-form has modified since Shakspere's day, drama-form ought to have modified too; but whereas Shakspere wrote little non-dramatic verse, and therefore did not overshadow the 'heaven of poetic invention', his magnificent dramatic product has daunted the whole literature of England, and in large part that of Germany, down to these days. Whom Shakspere daunts may be well daunted, to parody—is it Goethe's?—line on the God-deluded; but the fact remains that the thrall is thrall, and no free 'maker'. And in any case, the habit of producing poetry proper clearly tells against soundness of dramatic method, and *vice versa*. It cannot, indeed, be doubted that if Tennyson had devoted himself to the dramatic form from the first he might have been original and

---

[1] *Our Corner*, February 1885.

masterly in that as he has been in lyrism. All along he has given striking proofs of a power to seize and portray character in phases and wholes, as in his youthful masterpiece 'The Two Sisters', 'Lady Clara Vere de Vere', the 'English Idylls' generally, the 'Enoch Arden' group, and a number of shorter pieces. That the writer of all these poems could both group characters and project situations is abundantly clear; and the author of 'The Grandmother' and the two versions of 'The Northern Farmer' might even claim, so far as these pieces went, to be abreast of the best English fiction of his time, so fresh and masterly is their realistic 'nudity', as Zola would call it. But while these latter performances have barely as much poetic flavour as will keep them in the poetic category, verse as they are, the dramas constitute an absolute relapse into convention. They are methodistic and formal, as they needs must, in respect of their historical motives, where the character-poems are subtly and freely original; and the scrupulous attempt to make them realistic in the Shaksperean fashion only serves to emphasize the more their artistic insincerity. *The Promise of May*, where the poet has at last attempted a modern subject, is the final evidence of his failure as a dramatist; a failure absolutely inevitable, as we can now see, in the nature of the case, and, perhaps we should add, something of a fine failure in its way. The attempt has all along amounted to an exhibition of superior—indeed, very superior—dilettantism; and when, as is natural, the effort at a modern play is found to show most decisively the fallacy of the method employed, with its primitive transitions from verse to prose and its crude grouping of impossible abstractions beside thinnish actualities, we can only hope that the old poet will be content to leave drama alone for the rest of his days.

But if this criticism be admitted to hold good against the dramas, it is to be feared a similar judgment will ultimately be come to in regard to the *Idylls*. 'Superlative lollipops', Carlyle called them, in prompt resentment of their sentimental didacticism; going thus nearer the truth than did Dickens, whose first sensation on conning them was that of the blessedness of reading a man who could write. The whole question between those of us who sum up against the *Idylls* and those who adhere to Dickens's position, is as to whether the poet's art here, highly developed as it undoubtedly is, wealthy as it is in resource, and consummate as is its conduct, has moved on the lines of healthy evolution, or has diverged on a line of impermanent variation; whether, in short, these poems, pleasant as they have been to the sophisticated palate of the generation now passing away, will be pronounced successes a generation or more hence. In such a matter it is perhaps prudent not to prophesy; but on the other hand it is well to have the courage of our opinions; and I venture for my part[1] to lay it down that, lacking as they do those artistic virtues of naturalness and sincerity which vitalize other portions of Tennyson's work, they must in time be classed among his mistakes. And the cause and manner of the failure are I think apparent. He had succeeded in those character studies where his artistic volition played freely, either entirely creating or working on the actual; but to take the naïf old Arthurian stories and pinch and lace them into so many superfine moral commentaries for the present day, adding the hothouse sentiment of the nineteenth century to the quaintly childish idealism of the original, and grafting on the old romance a mawkish cultus which seemed to take its rise or have its end in a nauseous adulation of a living personage—this was to place art in a fatally false position, where no acquired resource could finally avail it. The poet is writing to fill a given scaffolding, and as a result we have a constant and laboured archaism of style instead of the telling simplicity and robust modernness of his best rhymed verse; a delicate and charming Euphuism in its way, but still a Euphuism, and therefore a doomed development. This might seem to be a case justifying Mr. Swinburne's dictum that when the thought goes wrong the verse follows it; but it is not the wrongness but the fashion of going wrong that is at the bottom of the matter. There is all the difference in the world between affectation and sincere wrong-headedness; and the thesis here maintained is that while the wrongheaded artist may give us fine poetry, he who gives way to an affectation cannot, for the reason that that is a vice striking directly at his art; that, in brief, the *Idylls* as a whole amount to a masquerade, which cannot succeed in creating the right illusion. Only a lengthened analysis, however, could give the full justification of such a judgment; and it must be left for the present in its summary form.

[1] But indeed I venture little. The more powerful impeachment of Mr. Swinburne (*Miscellanies*, pp. 247–253), which was not in my recollection when I wrote mine, goes much further, and, barring some characteristic exaggeration, is unanswerable. And since I wrote there has appeared in a newspaper article on 'Fifty Years of Victorian Literature', bearing the mark of a certain fine Roman hand, this corroborative judgment:— 'Lord Tennyson, before he moralized Malory, had given the world an inestimable amount of pleasure, merely by virtue of that beauty which made Poe regard him as the greatest of all poets. His blank verse sermons, on the other hand, are of no avail, and only disturb his narrative (*Daily News*, June 22, 1887). Yet Clough on their publication wrote: 'I certainly think these Idylls are the best thing Tennyson has done' (*Prose Remains*, ed. 1888, p. 250). The old order changeth.

It remains but to say a word on Tennyson's latest performances on what may be termed his normal lines; the verdict here again being necessarily summary. To put it bluntly, these productions seem to prove that while he largely retains his old faculty of tragic and humorous characterization, his power of creating 'rhythmical beauty' is for the most part gone; the old-time Tennyson giving us his swan-song, a worthy one indeed, in the nobly beautiful lines 'To Virgil'. Than these, indeed, he has done nothing more happily inspired and achieved. While, however, 'Rizpah' and 'The Spinster's Sweet'Arts' may be taken to prove the retention of his other powers—though some pieces, as 'The Flight', tell for an opposite view; the sequel to 'Locksley Hall' and the 'Epilogue' in the 'Tiresias' volume furnish positive proof, so far as positive proof will go, of the decline in his general sense of beauty. To some perhaps this will not amount to saying that there has been any substantial falling off in the Laureate's work. Mr. Swinburne has set the fashion of treating 'Rizpah' as his greatest achievement, on the strength, not so much of its poetic workmanship, as of the tragic impressiveness of its motive and the dramatic intensity of some of its expressions. These are indeed powerful and memorable enough; but those to whom poetry, as such, is a matter of beauty of speech, can hardly let Mr. Swinburne coerce them into giving the palm in Tennyson's work to a piece which, as a little reflection will show, might have been made about equally powerful in prose. Realism of character representation, as distinguished from naturalism in the structure of non-dramatic phrases, obviously tends towards prose as being the natural utterance of real persons, true poetic values lying rather in the direction of a beauty of speech which is utterly beyond actual use, though its triumph lies in seeming natural at its topmost flight, as the finished athlete's most strenuous feat seems done with joyous ease. If this be granted, 'Rizpah' must rank as a powerful study in an intermediate literary form rather than as belonging to the higher poetry; and this is of course entirely consistent with the view that the artist's cunning for that other work is now as good as gone. The 'Epilogue' was presumably meant to be beautiful—was, however, commonplace; and splenetic as is the later 'Locksley Hall', the poet cannot but have meant to give it some of the dower of beauty that he bestowed on the earlier poem. Spleen, however, remains uppermost, and only a few lines here and there break mellowly on the strident invective of what is as much a self-impeachment as an arraignment of the world. As in the couplet picturing a perfected earth:

442

Robed in universal harvest, up to either pole she smiles,
Universal ocean softly washing all her warless isles.

But, to say nothing of the epithet-stringing, the new poem contains
some outrages in the way of padding such as the Laureate never before
committed, as when, in order to get a rhyme, he speaks of the dead wife
as

Feminine to her inmost heart and feminine to her *tender feet*.

Mr. Browning, certainly, has padded as brazenly as this for many a
long day; but then Mr. Browning does it to the philosophic end of
making out that whatever is, is right, and is thus apt to be more easily
forgiven than one who employs such devices in an outpouring of
scorn against mankind. Padded denunciation is too powerfully suggestive of infirmity. In fine, we must go back to the poetry of the poet's
earlier days if we would have what is best in his art; and indeed this is
but what has always been in the service of the Muses. What is song but
one of the ways of birth to the urging force of all things, a flower of
the vernal blood or the summer-nourished brain, finding their fulfilment like every other cosmic energy? And though spring and summer
rain and blast yield thrilling interludes of radiant storm, and autumn
many a wondrous harmony and grave magnificence of ripened meaning, how shall the sun-forsaken winter tell of aught but the ebb of the
eternal tide, the passing of the protean spirit that is only to return in
other lives? In all of us, says the great critic, there is or was a poet
whom the man survives. Even so is it with *the* poet. Or, if the waning
pulse is ever to chime into the old music, it is to the spell of a passion
that recreates the past, not to the bitter musings of frost-nipped eld.
It is reviving youth in the poetic heart that sings here:

[Quotes 'To Virgil', stanzas ii, iii, v, and x.]

In some such temper, borrowing his own melodious acclaim, let us to
the last salute that singer of our youth who is the Virgil of our time.

34. W. E. Henley 'Tennyson'

William Ernest Henley, 'Tennyson', *Views and Reviews* (1890), pp. 154–58.

Henley (1849–1903) was a poet, dramatist, and critic.

In Keats's 'St. Agnes' Eve' nothing is white but the heroine. It is winter, and 'bitter chill'; the hare 'limps trembling through the frozen grass'; the owl is a-cold for all his feathers; the beadsman's fingers are numb, his breath is frosted; and at an instant of special and peculiar romance

> The frost-wind blows
> Like Love's alarum, pattering the sharp sleet
> Against the window-panes.

But there is no snow. The picture is pure colour: it blushes with blood of queens and kings; it glows with 'splendid dyes', like the tiger-moth's 'deep-damasked wings'—with 'rose bloom', and 'warm gules', and 'soft amethyst'; it is loud with music and luxurious with 'spiced dainties', with 'lucent syrops tinct with cinnamon', with 'manna and dates', the fruitage of Fez and 'cedared Lebanon' and 'silken Samarcand'. Now, the Laureate's 'St. Agnes' Eve' is an ecstasy of colourless perfection. The snows sparkle on the convent roof; the 'first snowdrop' vies with St. Agnes' virgin bosom; the moon shines an 'argent round' in the 'frosty skies'; and in a transport of purity the lady prays:

> Break up thy heavens, O Lord! and far,
> Through all the starlight keen,
> Draw me thy bride, a glittering star,
> In raiment white and clean.

It is all coldly, miraculously stainless: as somebody has said, 'la vraie *Symphonie en Blanc Majeur*'.

And at four-score the poet of 'St. Agnes' Eve' is still our greatest since the Wordsworth of certain sonnets and the two immortal odes: is still the one Englishman of whom it can be stated and believed that

444

Elisha is not less than Elijah. His verse is far less smooth and less lustrous than in the well-filed times of *In Memoriam* and the Arthurian idylls. But it is also far more plangent and affecting; it shows a larger and more liberal mastery of form and therewith a finer, stronger, saner sentiment of material; in its display of breadth and freedom in union with particularity, of suggestiveness with precision, of swiftness of handling with completeness of effect, it reminds you of the later magic of Rembrandt and the looser and richer, the less artful-seeming but more ample and sumptuous, of the styles of Shakespeare. And the matter is worthy of the manner. Everywhere are greatness and a high imagination moving at ease in the gold armour of an heroic style. There are passages in 'Demeter and Persephone' that will vie with the best in 'Lucretius'; 'Miriam' is worth a wilderness of 'Aylmer's Fields'; 'Owd Roä' is one of the best of the studies in dialect; in 'Happy' there are stanzas that recall the passion of 'Rizpah'; nothing in modern English so thrills and vibrates with the prophetic inspiration, the fury of the seer, as 'Vastness'; the verses 'To Mary Boyle'—(in the same stanza as Musset's *le Mie Prigioni*)—are marked by such a natural grace of form and such a winning 'affectionateness' to coin a word of intention and accomplishment as Lord Tennyson has never surpassed nor very often equalled. In 'Vastness' the insight into essentials, the command of primordial matter, the capacity of vital suggestion, are gloriously in evidence from the first line to the last. Here is no touch of ingenuity, no trace of 'originality', no single sign of cleverness; the rhymes are merely inevitable—there is no visible transformation of metaphor in deference to their suggestions; nothing is antic, peculiar, superfluous; but here in epic unity and completeness, here is a sublimation of experience expressed by means of a sublimation of style. It is unique in English, and for all that one can see it is like to remain unique this good while yet. The impression you take is one of singular loftiness of purpose and a rare nobility of mind. Looking upon life and time and the spirit of man from the heights of his eighty years, it has been given to the Master Poet to behold much that is hid to them in the plain or on the slopes beneath him, and beholding it to frame and utter a message so lofty in style and in significance so potent that it sounds as of this world indeed but from the confines of experience, the farthest kingdoms of mortality.

It is to note, too, that the Laureate of to-day deals with language in a way that to the Tennyson of the beginning was—unhappily—impossible. In those early years he neither would nor could have been responsible for the magnificent and convincing rhythms of 'Vastness', the austere yet passionate shapeliness of 'Happy', the effects of vigour and variety realized in 'Parnassus'. For in those early years he was rather Benvenuto than Michelangelo, he was more of a jeweller than a sculptor, the phrase was too much to him, the inspiration of the incorrect too little. All that is changed, and for the best. Most interesting is it to the artist to remark how impatient—(as the Milton of the *Agonistes* was)—of rhyme and how confident in rhythm is the whilome poet of 'Oriana' and 'The Lotos-Eaters' and 'The Vision of Sin'; and how this impatience and this confidence are revealed not merely in a piece of mysticism naked yet unashamed as 'The Gleam'—(whose movement with its constancy in double endings and avoidance of triplets is perhaps a little tame)—but also in what should have been a popular piece: the ode, to wit, 'On the Jubilee of Queen Victoria'. In eld, indeed, the craftsman inclines to play with his material: he is conscious of mastery; he is in the full enjoyment of his own; he indulges in experiments which to him are as a crown of glory and to them that come after him—to the noodles that would walk in his ways without first preparing themselves by prayer and study and a life of abnegation—are only the devil in disguise. The Rembrandt of *The Syndics*, the Shakespeare of *The Tempest* and *Lear*—what are these but pits for the feet of the Young Ass? and what else will be the Tennyson of 'Vastness' and 'The Gleam'? 'Lord,' quoth Dickens years ago in respect of the *Idylls* or of *Maud*, 'what a pleasure it is to come across a man that can *write!*' He also was an artist in words; and what he said then he would say now with greater emphasis and more assurance. From the first Lord Tennyson has been an exemplar; and now in these new utterances, his supremacy is completely revealed. There is no fear now that 'All will grow the flower, For all have got the seed'; for then it was a mannerism that people took and imitated, and now—! Now it is art; it is the greater Shakespeare, the consummate Rembrandt, the unique Velasquez; and they may rise to it that can.

35. J. C. Collins on
Tennyson's Assimilative Skill

John Churton Collins, from *Illustrations of Tennyson* (1891).

This book consists mainly of particular examples of the assimilative skill described in such passages as those here reprinted from near the beginning (pp. 2–9) and from the end (pp. 176–78). Collins (1848–1908) was a critic, scholar, and university teacher.

... Without going so far as Harpax in *Albumazar*, when he says—

> This poet is that poet's plagiary,
> And he a third's till they all end in Homer—

it is still interesting and necessary to remember that there have appeared in all literatures, at a certain point in their development, a class of poets who are essentially imitative and reflective. They have usually been men possessed of great natural ability, extensive culture, refined taste, wide and minute acquaintance with the literature which preceded them; they have occasionally been men endowed with some of the most precious attributes of original genius. The poets of Alexandria, the epic, lyric, and elegiac poets of Rome, are the most striking types of this class in ancient times. Tasso, Gray, and Tennyson are, perhaps, the most striking types in the modern world. In point of diction and expression, and regarded in relation to the mere material on which he works, Milton would also be included in this class of poets. But he is separated from them by the quality of his genius and his essential originality. What he borrows is not simply modified or adapted but assimilated and transformed. In the poets who have been referred to, with the occasional exception of Virgil, what is borrowed undergoes, as a rule, no such transformation. They may be compared indeed to

447

skilful horticulturists. They naturalise exotics. A flower which is the beauty of one region they transplant to another; and they call art to the assistance of nature. If a blossom be single they double it; if its hue be lovely it is rendered more lovely still. The work of such poets has a twofold value: it has—to borrow an expression from the schools— not only an exoteric but an esoteric interest. To sit down, for instance, to the study of the *Eclogues*, the *Georgics*, and the *Æneid*, without being familiar with the illustrative masterpieces of Greek poetry and the fragments of the older Roman literature, would be like travelling through a country, rich with historical traditions and splendid with poetical associations, without possessing any sense of either. The uncritical spectator might be satisfied with the sensuous glory of the scenery, the simple loveliness of cloud and landscape, and the thousand effects of contrast and perspective; but an enlightened man would feel something very like contempt for one who, with the Ilissus and the Mincio whispering at his feet, was sensible only of the natural beauties of the landscape round him. Nature has indeed made one world, Art another. Lord Tennyson has now, by general consent, taken his place among English classics; he too will have, like Virgil and Horace, like Tasso and Gray, his critics and his commentators; and, unless I am much mistaken, one of the most important and useful departments of their labour will be that of tracing his obligations to his predecessors, of illustrating his wondrous assimilative skill, his tact, his taste, his learn- ing. John de Peyrarède once observed that he knew no task more instructive than to compare Virgil's adaptations of Homer with the original passages—to note what details he rejected, what he added, what he softened down, what he thought proper to heighten. It was a perpetual study of the principles of good taste. In full confidence that what applies to Virgil in this case applies with equal justice to the work of our Laureate, I propose in this little book to inaugurate, so to speak, a branch of Tennysonian research which must necessarily be gradual and cumulative, but which will sooner or later become indispensable to a proper appreciation of his services to art. Every Englishman must be quite as jealous of the fame of the Laureate as our old friend Furius Albinus was of the fame of his beloved Virgil, and I have in truth as little fear as honest Furius of these my illustrations being mistaken for an insinuation of plagiarism against a poet of whom we are all of us so justly proud.

Tennyson, then, belongs to a class of poets whose work has a twofold value and interest—a value and interest, that is to say, dependent on its obvious, simple, and intrinsic beauties, which is its exoteric and popular side, and a value and interest dependent on niceties of adaptation, allusion, and expression, which is its esoteric and critical side. To a certain point only he is the poet of the multitude; pre-eminently is he the poet of the cultured. Nor, I repeat, will his services to art be ever understood and just appreciated till his writings come to be studied in detail, till they are, as those of his masters have been, submitted to the ordeal of the minutest critical investigation; till the delicate mechanism of his diction shall be analysed as scholars analyse the kindred subtleties of Sophocles and Virgil; till the sources of his poems have been laid bare and the original and the copy placed side by side; till we are in possession of comparative commentaries on his poems as exhaustive as those with which Orelli illustrated Horace, and Eichhoff Virgil. His poems must be studied not as we study those of the fathers of song—as we study those of Homer, Dante, Chaucer, Shakespeare—but as we study those who stand first in the second rank of poets. In dealing with him we have not to deal with a Homer, but with an Apollonius, not with an Alcæus, but with a Horace—not, that is to say, with a poet of great original genius, but with an accomplished artist, with one whose mastery lies in assimilative skill, whose most successful works are not direct studies from simple nature, but studies from nature interpreted by art. He belongs, in a word, to a school which stands in the same relation to the literature of England as the Alexandrian poets stood to the literature of Greece, and as the Augustan poets stood to the literature of Rome.

To illustrate what has been said. In the works of the fathers of poetry everything is drawn directly from Nature. Their characters are the characters of real life. The incidents they describe are, as a rule, such incidents as have their counterpart in human experience. When they paint inanimate objects, either simply in detail or comprehensively in groups, their pictures are transcripts of what they have with their own eyes beheld. In description for the mere sake of description they seldom indulge. The physical universe is with them merely the stage on which the tragi-comedy of life is evolving itself. Their language is as a rule plain, simple, impassioned. When they are obscure the obscurity arises not from affectation but from necessity, Little solicitous about the niceties of conception and expression, they are almost free from what the Greeks called κροκυλεγμός (dealing in trifles) and ψυχρότης (ambitious conceits). Their object was to describe and interpret, not to refine and subtilise. They were great artists not because they worked consciously on critical principles but because they communed with truth. They were true to art because they were true to Nature.

In the school of which we may take Virgil and Tennyson to be the most conspicuous representatives, a school which seldom fails to make its appearance in every literature at a certain point of its development, all this is reversed. Their material is derived not from the world of Nature, but from the world of Art. The hint, the framework, the method of their most characteristic compositions, seldom or never emanate from themselves. Take their *dramatis personæ*. The only powerful portrait in Virgil is a study from Euripides and Apollonius; the rest are shadows, mere outlines, suggested sometimes by Homer and sometimes by the Greek dramatists. Tennyson's Arthur, Guinevere, Elaine, and Launcelot are, regarded as characters, in no sense of the term creations. Derived from types which have long been commonplaces in fiction, they add nothing to the gallery of dramatic portaiture. His Ulysses is a study from Dante. His most subtly elaborated character, Lucretius, is the result of a minute and patient study of the *De Rerum Naturâ*. The archetype for his most charming female creation, Edith, he found in Wordsworth. His minor heroes and heroines, his Eleänores, his Madelines, his Marianas, are rather embodiments of peculiar moods and fancies than human beings. When Virgil sits down to write pastorals he reproduces Theocritus with servile fidelity. When he writes didactic poetry he takes Hesiod for his model. When he composes the *Æneid* he casts the first part in the mould of the *Odyssey* and the second part in the mould of the *Iliad*. He is careful also to introduce no episode for which he cannot point to his pattern. So with the Laureate. Tennyson's *Idylls* are a series of incidents from the Arthurian Romances. The plan of the work was suggested partly by Spenser and partly, perhaps, by Theocritus.[1] His 'Enid' is from Lady Charlotte Guest's version of the *Mabinogion*. Of his classical studies 'Œnone' was modelled on the Theocritean Idylls; 'Ulysses' and 'Tithonus' on the soliloquies in the Greek Plays. His *English Idylls* are obviously modelled on Theocritus, Southey, and Wordsworth. In Wordsworth's 'Michael' he found a

---

[1] The great work of Spenser is, like the *Idylls*, an elaborate philosophical allegory, the central figure of which is King Arthur; and it was, like the *Idylls*, to have contained twelve parts. The minor resemblances between the two works are important and curious. What Theocritus may have suggested was the idea of substituting a series of idylls for a continuous narrative, of composing an epic on the same principle as painters present history or biography, through a succession of frescoes painted on separate panels. The three poems on Hercules seem to imply that he had intended to deal with the Herculean legends in this manner.

model for 'Enoch Arden', and in Miss Proctor's 'Homeward Bound' the greater part of the plot. His 'Lady Clare' was derived from Miss S. E. Ferrier's novel, *The Inheritance*. His *In Memoriam* was suggested by Petrarch; his 'Dream of Fair Women' by Chaucer; his 'Godiva' by Moultrie; his 'Columbus' by Mr. Ellis; the women's university in *The Princess* by Johnson. His 'Lotos-Eaters' is an interpretative sketch from the *Odyssey*; his 'Golden Supper' is from Boccaccio; his 'Dora' is the versification of a story by Miss Mitford. His 'Voyage of Maeldune' is adapted from Joyce's *Celtic Romances*.

When Virgil has a scene to describe, or a simile to draw, he betakes him first to his predecessors to find a model, and then proceeds to fill in his sketch. With a touch here and a touch there, now from memory, now from observation, borrowing here an epithet and there a phrase— adding, subtracting, heightening, modifying, substituting one metaphor for another, developing what is latent in suggestive imagery, laying under contribution the wide domain of Greek and Roman literature— the unwearied artist patiently toils on, till his precious mosaic is without a flaw, till every gem in the coronet of his genius has received the last polish. It has been the pleasing task of a hundred generations of the learned to follow this consummate artist step by step, to discover his gems in their primitive state, and to compare them in that state with the state in which they are when they leave his finishing hand. Such an investigation is little less than an analysis of the principles of good taste, and from such an investigation the poet has infinitely more to gain than to lose. It is the object of this little book to show that much of Tennyson's most valuable work is of a similar character, that he possesses, like Virgil, some of the finest qualities of original genius, but that his style and method are, like the style and method of the Roman, essentially artificial and essentially reflective. With both of them expression is the first consideration. If the matter be meagre, the form is always elaborate; if the ideas are fine, the clothing is still finer. Their composition resembles the sculpture described by Ovid—*materiem superabat opus*—the workmanship is more precious than the material. There is, it is true, much in the *Georgics* the charm and power of which cannot be resolved into the impression made on us by rhythm and style, but the charm and power of two-thirds at least of the work depend mainly on expression. So with *Maud*, but without reservation; it is a mere triumph of expression, a *tour de force* in elaborate rhythmic rhetoric. One of the most highly finished passages Virgil ever produced was the description of a boy whipping his top; one of the finest descriptive passages in all Lord Tennyson's writings is the comparison between the heavy fall of a drunken man and the fall of a wave tumbling on the shore.[1] . . .

* * *

. . . And now I bring this my humble drudgery to a conclusion, and in doing so am anxious to repeat that the object with which I have undertaken it has simply been to illustrate the works of a classical English poet as the works of other classical poets, both in our own and in other languages, are illustrated, and to show how indissolubly linked is the poetry of England with the poetry of the Greek, the Latin, and the Italian classics. How far the immense extent of Lord Tennyson's indebtedness to his predecessors in various languages may be judged to detract from his claim to originality, is a question with which I have no concern. Many analogies and parallels no doubt resolve themselves into mere coincidences; many are examples of those poetic common-places which must necessarily abound wherever poetry finds volu-minous expression; but the greater part of them as obviously represent the material on which he has worked as the Homeric parodies in the *Æneid* indicate their originals. It is here that I trust my illustrations may be of service to those for whom they are intended to be of service, that is to say, to serious students of a poet who is worth serious study. From all the higher work of the critic, from all attempts at the kind of criticism which is supposed to reflect any sort of credit on a critic, I have refrained. *Nobis in arcto et inglorius labor*. But I should not like it to be supposed that because I have instituted a comparison between Lord Tennyson and Virgil, I have assumed that they stand on the same level. The distance which separates the author of *In Memoriam* and the *Idylls of the King* from the author of the *Georgics* and the *Æneid*, is almost as considerable as the distance which separates all other poets now living from the author of *In Memoriam*. It measures indeed the difference between a great classic whose power and charm will be felt in all ages, and in all regions coextensive with civilised humanity, and a poet who will be a classic intelligible to those only who speak his language and think his thoughts. In tone and temper Lord Tennyson is, to borrow an expression of M. Taine, the most 'insular' of eminent English poets, as he is assuredly the most conventional. And it is this

---

[1] See the lines in 'The Last Tournament', beginning—

'Down from the causeway heavily to the swamp
Fell, as the crest,' &c.

which explains the extraordinary fascination which for nearly half a century he has exercised over his countrymen. A gift of felicitous and musical expression which it would be no exaggeration to describe as marvellous, an instinctive sympathy with what is best and most elevated in the sphere of the commonplace—of commonplace thought, of commonplace sentiment and activity—with corresponding representative power, a most rare faculty of seizing and fixing in very perfect form what is commonly so inexpressible because so impalpable and evanescent in emotion and impression, and a power of catching and rendering the charm of Nature, of meadow, wood, and mountain, of sky and stream, of tree and flower, with a fidelity and vividness which resembles magic, and lastly, unrivalled skill in choosing, repolishing, and resetting the gems which are our common inheritance from the past: in these gifts is to be found the secret of his eminence. And these gifts will suffice for immortality. But it is well that we should not accustom ourselves to talk and judge loosely. It requires very little critical discernment to foresee that among the English poets of the present century the first place will ultimately be assigned to Wordsworth, the second to Byron, and the third to Shelley. Had the Poet Laureate fulfilled the promise of the 'Morte d'Arthur' he might have stood beside his master, and England might have had her *Æneid*. As it is, he will probably occupy the same relative position in English poetry as De Quincey occupies in English prose. Both are Classics—immortal Classics—but they are Classics in fragments.

Index